MW01141795

Insurance and Risk Management

Insurance and Risk Management

The definitive Australian Guide

4th Edition

JOHN TEALE

© 2019 John Teale

All rights reserved. No part of this work covered by copyright may be reproduced or copied in any form or by any means (graphic, electronic or mechanical, including photocopying, recording, recording taping, or information retrieval systems) without the written permission of the publisher.

Disclaimer

No person should rely on the contents of this publication without first obtaining advice from a qualified professional person. This publication is sold on the terms and understanding that (1) the authors, consultants and editors are not responsible for the results of any actions taken on the basis of information in this publication, nor for any error or omission from this publication; and (2) the publisher is not engaged in rendering legal, accounting, professional or other advice or services. The publisher and the authors, consultants and editors, expressly disclaim all and any liability and responsibility to any person, whether a purchaser or reader of this publication or not, in respect to anything, and of the consequences of anything, done or omitted to be done by any such person in reliance, whether wholly or partially, upon the whole or any part of the contents of this publication. Without limiting the generality of the above, no author, consultant or editor shall have any responsibility for any act or omission of any other author, consultant or editor.

Commonwealth legislation

© Commonwealth of Australia (2016)
All legislation herein is reproduced by permission but does not purport to be the official or authorised version. It is subject to Commonwealth of Australia copyright. The *Copyright Act 1968* permits certain reproduction and publication of Commonwealth legislation and judgements. In particular, s 182A of the Act enables a complete copy to be made by or on behalf of a particular person. For reproduction or publication beyond that permitted by the Act, permission should be sought in writing. Requests should be addressed to the Commonwealth Copyright Administration, Attorney General's Department, Robert Gorman Officers National Circuit, Barton, ACT 2600 or posted at *www. ag.gov/cca*.

ISBN: 978-0-646-81281-6

eISNB: 978-1-922270-23-8

Contents

Preface

As the title indicates, this book is about risk management and about insurance and ethics and provides an essential resource for all those involved in delivering high-quality advice about protecting both personal and property for all Australians, their families and businesses. Financial planning involves more than just solving accumulation of capital problems. It has evolved to include advising on strategies to protect assets against catastrophic events should they happen and reducing their financial impact. This book introduces the risk management process and shows how insurance fits into the process. It also outlines how the process is applied to small business, personal property and personal financial protection; that is, the book focuses on the practical application of the techniques.

Financial planning exists in a dynamic environment where legislative change is the only constant. From the introduction of the new *Corporations Act* (2001), the FOFA legislation and the new education requirements enforced by the Financial Advisers Standards and Ethics Authority (FASEA) signals the government's expectations of higher professional and ethical standards of financial planners.

The fourth edition goes a long way in meeting these increased expectations as it includes the new legislative reforms as well as the reforms contained in the *Insurance Contracts Amendment Act* 2013. (the Act). This Act introduces changes such as to: the duty of disclosure, subrogation, misstatement of age, the removal of unfair terms in insurance contracts and much more. This new edition also includes the FOFA reforms and advice to financial planners conducting due diligence. Many sections have been updated and additional cases and illustrated examples added. A new chapter has been included that explains the principles of ethics and its application In the decision making process.

Features and benefits

Insurance and Risk Management is the only Australian text book that focuses exclusively on the Australian Insurance Contracts Act 1984, Australian regulatory environment, Australian insurance environment, Australian insurance policies and as such, is an invaluable resource for Australian students and professionals. It:

- includes all the material that is required to be covered for graduates to gain entry into the Financial Planning Association of Australia

- meets the current education content requirements for FASEA

- provides a practical explanation of risk management and its application

- explains complicated and technical general and life insurance concepts in plain English

- outlines how the general and life insurance industries operate in Australia

- provides practical instruction that will enhance the financial planning and insurance curriculums

- provides a detailed explanation of the theory of ethics, and provides a guide to its application, and

- empowers readers to present life and general insurance risk management solutions in an authoritative and professional manner.

Insurance and Risk Management is is an invaluable resource for practicing financial planners, students and the public as the reader is taken from the basics through to a deeper level of understanding on a range of topics. Each chapter concludes with specific review questions, which makes the book particularly useful for:

- Diploma of Financial Planning students

- Advanced Diploma of Financial Planning students

- students studying for a degree in financial planning or as a major/minor area of study in an accounting or other degree

- students studying for a master's degree in financial planning or as part of a master's degree in business, or

- those who wish to know how a better understanding of risk management and the application of insurance can increase the financial security of their families and businesses.

Dr John Teale
November 2019

ACKNOWLEDGEMENTS

The author would like to thank the following copyright holders, organisations and individuals for their permission to reproduce copyright material in this text.

Images

- David Minty, 'General Insurance in Australia'. Presentation to UNSW actual students, 27 August 2002 (figure 9.4)

- Graeme Berwick, QR Consulting, Sydney. From Berwick, G 2001, *The executives guide to insurance and risk management,* (figure 10.4) adapted with permission

- Pearson Education Australia. From Gibson, A and Fraser, D 2015, *Business Law,* 9th edn, (figure 5.1) included with permission

- © Commonwealth of Australia, APRA, *www.apra.gov.au*. From *Statistics – Half Yearly General Insurance Bulletin* 2016

- © Commonwealth of Australia. Adapted from *Executive Briefing: Insurance in Australia, www.axiss.com.au,* (figure 4.1) reproduced with permission

Text

- Allens Arthur Robinson, 'Focus: The duty of utmost good faith –

- ING Australia Ltd: 12-060, included with permission, and

- © Commonwealth of Australia. From *www.medicare.gov.au:* 14-130, reproduced by permission

ABOUT THE AUTHOR

John Teale was a senior lecturer in financial planning at the Universities of Southern Queensland, Sunshine Coast and New England. He holds a PhD, a business degree with a triple major in economics, business and marketing, a masters degree in research, gained his insurance qualifications from the professional body a Diploma of Financial Planning from the Financial Planning Association of Australia (FPA) and is a Certified Insurance Professional (CIP). He commenced his academic career in 2003 and specialised in teaching Risk Management and Insurance and Superannuation and Retirement Planning.

Dr Teale has 39 years' experience working in the general and life insurance industries. He has worked in the field as a district inspector for a general insurance company and held senior executive positions, such as general manager of an insurance company. As general manager, he undertook overseas projects in Europe and Britain. He also owned and operated a financial services business for 18 years specialising in general insurance, life risk and financial planning.

 As an academic, Dr Teale has held committee positions with the FPA and up until recently a member of the FPA's Education Council that drew up the new accreditation and education requirements for higher education bodies to have their financial planning programs accredited with the FPA and which have been adopted by FASEA. He was also a member of the Financial Planning Standards Board's (FPSB), owner of the CFP© mark outside of North America, education working group. This working group has developed the curriculum framework and content for the 26 countries in which the FPSB has franchised its CFP program.

Dr Teale has helped many students enter the financial planning profession, undertaken consulting projects with financial planning groups and written a number of scholarly papers on self-managed superannuation funds, flood insurance, transitioning financial planning students into the profession, pedagogy in financial planning education and providing financial advice to the aging population. One paper 'Improving financial planning graduate employability through enterprise education (2013)' has been selected by the Social Sciences Research Network (SSRN) to be included in their inaugural edition of their Social Sciences Research eJournal, EduRn, first published in 2018.

CHAPTER 1

NATURE OF RISK AND ITS MANAGEMENT

THE CONCEPT OF RISK

1-000   Introduction

Why are we motivated to define and manage risk? The answer is that we cannot be certain what the future holds; ie, the future is not completely predictable. We know that we will have an array of experiences in the future, some of which may be pleasurable, some painful and some potentially fatal. Although most of us realise that we do not have any control over the future, we are motivated to avoid or minimise our exposure to fatal experiences.

Risk and uncertainty have existed since the beginning of time. Our ancestors worried about being eaten by large carnivores or about where they would be able to find shelter. As humans evolved, their concerns shifted (eg, whether the houses they built would burn or be blown down). Today, there are many other worries to contend with: eg, will the stock market crash and render many investments worthless or severely reduced in value as happened following the Global Financial Crisis of 2007-2008, thereby affecting quality of life after retirement; or investing in a company that did not carry insurance.

Uncertainty creates two separate problems. The first concerns the financial problems that may result from a loss of income or assets; the second concerns the emotional stress that result from worrying about these losses. In earlier times, these problems might be dealt with through appeals to various gods; today there is the comfort of government services, such as social security and aged pension, and insurance is available from an array of providers. If insurance was not available, would you start a business and put everything you own at risk?

1-010   Definition of risk

The loose, intuitive description of risk discussed above — the unpredictability of the future and the possibility of unfavourable outcomes — is suitable for everyday usage but is not sufficient when considering insurance theory. There are many definitions of risk that are used by different disciplines, such as economics, statistics or business. Each of these definitions uses different concepts because each group deals with a different subject. Therefore, even though each group uses the term *risk*, it may do so in a manner that is entirely different from how it is used within the area of insurance.

To make things more complicated, even in the area of insurance, practitioners use the term in several different ways depending on the circumstances. Risk may refer to a peril insured against (eg, fire is a risk to which most property is exposed) or to a person or property protected by insurance (eg, available statistics lead many insurance companies to consider that young drivers are bad risks, or that a jewellery store without adequate perimeter security is an unacceptable risk). The word *exposure* is commonly used in insurance to denote the person or property's vulnerability to loss (risk). Exposure is discussed on page 19.

In insurance theory too, *risk* has many definitions, including the chance of a loss, the possibility of a loss, uncertainty, the difference between actual and expected results, or the probability of an outcome different from the one expected. In this text the following definition of risk, which is an adaptation of the definition used by Vaughan and Vaughan (2003), will be used:

> Risk is a condition where there is a possibility of an adverse deviation from an expected outcome.

This definition has been chosen because it contains the three common elements in all definitions of risk: indeterminacy, loss and variability.

1. *Indeterminacy:* The outcome must be uncertain (ie, indeterminate). If risk exists, there must be at least two possible outcomes. If it is known for certain that a loss will occur, then there is no risk and you will lose. A good example is the reduction in value of a capital asset through depreciation. In this situation the outcome is known, so there is no risk.

2. *Loss:* At least one of the outcomes is less desirable than expected. This may be a loss of something that a person owns, for example as a result of a house fire, or a gain that is smaller than anticipated. If you had the choice between two blue chip shares and a Santos share, you would lose if you chose the one that increased in value the least.

3. *Variability in possible outcomes:* This draws attention to the degree of risk that exists in given situations. The degree of risk indicates the accuracy of predictions of an event based on chance. Therefore, the degree of risk will be lower where the prediction of an event based on chance is made with a high degree of accuracy. Conversely, there will be a higher degree of risk where there is a less accurate prediction of an event based on chance.

It is evident that risk is a condition of the real world and is a combination of circumstances that exist in the external environment. Also, because there is only the *possibility* of a loss, the probability of a loss actually occurring is between 0 (impossible) and 1 (definite); that is, risk is neither definite nor impossible. There is no requirement that the possibility be measurable, only that it exists and the probability of the loss occurring be between 0 and 1. For example, death is a condition with a probability of 1 ($p = 1$), because it is 100 per cent certain that everyone will eventually die, thus there is no risk of death.

Risk was defined above as the 'possibility of an adverse deviation from an expected outcome'. If a person owns a house, the expected outcome is that it will not be damaged by fire. The adverse deviation from the expected outcome is that it will be damaged by fire and a loss will have occurred. The possibility that the expected outcome will not be met is what constitutes risk.

1-020   Uncertainty and its relationship to risk

Risk was defined above as the chances of something happening in the future based on what we know about the past. Uncertainty is the reality that some outcomes aren't predictable just by looking at the past.

Dr Frank Murray an American economist drew a distinction between 'risk' and 'uncertainty'. His assertion is illustrated by imagining an urn containing marbles, 40 per cent of which are red and 60 per cent are not red. If you draw one marble from the urn, you don't know what colour the marble will be, but you know that there is a 40 per cent risk that it will be red.

The non-red marbles are yellow and black. You don't know how many there are of each. So when you are about to draw a marble from the urn, if you were asked what the risk is that it will be black, you have no way of really assessing the probability. It's not 40 per cent or 60 per cent; it is unknowable. The unknowable is what Dr Frank Knight characterised as uncertainty and there is a very big difference between risk and uncertainty.

Since uncertainty is present when there is doubt about future events. It is the opposite of 'certainty', which is knowing with conviction what will happen in the future. For example: 'I am certain that the flood water covering the bridge has not washed a section away'. This statement reflects a conviction about the outcome of the future event, possibly because the bridge was inspected. However, if the person said, 'I do not know if the flood water covering the bridge has not washed a section away,' he or she is expressing uncertainty about the outcome because of an absence of knowledge (or information) about the bridge. As discussed above, uncertainty means that the probability of the outcome occurring is between 0 and 1.

The existence of risk — a condition that entails the possibility of loss — creates uncertainty in the mind of individuals when risk is recognised. Uncertainty is subjective and is based on a person's perception of risk, which is influenced by their mental condition or state of mind regarding future events; that is, it is a psychological reaction to the lack of knowledge about the future. On the other hand, risk is objective and reflects the external state of the world.

Objective risk is the variation of actual loss from expected loss. This variance allows objective risk to be measured, which makes it an extremely useful tool for an insurer or corporate risk manager.

During decision making, risks are inherent in uncertain knowledge and information. Uncertainty creates risk that a poor decision will be made. When making a decision that involves uncertainty and risk, answers should be sought for the following questions:

- *What can go wrong?* A poor choice is made.

- *How likely is it to happen?* Probability depends on uncertain knowledge and on the interpretation of information.

- *What are the consequences?* Money, time, property loss.

A corollary is that the more uncertainty, the higher the risk that a poor decision will be made.

It should be appreciated that an individual's opinion of certainty or uncertainty may or may not necessarily coincide with reality. An individual can be certain of a particular risk when there is, in reality, no risk. A traveller may be certain that a particular road is closed by floodwater when in fact it is not. Similarly, an individual may not recognise the existence of risk when, in fact, the risk does exist. When there is a possibility of loss, risk exists irrespective of whether the individual is aware of the risk. Uncertainty will vary with the level of knowledge, expectations and attitudes of the individual. Because of this, different individuals may have different attitudes towards certainty under identical circumstances therefore; a person may be termed a risk seeker or a risk avoider. However, as knowledge and experience is gained a person's uncertainty is often reduced and less risk is perceived.

One thing is consistent in this discussion: without uncertainty, there is no risk. How uncertainty effects retirement savings is shown in the following illustrated example.

Illustrated example 1.1

Uncertainty must also be considered in planning one's retirement. Once retired, there is typically little chance of being able to earn back any capital lost. Similarly, there is no chance of stopping your spending while you wait for markets to rebound. You either have enough certain income, or you will be forced to sell assets during the storm, which is never a good outcome.

Uncertainty, more so than risk, poses a significant question to investors: If no-one can predict the future with any certainty, what can I do to ensure I survive the storm? Many investors decide the best way to survive is to invest in term deposits. If we look at risks (i.e. looking backward), this seems like a safe strategy.

Inflation has been between two and three per cent for nearly a generation and has actually been declining in recent times. What would happen if inflation did spike like it did in the 1970s? How would your retirement funds survive then? Retirees in 1970 would see 76 per cent of their savings eroded by inflation over the next 13 years (their life expectancy at the time). Warren Buffet once described the asset class most investors consider the 'safest' – cash – as extremely risky. Cash can't be extremely risky, but it's not risk-free either, and the risk is inflation – the unknown.

At a glance

- Risk has existed in various forms since the dawn of time.

- Risk is a possible adverse deviation from expectations.

- The term *risk* is used to identify the person or property exposed to loss.

- The probability of an adverse deviation from an expected outcome indicates the presence of risk.

- The probability of a loss occurring is between 0 and 1.

- Risk creates uncertainty about future events when risk is recognised.

- Uncertainty is subjective while risk is objective.

- Objective risk is measurable.

MEASUREMENT OF RISK

1-030   Introduction

We defined risk as 'an adverse deviation from an expected outcome'. In insurance terms, this definition implies a variation around an average expected loss. Therefore, the greater the variation around this average, the greater the risk of an adverse deviation from what is expected. This variability in possible outcomes implies that different situations will have 'more risk' or 'less risk' than others — that is, there will be different degrees of risk in given situations.

1-040   Degree of risk

The degree of risk (or variability) is related to the likelihood of occurrence and is a measure of the accuracy with which the outcome of an event based on chance can be predicted. Therefore, the more accurate the prediction of the outcome of an event based on chance, the lower the degree of risk. Conversely, less accurate predictions will result in a higher degree of risk. How insurance companies use this information to predict losses is shown in the following illustrated example.

Illustrated example 1.2

An insurance company wants to predict how many houses will be destroyed by fire in the next 12 months out of a sample of 5,000 randomly chosen houses. This gives a total of 5,001 outcomes ('no loss' is the additional outcome). When considering the degree of risk, the insurance company will be interested in factors that will increase or decrease either the frequency (the number of losses that occur in a given period) or the severity (the probable size) of the loss or both. Factors that would reduce the degree of loss would include if all homes were less than five years old and located within five kilometres of a fire station. Factors that would increase risk would include if houses were of timber construction, were more than 40 years old and had the original electrical wiring.

Further information about the frequency of loss could come from the insurance company's own statistical records. If they know that about one in 1,000 houses with a similar risk profile suffered a fire, they would be able to make an even more accurate prediction, and this would further reduce the degree of loss. Because insurance companies know the number and the total dollar value of losses that have occurred in similar samples, they are able to use this information to both predict and calculate a premium based on this prediction.

In the above example, the insurance company estimated that five out of the 5,000 houses will burn. If the company insures 50,000 houses, then it can predict that 50 of the insured houses may burn. However, it is unlikely that exactly 50 houses will burn, as actual experience will probably vary from expectations. If more than 50 houses burn, then this deviation will be unfavourable and will represent risk for the insurance company. Therefore, the insurance company will not only estimate the number of houses that will burn, but will also estimate the range of error.

The range of error indicates that the actual losses may be more or less than estimated. Therefore, although 50 losses may be estimated, the range of possible deviation may be that between 40 and 60 will burn, and the possibility that the number will be greater than 50 will represent the insurer's risk.

In statistical terms, this deviation from the average (or mean) is called the standard deviation, which represents the unit for measuring risk. In financial terms, a standard deviation greater than one is more risky than a standard deviation of less than one, with one representing the chosen index. For example, a standard deviation of 1.25 means that the particular security is 25 per cent riskier than say, the S&P/ASX 200,[1] which has a market risk of one.

In many situations, although the probability of loss is the same, the magnitude of the losses may be very different. For example, if one risk had a potential loss of $500,000 and another had a potential loss of $50,000, assuming each had the same probability of loss, the former would be considered to involve more risk. However, if the amount of the potential loss (exposure) is the same, the risk with the greater probability of loss would be considered the more risky.

We have introduced two terms used in the measurement of risk: the probability of loss and the size of the possible loss. Tying these two terms together introduces the concept of the *expected value of a loss.*

$$EV = P \times S$$

where: EV = the expected value of the loss

P = the probability of loss

S = the size of the possible loss

---

1   This index represents the investable benchmark for the Australian equities market. The S&P/ASX 200 is comprised of the S&P/ASX 100 plus an additional 100 stocks.

For example, if the amount at risk is $100,000,000 and the probability of loss is 1 per cent, then the expected value of the loss is $1,000, 000 (.01 x $100,000,000). What we have discussed is an introduction to the *law of large numbers*, which is the principle on which insurance in society is founded.

A brief review of some concepts of probability, central tendency and dispersion are examined in Appendix 1.1.

The law of large numbers

The law of large numbers is a mathematical principle that states that the greater the number of observations of an event based on chance, the more likely the actual result will approximate the expected result. In other words, as the sample of observations is increased in size, the relative variation from the mean (average) declines, and the sample mean will eventually approximate the population mean. An example is given in Appendix 1.2. The important point is that larger samples produce greater confidence in the estimates.

Suppose an insurance company's historical statistical records indicated that the company could expect one per cent of the houses in its domestic portfolio to burn. The law of large numbers states that the greater the number of houses insured by the company, the more likely it is that the one per cent will be achieved. This allows an insurance company to accurately predict the dollar amount of losses it will experience in a given period, although the insurer still faces some risk or volatility around the average. But the risk for an insurer with more exposures is relatively lower than that for an insurer with fewer exposures under the same expected distribution of losses, as presented in Appendix 1.2.

It must be emphasised that the law of large numbers allows only group results to be estimated. It will not allow us to predict accurately what will happen in a particular exposure, for example to your house or your life, in the group. The law of large numbers is an important concept and is examined further in Chapter 3.

At a glance

- An important aspect of risk relates to its variability of outcomes.

- Variability implies different degrees of risk in given situations.

- Insurance companies use the degree of risk to discover factors that will either increase or decrease the frequency or severity (or both) of loss.

- Insurance companies keep detailed statistical records of past losses and thus are able to predict future losses fairly accurately.

- Because predictions cannot be 100 per cent accurate, the statistician will estimate a range of error.

- Risk is measured by a statistical concept called standard deviation, which indicates more or less risk.

- The magnitude of a loss can also be an indication of risk.

- The expected value of a loss is the product of the probability of loss and the size of the expected loss.

RISK VERSES PERILS VERSES HAZARDS

1-050   Introduction

When discussing risk, it is not uncommon for people to substitute the terms *peril* and *hazard* and to be confused about their meaning. Perils are the immediate causes of loss. If your house is destroyed by fire, the peril, or cause of the loss is the fire. If your car is damaged in a collision with a tree, collision is the peril, or cause of loss. We are surrounded by potential loss because the environment is filled with perils such as fire, flood, windstorm, hail, theft, death, sickness, accidents or lightning.

1-060   Perils

Perils can be classified as natural perils, human perils and economic perils.

Natural perils

Natural perils are those causes of loss over which people have very little control, such as cyclones, volcanic eruption and tsunamis. Table 1.1 provides examples of the types of natural perils that can be encountered.

Table 1.1: Natural perils

Natural perils	
Usually insurable	Usually uninsurable
Storm and tempest	Flood coverage in a flood prone area
Natural combustion	Epidemic
Lightning	Tsunami
Heart attack	Damage by vermin

Table 1.1 shows that not all natural perils are easily insurable either because it is not possible to predict their occurrence and so allow underwriters to strike an economical premium (eg, epidemics) or because they have the potential to cause catastrophic losses (eg, tsunamis). However, flood insurance is now readily available in Australia for private property, small business and strata title properties.

Human perils

Human perils are those causes of loss over which individuals have full control, such as suicide, theft and war. Table 1.2 shows examples of the types of human perils that can be encountered.

Table 1.2: Human perils

Human perils	
Usually insurable	Usually uninsurable
Theft	War
Vandalism	Civil unrest
Negligence	Radioactive contamination
Fire and smoke	Terrorism
Fraud involving e-commerce	
Suicide	

Table 1.2 shows that not all human perils are insurable. Theft is a cause of loss and is generally insurable; however, although war is a human peril that leads to a loss, it is not insurable because of its catastrophic effects on an insurer. Suicide is a human peril that is controllable by the individual but is insurable, generally after a three-month waiting period for death insurance.

Economic perils

Economic perils (eg, employee strikes or arson for profit) are causes of loss over which humans can be considered to exert an influence and are considered uninsurable.

1-070   Hazards

A hazard is a condition that increases the probability (frequency) of losses, their severity or both. For example, if your car was involved in a collision and it was found that the tyres were bald, the collision is the peril, or the cause of the loss, and the bald tyres are the hazard, as they increase both the probability and the severity of the loss. There are two major groups of hazards — tangible and intangible — that affect the probability and severity of losses.

Tangible hazards include physical hazards; intangible hazards include moral hazards, morale hazards and legal hazards.

Tangible hazards

Physical hazards

Physical hazards are the tangible conditions present in the environment that affect the frequency and/or severity of loss. Examples of physical hazards include low humidity combined with hot and strong winds (which increases the probability of bushfires); defective wiring (which increases the probability of fire in a building); and inadequate perimeter security (which increases the probability of burglary).

The most important physical hazards that affect a property relate to its *location*, *construction* and *usage*. The location of the property affects its susceptibility to damage by fire, flood, earthquake and other perils. How location is affected by physical hazards is shown in the following illustrated example.

Illustrated example 1.3

John and Julie have retired to the country and built their dream home in a heavily timbered, isolated area so they can be close to nature. As the only access to their home is by a long gravel road, there is a high probability of severe loss by fire as it will be difficult for emergency services to respond if needed.

A building's construction can affect both the probability and the severity of loss. It is difficult to make a building completely fire proof, but some types of construction are more susceptible to damage than others. A building with a fibro external wall is more susceptible to damage by flying objects in a storm than one constructed of brick or reinforced concrete. A commercial building divided into units is less likely to suffer extensive damage by fire if the dividing walls between the units are constructed of double brick with rooftop fire parapets, as most fires are likely to be contained in one unit until the fire services arrive.

The use or occupancy of a building will also create physical hazards. A building occupied by a fibreglass manufacturer or motor vehicle paint shop will have a greater probability of loss by fire than a building occupied by offices.

People also have physical characteristics that affect loss. If a person is a heavy smoker and also has high blood pressure or is obese, there is a high probability that these health characteristics will result in large health expenses.

Intangible hazards

Intangible hazards relate to people's attitudes and non-physical cultural conditions that affect the probability and severity of loss. They are referred to as moral, morale and legal hazards and their existence can lead to physical hazards. Each of these hazards is examined in turn.

Moral hazards

A moral hazard refers to the deliberate creation of a loss to defraud an insurer. This could be triggered by a person who intentionally causes a loss or dishonestly inflates the size of a claim in an attempt to collect more than the amount to which they are entitled, or as a result of organised crime. These dishonest tendencies increase the probability of loss.

Insurers pay the cost of these claims out of the insurance pool that contains the premiums collected from a large number of insureds. These claims erode the premium pool so a provision must be included in the premium calculation to allow for these false claims. The result of moral hazard is that the premiums are higher for everyone. Fraud costs the Australian insurance industry more than $2 billion each year, or $73 for every insurance policy paid in Australia (EIU, 2004).

Moral hazards are present in all forms of insurance which insurers find difficult to control. They attempt to control this hazard by careful underwriting of the risk and by the imposition of policy provisions such as deductibles, waiting periods, exclusions and warranties. These terms are defined and discussed in later chapters.

Morale hazards (or attitudinal hazard)

A morale hazard refers to carelessness or indifference to a loss because of the existence of insurance. This hazard is not necessarily caused by dishonesty; it may owe more to a psychological tendency for people to act carelessly or show a lack of concern about either protecting their property before a loss or conserving their property after a loss, because they think that their insurance will cover the loss. Examples of such carelessness include drivers who leave their keys in their unattended car (thereby increasing the probability of theft) and shopkeepers who do not maintain their machinery (leading to its breakdown and claiming on their machinery breakdown insurance). Insurers attempt to control morale hazards by inserting clauses in their policies requiring policyholders to exercise care, such as requiring insureds to activate installed alarm systems when leaving their property for burglary/theft cover to remain in place.

Some morale hazards, created unintentionally, result in poor health and reduced life expectancy. For example, excessive smoking or drug taking, poor eating habits, insufficient exercise and obesity are all morale hazards that can increase the probability and severity of loss.

Legal hazards

Legal hazards refer to the increase in the probability or severity of loss that arises from court judgments or acts of Parliament (resulting in changes in the regulatory environment). For example, large liability awards made by courts some years ago resulted in many small businesses, clubs and community groups folding in the face of large increases in liability insurance premiums. More recently, federal legislation stipulating the adoption of a common definition of flood to be included in domestic home building and contents, and strata title policies, has resulted in substantial increases in insurance premiums for these policies.

Recognising the existence of hazards is important, because our ability to reduce their effects will reduce insurance and other costs, as well as the severity of retained losses. Hazard management is an important risk management tool. For example, many corporations around the world implement disaster control management to reduce the impact of biological or terrorist attacks. One visible example of disaster control management is increased baggage and passenger inspections at airports.

At a glance

- Perils are the immediate causes of loss.
- Perils can be classified as natural and human perils.
- Natural perils are those over which people have very little control.
- Human perils are those over which humans have full control.
- A hazard is a condition that increases the probability of losses, their severity or both.
- A hazard can be either tangible or intangible.
- Tangible hazards are physical hazards that are present in the environment.
- Intangible hazards relate to people's attitudes and non-physical cultural conditions. They can be moral, morale or legal hazards.

CLASSIFICATION OF RISK

1-080   Introduction

Because risk can be classified in many different ways, it is important that we understand the differences and how they relate to insurance. These classifications include:

- financial and non-financial risks
- dynamic and static risks
- pure and speculative risks
- fundamental and particular risks.

1-090   Financial and non-financial risks

Financial risk refers to those situations that involve financial consequences such as changes in commodity prices, interest rates, foreign exchange rates and the value of money. For example, a farmer who agrees to sell grain for a fixed price in six months may lose money if the price of grain were to increase. Furthermore, in some situations, risk results in financial loss, such as the loss of property through peril of fire, and in other situations it does not.

Non-financial risk refers to such factors as meeting community expectations (social), environmental impact and cutting greenhouse gas emissions (environmental), and compliance with local laws and international conventions (legal). While these factors may impact on the successful operation of a company or project and need to be taken into consideration by management, they are not matters that results in a financial loss, as caused by a peril such as fire. This text is concerned only with risk that involves financial loss.

1-100   Dynamic and static risks

Dynamic risks are risks resulting from changes in the economy. Changes in technology, price levels, consumer tastes, income and production may cause financial loss to members of the economy. Generally these dynamic risks benefit society over the long run because they result in adjustments to correct the misallocation of resources. These risks are not predictable, as they do not occur with any degree of regularity.

Static risks are risks that occur independently of economic changes. These losses generally result from natural perils and dishonesty of individuals. Unlike dynamic risks, static risks do not benefit society, as they involve destruction of assets or result from human failure. Static losses are generally predictable because they occur with a reasonable degree of regularity. Because of this predictability, static risks are generally insurable, while it is difficult to insure dynamic risks.

1-110   Pure and speculative risks

Pure risk refers to those situations that involve only the possibility of loss or no change in condition. With pure risks, the only possible outcomes are adverse (loss), neutral (no loss), but no chance of a gain (profit). If you own a motor vehicle, for instance, you face the possibility of the vehicle being damaged or not being damaged. Examples of pure risk include damage to property caused by fire, lightning, flood or earthquake; job-related injury; premature death; and catastrophic medical expenses.

Speculative risk refers to a situation where there is the possibility of a loss but also the possibility of a gain. While there is the possibility of a break-even position, this is generally considered a loss, as a speculation is made with the intention of making a gain. Gambling is a good example of speculative risk, as the punter deliberately assumes risk in the hope of making a gain. Entrepreneurs who start up e-commerce companies also face speculative risk as they assume considerable risk in the hope of developing a successful business and making a gain.

It is important to distinguish between pure and speculative risks, as insurers do not normally insure against speculative risks. This is because insurers cannot apply the law of large numbers in order to predict future loss experience. In some situations, society can benefit from a speculative risk but will be harmed if a pure risk exists and a loss occurs. Companies that speculate on developing new technology — for example, developing new and faster memory systems for computers — will benefit society if they are successful.

1-120   Fundamental and particular risks

A fundamental risk is a risk that affects the entire economy or large numbers of individuals, firms or groups within the economy. The resulting losses are impersonal in origin and consequence and are caused mainly by a natural phenomenom, such as earthquake, cyclone or flood or economic, social and political phenomena. Examples include war, rapid rises in inflation and cyclical unemployment, because large numbers of people are affected.

Fundamental risks are caused by circumstances largely beyond the control of the individuals who suffer the losses. Since they are not the fault of anyone in particular, it is considered that society rather than the individual has the responsibility to deal with them. For example, Australia is prone to widespread drought that results in financial hardship for many people and businesses. Hurricane Katrina in the United States in 2005, Hurricane Sandy in 2012, cyclone Tracey in 1974 and cyclone Yasi in 2011 caused widespread property damage from wind and flooding.

It is possible to include terrorist attacks as a fundamental risk because these attacks can result in substantial damage to property and loss of life. For example, the terrorist attack on the World Trade Center in New York on 11 September 2001, resulted in losses, both personal and property, estimated at US$32.5 billion (in 2001 dollars).

A particular risk is a risk that affects only individuals and not the entire community. These risks may be static or dynamic. Examples include car theft, fires in dwellings, theft, burglary and storm damage. Losses caused by particular risks are considered the responsibility of individuals and can be dealt with through the use of insurance or loss prevention strategies, for example.

At a glance

- Risks can be classified as:
  - » financial and non-financial
  - » dynamic and static
  - » pure and speculative
  - » fundamental and particular.
- Pure risk refers to those situations that involve only the possibility of loss or no change in condition (no loss).
- Speculative risk refers to a situation where there is the chance of a gain but also the chance of loss.

CLASSIFICATION OF PURE RISK

1-130   Introduction

We face countless risks in our daily lives and in business, but for the most part they are static risks. For someone managing risk, it is essential that they know the characteristics of the underlying potential losses. These can be described in terms of exposures, perils and hazards.

1-140   Exposures

It is not correct to use the word 'risk' to denote a property or person likely to suffer losses. The term exposure is used to describe the property or person facing a condition in which loss or losses are possible. For example, a business is exposed to the perils of fire, storm, burglary, etc, while a person is exposed to the perils of accidental death, injury or illness. This text uses the term *exposure* in this way.

Classifying pure risks begins by putting them into broad types of exposures that are not mutually exclusive and may overlap. Pure risks may cause an individual, family or business to be faced with such exposures as personal loss exposures, property loss exposures, liability loss exposures, catastrophic loss exposures, accidental loss exposures or failure to perform loss exposures. These risks can be classified as:

- personal
- property
  - » direct loss
  - » indirect loss (or consequential)
- liability
  - » failure to perform.

Personal risks

Personal risks are those risks that directly affect an individual. These personal loss exposures involve the possibility of a complete loss or reduction in our ability to earn income; incurring extra expenses; and a reduction of financial assets. Generally this is caused by the following perils:

- Risk of premature death

- Risk of dependent old age (insufficient income during retirement)
- Risk of sickness or accident (poor health)
- Risk of unemployment.

Risk of premature death

This is the risk of the death of a family bread-winner (family head) with unfulfilled financial obligations. These obligations can include leaving dependents with insufficient funds to finance daily living and education and unpaid mortgages.

The premature death of a family head can result in at least four costs. First, is the loss the human life value of the family head. The human life value is defined as the present value of the family's share of the deceased breadwinner's future earnings. Second, additional expenses may be incurred that may include uninsured funeral and medical expenses, probate, taxes, legal costs. Third, the surviving family may not have sufficient income to meet these expenses. Finally, noneconomic costs can also be incurred. These can include emotional grief, loss of companionship and a role model for children.

Risk of dependent old age

The major risk associated with old age is having insufficient income during retirement. On retirement, workers lose their earned income and must rely on their superannuation, savings, age pension and/or other income sources to fund their retirement. In Australia the emphasis on funding retirement is shifting from the age pension to self-funded retirement from accumulated superannuation. However, the Association of Superannuation Funds Australia Limited (ASFA) (2019) estimated that the average superannuation balance held by men at retirement in 2017-18 was $168,500 and $121,300 for women. It is estimated that a single retiree needs a yearly income of $27,913 to achieve a "modest' lifestyle and $43,787 for a "comfortable" lifestyle (requiring a lump sum of $545,000), while a couple requires $40,194 and $61,786 respectively (requiring a limp sum of $640,000) (ASFA Retirement Standard, 2019). Clearly, it will be difficult for many retirees to achieve even a "modest" lifestyle in retirement particularly if the breadwinner dies.

Risks of sickness or accident

The risks posed by these perils include the loss or reduction in earned income and catastrophic medical bills. While the majority of Australians have access to some form of health insurance, many expenses such as hiring or the use of specialist medical equipment may not be covered by all health insurance funds. Unless the person has adequate health insurance, private savings and personal assets, or other sources of income to meet these expenses they may be financially insecure.

Risk of unemployment

The risk of unemployment is a further threat to financial security. This risk can result from business cycle downturn, technological and structural changes in the economy, seasonal factors and imperfections in the labour market. In Australia increasing numbers of workers are being laid off in the mining, government and other sectors as the demand for mining products and government revenues decline.

Property risks

Property risks arise from the loss of property through its vulnerability to destruction or theft. These property loss exposures are associated with both real property, such as buildings, and personal property, motor vehicles and contents of a dwelling. The loss exposure can be due to accidental causes or catastrophic causes, such as floods or cyclones. These risks are of two distinct types of loss: *direct loss* and *indirect or consequential loss*. Direct loss arises through the physical damage, destruction or theft of the property. For example, if a house is destroyed during a storm, the owner loses the value of the property. Indirect or consequential loss refers to financial loss that results indirectly from a loss to the exposed property. How both direct and indirect losses can affect a business is shown in the following illustrated example.

Illustrated example 1.4

Benjamin owns a commercial building that he partially occupies as an auto-electrician, and he rents out the remainder. If the building was destroyed through the direct loss of fire, this would result in a financial loss through physical damage and a loss of profits, called consequential loss, because Benjamin might not be able to conduct his business, and he would also incur a loss of rent while the building was being rebuilt.

A further type of indirect loss would result from the extra expenses incurred to rent alternative temporary premises to continue business operations so as to retain customers. Benjamin might rent a shed so that he could continue his business, and in doing so might reduce his loss of profits claim. The extra expenses incurred to allow Benjamin to continue his business might be covered by his policy.

Liability risks

Liability risks result from the intentional or unintentional injury to other people or damage to their property through negligence — that is, by carelessness or failure to take necessary precautions. These risks can be personal or can arise through business activities. For example, a person injured while water skiing may sue the boat owner for damages owing to the owner's failure to exercise due care, or a shopper may sue a supermarket for injuries suffered from slipping on a wet floor.

Loss exposures also include both the catastrophic loss exposures associated with fundamental risk and the accidental loss exposures associated with particular risk, both of which were discussed in the previous section.

Failure to perform risk results from the failure of others to perform a service as promised. Their failure to carry out their obligation may cause financial loss to the other party. For instance, a building contractor may fail to complete a shopping centre on schedule, causing financial loss to the owner through loss of rental income. Also, the rapid rise of e-commerce introduces new risks relating to the failure of others to perform as promised or to a standard that would be reasonably expected.

We are surrounded by risk in one form or another and most vigilant people are constantly looking for ways to either reduce or eliminate risk. Some fundamental risks such as policing and bushfire control are met by semi-government and government bodies, while other risks are considered the responsibility of individuals. The question arises as to how the various risks are to be dealt with and in what order. A systematic approach to dealing with risks is needed, and this is discussed in Chapter 2.

1-150   Study questions

1.1   Explain the meaning of risk. In your explanation, state the relationship between risk and uncertainty.

1.2   Risk may be sub-classified in several ways. List the three principal ways in which risk may be sub-classified and explain the distinguishing characteristics of each class.

1.3   How does objective risk differ from subjective risk?

1.4   Explain in insurance terms why some situations have 'more risk' or 'less risk' than others.

1.5 Explain what is meant by the expression the range of error and how this relates to an insurer's risk.

1.6 Briefly explain the law of large numbers and how this mathematical principle is relevant to an insurer's operations?

1.7 Distinguish between 'perils' and 'hazards', and give two examples of each.

1.8 Hazards can be classified into two major groups. Explain the hazards contained in these groups.

1.9 Why may it be difficult in a particular situation to distinguish between moral hazard and morale hazard?

1.10 Some people with top-level health coverage visit doctors more often than required. Is this tendency a moral hazard or simply common sense? Explain.

1.11 Explain the difference between dynamic and static risks. Give an example of each.

1.12 Explain the difference between pure and speculative risk and between fundamental and particular risk.

1.13 Inflation causes both pure and speculative risks in our society. Give some examples of each.

1.14 List four types of risk that an individual or organisation faces.

1.15 What is the difference between a direct loss and an indirect or consequential loss?

1-160 References and further reading

References

Articles and Books

Baranoff, E 2004, *Risk management and insurance,* John Wiley & Sons Inc, USA, p3.

Economist Intelligence Unit (EIU) (2004), The truth about fraud, November. Accessed 27 January 2016. Available at http://www.iag.com.au/economist-intelligence-unit-eiu-report-truth-about-insurance-fraud

Association of Superannuation Funds of Australia Limited (ASFA) 2014, *An update on the level and distribution of retirement savings.* Accessed: 26 January 2016. Available at file:///C:/Users/Owner/Downloads/1403-LevelAndDistributionRetirementSavings.pdf.

Vaughan, EJ & Vaughan, TM 2003, *Fundamentals of risk and insurance,* 9th edn, John Wiley & Sons Inc, USA, p3.

Releases

Association of Superannuation Funds of Australia (AFSA) 2019, *The AFSA Retirement Standard.* Accessed: July 2019. Available at *http://www.superannuation.asn.au/resources/retirement-standard*

Further reading

Baranoff, E 2004, *Risk management and insurance,* John Wiley & Sons Inc, USA. Chapter 1.

Bernstein, PL 1996, *Against the gods: The remarkable story of risk,* John Wiley & Sons Inc, USA.

Redja, GE 2003, *Principles of risk management and insurance,* 8th edn, Pearson Education Inc., USA. Chapter 1.

Vaughan, EJ & Vaughan, TM 2003, *Fundamentals of risk and insurance,* 9th edn, John Wiley & Sons Inc, USA. Chapter 1.

1-170   Appendix 1.1

Probability and statistics

To determine expected losses, insurance actuaries apply probability and statistical analysis to given loss situations. The probability of an event is simply the long-run frequency of the event, given an infinite number of trials with no changes in the underlying conditions. The probability of some events can be determined without experimentation. For example, if a 'fair' coin is flipped in the air, the probability the coin will come up 'heads' is 50 per cent and the probability it will come up 'tails' is also 50 per cent. Other probabilities, such as the probability of dying during a specified year or the probability of being involved in a motor vehicle accident can be estimated from past data.

A convenient way of summarising events and probabilities is through a probability distribution. A probability distribution allows future expectations to be measured as well as the variability of those expectations. It lists events that could occur and the corresponding probability of each event's occurrence. Probability distributions may be discrete, meaning that only distinct outcomes are possible, or continuous, meaning that any outcome over a range of outcomes could occur. For example, speed and temperature are continuous measures as all values over the range of values can occur.

Probability distributions are characterised by two important measures: central tendency and dispersion. Although there are several measures of central tendency, the measure most often used is the mean (μ) or the expected value (EV) of the distribution. Other measures of central tendency are the median, which is the middle observation in a probability distribution and the mode, which is the observation that occurs most often.

The mean or expected value is found by multiplying each outcome by the probability of occurrence and summing the resulting products. This is shown as:

$$\mu \text{ or } EV = \Sigma X_i P_i$$

For example, assume that an actuary estimates the following probabilities of various losses for a certain risk:

Amount of loss (X_i)	Probability of loss (P_i)	$X_i P_i$
$0	.30	$0
$360	.50	$180
$600	.20	$120
	$\Sigma X_i P_i$	$300

The mean or expected loss of this probability distribution is $300. However, although the mean value indicates central tendency it does not indicate the riskiness or dispersion of the distribution. Consider a second probability-of-loss distribution:

Amount of loss (X_i)	Probability of loss (P_i)	$X_i P_i$
$225	.40	$90
$350	.60	$210
	$\Sigma X_i P_i$	$300

The second probability distribution also has a mean of $300. However, the first distribution is riskier because the range of possible outcomes is from $0 to $600.

With the second distribution, the range of possible outcomes is only $125 ($350 - $225), so the outcome with the second distribution is more certain.

Two standard measure of dispersion are employed to characterise the variability or dispersion about the mean value. These measures are the variance (σ^2) and standard deviation (σ). The variance of a probability distribution is the sum of the squared differences between the possible outcomes and the expected value, weighted by the probability of the outcomes. This is shown as:

$$\sigma^2 = \Sigma P_i(X_i - EV)^2$$

So the variance is the average squared deviation between the possible outcomes and the mean. Because the variance is in 'squared units', it is necessary to take the square root of the variance so that the central tendency and dispersion measures are in the same units. The square root of the variance is the standard deviation. The variance and standard deviation of the first deviation are as follows:

$$\sigma^2 = .30(0 - 300)^2 + .50(360 - 300)^2 + .20(600 - 300)^2$$

$$= 27,000 + 1,500$$

$$= 46,800$$

$$\sigma = \sqrt{46,800} = 216.33$$

For the second distribution, the variance and standard deviation are:

$$\sigma^2 = .40(225 - 300)^2 + .60(350 - 300)^2$$

$$= 2,250 + 1,500$$

$$= 3\,750$$

$$\sigma = \sqrt{3,750} = 61.24$$

It can be seen that while the means of the two distributions are the same, the standard deviations are significantly different. What can be deduced from this? Higher standard deviations, relative to the mean, are associated with greater uncertainty of loss, therefore, risk is higher. Lower standard deviations, relative to the mean are associated with less uncertainty of loss, therefore, risk is lower.

This example is contrived to illustrate the application of the measure of central tendency and dispersion. In practice, estimating the frequency and severity of loss is difficult. Insurers employ both actual loss data and theoretical loss distributions such as binomial and Poisson in estimating losses. An example of the use of binomial distribution is shown in Appendix 1.2.

1-180   Appendix 1.2

More exposures less risk

Assume that the riskiness of two groups is under consideration by an insurer. One group is comprised of 1,000 units and the other of 4,000 units. Each group anticipates incurring 10 per cent losses within a specified period such as one year. The first group, therefore, is expected to have 100 losses; the second group expects 400 losses. This example demonstrates a binomial distribution that is, one where two possible outcomes exist, loss or no loss. The average of a binomial equals the sample size times the probability of 'success'. Success is defined as a loss claim where:

n = the sample size

p = probability of 'success'

q = probability of 'failure' = $1 - p$

$n \times p$ = mean

For group 1 in the sample, the mean is 100:

$(1,000) \times (0.10) = 100$

For group 2 the mean is 400:

$(4,000) \times (0.01) = 400$

The standard deviation of a distribution is a measure of risk or dispersion. For a binomial distribution, the standard deviation is

$\sqrt{n \times p \times q}$

In our example, the standard deviations of Group 1 and Group 2 are 9.5 and 19 respectively.

$\sqrt{(1,000) \times (0.10) \times (0.90)} = 9.5$

$\sqrt{(4,000) \times (0.10) \times (0.90)} = 19$

Therefore, while the mean, or expected number of losses, quadrupled with the quadrupling of the sample size, the standard deviation only doubled. Through this example, it can be seen that the proportional deviation of actual from expected outcomes decreases with increased sample size. The relative dispersion has been reduced.

The coefficient of variation (the standard deviation divided by the mean) is often used as a relative measure of risk. In this example, Group 1 has a coefficient of variation of 9.5/100, or 0.095. Group 2 has a coefficient of variation of 19/400 = 0.0475, indicating reduced risk.

Taking the extreme, consider an individual (n = 1) who attempts to retain the risk of loss. The person either will or will not incur a loss and even though the probability of loss is only 10 per cent, how does that person know whether he or she will be the unlucky one out of ten? Using the binomial distribution, that person's standard deviation (risk) is $\sqrt{(1)} \times (0.10) \times (0.090) = 0.30$, a much higher measure of risk than that of the insurer. The individual's coefficient of variation is 0.30/0.10 = 3, demonstrating the higher risk. More specifically, the risk is 63 times (3/0.0475) that of the insurer, with 4,000 units of exposure.

CHAPTER 2

INTRODUCTION TO RISK MANAGEMENT

THE CONCEPT OF RISK MANAGEMENT

2-000   Introduction

Insurance is an important component of risk management. The risk management decision is dependent on the nature of the risk, the frequency and severity of loss, and external market conditions. Many pure risks have insurance solutions however, in some cases we may decide not to use insurance and instead avoid the risk altogether, self-insure it, transfer it, or reduce it. As this text focuses on the use of insurance to manage risk, it is important that you understand when it is most appropriate to use. The importance of risk management is shown in the following illustrated example.

Illustrated example 2.1

On 1 May 2005 a fire occurred in one of the Taiwanese manufacturing facilities of Advanced Semiconductor Engineering, Inc. (ASE), one of the world's largest operations for the assembly and testing of integrated circuits. The fire started in the materials processing plant at the company's Chungli substrate plant and resulted in a property loss approaching US$400 million. ASE did not have any business interruption cover in place and suffered in excess of US$10 million per month in lost capacity. Within days of the accident, the share price dropped 10 per cent in value (Cusack 2005).

ASE is liable for compensation for compensation to its customers for non-compliance with its contractual obligations. The organisation provides semi-conductors to customers, such as Inter and Motorola. Because of its failure to complete its contracts, some of ASE's customers indicated that they were considering seeking alternative sources of supply.

2-010   Risk management defined

The term *risk management* can be interpreted in different ways depending on the nature of the risk, the frequency and severity of losses, and external market conditions. Its meaning can vary depending on whether physical assets are being protected, physical injuries are being prevented to reduce a firm's potential legal liabilities, the impacts of a firm's investment and commercial decisions are being limited, or complex financial instruments are being used, such as derivatives to manage currency risks. Because of these different meanings, it is important to define risk management for the purposes of this text.

The Australian/New Zealand Standard on Risk Management (AS/NZS ISO31000:2009) provides a generic framework for the identification, measurement and control of those risks that may threaten the profitability, reputation or long-term survival of a firm. This standard also provides a definition of the process of risk management:

> *"the systematic application of management policies, procedures and practices to the tasks of communicating, establishing the context, identifying, analysing, evaluating, treating, monitoring and reviewing risk"*. (AS/NZS ISO 31000:2009)

The purpose of a risk management program is to manage a firm's exposures to loss and to protect its assets. Risk management can be used by whoever faces potential losses, be they large or small firms, non-profit organisations, individuals or families.

But who is ultimately responsible for a company's risk management program? Most large organisations employ a risk manager to carry out this task, but senior executives and boards are increasingly recognising their responsibility for risk management. Senior managers and boards have both a moral and a statutory responsibility to maintain shareholder value, which is the present value of future cash flows. Therefore, implicit in shareholder value is an assessment of the company's risk profile and of the executive's ability to manage the risk–reward equation that generates that profile. A failure to effectively carry out these duties could make the company's officers potentially liable to stakeholders under statute for any resultant losses. Therefore, risk management is an important function in large organisations; and, as you will see throughout this chapter, it is equally important for small businesses and individuals.

This chapter discusses the treatment of pure risks or loss exposures as defined in Chapter 1 — ie, risk that can be treated through the application of insurance, and not speculative risks such as those involving currency exchange, interest rates and commodity prices. A wide variety of texts are available that describe the treatment of speculative risks, and a reference to such texts is made in the 'Suggestions for further reading' section at the end of this chapter.

At a glance

- The meaning of risk management varies depending on its uses.
- A framework for risk management and its meaning is provided by AS/NZS ISO 31000:2009.
- Senior management is ultimately responsible for a company's risk management program.

RISK MANAGEMENT PROCESS

2-020   Introduction

Risk management activities are part of an ongoing process, which can be divided into a series of individual steps that need to be accomplished in order to manage risks. Planning for losses occur before the occurrence of the loss, while losses involving emergencies, such as a fire in a vital production plant, require action while the loss is occurring. Finally, once the loss has occurred, insurance claims need to be completed and lodged with the insurance company, and details of the loss must be analysed.

The risk management process involves the following steps:

1.   Define objectives.

2.   Identify potential loss exposures.

3.   Evaluate and analyse potential loss exposures.

4.   Select the most appropriate risk management techniques.

5.   Implement and monitor the program.

2-025   Step 1: Defining objectives

The first step in the risk management process is to formulate the objectives of the risk management program. Without these written objectives many risk management programs are fragmented and inconsistent. The statement of objectives is followed by identification of the principles and procedures designed to achieve these objectives. The objectives can be classified as:

- pre-loss objectives
- post-loss objectives

Pre-loss objectives

These are important objectives that are addressed before the loss occurs. They include making a commitment to the risk management process, economy, reduction of anxiety and meeting legal obligations.

The first objective focuses on the firm preparing for potential losses in the most economical way. This objective involves an analysis of the cost of safety programs, insurance premiums paid and the costs associated with the different techniques for handling losses.

The second objective focuses on the reduction of anxiety. Certain loss exposures can cause considerable worry and anxiety for managers, small business owners and individuals. For example, the threat of a catastrophic legal action resulting from a defective product can cause greater anxiety than a small loss from a minor fire.

The final objective focuses on ensuring that all legal obligations are met. For example, government regulations may require a firm to install safety devices to protect workers from harm, to govern the storage of flammable liquids within a firm's premises, to dispose of hazardous waste products properly and to label consumer products appropriately. Workers compensation insurance must be in place for all the firm's workers.

Post-loss objectives

These objectives can include survival, continuing operation, stability of earnings, continued growth and social responsibility.

The most important post-loss objective focuses on the survival of the firm (or family unit). Survival means that after a loss occurs, the firm can resume at least partial operations within a reasonable period of time.

The second post-loss objective is to continue operating. For most firms, the ability to continue operating after a loss is extremely important. This may mean shifting the business to temporary accommodation while the damaged premises are being repaired. For example, bakeries, dairies, the local panel workshop and other small business must continue to operate after a loss otherwise business will be lost to competitors, customer loyalty eroded and in some cases, contracts for the supply of product (eg, milk) broken with possible legal consequences for the producer resulting from a failure to supply as contracted.

The third post-loss objective focuses *on maintaining stable earnings.* For large companies it is important to maintain earnings per share to maintain shareholder confidence and for small business and individuals to meet ongoing financial obligations.

The fourth post-loss objective focuses on the continued growth of the firm. A company can grow by developing new products and markets, or by acquiring or merging with other companies. Management (or the risk manager) must consider the effects that a loss could have on the firm's ability to grow.

Finally, the objective of social responsibility focuses on minimising the effects that a loss will have on other persons and society. A severe loss can adversely affect employees, suppliers, creditors and the community in general. For example, a severe loss that shuts down a manufacturing plant in a small town for an extended period can cause considerable economic distress in the town.

An application of these principles is shown in the following illustrated example.

Illustrated example 2.2

A risk management manual for a hospital might concentrate on hygiene issues and then include objectives relating to the insurance aspect of the hospital's risk management program, followed by identifying specific rules relating to losses to be retained and those to be insured.

Objectives

1. Treat all potential losses as if they are retained by the firm (ie, losses not transferred to an insurance company).

2. Retain those risks that will not significantly affect the firm's financial strength in the event of a loss.

3. Insure all risks that are not retained.

Insurance rules

This section contains the specific rules for dealing with these losses and specifies the losses the firm will retain, such as:

*   losses to buildings and contents up to $500,000

*   losses up to $1,000 for physical damage to company-owned motor vehicles

*   losses to all products transported on land.

General guidelines

The specific categories of exposures that are to be insured are detailed here, such as:

*   all losses to buildings and contents exceeding $500,000

*   all liability losses, both general and product

*   all losses to electronic equipment and its information.

Once the statement of objectives is formulated, the second step in the risk management process involves identifying the potential loss exposures.

2-030   Step 2: Identifying potential loss exposures

Identifying the risk management exposures can be difficult because there is so much to observe. The discovery process is critical to learning and understanding an organisation's tolerance for risk. Additionally, it is necessary to review an organisation's overall risk exposures. This process is called risk profiling. Both the types of risk and the severity of risk will differ vastly between industries. For example, BHP has a large potential legal liability for environmental damage, and intellectual property piracy and property rights issues could have a major impact on the operations of Microsoft, particularly in China.

The process of understanding an organisation's tolerance for risk begins with arranging potential loss exposures into the following categories:

- *Direct property loss exposures.* These can include losses to building, plant, equipment, computers, data and software, vehicles and mobile equipment.

- *Business income loss exposures.* Loss of business income from a covered loss and extra expenses following a property loss.

- *Liability loss exposures.* These can include defective products, environmental pollution, sexual harassment of, or discrimination against employees, wrongful dismissal, premises and general liability exposures, liability arising from the use of company vehicles or unregistered mobile equipment such as on-site fork lifts, misuse of Internet or e-mail transmissions plus officers and directors liability exposures.

- *Human resources loss exposures.* These include losses caused by the death, total and permanent disability or unplanned retirement of key personnel and job related injuries or disease experienced by employees or business partners.

- *Crime exposures.* These include holdups, robberies, burglaries, employee theft and dishonesty, fraud and embezzlement, internet and computer crime exposures, theft of intellectual property.

- *Foreign loss exposures.* These can include acts of terrorism, plants, business property, inventory, foreign currency risks, kidnapping of key personnel and political risks.

- *Intangible property loss exposures.* These can include damage to a company's public image, loss of goodwill and market image, loss or damage to intellectual property.

Failure to comply with government laws and regulations should also be considered.

Identifying potential loss exposures includes the characteristics of the three major categories discussed in Chapter 1: perils, exposures and hazards (see ¶1-050). This can be a difficult task because it is an ongoing process, necessitated by our dynamic environment, which continually generates new risk exposures, such as identity theft, computer fraud and effects of global warming.

Direct property losses

The first step is to gain as much information as possible about the firm and its operations. A physical inspection of the property, plant and machinery can reveal invaluable information about potential loss exposures. Information about previous loss exposures can be gained from the following sources:

- *Checklists.* Property checklists enable property to be identified and value assigned to potential losses.

- *Risk analysis questionnaires.* These questionnaires ask wide-ranging questions and can be distributed to key employees to identify major and minor potential loss exposures.

- *Flow charts.* These charts show the production and distribution process graphically. By analysing the charts, it is possible to identify bottlenecks in production, sole-source suppliers or concentrations of valuable property. Flow charts also reveal the consequential impact of losses. For example, a fire at a key supplier who is the company's only source of raw materials may bring the entire production process to a halt if alternative sources of supply have not been arranged.

- *Financial statements.* Analysis of these statements will identify the important assets that must be protected.

- *Historical loss data.* An analysis of this data will reveal any loss trends and loss exposures.

Loss of income

Indirect losses

Indirect losses can be difficult to identify and quantify. It is relatively easy to identify and value a particular machine, but it may be difficult to quantify the loss of profits that may result from the machine's remaining idle for two or three months. This will particularly be the case where the firm's sales are cyclical and a judgement about the possible size of the loss must be made. These indirect (or business interruption) losses have the potential to cause an organisation to fail, so management must understand the business interruption exposures the organisation faces and ensure that these risks are actually transferred where intended. Indeed, of those companies who experience a catastrophic loss, 30 per cent will fail within the first 24 months and an additional 29 per cent will fail beyond 24 months (META Research Report 2002).

Direct loss

The potential loss of income following a loss is the difference between the forecast of pre-loss income under normal circumstances and the estimate of the post-loss income. It is important to recognise that a direct loss to property usually has the potential to cause an indirect loss of income that in many cases could be far greater than the direct loss. The financial consequences of failing to recognise that a direct loss can cause indirect losses are shown in the following illustrated example.

Illustrated example 2.3

The management of Precision Engineering had a policy of backing up their computers at the end of each working day and securing the back-up tapes in their safe. A fire in the office building totally destroyed the building and all contents, including the back-up tapes. The total value of the direct property loss of the destroyed contents, including computers, amounted to $80,000, but the cost of the indirect loss involving the reconstruction and rewriting of the company's records amounted to $150,000.

Legal liability losses

Losses resulting from legal liability exposures arise from three sources:

1. the amount of legal damages awarded by a court to the injured party

2. the legal defence costs (which may include paying a proportion of the plaintiff's costs)

3. the cost of loss prevention of potential legal liability actions.

Identifying potential sources of legal liability can be an expensive and time-consuming process. Risk managers realise that their firms operate in an increasingly litigious society in which many claims are brought against businesses with the sole objective of obtaining a cash settlement from the firm's insurer rather than for genuine injuries suffered. The insurer may make a cash settlement if it considers that the cost of investigating and defending the action is higher than the actual amount of the third party claim. Examples of sources of liability losses are: physical or personal injury to customers, employees, clients or guests; damage to property belonging to a third party; intentional damage to a person's reputation; sexual harassment; wrongful dismissal; and vicarious liability arising when a firm hires or authorises another party to act on its behalf and this party injures a third party.

Loss of key personnel

Most businesses have a key person or persons in the organisation whose resignation, unplanned retirement, death or disablement could seriously affect the cash flow of the business. They could be a salesperson servicing high net worth clients, a research chemist or even the board of directors, who could all be killed in a single accident.

Key personnel can be identified from a firm's organisational chart, with the cost exposure represented by the cost of finding, hiring and training a replacement. Estimating the costs of key employee losses can be difficult, because finding a replacement is a function of the job market and a suitable person may not be available. This is particularly the case where the key employee has specialist knowledge, for example as the operator of specialist machinery. Such an employee's replacement may take several years to fully train.

The result of the death or permanent disablement of a key person could be:

- creditors demanding repayment of loans and creditors withholding payments

- customers and suppliers losing confidence in the firm

- lenders being unwilling to extend credit, or

- outstanding loans owed by the key person to the business called up for payment.

While it is important to identify all potential risk exposures, it is also important to estimate the impact that these loss exposures will have on the firm.

2-035   Step 3: Evaluating and analysing potential loss exposures

The third step in the risk management process is to evaluate and measure the impact that the identified losses will have on the firm. To do this it is necessary to estimate both the *frequency* and the *severity* of each type of loss exposure, as discussed in Chapter 1. There are two reasons for evaluating the frequency and severity of each loss type: first, to allow the various losses to be ranked according to their importance and second, to prioritise the selection of the most appropriate method, or combination of methods, of handling each exposure.

While it is necessary to evaluate both frequency and severity of losses, severity is the more important because a single catastrophic loss may bankrupt a firm. It was demonstrated in illustrated example 2.1 that a single fire loss occurring at a materials processing plant resulted in a crippling loss of profits due to the firm's inability to produce its products, and a potentially catastrophic claim for compensation and possible loss of customers because of their inability to fulfil their contracts. Therefore, it is necessary for the risk manager to map out all possible losses that can result from a single event.

Risk managers need to estimate both their maximum possible loss and their maximum probable loss. The maximum possible loss refers to the worst loss that could possibly happen to the organisation during its lifetime. The maximum probable loss refers to the maximum amount of damage a peril could cause under normal conditions. Therefore, a maximum probable loss value represents the largest probable financial loss to which the insured is potentially exposed. The operation of these principles is discussed in the following illustrated example.

Illustrated example 2.4

The risk manager of a large manufacturing firm estimates that if the plant was to be destroyed by flood, the cost of its replacement, including removal of debris, demolition and other costs would total $5 million. Therefore, the maximum possible loss is $5 million. The risk manager may estimate that a flood causing more than $3 million damage is so unlikely that it would not occur more than once in 100 years.

If the risk manager chose to ignore the amount of flood loss above $3 million, then the maximum probable loss is $3 million.

There is a $2 million difference between the maximum possible loss and the maximum probable loss. While the maximum probable loss of $3 million is more likely to occur, the risk manager must be mindful that the maximum possible loss of $5 million might also occur and prove catastrophic for the firm.

Catastrophic losses are difficult to predict because they occur infrequently. However, if they do occur their potential impact on the firm must be recognised. In contrast, losses that occur on a regular basis, such as damage to motor vehicles and trucks, can be predicted with greater accuracy.

Now that maximum possible cost of the exposures has been estimated, it is necessary to rank these potential risk exposures on the basis of how critical each occurrence will be to the future financial wellbeing of the company.

Ranking losses based on their criticality

Having estimated the potential size (severity) of the losses that are likely to occur and the probability (frequency) of their occurrence, it is now possible to rank the loss exposures according to their criticality. That is, will the occurrence be of minor importance and so be covered by current resources, or will it be so financially catastrophic that it will lead to the demise of the company? This ranking can be made by assigning a priority to each risk, based on whether it is critical, significant or insignificant.

- *Critical risks*: These are likely to result in catastrophic losses where the maximum possible loss cannot be covered by current resources, or any level of borrowing, and so could result bankruptcy — eg, extended industrial action at the company's only production plant; or, for individuals, a total loss of a house through fire.

- *Significant risks*: With these risks existing credit arrangements can cover the maximum possible loss — eg, flood damage at one of the company's warehouses; or, for individuals, major accident damage to a car.

- *Insignificant risks*: With these risks the maximum possible loss can be covered from existing current cash assets — eg, minor damage to packaging caused by vermin, or damage from vandalism; or, for individuals, minor panel damage to a motor vehicle.

By ranking risks in this manner, it is possible to construct a risk matrix that clearly highlights their probability of occurrence and severity. Figure 2.1 is a matrix that illustrates the possible risks faced by a medium-sized manufacturing business.

Figure 2.1: Risk matrix

PROBABILITY				
HIGH	Foreign exchange fluctuations	Credit risk of overseas customers	Industrial action
MEDIUM	Damage to goods in transit	Fire damage to Inverell storage facility	Loss of key personnel
LOW	Damage by vermin Vandalism	Product tamper Sabotage	Fire at the main production facility
	Insignificant	**Significant**	**Critical**

SEVERITY

Source: Adapted from Berwick 2001.

Some corporations own and operate hazardous operations in different parts of the world and must place greater emphasis on risk assessment such as injury to the surrounding population that a severe loss at one of these facilities could cause and the resulting damage to the corporation's reputation as shown in the following case example.

Case example

On 3 December 1984 a large quantity of toxic methyl isocyanine gas leaked from the Union Carbide (UCC) pesticide plant in Bhopal, India. This leakage caused 3,300 deaths, and more than 20,000 people were injured from exposure to the gas.

Massive litigation followed, and the widespread publicity triggered protests and worldwide sanctions against the company, which had a devastating impact on its profitability. Before the disaster, UCC's stock traded at between US$50 and US$58; in the months immediately following the accident it traded at US$32 to US$40. A takeover attempt in late 1985 forced UCC to start selling assets, so that by 1992 UCC was only half its pre-Bhopal size. Additionally, it was forced to take on nearly US$3 billion in debt, so that at the end of 1986 debt accounted for a staggering 80 per cent of capitalisation. This debt persisted, accounting for 50 per cent of capitalisation in 1991.

In 1984 sales revenue was US$9.5 billion, net income was US$323 million and total assets were US$10.5 billion. By 1987 sales revenue had fallen to US$6 billion, assets had fallen to US$6.5 billion and shareholders' equity had dropped from US$4.9 billion to less than US$1 billion. This dramatic fall in fortunes resulted from an event at a plant that contributed less than .5 per cent to company profits. The disaster represented a life-threatening risk to the company as well as to the citizens of Bhopal (Shrivastava 1987).

Had Union Carbide carried out a risk assessment as described above, management might have realised that the continued operation of this plant was too risky given its small contribution to company profits.

Once potential loss exposures have been identified, evaluated and measured, decisions about selecting the appropriate tools to manage these risks can be made.

2-040   Step 4: Selecting appropriate risk management techniques

The fourth step in the risk management process is the selection of the most appropriate tools for managing the risk exposures. These risk exposures result in costs, because all organisations are exposed to unexpected losses. These costs could include paying insurance premiums, paying for uninsured losses, paying for security of personnel and property, and paying for loss reduction techniques such as installing automatic sprinkler systems. Successful loss control will reduce the frequency or severity of these loss costs. However, despite loss control efforts some losses will still occur, so an effective risk-financing program must be implemented in order to minimise the effects of these losses on company profits.

Loss control techniques can be grouped into two broad approaches: *controlling* the risk and *financing* it. Risk control is defined as those techniques used to reduce the frequency and severity of the incurred loss.

Risk control

Risk control activities include the following risk management tools:

- risk avoidance
- loss prevention
- loss reduction.

Risk avoidance

In some instances, the best method of handling a loss exposure is to avoid any possibility of the loss occurring. Risk avoidance means that by abandoning an existing loss exposure, or never acquiring it in the first place, any chance of loss is eliminated. Union Carbide could have avoided the loss of life and injury to the citizens of Bhopal and the resulting devastation to its profits and assets, by closing the Bhopal plant before the disaster occurred. Some firms avoid investing in some foreign countries such as Nigeria because of the risk of employees being kidnapped and held hostage or property being confiscated.

Some risks are unavoidable: firms cannot avoid the risk of liability claims, and individuals cannot avoid the risk of natural death. In other instances, the avoidance of one loss exposure may create another. For example, some people choose to travel by car instead of by air because of their fear of flying. They may have avoided the risk of being killed in a plane crash, but they have exposed themselves to death or injury in a car crash. Where a risk cannot be avoided prevention measures should be put in place to reduce the probability of a loss.

When the chance of loss is high and loss severity is also high, the risk should be avoided unless the risk can be reduced.

Loss prevention

Loss prevention refers to activities that reduce the frequency of loss. Examples of loss prevention include the use of tamper-resistant packaging, driver training, speed control devices on trucks, and the implementation of quality control checks.

Loss prevention techniques should be used to treat all exposures, provided the costs do not exceed the benefits. However, the foremost goal of loss prevention is to reduce the probability of death and eliminate the chance of personal injury. Therefore, large firms employ loss control engineers to investigate sources of loss or injury and to implement corrective action.

Most companies realise that effective loss prevention reduces their insurance premiums. Some companies pay millions of dollars in insurance premiums, so effective loss prevention could equate to a saving of tens of thousands of dollars. For a small business involved in a hazardous occupation, effective loss prevention may be the difference between obtaining insurance and having an insurance application declined.

Loss reduction

Loss reduction refers to activities that reduce the severity of loss after it occurs. It is inevitable that some losses will occur, so loss reduction techniques can be implemented to minimise the impact of these losses. For example, automatic fire sprinkler systems are not designed to prevent fires but to prevent the spread of fires and hence reduce their severity. Underwriters will usually apply a premium discount if automatic fire sprinkler systems are installed, because of their loss prevention capabilities. Other loss reduction techniques include the installation of fire doors and fire-rated walls to slow the spread of a fire, and salvage operations. In addition to these underwriter requirements, in many jurisdictions these preventative measures are required by law. For example, legislation took effect on 1 July 2007 that requires all Queensland homes and units to be fitted with smoke alarms.

The basic rule is: *when the severity of loss is high and when the loss cannot be avoided, then loss reduction techniques need to be implemented.*

As is the case with loss prevention, the costs of loss reduction activities can be justified only when the savings they produce are greater than the cost of the activities.

Another important loss reduction technique is physical separation. Firms often locate manufacturing factories in different geographical locations to avoid a catastrophic loss. The destruction of one plant of a group owned by a firm would be far less damaging than the destruction of its only production facility. Firms with several buildings on the one site will locate them sufficiently far apart that it would be difficult for a fire in one to spread to the others.

Now the possible causes of risks have been identified and measured and exposures quantified, avoided, reduced or controlled, management must decide on the most effective method of financing the remaining risk exposures.

Risk financing

Risk financing refers to those techniques that ensure that funds will be available to finance losses when they occur. The main techniques used are *risk retention* and *risk transference*. If risks cannot be controlled by risk avoidance, loss prevention or loss reduction techniques, then the risks must be retained or transferred. In many cases, a portion of a risk may be retained and the remainder transferred, such as when a deductible is voluntarily attached to an insurance policy.

Risk retention

Risk retention occurs when an individual or business firm retains all or part of a given risk. Risk retention is generally appropriate when the frequency of loss is low and its severity is low. Risk retention can also be appropriate for high-frequency, low-severity risks where potential losses are of low value. Risk retention can be either *active* or *passive*.

Active risk retention refers to the situation where an individual recognises the risk and deliberately elects to retain all or part of that risk. This may be achieved by a firm or individual electing to carry the first $500 of any loss as a policy excess (or deductible). An excess (or deductible) is a provision in the policy whereby a specified amount is deducted from the loss payment otherwise payable to the insured. Alternatively, the risk manager may decide to self-insure the entire risk thereby saving what they would have paid as an insurance premium. Active risk retention is used because a policy excess will eliminate small policy claims and the administrative expense of adjusting these claims resulting in reduced premiums. It is also used where insurance is either unavailable or too expensive.

Passive risk retention refers to those situations where a risk is retained unknowingly or through ignorance, indifference or laziness. Passive risk retention is potentially disastrous as it is not possible to employ any risk management techniques. For example, a contractor may unknowingly assume liability for all material losses to a building because the insuring clause in the contract was not read carefully enough and he failed to insure the risk.

When an organisation deliberately retains an insurable risk, the organisation has *self-insured* the risk. This means that the company actively retains the risk without insurance and elects to absorb the financial losses from any claims. The success of such a strategy will depend on the accuracy of the loss predictions and on the company's reserving adequacy to pay for the losses. Organisations are more likely than individuals to use the law of large numbers, so retention is often an attractive option.

When large organisations do utilise risk retention, they are able to use stop loss reinsurance mechanisms to protect them against a catastrophic single loss or an unusual accumulation of smaller losses above retained amounts. Stop loss coverage is provided by a reinsurance company as reinsurance coverage and commits the reinsurer to paying part of a claim only after the company's retained amount has been exceeded. The use of reinsurance to protect a company against an unusually large claim is shown in the following illustrated example.

Illustrated example 2.5

Widget Manufacturing Pty Ltd has a number of manufacturing plants located in different parts of the country valued at $10 million with a maximum probable loss at any one plant of $1 million. Management have decided that the chance of loss above $1 million is so remote that they will retain the entire risk. However, just to be sure they reinsure all losses exceeding $1 million from any single event or series of events. By doing this, management are able to restrict their loss to $1 million and avoid a catastrophic loss from an unusual event or series of events.

Insurance companies also use reinsurance to transfer part of their risk so as to diversify their exposure and so make the insurance transaction safer for the original consumer as well as the original insurer. Reinsurance is discussed in greater detail in Chapter 9 at 9-050.

Another way a large company can self-insure is through the use of a captive insurance company. A captive insurance company is an insurance entity established by companies whose core business is not insurance related. The purpose of a captive (sometimes referred to as captives) is to enable these companies to retain a portion of their risks, which they would otherwise have to transfer to another external insurer.

Captive insurance companies can provide one or more of the following potential advantages:

- *A more efficient and cost-effective way of managing certain risks.* Risks characterised by reduced probability of occurrence but relatively high severity (loss costs) — such as loss of a production site or a product recall — have a fairly predictable aggregate loss potential and are suitable for a captive insurance company. Losses resulting from high probability and low severity, such as minor damage to buildings, machinery and equipment, can be paid out of a company's current cash flow or be transferred to a captive. This can be more efficient than incurring the administration and transaction costs associated with transferring these low and medium risks to an insurance company.

- *Providing cover for uninsurable risks.* Captives can be used to protect exposures for which there is no cover available in the traditional insurance market, such as political uncertainties and patent infringements.

- *Balancing risk exposures and stabilising insurance costs.* By carrying a broad range of risks, captives allow the development of a 'portfolio' of risks, which helps to balance the overall exposure. Captives also minimise the parent's dependency on the volatile insurance market and therefore help stabilise insurance costs.

- *Creation of a profit component.* By maintaining a favourable loss history, the funds allocated for claims payments generate investment income, some of which can be paid back to the parent company through profit-sharing arrangements.

- *Greater risk transparency.* The incentive of profit sharing encourages the parent company to implement a comprehensive and systematic risk management program throughout the group, which in turn creates greater risk transparency.

While there are significant advantages for a business in establishing a captive insurer, there are other factors that must also be considered. First, commercial insurance companies and insurance brokers can provide services such as loss prevention inspections and advice, and claims adjustment services. If a captive insurer is used, then these services must be sourced elsewhere, such as external consulting firms. Second, competent staff must be recruited to run the captive insurer and these may be difficult to find. Third, the cost of establishing and operating a captive insurer can be quite substantial.

Many companies arrange their insurance by carrying a policy excess (or deductible) on their insurance policies. As mentioned above, some companies elect to retain a certain amount of the risk and insure the remainder. In some classes of insurance, such as liability insurance where the insured has a retention, a distinction is usually made between a policy deductible and retention programs, as the loss and legal defence costs together must exceed the retention level before the insurer will make a payment. If the insured carried a deductible only on their liability insurance, then only the loss would be considered when determining the insurer's liability. However, there is no difference in the terms in property insurance. The operation of a policy deductible is shown in the following illustrated example.

Illustrated example 2.6

As an example, suppose the Abacus Manufacturing Company had an insurance policy with a sum insured of $10,000,000 and a policy deductible of $100,000. The company suffered a large fire resulting in property damage of $1,000,000, so the insurer will be liable for only $900,000 ($1,000,000 less $100,000 deductible). The company reduced their premiums by carrying $100,000 deductible on their insurance policy, but had to bear the risk of absorbing the $100,000 or any loss less than $100,000, irrespective of the number.

A deductible to save on insurance premiums is used in many classes of insurance, such as domestic home and contents, motor vehicle and business insurance. However, the process of increasing deductibles to lower insurance premiums must not be carried beyond the capacity of the individual or business to fund the retained loss.

The basic rule: *when the chance of loss and loss severity is low, the risk should be retained*. A loss could also be retained when the chance of loss is high but the severity is low, provided that effective loss control strategies are employed.

Risk transference

Risk transference occurs when financial risk is transferred to an insurance company through the purchase of insurance.

The basic rule: *when risks have a low frequency but high severity they should be transferred*, as events of this nature represent significant risks for an organisation. For example, liability losses arising from the manufacture of defective parts are low-probability but potentially high-value events, as is a loss caused by the interruption of business due to damage to a factory or terrorist attacks such as the September 11 attacks in the United States.

The above risk management techniques can be arranged into a matrix to make it easier to select the appropriate risk management method. This matrix is shown in table 2.1.

Table 2.1: Risk management on the basis of frequency/severity considerations

Type of loss	Loss frequency	Loss severity	Appropriate risk management method
1	Low	Low	Retention
2	High	Low	Control/Retention
3	Low	High	Transfer
4	High	High	Avoid/Control

The first loss in table 2.1 can best be handled by retention, because the loss occurs infrequently and when it does the loss can be absorbed as a charge against current income. Type 2 losses are more serious although loss control may be implemented to reduce their frequency. Because the losses are predictable, the retention technique can be used, although stop loss reinsurance should be purchased to transfer losses that exceed a predetermined amount over a financial year.

The third type of loss can be met by insurance, as it is consistent with the situation where insurance pooling is theoretically suited. Type 4 losses should be avoided as the cost of insurance would be prohibitive and wealth reduced if the risk was retained, although in some cases the risk cannot be avoided because the process is vital to the production process then the frequency of loss may be reduced through control measures.

Not all risks will fit neatly into one of the matrix cells. In those instances where the high/low classification is not appropriate, the approach needs to be modified to meet the particular circumstances. For example, the appropriate risk management method for a type 4 loss exposure is to take out adequate insurance to provide funds in the event of a loss to reinstate or replace the damaged asset. However, if the cost of the insurance is too high, then management may elect to carry a large policy excess to reduce the premium. In this instance, management would initiate control measures to lessen the probability of loss.

Additionally, some risks can be transferred through the formation of a limited liability company, while other risks may be transferred by hedging or through contractual arrangements.

The shareholders of a limited liability company are liable only for the losses incurred by the firm up to the amount of their investment (shareholding). This means their private assets are safe, as they do not form part of the assets of the company if it should become bankrupt. On the other hand, a sole proprietor or a partnership is liable for all losses incurred when such liabilities exceed the firm's assets. Thus, the sole proprietor or partnership carries the business risk.

Risk can also be transferred through the process of hedging, where an individual guards against adverse price changes in one asset by purchasing or selling another asset whose price changes in an offsetting direction. For example, a wheat farmer expects to harvest a crop in September, and knows that costs are $180 per tonne. The farmer is concerned that the price of wheat may fall between planting and harvesting, and can enter into a contract to sell (to make future delivery). Such a contract is a hedged position, because the farmer has a long position (the wheat in the ground) and a short position (the sale of the contract for future delivery).

This position reduces the farmer's risk of loss from a price decline. Suppose September wheat is selling in June for $200 per tonne. If the wheat is sold for September delivery, the farmer stands to guarantee a profit of $20 per tonne, because the buyer of the contract has agreed to pay $200 per tonne upon delivery in September. If the price of wheat declines to $160 the farmer is guaranteed $200, but if the price rises to $220 the farmer receives $200 and the holder of wheat declines to $160 the farmer is guaranteed $200, but if the price rises to $220 the farmer receives $2 the contract makes a profit of $20 per tonne.

Finally, some risks can be transferred through contractual arrangements such as by a guarantee included in a contract of sale. An example is the warranty that comes with the purchase of a new car. In this case, the new owner has transferred a large part of the risk of purchasing a new car back to the manufacturer. Another example would be where a contractor requires a subcontractor to provide the contractor with liability protection if they are sued because of the subcontractor's negligence. Insurance is the most common contractual form of planned risk transfer as a financing technique employed by most businesses and individuals. Insurance is particularly relevant when frequency of loss is low and the severity of a potential loss is high.

Many business and individuals face situations that meet these criteria and insurance is widely used to transfer this risk. Insurance is the foundation of the risk management programs of many small to medium enterprises (SMEs), while commercial insurance is widely used by large organisations. In other cases, various laws influence insurance decisions. Queensland's *Motor Accident Insurance Act 1994*, for example, requires all owners of motor vehicles used on public roads to have compulsory third party insurance. Insurance as a risk transfer device provides further advantages as it allows businesses to access insurers' or insurance brokers' services, such as loss control inspections or loss settlement expertise.

Arranging insurance can be a complicated affair. Tasks can include:

- assembling the data

- tendering an insurance program

- selecting a broker or agent (or an insurance company for those businesses and individuals who wish to deal direct).

Of course, once the insurance has been put in place, the risk manager must be sure that the terms and conditions of the policies are complied with. For example, the policy may make the installation of a combined back-to-base burglar/smoke alarm system a condition of the burglary/property insurance policy, and this condition must be met to ensure that the contract is not breached.

Losses inevitably occur. The risk manager will report the loss to the firm's insurance broker, agent or company and negotiate the settlement with the insurance company's loss adjuster. Clearly, the use of insurance as a risk management tool involves much more than simply arranging insurance cover.

2-045   Step 5: Implementing and monitoring the program

Implementation involves decisions being made as to whether to retain, control, transfer or avoid the risk. If the decision is made to retain a risk, then management need to decide whether to accumulate a reserve or to arrange stop loss reinsurance to provide funds to cover future losses. If the decision is to transfer the risk through insurance, then the type and amount of insurance needs to be decided and the insurance company or insurance broker selected. If the decision is to control the risk through loss prevention, then a loss prevention program needs to be developed, implemented and communicated to employees.

Monitoring the risk management program involves both evaluation and review, by which management controls the program. This continuous process is important, as risks are constantly changing, and even where risks have been transferred it is important to maintain the risk management program. The monitoring process would examine the decisions that were implemented to see if they were the correct ones and if they were properly implemented. Also, the underlying problems that were identified would be examined to see if they have changed and if the management plans need to be changed to reflect this. If either of these conditions arises, then the process returns to the step of identifying and measuring the loss exposure and the relevant risk management tools, and the cycle repeats. Therefore, risk management is an ongoing systems process that never ceases.

At a glance

The risk management process involves five steps:

1. Defining the objectives
2. Identifying and measuring potential loss exposures
3. Evaluating potential loss exposures
4. Selecting the most appropriate risk management techniques
5. Implementing and monitoring the program.

RULES OF RISK MANAGEMENT

2-050   Introduction

With the evolution of risk management as a functional area of management science, attention has been directed to formalising concepts and techniques so as to provide guidance to the decision-making process. There are four general principles that can be used as guidelines when applying the techniques of risk management, particularly when considering insurance. These are:

1.   Don't risk more than you can afford to lose.

2.   Consider the odds.

3.   Don't risk a lot for a little.

4.   Insure the big risks; retain the small risks.

Don't risk more than you can afford to lose

The first rule may be reduced to determining which risks cannot be retained. If the maximum possible loss from a given exposure is so large that it could result in financial distress, then retention is not an option unless the severity can be reduced to a manageable level. If this cannot be done, then the risk must be transferred or avoided if possible.

Consider the odds

The second rule gives guidance on which risks should be retained and implies that management, or individuals, are able to accurately determine the probability of loss. However, even if management knows that the probability of loss is low, the decision still needs to be based on severity. This is because insurance works well only for low-probability risks that are severe in their impact. Because of the low probability of loss, insurance companies are able to collect a small premium from the many insureds who do not suffer losses to pay for the losses suffered by the unfortunate few.

If, on the other hand, many insureds suffer losses, then the insurance company would have to charge a premium to cover these losses plus a margin to cover expenses. Therefore, if a risk has a high probability of loss, then insurance will not be cost effective for the insurance company. Thus, risks like doctor's appointments would not normally be insured. This rule has a useful application when considering risk retention. For example, if minor loss or damage under a business policy of, say, under $1,000 has a high frequency, then insurance will be a 'bad buy'. On the other hand, if damage above $5,000 is unlikely, then insurance is a 'good buy'. Therefore, the insured has the opportunity of selecting a policy excess of, say, $1,500 so that the unlikely but severe events (the good buys) are insured, but the bad buys (the likely events) are retained. By taking this action, the insured will be able to maximise the premium discounts and thus save money.

Don't risk a lot for a little

The third rule requires a cost–benefit analysis of the relationship between possible losses and the opportunity cost of insurance. The last dollar of premium should buy more than the weighted dollar of coverage.

Insure the big risks; retain the small risks

Finally, the fourth rule suggests that where avoidance, retention or loss control is not an option, then the risks that may result in financial distress should be transferred by way of insurance. Small risks that occur with reasonable frequency are best charged against current income as insurance is usually not cost effective.

At a glance

There are four rules that relate to risk management:

- » Don't risk more than you can afford to lose.
- » Consider the odds.
- » Don't risk a lot for a little.
- » Insure the big risks; retain the small risks.

RISK MANAGEMENT FOR INDIVIDUALS

2-060   Introduction: Risk management for individuals

In the preceding paragraphs, risk management has been described mainly in terms of solving business problems. However, a similar process can be used for individuals and families, although it must be realised that individuals and families do not usually have the resources, sources of finances and access to risk management expertise that is available to organisations and SMEs. Therefore, although loss retention and risk avoidance can still be used, insurance will be a more likely risk management device than these risk management tools.

Essentially, the risk management process described above applies also to individuals and families — that is, they need to:

1.   define their objectives

2.   identify and measure potential loss exposures

3.   evaluate potential loss exposures

4.   select the most appropriate risk management techniques

5.   implement and monitor the program.

Therefore, the objective of the risk management plan is to ensure that a catastrophic loss will not jeopardise the financial plan.

2-070   Defining personal objectives

When developing a risk management plan for an individual or family, it should be recognised that the plan must form part of an overall financial plan. Therefore, the risk management objectives must support this financial plan by ensuring that a catastrophic loss will not jeopardise its achievement.

The overall financial plan objectives might be as follows:

To accumulate $2.5 million in assets, excluding the family home, within the next 15 years.

The financial plan will then detail the necessary steps to achieve these objectives. However, the world is full of risk and an unforeseen loss such as death of the breadwinner or long term disability could jeopardise these plans.

The risk management objectives could be:

1. *To ensure that sufficient funds are available to guarantee the retirement income should the breadwinner die or be permanently disabled.*

2. *To ensure that the breadwinner's income is not interrupted by illness or accident.*

3. *To ensure that the family's finances are not compromised by a serious medical condition occurring to either parents.*

4. *To ensure that medical expenses do not erode the family's savings.*

The statement of the individual's or family's objectives is the starting point of the risk management process. It is then necessary to establish the individual's or family's risk profile, which includes establishing their financial capacity to absorb a loss before an effective risk management strategy can be implemented.

2-080   Identifying and measuring potential loss exposures

The development of an individual's or family's risk profile begins with the identification of the types of risks that could jeopardise a financial plan. The types of losses that individuals and families face can fall into three categories:

1. personal income losses resulting from human life contingencies

2. direct and indirect property losses

3. liability losses.

Personal income losses arise from a number of causes, such as the premature death or long-term disability of the breadwinner or primary carer of young children, in which case alternative childcare arrangements need to be made and paid for. Losses could also be the result of high medical bills arising from an extended period of disability. The primary carer is often overlooked but should that person suffer long term disablement then the cost of care and medical treatment for that person could cause a severe drain on the family's finances and disruption to the breadwinner's work and income. There will also be considerable stress for both parties should they have inadequate income to finance the person's recovery.

Direct property losses arise from such major perils as fire or storm and tempest; both these perils can be severe and result in the total loss of a home and so jeopardise a financial plan. Direct losses could also include damage to motor vehicles or pleasure craft resulting from collision or impact. Theft of personal property such as jewellery, money, paintings and artwork, computer equipment, cameras, coin and stamp collections, and antiques are also direct property losses.

Indirect property losses are consequential to the main loss and include the cost of alternative accommodation while the home is being repaired or rebuilt or the cost of car hire while a damaged car is being repaired. Householders insurance will protect the individual or family against a wide range of perils associated with domestic property damage, while comprehensive motor vehicle insurance will cover the cost of car hire following the theft of a car for a limited time.

It is important to identify all potential property losses and measure the effect that these losses will have on the individual's or family's financial plans. In some cases, it may be necessary to approach professional valuers to appraise items such as antique furniture or jewellery to determine their value and provide evidence of ownership.

When developing personal risk management plans it is necessary to have a full understanding of all personal insurance policies, especially householders, motor vehicle, medical, and life and disability insurances. These policies are discussed in detail in Chapters 13, 14 and 12.

Liability insurance is provided for amounts up to $10 million and $20 million in most Australian householders insurance policies to cover the policyholder and family against liability losses arising out of personal acts causing property damage and bodily injury to others. Legal liability losses can also arise out of defamation, from the negligent operation of vehicles used for personal use such as motor vehicles, motor cycles, golf buggies, pleasure craft or recreational vehicles. Also, does the liability cover extend beyond the land boundary to the footpath and elsewhere in the Commonwealth?

Legal liabilities arising out of business activities need to be covered by business insurance while liability arising from faulty advice needs to be covered by professional indemnity insurance. Some householders insurance policies will provide cover for legal liability and property damage for home offices, but the policy should be carefully checked for adequacy of cover. If the cover is inadequate, then an extension should be made to an existing business policy or a separate business policy should be taken out.

Income losses resulting from human life contingencies such as death and total or partial disability are difficult to measure and are discussed in more detail in Chapter 13. These losses also result from having insufficient physical assets and income during retirement and from large uninsured medical bills. Most people do not have access to emergency cash, and a period of unemployment or illness resulting in the cessation of income could result in loss of the family home and ruined financial plans. Generally, as a "rule of thumb" it is recommended that a family should have at least six month's living expenses saved in an emergency fund. Therefore, if the monthly expenses are $2,000 then $12,000 should be held in this fund.

Once the potential losses have been identified and measured, an individual or family needs to evaluate how often these losses are likely to occur and their ability to absorb the cost should the losses eventuate.

2-090   Evaluating potential loss exposures

The third step is to estimate the frequency and severity of all potential loss exposures. A risk matrix, as illustrated in figure 2.1, can be constructed as an aid in this process. For example, the cost of minor dents and scratches to a motor vehicle fall into the upper left cell of the risk matrix and can be retained by carrying a policy excess on a comprehensive motor vehicle policy. On the other hand, while severe losses to a house by fire or storm and tempest are relatively rare, the resulting damage has the potential of being a catastrophic loss for a homeowner. When considering both frequency and severity, a potential loss such as this would fall into the top right-hand cell of the risk matrix. These potential losses must be transferred through insurance because of their potentially catastrophic nature.

The risk evaluation is an important step because it highlights the possible effect that a particular loss may have on the individual's or family's financial plan. Once they have been identified and organised into a risk matrix, the most appropriate technique for handling these potential loss exposures can be selected.

2-100   Selecting the most appropriate risk management techniques

The fourth step is to select the most appropriate method of handling each potential loss exposure identified in the risk matrix. As discussed above, there are two main approaches to handling potential loss exposures: *controlling* the loss exposure through avoiding any possibility of loss, preventing a loss from occurring, reducing the severity of a loss when it occurs and retaining part of the loss; or *financing* the potential loss exposure by transferring the exposure through insurance or by contract. The matrix shown in table 2.1 will be an invaluable aid in this process.

- *Avoidance.* By avoiding the risk, an individual or family will prevent any possibility of a loss occurring. For example, an individual or family can avoid potential catastrophic loss caused by flood by not purchasing a house in a flood-prone area. An individual can avoid the risk of personal injury by returning home by taxi instead of running the risk of being robbed and injured by walking home through dark streets.

- *Prevention and reduction.* These are risk control measures designed to reduce both the frequency and the severity of loss. For example, the risk of a motor vehicle accident can be reduced by having a car regularly serviced, by not driving it if the brakes are faulty and by not speeding. Having a reliable vehicle will further reduce the risk of personal danger resulting from the car's breaking down in a lonely, isolated area. The potential for fire damage can be reduced by fitting smoke detectors to give the occupants of a house early warning of a fire, allowing time for them to exit the house before they are injured and for the fire brigade to control the fire before it takes hold.

- *Risk financing.* Personal risk management relies heavily on transferring the potential loss to an insurance company through the use of insurance. This will be examined further in Chapter 13, which discusses life insurance, and Chapter 14, which discusses general insurance.

A further method of risk financing is to retain a part of the risk exposure. In most instances, an individual or family will not be in a position to retain the entire risk exposure or a substantial portion of the exposure because of the risk of catastrophic loss. However, they may be able to retain some of the risk exposure by carrying a deductible on their insurance policies.

Passive risk retention is potentially catastrophic because risk management techniques will not have been applied. This can happen through ignorance of the law and legal responsibilities or a failure to read and understand the conditions and exclusions that are contained in an insurance policy. For example, it may be a condition of a motor vehicle policy that the car should not be fitted with performance-enhancing equipment. If the car is later modified in this way and is damaged in a collision, the insurance company will generally not pay the claim if this modification contributed or caused the accident.

Once the personal risk management plan has been developed, it is important to take the necessary steps to implement it and to continually monitor and review the plan so that it can take account of changing circumstances.

2-110 Implementing and monitoring the personal risk management plan

Implementation of the personal risk management plan is an important step, because if it is not implemented according to what has been decided it may be largely ineffectual. It is advisable to assign responsibility both for the various tasks and for a time limit for their completion.

Illustrated example 2.6

Kim will contact the local fire services department to have the house assessed for potential fire hazards and to advise on the placement of smoke detectors, and the design of an evacuation plan. This action is to be completed within 14 days.

The plan must be revisited on a regular basis — say, every two years or at the time of a major life event such as the birth of a baby, a promotion or the purchase of an investment property — so as to determine whether the current insurance policies are still adequate to cover the major risk exposures.

This chapter examined the steps in the development, implementation and monitoring of a risk management plan for businesses, individuals and families. Insurance was identified as the main method of transferring risk because for a small cost — the premium — the insured is assured that the insurance company will pay for a catastrophic loss, which could not be carried by a firm, individual or family. The basic elements of insurance and its benefit to society are examined in the following chapter.

2-120   Study questions

2.1   Define risk management. How does risk management differ from insurance management?

2.2   How would you explain the objectives of a risk management program both before and after a loss occurs?

2.3   What is the traditional process of risk management for an organisation?

2.4   Identify and briefly explain the two broad approaches to dealing with risk.

2.5   Identify and briefly describe the five basic techniques for dealing with the pure risks facing a firm. Give an example of each technique.

2.6   Using the risk management matrix, explain the following:

a)   when would you buy insurance?

b)   when would you avoid the risk?

c)   when would you retain the risk?

d)   when would you use loss control?

2.7   Define the terms loss prevention and loss reduction, providing examples of each.

2.8   A jeweller has seen the price of gold rise to more than A$1 500 per ounce and is concerned about what the price will be when he or she needs to replenish gold stocks in three months' time. What financial instrument might the jeweller use to cap his or her price of gold?

2.9   Explain the rules of risk management.

2.10   Identify and explain the three types of losses that individuals and families face.

2.11   Explain how an individual would use risk retention as part of his or her risk management program. Give an example of how this would work.

2-130   References and further reading

References

Articles and Books

Cusack, R 2005, 'How much is enough? Insuring against business interruption', *Currency*, Spring, p 3.

Shrivastava, P (1992) *Bhopal: Anatomy of a crisis,* Cambridge, MA: Ballinger.

Reports

Comcover, *AS/NZS ISO 31000:2009, Risk Management – Principles & Guidelines.* Accessed: 27 January 2016. Available at http://www.finance.gov.au/sites/default/files/COV_216905_Risk_Management_Fact_Sheet_FA3_23082010_0.pdf

META Research Report, 2002 in Cusack, R 2005, 'How much is enough? Insuring against business interruption', *Currency*, Spring, pp. 2–5.

aon.com.au.

Further reading

Baranoff, E 2004, *Risk management and insurance*, John Wiley & Sons Inc, USA. Chapter 3.

Berwick, G 2001, *The executives guide to insurance and risk management*, Quality Results Pty Ltd, Sydney. Chapter 1.

Culp, CL 2002, *The art of risk management*, John Wiley & Sons Inc, New York.

Redja, GE 2003, *Principles of risk management and insurance*, 8th edn, Pearson Education Inc., USA. Chapter 3.

Vaughan, EJ & Vaughan, TM 2003, *Fundamentals of risk and insurance*, 9th edn, John Wiley & Sons Inc, USA. Chapter 2.

CHAPTER 3

INSURANCE AND RISK

Types of insurance

WHAT IS INSURANCE?

3-010   Insurance defined

There is no single definition of insurance. Different insurance texts provide different definitions, although they all tend to incorporate the points discussed below. Definitions of insurance for legal purposes have usually been expressed in terms of contracts of insurance. The *Insurance Contracts Act 1984* (Cth) (IC Act) provides little assistance as it defines a contract of general insurance as a 'contract of insurance that is not a contract of life insurance' (s 11(6)). Since this definition is not helpful for our purposes, it will be necessary to look outside of the IC Act for a more useful definition.

The usual starting point for a definition of a contract of insurance is to refer to

Channell J's three-point test in *Prudential Insurance Co v Inland Revenue Commissioners* (1904) (2 KB 658, pp. 662–3):

1. It must be a contract whereby for some consideration (premiums) the insured secures himself/herself some benefit (the payment of a sum of money or its equivalent) upon the happening of an event.

2. The event should involve some amount of uncertainty, either as to whether it will ever happen or, if the event must happen at some time, as to when it will happen.

3. The event must be of a character more or less adverse to the interests of the insured. (Marks & Balla 1998, p 7)

All elements of the three-point test must be present for a valid definition of an insurance contract. Therefore, an insurance contract is defined in this text as:

> *a contract whereby one person or party (the insured) agrees to pay money (the premium) to another person (the insurer) in order to secure some benefit, usually in the form of payment of a sum of money or its equivalent on the uncertain happening of a specified event that is generally adverse to the interests of the insured.*

This definition identifies several important elements that must be contained in a contract of insurance:

1. For insurance to be effective there must be a binding contract in which the consideration is usually monetary (the premium), although it could take another form.

2. The insurer must be legally bound to pay a sum of money (paying a death benefit), or its equivalent (to rebuild a home).

3. There must be uncertainty as to whether or not the specified event will occur or, as in the case of life insurance, as to when it will occur.

4. Under common law, an insured must have an insurable interest in the subject matter of the insurance — that is, in the physical property or life insured. This requirement has been largely modified by the IC Act, under which an insured is not required to have an insurable interest in the life insured, in the case of life insurance; nor is an insurable interest required in the case of general insurance, provided the insured suffers a pecuniary or economic loss on the happening of the event, even though the insured does not have a legal or equitable interest in the subject matter of the insurance (ss 16; 17). Common law still applies to marine insurance contracts, with the exception of pleasure craft and inland marine insurance in Australia. Marine insurance is a complex subject and will not be examined in great depth in this text.

    Insurable interest is examined in greater depth in Chapter 5 (see 5-020).

5. The event insured against should be outside the control of the one assuming the risk (the insurer). This means that agreements such as manufacturers' guarantees or warranties and service or repair contracts are removed from any definition of a contract of insurance.

    The word 'control' is somewhat misleading, as a manufacturer has little control over a product after it is sold. Therefore, it may be more appropriate to "consider whether the alleged insurer is responsible (directly or indirectly) for producing the event giving rise to the claim" (Marks & Balla 1998, p 10).

This section examined the legal requirements of an insurance contract; now it is necessary to examine how insurance works.

At a glance

- Insurance is generally defined in relation to insurance contracts.

- There are five elements that must be contained in an insurance contract:

    1. For the contract to be binding the premium must be paid.

    2. The insurer must be legally bound to pay a sum of money or its equivalent.

    3. There must be uncertainty as to the happening of an event or its timing.

    4. Insurable interest is not a prerequisite to entering into a binding contract.

    5. The event must be outside of the control of the insurer.

HOW INSURANCE WORKS

3-010 Introduction

The transfer of risk from those exposed to risk to an insurance company reduces the level of risk to society as a whole. By transferring risk to insurers, the risk of 'loss' or 'no loss' that individuals face changes. The premiums these individuals pay provide security of the 'no loss' while the insurers are exposed to some risk. This risk arises from missing their loss prediction represented by the standard deviation and which is influenced by the number of exposures. As was shown in chapter 1, the larger the number of exposures insured, the lower the insurer's risk of missing the prediction of future losses. Therefore, the transfer of risk to insurers lowers the risk to society as a whole through the law of large numbers. In addition, insurance preserves both an individual's wealth and the wealth of businesses through its ability to maximize the value of assets. Insurance placed with a reputable and well-rated insurance company assures the preservation of assets and economic value.

An insurance plan or arrangement works if it contains the following characteristics:

1. Risk is transferred from the individual to an insurance company.

2. Losses are shared with a group (pooling) or an insurance company.

3. Losses must be accidental and beyond the insured's control.

4. Payment of fortuitous losses is made through indemnification.

3-020 Risk transference

The definition of an insurance contract provided above does not explain how insurance is created. An essential element in the creation of insurance is risk transference.

Risk transference involves the transfer of pure risks from an insured to an insurer, who is in a better financial position than the insured to pay for any loss. It is this transfer of pure risks to an insurer who assumes the financial aspects of the risks that creates insurance. The insurer assumes risk through its promise to compensate the insured by the payment of money or its equivalent for any loss, as covered by the terms of the insurance policy, but with the amount of the loss limited to the value of the sum insured. The insurer receives an amount of money (the premium) from the insured to accept the risk and to create a valid contract (the insurance policy). By paying the premium, the insured has paid a small certain expense in order to transfer the risk of a large uncertain financial loss. The insurance policy is evidence of the insurer's acceptance of the transfer of a particular risk, such as a building, and stipulates the types of losses that will be paid for by the insurer.

Most insurance contracts define an insurer's obligation in terms of money, while others provide a service. For example, a householders policy obliges the insurer not only to pay money to repair, reinstate or replace the damaged property, but also to provide alternative accommodation for the insured if the property is untenable. A life insurance policy promises to pay a specified sum of money on the death of the life insured.

On the other hand, a health insurance policy generally promises to provide medical and hospital services such as a private room and board and other medical services if the insured falls ill or is injured. In all these instances, the burden that the insurer assumes is financial. While an insurance policy can provide money to compensate for a loss, it cannot compensate for the sentimental value that an item may hold, nor can the receipt of money compensate for the death of a loved one. The benefit that insurance provides to society is to reduce the financial uncertainty created by risk.

3-030   Pooling of losses

Our definition of insurance has established that the premium paid by the insured compensates the insurer for assuming the transfer of pure risk. The bulk of the premiums are used to compensate individuals who incur insured losses. These individuals are members of a large group of insureds who share the group losses through the premiums they pay. This is the basis of pooling. Pooling involves spreading the losses suffered by the few over the entire group, so that average loss is substituted for actual loss.

The premiums charged by an insurance company are intended to reflect each individual's losses. Therefore, actuaries estimate both the probability (likelihood) and the severity (size) of losses. These estimates are made for different categories of insureds so that they are grouped with respect to their probability and severity of loss. For example, one category of insureds could be represented by those who are overweight and smoke. As discussed in Chapter 1, actuaries then use this information to arrive at an average or expected loss.

These groups form only a sample of the total population, so the calculations tend to be more accurate when the number of observations (or empirical data) is large enough to allow the mean (or the expected loss) of the sample to approximate the mean of the population. This is the basis of the law of large numbers. It means that the actuary is able to predict future losses of the group with greater accuracy and thus reduce *objective* risk. However, in some instances the actuary will also exercise subjective judgement when setting rates.

This *subjective* judgement is based on past experience and will result in either a loading or a discount being applied to the premium to form the base premium. Once the base premium has been set by the actuary, further costs must be added to give a final premium, as shown in figure 3.1.

Figure 3.1: Four building blocks of an insurance premium

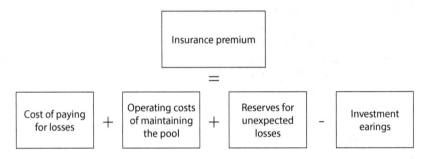

The following illustrated example shows how an insurance premium is calculated.

Illustrated example 3.1

Assume that an insurance company insures 1,000 industrial sheds with an average value of $100,000, forming a total worth of $100,000,000 (1,000 x $100,000). The actuary knows from past experience that the probability of loss (damage) from fire will equal two per cent for similar industrial sheds. Some of these sheds will be totally destroyed while others will be partially damaged.

The value of all these past losses is aggregated and divided by the dollar value of the insured property to give the average figure of two per cent. Therefore, the expected value of a loss for these 1,000 sheds will be $2,000,000 ($100,000,000 x 2% (or 0.02). Once this figure is obtained, the actuary is able to calculate the base insurance premium.

The base insurance premium represents the amount of premium required to cover the expected value of losses. For this insurance pool the base premium will be $2,000 per shed ($2,000,000 in losses divided by 1,000 insured sheds). Table 3.1 summarises these figures.

Table 3.1 Industrial shed insurance pool

Number of insured industrial sheds	1,000
Value of each shed	$100,000
Total value of property in the insurance pool	$100,000,000
Expected value of losses at 2% of total value	$2,000,000
Expected value of loss per industrial shed ($2,000,000/1,000)	$2,000
Loss per $100 of property value ($2,000,000/1,000,000) (Note: 1,000,000 = 100,000,000/100*) ($100 is used because premium rates are expressed in terms of a rate per $100 of sum insured) *$1,000,000 = Total value of property in the pool ($100,000,000)/ $100	$2

In table 3.1 the base rate of $2 was calculated on the basis of a total loss of the sheds. (Although this rate will apply to a partial loss, the rate is calculated on the assumption of a total loss.) If this was to happen, then the insurance company would recoup $2,000,000 from premiums to cover the losses. Since it is unlikely that all damaged sheds will cost exactly $100,000, the actuary will calculate the cost of insurance based on each $100 of value. Therefore, each $100 of insurance should cost $2 to insure ($2,000,000/1,000,000, or dollar value of losses per $100 of exposure). This means that if a particular industrial shed was valued at only $60,000, the insured would pay a base premium of $1,200 to belong to this pool (600 x $2, or 60,000/100 hundreds of dollars of value times premium cost per $100). Similarly, an industrial shed worth $30,000 would cost $600.

In order to remain viable and earn sufficient profits to pay a dividend to shareholders, the actuary must add an amount to cover all the costs of salaries and all other operating costs and costs of acquiring the business, such as agents' commissions. Assume that these expenses are expected to add 30 per cent to the $2 insurance rate, making the rate $2.60 for each $100 of industrial shed covered. Additionally, the actuary will allow a margin to provide sufficient funds to cover an adverse variation for the expected value of losses. Suppose this reserve adds a further 10 per cent to the $2 loss cost, which makes the premium $2.80 per $100 ($2.60 + 0.20) for insurance on the industrial shed.

Finally, the actuary will make an allowance for investment earnings on the collected premiums. Suppose the insureds pay their premiums on 1 January each year and, on average, the insurance company pays claims on 1 July. Therefore, the insurer earns interest on one half-year's premiums. Assume an annual interest rate of six per cent, then the interest earned will be three per cent on the half-year's premiums, which will reduce the premiums, and the final premium that the insurance will charge per $100 will be $2.74 ($2.80 − 0.06).

3-040   Losses must be accidental and beyond the insured's control

The third characteristic of insurance is that the losses must be beyond the insured's control; that is, the losses must be accidental or *fortuitous*. Fortuitous losses have unexpected or unanticipated causes and result from chance. The loss must not occur as a result of the insured's deliberate actions, such as deliberately burning a house down in order to collect the insurance. Such intentional losses are against public policy and can result in criminal charges of arson being brought against those responsible.

The law of large numbers is based on the assumption that the losses will be accidental and will occur randomly. For example, a building contractor accidentally reverses his utility into a power pole causing considerable damage to the vehicle. Because the damage was caused by accidental means, the builder is able to make a claim on his motor vehicle policy for the cost of repairs. This is an example of a non-fraudulent loss caused by the insured's negligence and is insurable. Insurance policies do not generally cover intentional losses.

Non-accidental losses that reduce economic value, such as wear and tear, are not caused by accidental means and so are not insurable events and are specifically excluded from insurance policies.

As mentioned previously, intentional loss caused by the insured's deliberate actions is not covered by insurance. It is interesting to note that death caused by suicide is considered to be non-accidental for only the first 13 months from the commencement date of the policy, or following an increase in the sum insured and is therefore not covered by the policy. After 13 months a suicide is considered to be accidental and is covered by the policy.

3-050   Payment of fortuitous losses through indemnification

The final characteristic of insurance relates to the principle of indemnification for losses. Indemnity is a legal principle that ensures the insured is restored to the same or approximately the same position after a loss as was enjoyed immediately prior to the loss, subject to policy terms. This means that if a person's home is damaged by fire, their householders policy will indemnify them by restoring them to their previous position by carrying out repairs. Similarly, if a person's motor vehicle suffers panel damage as a result of an accident, their motor vehicle policy will indemnify them through the repairs that are carried out to restore the vehicle to its pre-accident condition.

In both of these examples, the repairs could result in the insured being restored to a better position, so it is not unusual for an amount to be deducted from the claim to avoid 'betterment'. Finally, if a person suffers an injury or serious illness, his/her income protection insurance policy will indemnify the person by paying up to 75 – 85 per cent of lost wages until the person can resume work (provided he/she was insured for that amount).

At a glance

An insurance plan must contain four characteristics:

1. Risk is transferred from an individual to an insurance company.

2. Losses are shared with a pool or insurance company.

3. An insured must not contribute to the loss.

4. Losses are settled on the principle of indemnification.

IDEAL REQUIREMENTS OF AN INSURABLE RISK

3-060   Introduction

It has been stated that insurers only insure pure risks. Not all pure risks are insurable, however. This section examines the requirements that must generally be met if a pure risk is to be insured. From a practical perspective, not all risks have these requirements, but it is still possible for the risks to be insured. However, the bulk of insured risks fulfil most, if not all, of the requirements.

Insurers would consider a risk perfectly suited for insurance if it meets the following six requirements:

1.   There must be a large number of similar exposure units.

2.   The loss must be accidental and unintentional.

3.   The loss should be determinable and measurable.

4.   The loss should not be catastrophic.

5.   The chance of loss must be calculable.

6.   The premium must be economically feasible.

3-070   Large number of similar exposure units

It has been noted that insurance is based on the law of large numbers, and that insuring a potential loss exposure requires a large number of *similar* units. The use of the word 'similar' is deliberate, because the exposures assumed by insurers are usually not identical. No two houses are identical, even though they may appear so. Their location will be different, so some may be more exposed to bushfires than others, and the houses will be occupied by different families, some of whom may be fire-prevention conscious while others are not. However, the units in a group must have reasonably similar characteristics if predictions about future losses are to be accurate. For example, brick veneer homes will be considered similar for insurance purposes. Therefore, the loss costs associated with this group can be fairly spread over all insureds in the group. If the group included timber houses, which experienced higher losses than the brick units, then the loss costs would be unfairly distributed over the group as the brick units will be subsidising the wood units.

Some insurances are sold that do not meet the desirable requirement of an insurable risk — that is, that there be a large number of similar exposures — but these transactions are still insurance. For example, a famous singer may insure against the risk of losing her voice or a pianist may insure his fingers against loss of use. These risks are generally insured in a specialist market with the underwriters at Lloyd's of London. The Lloyd's underwriters rate each risk individually and charge a loaded premium — that is, at a rate higher than probability requires.

3-080   Accidental losses

The second requirement is that losses must be accidental and unintentional, because the risks assumed by an insurer must involve the possibility of loss, not the certainty of it (such as by arson for profit); that is, they must occur as a matter of chance. This is important for two reasons. First, if insurers paid intentional losses, then the moral hazard would be substantially increased and premiums would have to be loaded to allow for the extra risk.

The premiums might become so expensive as to cause many insureds not to insure, thus substantially reducing the number of exposure units in the group. As a result, the insurer might have an insufficient number of exposure units to predict future losses. Second, predictions of potential losses are based on a probability distribution, which has been estimated on past experience. A principal assumption made in this estimation is that losses are fortuitous occurrences and that future losses will also be a matter of chance. If the losses were caused deliberately and were not random events, then the prediction of future events would not be accurate.

3-090   Determinable and measurable losses

The third requirement of an insurable risk is that the loss must be definite and verifiable. This means that the loss must be verifiable as to cause, time and place and be measurable in economic terms. Otherwise, there would be many arguments between insureds and insurers about whether a loss has occurred. A good example that illustrates how these requirements work is to consider the payment of a death claim under a life insurance policy. It is relatively easy to determine the cause and time of death. If the deceased is insured, then the damage can be measured in economic terms by the payment of the policy sum insured.

The requirement that a loss caused by an insurable event be measurable in economic terms means that some events cannot be insured. For example, the emotional distress associated with the death of a loved pet cannot be insured under a householders insurance policy because it is not possible to assign an economic value to the distress. In contrast, it is possible to insure racehorses and other valuable livestock against loss because the damage can be measured in economic terms. For a racehorse this could include lost prize money or stud value.

3-100   Non-catastrophic losses

The fourth requirement of an insurable event is that the loss should not be catastrophic. A catastrophe loss refers to a type of loss that is extremely serious and random. In other words, it is one that has a devastating effect and cannot be foreseen. Therefore, it is very difficult to prepare for without insurance. (Insuranceopedia, n.d.). For example; earthquakes, sudden loss of life, volcanic eruptions, etc.

The concept of pooling was discussed earlier when it was noted that where an insurer assumes a group of risks, it expects only a small percentage of the group to experience loss at any one time. If most of the group of risks suffer losses at the same time, the pool may have insufficient funds available to pay all claims and so the pooling technique will break down. For example, Hurricane Katrina caused widespread wind and flood damage to areas adjacent to the American Gulf Coast, and estimates place private insurers' losses as high as US$25 billion.

If one insurer had insured the bulk of the property in the Gulf area, they would have suffered a catastrophic loss. This is an example of *dependent* exposure units. Exposure units are dependent if loss to one affects the probability of loss to another exposure unit. Therefore, loss of homes by wind or fire in one location increases the probability of wind or fire damage to other homes in that area. The only options for the insurer are to cease business or to raise premiums, possibly to unaffordable levels. If it is not possible to predict losses with reasonable accuracy, then it is impossible to set adequate premium rates and to accumulate reserves.

While insurers ideally wish to avoid catastrophic losses, this is not always possible, because catastrophic losses periodically result from wars, bushfires, cyclones, floods, earthquakes and terrorism. Additionally, as Australian insurance companies expand overseas as direct insurers, for example into the North American market, they become exposed to new, potentially catastrophic events caused by hurricanes like Katrina, tornadoes and terrorism.

There are several methods of dealing with the problem of catastrophic losses. The first is to transfer much of the risk through reinsurance, so the insurer will be indemnified when losses exceed a predetermined amount. Reinsurance is a system whereby the insurers who deal with the insuring public (direct insurers) transfer (cede) all or part of an insured risk to other insurers known as reinsurers. In other words, the ceding company pays the whole or part of the premium it has received to the reinsurers, who agree to reimburse to the ceding company the claims for which they are liable under the original insurance. Reinsurance is examined in greater detail in Chapter 9 (see 9-080).

Second, insurers can suffer catastrophic losses if they have a large portfolio of risks concentrated in one area. Concentration refers to the situation in which a large number of risks representing a high dollar exposure for an insurance company are insured in small geographic areas, such as in a town, city or country area. Therefore, a catastrophic event such as Hurricane Katrina could result in financial distress for an insurance company that had concentrated its business in the Gulf area.

Insurers can avoid the risk of concentration by diversifying their exposures over a large geographic area. This means that an insurer with a heavy insurance property exposure in the Gulf region would attempt to balance this exposure with risks written in less hurricane-exposed areas. Such diversified insurance will help to reduce the impact of catastrophic losses on the company's financial stability.

A third type of catastrophic exposure arises where an insurer has an exceptionally high loss exposure concentrated in a single risk. The 11 September 2001 terrorist attack on the World Trade Center in New York resulted in estimated insured losses to the Twin Towers insurers of US$3.6 billion. The response from the insurance industry was to exclude terrorism coverage from new policies.

When insurers and reinsurers see that a peril has a greater probability of occurring than previously perceived, they realise that they cannot predict such future losses accurately. The response from the insurance industry is to exclude terrorism from new policies. However, it must be recognised that this peril cannot be excluded during the currency of the policy, only on its renewal. This subject is discussed in detail in Chapter 5.

3-110 Calculable chance of loss

The fifth requirement of an insurable event requires the chance of loss to be calculable. Insurers are able to calculate the average frequency and severity of future losses based on past experience. The probability distribution of future losses is greatly influenced by the regularity of the events, which makes them predictable. As was discussed in the previous section, lack of experience and regularity means that when insurers can no longer accurately predict future losses, they will either exclude the peril or avoid providing insurance coverage for the peril because of the potential for a catastrophic loss.

3-120 Economically feasible premiums

It was stated in Chapter 2 that losses that have a low frequency of occurrence but a high severity are best transferred through insurance. Therefore, for insurance to be economically feasible for an insured the size of the possible loss for the insured must be significant and the cost of insurance must be small in comparison to the possible loss. Large losses are the key because insureds cannot bear them, and low probabilities for large losses make insurance premiums low in comparison to the size of the possible loss. Therefore, the majority of homeowners insure their homes because the cost of their insurance premiums is relatively low compared to the loss that the homeowner could suffer.

The chance of loss must be low if the premium is to be economically affordable. For example, the cost of a $100,000 life insurance policy covering death only on a 30-year old non-smoking male is approximately $152.40 per year. In contrast, the cost of a $100,000 life policy on a non-smoking male aged 95 would be approximately equal to the face value of the policy and so be unaffordable, if it could be obtained.

Based on the above criteria, most property, liability and personal risks can be insured by private insurers, because the requirements of an insurable risk are generally met. In contrast, financial risks, political risks and most market risks are uninsurable by private insurers. This is because, first, they are speculative; second, the potential of catastrophic loss is high (for example, war is a risk associated with political risk); and third, a proper premium cannot be calculated, because the chance of loss cannot be accurately predicted.

3-130   Insurance and gambling compared

It is often said that insurance is just a gamble. This is not the case, however, for two important reasons. First, gambling not only creates risk (uncertainty) as to the outcome, but it also creates a new speculative risk. For a gambler to win, someone else must lose; it is a win–lose situation. This means that gambling is socially unproductive. For example, if someone bets $500 on roulette and wins, the casino loses. On the other hand, if the gambler loses, the casino wins. The gamble creates a new speculative risk where previously none existed. In contrast, if the $500 is paid as a premium for fire insurance, the payment of the $500 premium transfers the fire risk to the insurer.

The risk of fire already exists, so no new risk is created. Insurance is always socially productive because it is a win–win for both the insurer and the insured if the loss does not occur. Indeed, the insured and insurer have a common interest in the prevention of the loss. If gambling events were insurable, the gambler would never lose: 'heads, I win; tails, I collect on my insurance'. The more gamblers bet, the more they stand to win.

Second, if a loss does occur, insurance will restore the insured financially either wholly or in part to their former position. In contrast, consistent gambling generally never restores losers to their former financial position.

3-140   Adverse selection

When one party to a transaction possesses relevant information that the other party has no way of knowing, the party with the superior information can potentially take advantage of the position. The possession and use of this asymmetric information is called adverse selection. Adverse selection arises when one person with a greater than average chance of loss seeks insurance at average (standard) rates. If this was allowed to continue unchecked, higher than expected losses would result and the premium pool would be severely depleted. In other words, the insured is paying less than the mathematically calculated fair price based on the law of large numbers.

However, if an insured is paying more than the mathematically calculated fair price, the insured provides a subsidy for the person seeking adverse selection. This is what is known as subsidisation. Subsidisation occurs if each person does not pay a fair price for his or her insurance. For example, owners of businesses with higher than average burglary claims will seek out insurers who will insure them at standard rates. Similarly, when life insurance companies started offering discounts for non-smokers, smokers sought life insurance coverage from those companies who still charged the same rates for smokers and non-smokers. Undoubtedly it was this adverse selection by smokers that caused all life insurers to offer discounts for non-smokers.

Adverse selection can be controlled by two methods. First, it can be controlled by careful underwriting. Underwriting is the process of classifying potential insureds into various risk categories so that an appropriate premium will be charged. Second, adverse selection can be controlled by policy conditions. For example, a three-month waiting period from the start of the coverage in a trauma policy exists to prevent claims for heart attack from insureds who know they are at risk. Similarly, prospective insureds must declare pre-existing medical conditions when applying for life and health insurances.

3-150   Insurance and hedging compared

The concept of hedging was discussed in Chapter 2 (see 2-040), where it was shown that risk could be transferred to a speculator through the purchase of a futures contract. Similarly, risk transfer by contract is an important part of an insurance transaction, but not all methods of risk transfer involve insurance. On the face of it, it would appear that a futures contract (hedging) and insurance are one and the same.

There are two important differences that make a hedging contract uninsurable. First, insurance involves the transfer of insurable risk and not speculative risk (such as the decline in the value of agricultural products), which is not insurable, as is the case with hedging. Second, insurance involves the reduction of objective risk through the increased predictability of the law of large numbers. In the case of hedging, risk is transferred to speculators who believe that they can make a profit through price fluctuations. Risk is transferred but not reduced, and predictions of possible loss are not based on the law of large numbers.

At a glance

- There are six requirements for a risk to be insurable:

  1. There must be a large number of similar exposure units.
  2. Losses must be due to accidents and be unintentional.
  3. Losses should be determinable and measurable.
  4. Losses should not be catastrophic.
  5. The chance of loss must be measurable.
  6. The premium must be economically feasible.

- There are two differences between insurance and gambling:

  1. Gambling creates uncertainty and also creates a new speculative risk.
  2. If a gambler wins, someone else must lose.

- Adverse selection occurs when someone seeks average or standard premium rates when they are not entitled to them.

- There are two reasons why a hedging contract is uninsurable:

  1. Hedging involves the transfer of a speculative risk, which is not insurable.
  2. A hedging contract involves the transfer of risk to a speculator and objective risk is not reduced by the law of large numbers.

PRINCIPLES OF RISK CLASSIFICATION

3-160   Introduction

In the previous section it was shown how those who paid a fair, mathematically calculated premium subsidised those who practised adverse selection. Additionally, it was shown how adverse selection, if left unchecked, could severely deplete the insurance pool and result in premiums being increased, possibly to unaffordable levels. Much controversy has surrounded insurers' desire to further classify potential insureds on the basis of their genetic profile so that actuaries can further refine their premiums. The problem then is how to construct risk classes that will ensure that insureds will bear a mathematically fair share of the pool's losses and expenses when calculating premium rates.

Generally, premium rates are evaluated according to four criteria:

1.   separation and class homogeneity

2.   reliability

3.   incentive value

4.   social acceptability.

3-170   Separation and class homogeneity

It was mentioned above that adverse selection is a serious problem faced by insurers. Underwriters combat adverse selection by establishing risk classes and mathematically calculating appropriate premium rates for each class. Risk classification involves placing insureds or property into groups or classes so that a fair premium based on the law of large numbers can be calculated for each class. For instance, life insurance groups people into classes based on age, sex, height, weight, and smoking and non-smoking habits. This results in an overweight smoker paying a higher premium for life insurance than a non-smoking person with the correct height/weight ratio.

3-180   Reliability

Once the risk class has been established, information relating to this class should be easy to obtain and should not be subject to manipulation by insureds. For example, information about a person's height and weight is easy to obtain, but other information about a person's medical history can be manipulated by the insured to provide false information. Smokers often claim to be non-smokers in order to obtain cheaper life insurance premiums. Insurers are able to verify much of the information provided by insureds by requiring them to undergo a medical examination. In addition, false answers on a proposal form generally come to light when there is a claim and the insured's doctor reports on the condition giving rise to the claim.

3-190   Incentive value

While risk classes are constructed in ways to allow insurers' to obtain a mathematically fair premium, insureds should be rewarded for having below-average loss experience or potential by receiving lower premiums or discounts. For example, a business that installs a back-to-base burglar alarm system and other perimeter security generally will be charged a lower burglary premium than those that don't. Additionally, insureds with a loss-free driving record will earn a no-claim bonus (discount) on their premiums.

3-200   Social acceptability

The methods insurers use to construct the risk classes can pose problems, because certain premium rating factors such as race and genetic testing may not be acceptable to society.

Genetic testing

The possible requirement for an applicant for life insurance to undertake a genetic test in order to assess their likelihood of either dying from or contracting certain illnesses has caused considerable debate in Australia, as it has in other countries. By allowing insurers access to a person's genetic code, underwriters are able to more accurately charge an appropriate premium for a certain risk. However, the availability of genetic testing raises the prospect of an applicant's cover being denied on the basis of genetic discrimination. For example, some applicants may possess a gene that makes them prone to alcoholism, but they will pay a loaded premium even if they do not drink.

The Australian life industry has agreed to abide by the industry standard (IFSA Standard 11.00 — Genetic Testing Policy) for life insurance and genetic testing developed by Investment and Financial Services Association (IFSA) (now the Financial Services Council (FSC), which represents all life insurers operating in Australia. Under their code of practice, insurers will not require applicants for life insurance to undergo a genetic test. However, s 21 of the IC Act imposes a duty of disclosure on applicants for insurance; as such, it requires an applicant to disclose if they attended counselling because they knew that a parent carried a potentially fatal gene or had a prior predictive genetic test and knew its results.

The insurer may then use this information when assessing the application for life insurance and restrict cover if it is unfavourable. However, as from 21 June 2019 life insurers are no longer allowed to require applicants for insurance to disclose the results of any genetic tests they may have had.

The Australian ban will last until June 30, 2024, with a review to be conducted in 2022. The review is deemed necessary by the life insurance industry as the field of genomics is advancing rapidly. The ban is limited by the size of the policy which currently stands at $500,000. For amounts above that, the insurer can continue to ask for genetic results. Other countries with similar rules also have monetary limits.

There is also a limit of $500,000 for total and permanent disability cover, $200,000 for trauma or critical illness cover and $4,000 a month in total of any combination of income protection, salary continuance or business expenses cover. Since life policies are "guaranteed renewal", there is no requirement to disclose the result of any subsequent genetic testing.

The change does not stop someone from disclosing favourable genetic test results to a life insurer.

Further information about genetic testing and life insurance canbe viewed in "FSC Standard No. 11: Moratorium on Genetic Tests in Life Insurance https://www.fsc.org.au/resources/1779-standard-11-moratorium-on-genetic-tests-in-life-insurance. Accessed 7 August 2019.

At a glance

Four criteria are used to evaluate premium rates:

- separation and class homogeneity
- reliability
- incentive value
- social acceptability.

TYPES OF INSURANCE

3-210   Introduction

In this final section, the various categories into which insurance transactions can be placed will be examined. These classifications are based on the perils insured against and can be grouped into two classes: private insurance and social insurance.

3-220   Private insurance

Private insurance consists of mainly voluntary insurance programs offered by private insurers to provide compensation to individuals and business owners when an insured loss occurs. This insurance is offered by both private and government insurance offices. Private insurance is based on the concept of individual equity, which means that the benefits received are related to the premiums paid by the individual. The two distinguishing characteristics of private insurance are that it is usually voluntary and the transfer of risk is evidenced by contract.

On the other hand, social insurance is compulsory insurance, often operated by the government, whose benefits are determined by law and which attempts to achieve social adequacy.

The major groupings within private and social insurance are as follows:

- Private insurance
    - » life insurance
    - » health income insurance
    - » general insurance (ie, property and liability insurance)
- Social (government) insurance, which includes
    - » social security
    - » welfare
    - » unemployment.

A brief introduction of the major products in each category follows, with a more detailed description deferred to later chapters.

Life insurance

There are 28 registered life insurance companies in Australia (APRA 2015). These insurers play an extremely important role in society by providing financial security to individuals and families.

Life insurance covers a variety of products, including policies that provide payment upon death, continuous disability or trauma. The underwriting of life insurance relies on the collection and use of health information to assess an applicant's risk of mortality and morbidity, and is mutually rated. Morbidity refers to sickness, injury or failure of health.

Term life insurance

Term life insurance provides for the payment of an agreed lump sum in the event of death of the insured during a specified period. The death benefits are paid to designated beneficiaries or the deceased's estate. The policy proceeds can be used to pay for funeral expenses, uninsured medical and hospital expenses, education expenses for surviving children, living expenses for the surviving spouse and for other uses. If the life insured survives to the end of the period, no amount is payable by the insurer. These policies do not contain any investment element and can be obtained for a relatively low premium if the insured is in good health.

The proceeds or other lump sum paid from a life insurance policy can also be used to provide guaranteed regular income payments for life through the purchase of an annuity. An annuity is a guaranteed regular payment that continues for a fixed period or for the life of the insured. The person who receives the annuity is called the annuitant. The fundamental purpose of an annuity is to provide a lifetime income that cannot be outlived. It protects against the loss of income because of excessive longevity and exhaustion of savings.

Income protection insurance

Income protection (or disability income) insurance provides for regular sums to be paid while an insured is unable to work because of sickness or injury. The monthly income benefits are generally paid for a designated period, such as to age 65, following a minimum waiting period of 14 days. These policies are guaranteed renewable and once accepted by the insurance company cannot be cancelled or altered by the company. They can be cancelled only by the insured, generally by non-payment of the renewal premium.

Trauma insurance

Trauma (or crisis) insurance provides for the payment of an agreed lump sum if the insured person is diagnosed with one of a list of specified conditions such as heart attack, cancer or stroke.

This section has introduced the major life insurance products. These and other life products are discussed in greater depth in Chapter 12.

Health insurance

A long-term loss of income resulting from sickness or accident can cause greater financial difficulties for individuals and families than death. Health insurance is insurance against loss caused by accidental bodily injury or sickness. The 'loss' resulting from this insurance can relate to doctors' bills, hospital bills, the cost of medication and long-term care, and loss of wages resulting from the accident or sickness. Uninsured losses that could have been covered by health insurance may be sufficient to result in the abandonment of a financial plan. Health insurance is examined in greater depth in Chapter 14.

General Insurance

This type of insurance is offered by fire and general insurance companies and provides protection against loss or damage to property and losses arising from legal liability. These insurances can be classified by the types of policies sold. The major categories are:

- fire insurance
- multiple line insurance
- marine insurance
  - » ocean marine insurance
  - » inland marine insurance
- aviation insurance
- motor vehicle insurance
- liability insurance
- equipment breakdown insurance
- burglary, robbery and theft insurance
- workers compensation insurance
- fidelity insurance and surety insurance.

Each category is briefly discussed in turn, but these and other general insurance products are discussed in greater depth in Chapter 13.

Fire insurance

Fire insurance provides protection against damage to or destruction of property (real or personal) due to fire. A fire policy may also provide protection against perils such as lightning, explosion, storm, aircraft, earthquake, water damage and sprinkler leakage.

There are two approaches to classifying the perils covered by a fire policy. The first approach is to provide cover under a named peril coverage. A named peril policy provides coverage against loss arising from specific perils such as fire, lightning, explosion, impact by aircraft, etc listed in the policy document. The policy will indemnify the insured only if a loss is caused by these perils.

The second approach is called open peril coverage. Open peril coverage provides cover for all accidental loss or damage to the insured property unless the peril is excluded from the policy. The policy contains a list of excluded perils, such as wear and tear, and unless excluded the peril will be covered subject to any policy excess.

Coverage is generally available for both 'direct loss' (ie, loss or damage to the insured property) and 'indirect loss' (ie, loss of business income and any extra expenses incurred as a result of the loss of use of the insured property).

Multiple line insurance

Multiple line insurance combines property and other general insurance coverage in one contract. For example, business insurance packages combine coverage for fire, business interruption, liability, burglary and theft, fidelity guarantee, motor vehicle and general property coverage in one contract. Similarly, a householders policy also combines fire insurance and other perils with liability insurance in one contract. Home building and home contents insurances are prescribed contracts under the IC Act and prescribed cover applies. This is discussed further in Chapter 13 (see 13-150).

Many large businesses are insured under an industrial special risks policy. An industrial special risks policy covers all physical loss, destruction or damage that is not otherwise excluded, including loss resulting from interruption or interference to the business anywhere in the world. These policies cover a wide range of property, including personal property of employees, against a variety of perils such as burglary or theft of money, subject to policy limits and excesses. These are specialist policies designed for large commercial risks that allow specific cover to be designed for those risks. The discussion of these types of policies is beyond the scope of this text and is not discussed further.

Marine insurance

Marine insurance provides protection for the hulls of vessels and their cargo against loss or damage during transportation. Coverage can be from 'warehouse to warehouse', thereby providing protection against perils associated with overland transportation prior to loading onto the vessel as well those on the ocean.

Inland marine insurance provides protection against loss or damage to property that is transported by carriers such as motor vehicles and railways. These policies can be arranged to cover a one-off transportation or as an open annual policy to cover all goods transported during the year.

Marine insurance, with the exception of private pleasure craft insurance, is beyond the scope of this text and is not examined.

Aviation insurance

Aviation insurance provides cover to aircraft, loss of air freight and liability to passengers in aircraft, and personal accident insurance for passengers and crew. Aviation insurance is not examined further in this text.

Motor vehicle insurance

Motor vehicle insurance falls into two categories:

* *motor vehicle insurance – property*
* *motor vehicles – compulsory third party insurance.*

Motor vehicle insurance – property provides protection against several types of losses. Comprehensive motor vehicle insurance covers accidental loss or damage, including fire and theft to the insured vehicle, plus claims by third parties in relation to property damage. Motor vehicle insurance is a prescribed contract under the IC Act and standard cover applies. This is discussed further in Chapter 13 (see 13-050).

Third party property damage insurance covers liability for damage to other people's property. This type of policy does not provide any cover to the insured's own vehicle. Standard cover has been prescribed under the IC Act for motor vehicle property damage insurance, which is discussed further in Chapter 6 (see 6-040).

Motor vehicles – compulsory third party (CTP) insurance provides cover for the owners of motor vehicles and anyone else driving the vehicle against liability incurred in respect of the death of or bodily injury to other persons, such as other drivers, passengers, pedestrians and cyclists involved in the accident. This type of insurance is compulsory in Australia, Although not all injured people will be eligible for coverage and will rely on cover with the National Injury Insurance Scheme (NIIS) operating in each state and territory (See 14-055).

The NIIS will provide compensation for anyone catastrophically injured in a motor vehicle accident and will be eligible to receive reasonable lifetime treatment, care and support. Because CTP insurance is a fault-based scheme people who are considered to be at fault, or in situations where there is no negligent person involved in an accident or when one cannot be identified for example, a hit and run accident, or the negligent driver does not have CTP insurance, do not receive compensation under CTP insurance. Therefore, the NIIS scheme complements existing CTP insurance by insuring that all catastrophically people will receive the care and support that they need.

Not all countries have the same CTP system for example, the legal situation is different in New Zealand, where owners of motor vehicles are not required to hold compulsory third party insurance as personal injury is covered under the *Accident Rehabilitation and Compensation Insurance Act 1992* (NZ), which provides a no-fault compensation scheme for personal injury. All people, including visitors, are eligible for the benefits. However, under the same Act, the right to sue for compensation was abolished.

Liability insurance

Liability insurance protects the insured against the consequences of being held legally liable for personal injury or damage caused to third parties. Liability hazards can arise from the sale and distribution of products, the ownership of property, manufacturing and construction businesses, and many other exposures.

Equipment breakdown insurance

Equipment breakdown insurance can be divided into two categories:

- machinery breakdown insurance
- electronic equipment insurance.

Machinery breakdown insurance covers the cost of repairs to machinery following breakdown. This policy can be extended to cover consequential loss of profits following a breakdown. These policies also cover damage to pressure vessels such as compressors caused by explosion and the insured's legal liability for personal injury and damage to third party property. Cover is generally not offered by insurers until the equipment proposed for insurance has been inspected by either the insurer or a specialist firm operating on their behalf. These inspections are often a valuable additional benefit for the insureds.

Electronic equipment insurance indemnifies insureds for the cost of repairs following electronic breakdown to computers and other electronic equipment. The cover can be extended to cover loss of data and the cost of rewriting records both of which can be a significant cost following a loss.

Burglary, robbery and theft insurance

Burglary and theft insurance protects an insured against loss of property, money and negotiable instruments through burglary, larceny and theft. Theft by employees is generally excluded from the cover, as protection against criminal acts of employees is provided under fidelity guarantee covers.

Workers compensation insurance

Workers compensation insurance covers workers who suffer work-related injury or disease resulting from illness or accident. In some Australian states this insurance is offered by private insurance companies, while in others state governments are the only providers of this insurance. In all cases, state governments specify the content of coverage.

Fidelity insurance and surety insurance

Fidelity insurance protects organisations from loss of money, securities or inventory resulting from crime. Common fidelity claims allege employee dishonesty, embezzlement, forgery, robbery, safe burglary, computer fraud, wire transfer fraud, counterfeiting and other criminal acts.

Surety insurance provides protection to the principal client (project owner) against default or non-performance of a contractor. It is a contract used mainly in the construction industry and involves three parties:

- the *principal:* the primary party who will be performing the contractual obligation, such as a construction company that agrees to build an office building for a government department. The construction company may be required to arrange a performance bond before the contract is awarded.

- the *obligee:* the party, such as a bank, who benefits from the bond if the principal fails to perform. In the above example, the bank would be reimbursed for any loss that resulted from failure of the construction company to complete the building on time or according to contract specifications.

- the *surety* (or *obligor*): the party, such as an insurance company, who agrees to answer for the debt, default or obligation of another. Continuing the above example, if the construction company (principal) fails to perform, the bank (oblige) would be reimbursed for any loss by the insurance company (surety).

3-230   Social (government) insurance

Social insurance programs are government programs that pool certain risks and are required by law to pay certain benefits to qualifying persons in the event of certain predesignated losses.

Social insurance programs are designed to provide a 'floor of protection' or a 'safety net' to persons who are not able to cope individually with certain fundamental risks. The principle behind social insurance is that it is a fundamental obligation of a civilised society to provide a basic level of risk security. The first modern social insurance program originated in Germany in 1880 and operated on the premise that since the poor have inadequate resources to provide for themselves in adversity, such as cessation of income following work-related injuries, it was the responsibility of government to provide these basic benefits.

Certain conditions must exist for a program to qualify as social insurance:

- coverage is normally compulsory by law
- targeted recipients will receive more than they contribute because benefits are not tied to direct contributions
- the method of determining eligibility and the level of benefits is established by law
- the program is either run or regulated by government.

The organisation of social insurance is based on two philosophies:

1. social insurance approach
2. welfare approach.

In the social insurance approach, people are required to contribute regularly to a specific fund that will pay benefits under set circumstances regardless of the actual needs of the members. The cost of the scheme is borne by the members or their employers. Examples are the Accident Compensation Corporation of New Zealand and Workers Compensation in Australia.

In contrast, in the welfare approach, eligibility for benefits is based on need. Welfare benefits are financed through general revenue that normally comes from federal funds. The benefits received from welfare are based not on contributions made by or on behalf of the recipients, but on actual need of the members. Although public assistance programs provide economic security, they are not insurance programs because the principles of assessing and pooling risk do not apply.

3-240   Study questions

3.1   A purchaser has just purchased a new plasma television set with a one-year warranty. Has the insurer issued an insurance contract? Explain.

3.2   Explain why the pooling technique is essential to insurance.

3.3   Bryan and Mary are members of a community of 1,000 farmers who wish to join together to form an insurance pool to protect themselves against the loss of their machinery sheds by fire. After examining the past records of the rural fire brigade, they determine that fire losses caused damage each year equal to one per cent of the value of similar machinery sheds. That is, some sheds were totally destroyed while others were only partially damaged. Explain the following:

   (a)   If each farmer had a machinery shed worth $120,000, what would it cost each farmer to be a member of the pool? (Detail any assumption made.)

   (b)   Are there enough exposures to predict only one loss per year? Explain.

3.4   The transfer of risk is a requirement of insurance. The term risk refers to uncertainty about future outcomes. Since a life insurance company is aware that death is a certainty, does life insurance meet the ideal requirements of insurance?

3.5   Explain if it is possible for a small insurance company to survive without a large number of exposure units.

3.6   How does insurance differ from gambling?

3.7   How does insurance differ from hedging?

3.8   Komfy Furniture store is faced with many perils that threaten its operations every day. Explain why each of the following perils may or may not be insurable. In each case, discuss possible exceptions to the general answer given:

   (a)   the loss of stock because of theft when the thief is not caught and Komfy cannot establish exactly when the loss occurred

   (b)   injury to a child who falls to the floor while jumping on a bed

   (c)   injury to a customer when the store's delivery truck backs into him while delivering furniture.

3.9   The New London Insurance Company insures 80 per cent of all the property in the Docklands commercial area. Docklands is two square kilometres in area and has a total insured value (of all commercial and residential buildings) of US$26.5 billion. Explain the principal exposure faced by the New London Insurance Company.

3.10   Identify three uninsurable exposures and explain why each is uninsurable.

3.11   Explain the four major principles of risk classification.

3.12   Incentive value is a term used to evaluate premiums. Explain what this term means.

3.13   Explain the differences between a social and a private insurance plan.

3.14   Describe the three general categories into which private (voluntary) insurance is divided.

3.15   Life insurance companies argue that genetic testing allows them to more accurately categorise applicants so that insureds without a genetic predisposition to potentially fatal diseases will not subsidise the premiums offered to those with the predisposition. Surely this conforms to the principles of risk classification. Pose any arguments against genetic testing?

3-250   References and further reading

References

Businessopedia (n.d.). https://www.insuranceopedia.com/definition/1134/catastrophe-loss.

Articles and books

Marks, F & Balla, A 1998, *Guidebook to insurance law in Australia,* 3rd edn, CCH Australia Limited, Sydney, p 7.

Releases

Australian Prudential Regulation Authority (APRA) 2015, *Registered Life Insurance Companies, August.*

Legislation

Accident Rehabilitation and Compensation Insurance Act 1992 (NZ)

Insurance Contracts Act 1984 (Cth)

Further reading

Australian Law Reform Commission, *Essentially yours: The protection of human genetic information in Australia*, Report 96, Canberra.

Baranoff, E 2004, *Risk management and insurance,* John Wiley & Sons Inc, USA. Chapter 2.

Dorfman, MS (2005), Introduction to risk management and insurance, 8th edn, Pearson Education, Inc., New Jersey, USA.

Redja, GE 2003, *Principles of risk management and insurance,* 8th edn, Pearson Education Inc., USA. Chapter 2.

Vaughan, EJ & Vaughan, TM 2003, *Fundamentals of risk and insurance,* 9th edn, John Wiley & Sons Inc, USA. Chapter 3.

CHAPTER 4

REGULATION AND COMPLIANCE

REGULATION OF THE INSURANCE INDUSTRY

4-000   History of regulation

The process of deregulation began with the Campbell Committee Report of 1981, which reported on the regulation and control of the Australian financial system and made recommendations on its improvement, and the Financial Systems Enquiry (FSI), which culminated in the Wallis Inquiry Report in 1997 (the Wallis Report).

While the Campbell Committee Report ushered in fundamental changes to the Australian financial system, the Wallis Report focused on reviewing the process of deregulation and refining the regulatory system. Under the pre-Wallis system, regulation of the financial system was based on the types of institutions involved; for example, the insurance industry was regulated by the Insurance and Superannuation Commission (ISC). The Wallis Report recommended the creation of a structure based on regulatory functions involving the Reserve Bank of Australia (RBA) and two new bodies, the Australian Securities and Investments Commission (ASIC) and the Australian Prudential Regulation Authority (APRA). The Australian Competition and Consumer Commission (ACCC) is also important in this area although it is not directly part of the Wallis recommendations.

The *Financial Services Reform Act 2001* (Cth) (FSR Act) and the *Financial Services Reform (Consequential Provisions) Act 2001* (Cth) represent the final legislative response to the Wallis Report. The FSI and the consequent Corporate Law Economic Reform Program (CLERP) subjected the regulatory framework of the financial services industry to intense scrutiny in order to enhance Australia's international competitiveness by improving the efficiency of corporate regulation and reducing the regulatory burdens on business. The recommendations of the CLERP papers were incorporated into the FSR Act. The FSR Act aims to establish an integrated regulatory framework for all financial products to enhance efficiency and competitiveness and to encourage innovation. The FSR Act came into effect on 11 March 2002 with a two-year transition period for many of the new provisions.

As part of this deregulation process, regulators tend to have four main concerns. The first relates to the need to make insurance contracts easier to understand and to allow consumers to compare their various terms and conditions. Second is the intention to move away from controls that limit competition between insurers, such as controls on premium prices and policy terms and conditions, to controls on the financial position of insurers.

The third concern is the trend away from requirements for prior approval of terms and conditions of insurance contracts towards reliance on general prohibitions against certain terms, industry agreements — such as the Australian tariff rating schedules, which operated prior to the introduction of the *Trade Practices Act 1974* (Cth) (the provisions are now incorporated into the *Competition and Consumer Act 2010* (C&C Act)) and general consumer protection laws. Finally, there are moves to enhance the quantity and quality of information that insurers must disclose relating to their financial position and attempts to increase the responsibility of directors and managers regarding the prudential health of their company (OECD 1998).

The development of insurance law in Australia began with the introduction of the *Insurance Contracts Act 1984* (Cth) (IC Act), which stemmed from the Australian Law Reform Commission (ALRC) report *Insurance Contracts*, published in 1982. The IC Act sought to reform the law to redress a wide range of anomalies, quell a crescendo of complaints from dissatisfied insureds and replace out-dated law with law more compatible with changing social and economic conditions. This law also sought to improve standards of consumer protection. Three major inquiries were conducted in the early 1990s. In 1992 the Trade Practices Commission reported on life insurance and superannuation; the Senate Select Committee on Superannuation reported in June 1993; and the ALRC reported about the same time on collective investments. All were critical of the selling practices and standards of product disclosure in the insurance industry.

Codes of practice

As a further step to improve standards, the ISC put forward a draft code of practice for comment and debate. On 3 August 1995, the Code of Practice for Advising, Selling and Complaints Handling in the Life Insurance Industry (the Life Code of Practice) was issued (later superseded by the FSR Act). A General Insurance Code of Practice was also implemented, which was replaced on 18 July 2005 with a new Code of Practice in response to the FSR Act. The initial intention was that these Codes would constitute best practice in the industry and that later legislative reform would make them mandatory. However, a change in government and policy, and the recommendations of the Wallis Inquiry, left the Codes as best practice benchmarks only. Despite the lack of legislation, the Codes are taken seriously by the industry.

Within a few months of the introduction of the Life Code, the ISC issued circular G.II.2 *Code of Practice Requirements*, which provided some clarification and refinement of the Code. Meanwhile, the ISC and the Australian Securities Commission (ASC) had become concerned about the disparity in the regulation of insurance advisers/marketers and securities advisers.

Exposure drafts were released for comment and an agreed approach devised. Consequently, the ISC released circular G.II.6, which made slight amendments to the Life Code and the ASC released policy statement PS124 'Investment advisory services: mixed advice on securities and life insurance products'. These amendments introduced greater consistency ('harmonisation') in regulation and practice including:

- disclosure of capacity and Advisory Services Guide (ASG). These requirements meant that advisers had to disclose the products they were authorised to deal in and the ASG disclosed such matters as information that identified who the consumer was dealing with and the identity of those who were responsible for the adviser's actions.

- disclosure of the names of principals

- use of the term 'independent'

- needs analysis and appropriate advice

- bases for exclusions from advisory process and sales conduct requirements.

Finally, the intense scrutiny of the regulatory framework of the financial services industry by CLERP and the subsequent Financial Services Reform (FSR) Bill led to the enactment of the FSR Act, as discussed above. The FSR Bill inserted a new Ch 7 in the Corporations Act, including ss 760A to 1101J, which mandate the behaviour and practice of financial advisers, including those who sell insurance products into the future.

The behaviour and practice of advisers are also governed by the C&C Act and the IC Act, as discussed above, as well as the *Insurance Act 1973* (Cth) and common law. These are discussed in later sections and subsequent chapters.

4-010   Insurance intermediaries Australia

Before the introduction of the IC Act, the activities of agents and brokers were regulated by the *Insurance (Agents and Brokers) Act 1984* (Cth) (the IAB Act), which was administered by the Insurance Commissioner in Canberra. On 27 September 2001, the FSR Act received royal assent, which repealed the IAB Act and introduced a regulatory process, bringing agents and brokers within the same regulatory regime as others involved in the financial services industry.

Insurance agents and brokers

A great proportion of insurance business is conducted through intermediaries, whether employees of insurance companies, agents or brokers. While the FSR

Act does not generally refer to 'insurance agents' and 'insurance brokers', the terms *agent* and *broker* are still in use in the market and the difference between the two terms needs to be clarified. Common law recognises the ability of one person to appoint another to undertake activities, which will be binding on the person. The person who is appointed is an agent and the person appointing the agent is the latter's principal. A principal will be liable for the conduct of an agent in the course of carrying out their duties as an agent, even if carried out in an unauthorised manner. For example, if an insurer appoints a person as its agent to arrange contracts of insurance, the insurer may instruct the agent not to arrange insurance beyond a certain limit. If the agent arranges insurance beyond that limit, the insurer will be bound by the arrangement made by the agent.

An agent is appointed by a principal with the express and apparent authority to act on behalf of the principal. For example, in *Derham v AMEV Life Insurance Co Ltd (1981)* 56 FLR 34; (1982) 2 ANZ Insurance Cases 60-459 an insurer was held to have been liable for the actions of its agent where the agent's conduct was within his apparent authority. The insured took out life policies with AMEV, having been induced to do so by a fraudulent misrepresentation made by the agent of AMEV as to the investment benefits associated with the company's policies. The insured issued proceedings to recover money paid to AMEV in relation to these policies. AMEV denied liability on the basis that the agent had no authority to make the representations. The insured said that even if it was the case that the agent had no authority to do what he did, it did not matter as the agent's conduct was within his apparent authority. The Supreme Court of the ACT found in favour of the insured. AMEV had provided the agent with business cards, letterheads and other documents bearing its name, including a receipt book. In so doing, the insurer had represented to the insured that the agent had the authority to solicit business and receive premiums. The insurer was ordered to return to the insured the premium paid on certain life policies.

In some cases, such as when completing proposal forms on behalf of insureds or intending insureds (applicants), insurance agents and insurers' employees are, under common law, agents for the applicants. However, s 917B of the *Corporations Act 2001* (Cth) provides that an insurer is responsible for the conduct of its agent or employee when completing proposal forms on behalf of applicants where it is reasonable for the insured to rely upon the agent to do so.

Under s 9 of the now-repealed IAB Act, the principles of which are carried forward in the Corporations Act, a person would not be considered an agent of a principal if he or she did not receive a 'reward' in the form of money or money's worth for arranging insurance. For example, if a solicitor or friend assisted in arranging a contract of insurance, but did not receive any remuneration for doing so, they would not fall into the definition of an agent.

Under common law, insurance brokers are held to be agents of insureds and intending insureds, even though they are mostly remunerated by commission (brokerage) by insurers. Under s 9 of the IAB Act, an insurance broker is defined as a person who carries on the business of arranging contracts of insurance, whether in Australia or overseas, as agents for intending insureds. Therefore, for a person to be considered an insurance broker he or she must be carrying on the 'business' of arranging insurance contracts. Tax law clearly distinguishes between carrying on a business and pursuing some other activity such as a hobby. This is important when determining whether or not any income generated is assessable for tax purposes.

When carrying on a business, there is usually the intention of making a profit, although the activity may not initially produce a profit or be intended to. The activity must be carried out in some structured and regular fashion. With an insurance broker, the carrying on of some business is likely to involve some regular activity such as arranging insurance contracts where some form of remuneration is derived, usually in the form of commission. Therefore, an insurance broker who is retained by a client to arrange insurance is clearly in a principal–agent relationship.

Under the Corporations Act, which requires an entity to hold an Australian Financial Services Licence in order to advise or arrange a financial product, the terms *insurance broker, insurance broking, general insurance broker* and *life insurance broker* can be used to describe a business only if that is a condition of the licence.

However, in some instances a broker will be an agent of the insurer, such as when they act under a binder agreement (defined in s 761A of the Corporations Act). A binding agreement is an authority provided by an insurer to an insurance intermediary to enter into contracts of insurance on behalf of the insurer (ie, as agent for the insurer). An intermediary may also be authorised to deal with and, as the insurer's agent, settle claims against the insurer. If a broker has authority only to issue cover notes, then there is no 'binder'.

The distinction between insurance agents and insurance brokers was explained succinctly by Justice Lush in *Norwich Union Fire Insurance Society Limited v Brennans (Horsham) Pty Ltd* (1981) VR 981; (1981) 1 ANZ Insurance Cases 60-446:

> "... [an insurance broker] *is a person, firm or company, which carries on an independent business of placing insurance upon the instructions of clients and*

whose basic relationship of agency is with the client, and it is the insurance agent whose function it is to procure persons to insure with his principal, the insurer, and whose basic relationship of agency is therefore with the insurer."

Receipt of premiums

Monies paid to a licensee from an insured are regulated by s 981A of the Corporations Act, 'Dealing with Client's Money'. Licensees (including insurance brokers) are required to deposit premiums paid to them by insureds into an account with an Authorised Deposit-taking Institution (ADI) such as a bank or building society (s 981B), to be held in an account titled insurance broking account for the holding of these premiums until paid out to insurers. Under the 'broking agreement' between broker and insurer, the insurer will grant the broker credit terms such as 30, 60 or 90 days from the inception of the insurance, before the monies have to be paid to the insurer.

These credit terms are given to allow the broker to complete the relevant proposal form, 'close' the business to the insurer, which includes advising insurers that premiums on renewal invitations of existing policies have been paid — that is, advise the insurer that they are *on risk* — and complete the accounting and policy recording within their computer system. The insurer will send a statement of account to the broker that contains entries of all business 'closed' to the insurer. The broker is required by the Corporations Act to pay all monies relating to the policies issued by the broker before the expiry of the credit terms, including those policies that may not appear on the insurer's statement of account (s 981C).

General insurance brokers, not life insurance brokers, issue renewal notices to clients for policies coming due for renewal and payment in the near future. The Corporations Act requires that insurers must forward a renewal notice to the insured three weeks prior to the due date of the policy. The insured pays the renewal premium to the broker, who will account to the insurer as described above. All renewal notices issued by brokers must clearly show any 'broker fees' that may be charged, which are in addition to the insurer's premium.

The FSR Act, which amended the Corporations Act, also repealed the IAB Act. Section 14 of the IAB Act provided that the insurer, rather than the insured, was to bear the risks of funds held by an insurance broker. Section 985B of the Corporations Act provides that the payment of funds by an insured to a financial services licensee (eg, an insurance agent or broker who is not an insurer) will constitute a discharge of the liability of the insured to the insurer so long as there is an existing liability of the insured to the insurer. Thus, if the broker goes into liquidation or absconds with the premium, the insured is not liable under the Corporations Act to pay it a second time. The following case example provides an example where an insured was not protected under s 14 of the IAB Act against the failure of their insurance broker to pass their premium and renewal instructions on to their insurer.

Case example

Manufacturers Mutual Insurance Ltd v John H Boardman Insurance Brokers Pty Ltd

(1994) 8 ANZ Insurance Cases 61-215; (1994) 179 CLR 650

Facts: Boardman Insurance Brokers (Boardman) arranged insurance coverage on property owned by their client, Metrot with MMI Insurance. Twelve months later, MMI sent a renewal notice to Boardman inviting Metrot to renew the policy for a further twelve months. Metrot instructed Boardman to renew the policy and paid the renewal premium to Boardman. Boardman not only failed to instruct MMI to renew the policy, but also failed to pay the premium to MMI in accordance with the terms of the broker's agreement. As a result, the insurance policy with MMI lapsed. Approximately seven months later the premises were damaged in the Newcastle earthquake of 1989. The insured lodged a claim with MMI, which was rejected on the basis that the policy had lapsed. Consequently, Metrot sued MMI.

Issue: Was the insured's payment to the broker considered a renewal of the policy under s 14(2) of the IAB Act?

Decision: Both the Supreme Court of NSW and Court of Appeal ruled in favour of Metrot, but MMI appealed to the High Court, which ruled that for s 14(2) of the IAB Act to operate, there must have been a contract. Since s 14(2) did not displace the common law there was no contract because Metrot's acceptance had not been communicated to MMI. Under common law, insurance brokers are agents of the insured and as such Metrot's renewal instructions to Boardman did not constitute a renewal of the policy and hence, there was no contract until the instructions had been communicated to MMI. Metrot lost this case in the High Court.

The following case example shows the protection provided by the IABA to insureds for a further liability to their insurance company for premiums they paid to their insurance broker where these premiums were not passed on to their insurance company.

Case example

Norwich Union Fire Insurance Society Ltd v Brennans (Horsham) Pty Ltd

(1981) 1 ANZ Insurance Cases 60-446; (1981) VR 98

Facts: The insured paid premiums to an insurance broker for certain policies. The premiums were not passed on to the insurer. The insurer sued the insured for premiums it alleged were due and owing. The insured argued that the intermediary had acted as the insurer's agent in receiving the premiums. The issue was whether the intermediary had been authorised by the insurer to collect premiums on its behalf.

Issue: Where the broker goes into liquidation, is the insured liable to pay a second time?

Decision: The Victorian Supreme Court held that the practice adopted by the insurer in its dealings with the broker was such that the intermediary was its agent for the purpose of receipt of the premiums.

The court referred to:

- the practice of debiting premiums to a running account between the intermediary and the insurer

- the fact the defendant's premiums were debited into that account

- the fact that renewal notices were sent to the intermediary, which the court saw as authorising the intermediary to collect premiums

- the fact that the insurer made no demand on the intermediary for payment of the premium until after the intermediary ceased business, which was around eight months after the date of renewal.

In contrast to the *Boardman* case discussed above, renewal instructions had been given to Norwich Union so a contract under common law existed. In this instance the insured had protection under s 14 of the IAB Act as it varied common law where payment of premiums by the insured to a broker does not discharge the insured's liability.

Conflict of interest

A broker has a duty to avoid a conflict of interest between its obligations to the insured and any agreement with the insurer. The following case example confirms the agency relationship that exists between a client and their broker.

Case example

Anglo-African Merchants Ltd v Bayley

(1970) 1 QB 311

Facts: Certain goods covered by a policy of insurance were lost. The insurer asked the broker to obtain an assessor's report but the broker refused to disclose it. The insurer argued that while the broker was the agent of the insured in relation to arranging of cover, this did not extend to the making of a claim.

Issue: Does the broker's agency relationship with the insured extend only to arranging cover and not to the making of a claim?

Decision: The court rejected the insurer's argument and held that the insured was entitled to a copy of the report. It held that the broker was the agent of the insured, and once engaged by an insured, it was under a duty to do nothing inconsistent with such engagement without the consent of the insured.

Requirement to hold insurance

Until 31 December 2006, Class Order (CO) 06/495 required insurance brokers to hold professional indemnity insurance according to the provisions of s 9(B) of the repealed IAB Act, the extent of cover required (reg 2B) and the level of any policy excess (reg 2B(3)). This was a transitional arrangement put in place while the Australian government considered its position on a final compensation regime. In January 2007, ASIC released Regulatory Guide (RG) 167, which states that "… under regulation 7.6.02AA(1) and (2) [of the Corporations Regulations 2001], as a matter of law, insurance brokers must continue to have professional indemnity insurance" (RG167.49B).

Insurance agents, on the other hand, are authorised representatives of an insurance company (licensee) and are not required to hold professional indemnity insurance. However, in practice agents will be required to hold professional indemnity insurance under the terms of their agency agreement with their principal.

4-020   Regulatory control of intermediaries

Insurance intermediaries are regulated by the Corporations Act, which is administered by ASIC. This targets standards of conduct and competence in the industry and provides for disclosure to insureds.

A person who carries on a 'financial services business' (s 761A) must have an Australian Financial Services Licence (AFSL) (s 911A) issued by ASIC. This licence is required for all those providing financial services, including stockbrokers and financial advisers, which include general and life insurance brokers. Representatives and sales staff must also be authorised and supervised by the insurer or licensee (ss 916A; 912A(1)(ca)). Financial services licensees are responsible for the conduct of their representatives including loss or damage suffered by a client through the actions of the representative – for example, a representative issuing cover for a risk that he or she was not authorised to issue, as described above.

On 26 October 2005, ASIC created a special class of representatives called *distributors*. Distributors are authorised to arrange general insurance products issued on behalf of a financial services licensee and are excluded from holding an AFSL (CO 05/1070). (Note: class orders apply to a class of persons who carry on a particular activity in certain circumstances, such as operators of a managed investment scheme or financial services licensees.) A distributor is a person or corporation who is not an authorised representative of the licensee but is given written consent by the licensee authorising them to provide financial services in relation to risk insurance products on behalf of the licensee. A distributor will deal only in a general and a life insurance product or a bundled consumer credit insurance product or both. For example, car rental firms offer their customers car insurance when they rent a car. The car rental firm is appointed as a distributor by the insurance company providing this insurance to carry out the service.

The Corporations Act distinguishes between retail and wholesale insureds (s 761(G)), and provides a greater level of protection for retail clients. The distinction between the two and the level of protection provided by the Corporations Act are discussed later in the chapter.

At a glance

- Insurance agents and brokers have been subject to Commonwealth regulation since the introduction of the *Insurance (Agents and Brokers) Act 1984* (now repealed).

- Insurance agents represent the insurance company, and their first duty of care is to their principal.

- Insurance brokers represent their client as their agent unless they act as agents for an insurer under a binding agreement.

- Clients' monies held by insurance brokers must be paid into a special bank account.

- The payment of premiums to an insurance broker is regarded as payment to the insurer.

- Payment of claim monies to insurance brokers does not relieve the insurer's liability to their insured.

- The activities of Australian insurance agents and brokers are regulated by Chapter 7 of the *Corporations Act 2001*, and they must hold an Australian Financial Services Licence (AFSL) or be an authorised representative of an AFSL holder in order to advise on financial products or provide financial services.

- The Corporations Act draws a distinction between retail and wholesale clients, and requires disclosure to be made through a Financial Services Guide (FSG), Statement of Advice (SoA) and Product Disclosure Statement (PDS).

CONSUMER PROTECTION AND INSURANCE

4-030   Introduction

The aim of consumer protection in the financial services industry is to protect investors, superannuants (ie, someone who has retired and is receiving a pension) and insurance policyholders from being exploited through unconscionable, misleading or deceptive conduct. This section examines the consumer protection laws that apply to the financial services industry in Australia.

4-040   Consumer protection in Australia

Insurers, insurance agents and brokers may be liable to their clients under either the Australian Consumer Law (ACL) that is set out in Sch 2 of the C&C Act, the *Australian Securities and Investments Commission Act 2001* (Cth) (ASIC Act) or the Corporations Act.

The ACL came into force on 1 January 2011 and is the new law governing consumer protection and fair trading in Australia. It replaces nine different state, territory and federal consumer protection laws and applies to corporations and individuals acting in their own right such as sole traders and partnerships. The ACL is a single national law and is enforced by all Australian courts and tribunals, including the courts and tribunals of the States and Territories; and is administered by the ACCC and each State and Territory's consumer law agency. The ACL can also be privately enforced with consumers being able to enforce its provisions through the various consumer tribunals as well as through state and Commonwealth courts.

Section 18 of the ACL prohibits misleading and deceptive conduct while s 21 provides protection against unconscionable conduct in connection with the supply or acquisition of goods or services to a person or to or from a corporation. However, insurance contracts are excluded from the ACL.

Section 131 of the C&C Act and hence, the ACL states that this Act does not apply to 'financial services or financial products'. A *financial service* and the related concept of a *financial product* are defined in s 766A and s 763A respectively of the Corporations Act. The general definition of a financial product, as defined in the Corporations Act, includes managing a financial risk, such as taking out a general insurance or life insurance product (s 763C). A person who deals in a financial product is providing a financial service (s 766C). Therefore, an insurance problem that does not involve a 'contract of insurance', such as issues involving the pre-contractual negotiations, would be covered by the ACL.

Many sections in Subdiv A of the ACL, dealing with unconscionable conduct and consumer protection, are paralleled in the ASIC Act, which means that an insurance problem that involves a 'contract of insurance' would be covered by the ASIC Act.

Although it is not defined in the ASIC Act, unconscionable conduct is taken to mean taking advantage of a client in a transaction in a way that offends the conscience. Additionally, the ACL recognises that there may be circumstances where the *manner* in which a contract was executed was unconscionable, such as where a disparity in bargaining power exists. Mason, J in *Commercial Bank of Australia v Amadio* [1983] HCA 14; 151 CLR 447 at [3] held that "relief on the ground of unconscionable conduct will be granted when unconscientious advantage is taken of an innocent party whose will is overborne so that it is not independent and voluntary ... [or where the innocent party] is unable to make a worthwhile judgment as to what is in his best interest."

Insurers may be at risk if they:

- compel their clients to confirm conditions not reasonably necessary for the protection of the legitimate interests of the company

- use documentation that is unnecessarily complex

- contract with parties with reading or mental disabilities without taking special care

- exert undue pressure or influence such as intimidating or pressuring insureds to agree to settle a claim.

Four areas in which an insurer might breach the provisions of s 21 of the ACL are:

- representations that insurance cover contains benefits it does not have

- false or misleading statements regarding the need for insurance

- conduct liable to mislead regarding the nature or suitability of any product

- misleading advice about the rights to claim.

Section 12DB(1) of the ASIC Act identifies a number of situations where a corporation can be seen to making misleading or deceptive representations. These include where the corporation is deemed to:

- falsely representing that services are of a particular standard, quality, value or grade

- falsely representing that a particular person has agreed to acquire services
- making false or misleading representations that purport to be a testimonial by any person relating to a service
- representing that services have sponsorship, approval, performance characteristics, uses or benefits they do not have
- representing that the person has a sponsorship, approval or affiliation it does not have
- make a false or misleading representation with respect to the price of services
- make a false or misleading representation concerning the need for any services, or
- making a false or misleading representation concerning the existence, exclusion or effect of any condition, warranty, guarantee, right or remedy.

An example of misleading and deceptive conduct appears in the case *Gokora Pty Ltd v Montgomery Jordan & Stevenson Pty Ltd* (1986) 4 ANZ Insurance Cases 60-727. Insurance brokers were instructed to arrange insurance on a truck. A cover note was written and, when that expired, a secretary assured the client that a policy would be posted to him, even though she knew that no such policy had been contracted. That statement was deemed misleading or deceptive conduct by the brokers.

Examples of breaches of s 21 of the ACL are misleading or deceptive claims in promotional brochures or advertising and clauses in contracts at odds with the requirements of the IC Act or any other legislation.

As was noted by the High Court in *Concrete Constructions (NSW) Pty Ltd v Nelson* [1990] ATPR 41-022 "…the precise boundaries of the territory within which s 21 operates remain undetermined". This means that insurers and brokers, and indeed all business people, need to be vigilant that nothing they do could be interpreted as false or misleading conduct. Insurance advisers need to be particularly careful about making statements about future events, such as the likely returns from an investment. Where there are insufficient grounds for making such statements, they may be held to be misleading. The burden of proof that they are not misleading is on the adviser.

Sections 29 and 151 of the ACL, make it unlawful for a business to make false or misleading representations about goods or services when supplying, offering to supply, or promoting those goods or services and this may impact on insurance marketing. Examples that may breach the ACL are implying that a particular policy is well suited from among many for the purpose, when in fact only one policy had been considered, or where the purpose was not fully investigated. These examples would also breach the Corporations Act and the General Insurance Code of Practice.

ASIC Act and contracts of insurance

As mentioned earlier, the unconscionable conduct and consumer protection provisions relating to financial services are covered by s 18 and s 21 of the ACL in relation to pre-contractual matters and by the ASIC Act for post contractual matters. A 'financial service' and the related concept of a 'financial product' are defined in the ss 12BA–12BAA of the ASIC Act. A 'contract of insurance', including a life policy and a sinking fund, is a financial product (s 12BAA(7)(d)(e)), while the application for, or acquisition or issue of, a contract of insurance is the provision of a 'financial service', regulated by the ASIC Act and the Corporations Act. Therefore, any insurance problems that involve a contract of insurance are covered by the ASIC Act and the Corporations Act.

As a consequence, the ASIC Act does not apply to non–'financial product' situations and the ACL would apply in the following situations as they do not constitute an application for, or the acquisition or issue of, a 'contract of insurance':

- an applicant during pre-contractual negotiations before the making of a contract of insurance

- an insured's conduct during the performance of a contract of insurance

- an insured's conduct during unsuccessful negotiations that do not result in a concluded contract of insurance

- an agent or broker during negotiations or other non-contractual discussions with an insurer.

It should be noted that an agent or broker might be able to claim against an insurer for a breach, such as misleading conduct, in relation to financial services. Therefore, the ASIC Act and the ACL can provide remedies to anyone who suffers loss or damage because of unconscionable conduct by an insurer.

The ASIC Act does not regulate unfair contract terms in relation to insurance contracts as these are regulated by the IC Act.

Corporations Act and contracts of insurance

Actions that arise during the post-contractual stage of an insurance contract will generally arise as a result of an insurer who delays or fails to indemnify an insured under a contract of insurance. It has been mentioned above that the action for unconscionable conduct may be able to be taken under the ASIC Act. An aggrieved insured may also be able to take action under the Corporations Act. The remedies available to insureds are discussed next.

Remedies available under the Acts

While an insured is able to take action for unconscionable conduct under general law, damages are not available. At general law, a person subject to unconscionable conduct may seek to have the transaction set aside; have the transaction partially nullified; and/or seek specific performance. Under the ASIC Act and the Corporations Act, however, an applicant has a much wider range of remedies. They may include:

- obtaining an injunction (s 12GD ASIC Act; s 1324 Corporations Act)
- seeking damages (s 12GF ASIC Act; s 991A Corporations Act).

A contravention of the prohibition on misleading and deceptive conduct is subject to remedies including injunctions, damages and compensatory orders, as set out in Ch 5 of the ACL. Civil penalties and criminal sanctions do not apply to s 18 of the ACL, because of its very broad scope. Section 18 of the ACL creates a norm of business conduct, and allows persons to seek remedies for harm caused by breaches of that norm, rather than giving rise to a contravention that attracts punitive sanctions.

The remedies available for breach of the s 21 of the ACL unconscionable conduct provisions will not expose an insurer to criminal prosecution but may expose them to injunctions, damages, compensatory orders and other remedies, such as non-punitive orders and adverse publicity orders. There are also civil pecuniary penalties with maximum penalties of $1.1 million for a body corporate and $220,000 for a person other than a body corporate, as well as disqualification orders, redress for non-parties and public warning notices.

At a glance

- In Australia insurance intermediaries may be liable to their clients under the Australian Consumer Law (ACL) which forms part of the *Competition and Consumer Act 2010* (C&C Act).

- The ACL applies in all Australian states and territories and replaces existing state and territory consumer protection laws.

- The ASIC Act and ACL deal with unconscionable conduct and misleading and deceptive conduct and statements in relation to financial services.

- An insurance problem involving a contract of insurance is covered under the ASIC Act, but a problem occurring in the pre-contractual stage will be covered by the ACL.

REGULATORS IN AUSTRALIA

4-050 Introduction

The financial services regulatory framework that has been adopted in Australia has led to Australia being described as a global leader in financial services regulation (Axiss Australia 2007). Australia has adopted a three-pillar institutional framework, as shown in figure 4.1. Under this framework, responsibility for supervision of the sector is made along functional instead of institutional lines, as was the case prior to the restructuring of the financial system. Overall responsibility for the supervision of the regulatory system rests with the treasurer of the day. A Council of Financial Regulators has been established, which acts as an informal body to coordinate the activities of the financial regulatory bodies. This body ensures a high level of cooperation and collaboration among its members, who include the RBA, which chairs the council, APRA, ASIC and the Australian Treasury. The council is a non-statutory body that has no regulatory functions separate from its members (RBA 2007a).

4-060 Reserve Bank of Australia

The Reserve Bank of Australia (RBA) is responsible mainly for monetary policy with the objective of achieving low and stable inflation over the medium term. Its other major roles are maintaining financial stability and promoting safety and the efficiency of the payment system (RBA 2007b). This body is not a regulator of the general and life insurance industries and is not discussed further.

Figure 4.1 Australia's financial services regulatory framework

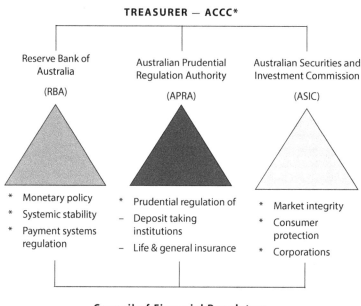

+ACCC = Australian Competition and Consumer Commission

Source: Adapted from Axiss Australia 2007, *Executive Briefing*: Insurance in Australia, p 18.

The two regulators of interest to the financial services sector and the insurance industry, as shown in figure 4.1, are APRA and ASIC, with ASIC being the principal regulator for the advising and consumer protection side of the industry.

4-070   Australian Prudential Regulation Authority

The Australian Prudential Regulation Authority (APRA) was established on 1 July 1998 under the provisions of the *Australian Prudential Regulation Authority Act (1998)* (Cth) as a sole Commonwealth agency concerned with the prudential regulation of the Australian financial services industry. This includes banks, credit unions, building societies, general insurance and reinsurance companies, life insurance, friendly societies and superannuation funds. Currently, it has the prudential supervision of the management of institutions holding approximately A$6.4 trillion (as at August 2018) in assets for Australian depositors, policyholders and superannuation fund members. APRA took over the former prudential regulator roles of the Reserve Bank of Australia and the Insurance and Superannuation Commission.

Prudential regulation is about prudential management so that the institutions are financially sound and can meet their financial obligations to depositors and policyholders when they fall due. APRA is concerned that institutions have sound systems in place to ensure fraudulent transactions are difficult and to identify, measure and manage other risks. It does this by issuing prudential rules and standards and providing advice through letters, circulars and notes on how general and life insurers can meet their responsibilities. Insurers must also submit regular returns to APRA indicating their financial position and solvency and provide the required statistics. Although APRA endeavours to ensure that financial institutions will meet their financial promises, no system of prudential supervision and regulation is infallible (as was demonstrated with the HIH collapse).

APRA seeks to reduce the likelihood of a financial institution failing however, it cannot, and does not, guarantee that failure may never occur. In the unlikely event an APRA-regulated institution were to fail, APRA has the role of administering the Financial Claims Scheme when activated by the Australian Government. This Scheme allows depositors of a failed deposit-taker to access their funds (up to a limit) in a timely manner, or provides general insurance policyholders with access to funds (up to a limit) to meet an eligible claim.

An example of APRA's regulatory powers is provided by the amendment made to the *Insurance Act 1973* requiring that direct offshore unauthorised foreign insurance companies conducting business in Australia either directly or through a broker or agent must be authorised by APRA under the Act, regardless of whether or not the person or company holds an authorisation in an overseas jurisdiction.

APRA administers the following legislation:

- *Insurance Act 1973*
- *Life Insurance Act 1995*
- *Insurance Contracts Act 1984*
- *Australian Prudential Regulation Authority Act 1998*
- *Insurance Acquisitions and Takeovers Act 1991*
- *General Insurance Reform Act 2001*.

4-080   Australian Securities and Investments Commission

The Australian Securities and Investments Commission (ASIC) was established by s 7 of the *Australian Securities and Investments Commission Act 1989* (Cth) (the ASIC Act) first as the *Australian Securities Commission* (ASC) in 1991 and then as ASIC on 1 July 1998. ASIC is an independent Commonwealth Government body, operating under the direction of three full-time Commissioners appointed by the Governor-General after nomination by the Treasurer. ASIC reports to the

Commonwealth Parliament, the Treasurer and the Parliamentary Secretary to the Treasurer.

ASIC enforces and regulates company and financial services laws to protect consumers, investors and creditors. Also, it keeps the public informed regarding these matters through media releases and its annual report. It is responsible for licensing, conduct, product operation, product disclosure and marketing, and dispute resolution. ASIC regulates Australian companies, financial markets, financial services organisations and professionals who deal and advise in investments, insurance, superannuation, credit and deposit taking.

ASIC administers the (retail) consumer protection requirements in relation to financial products, which include:

- securities such as shares, debentures and notes
- futures contracts
- life and general insurance contracts
- superannuation and retirement savings accounts
- depository financial products.

It does not have control over:

- credit products generally and their fees
- prudential regulation
- banking industry structure and delivery issues
- real estate agents and property developers
- finance companies, pastoral houses and mortgage originators.

ASIC administers the following legislation, as well as relevant regulations made under the following Acts:

- *Corporations Act 2001*
- *Australian Securities and Investments Commission Act 2001*
- *Insurance Contracts Act 1984*
- *Superannuation (Resolution of Complaints) Act 1993*
- *Superannuation Industry (Supervision) Act 1993*
- *Retirement Savings Accounts Act 1997*
- *Life Insurance Act 1995*
- *Insurance Act 1973*
- *Medical Indemnity (Prudential Supervision and Product Standards) Act 2003.*

Other regulators also administer some parts of these Acts. For example, parts of the last five Acts dealing with prudential regulation are also administered by APRA.

ASIC is concerned with the maintenance of confidence in the financial system by monitoring and promoting market integrity and consumer protection. It does this by monitoring products, markets, practices, management, complaints, approved industry standards and codes of practice in order to achieve this. The ASIC Act gives it the powers to provide consumer protection by bringing action against corporations who engage in:

- misleading or deceptive conduct (s 12DA)

- false or misleading representations (s 12DB).

Of particular interest to the financial services industry, including life and general insurance, is the requirement under s 12DF for corporations not to engage in conduct that is liable to mislead the public regarding the nature, characteristics, suitability for their purpose or quantity of the financial services. Also, under s 12DM a corporation is prohibited from demanding payment for unsolicited financial services.

ASIC releases regulatory guides about how they will administer the Corporations Act and other legislation for which they are responsible and what it expects of participants in the various sectors of the financial industry. It also releases class orders that apply to a class of persons who carry out a particular activity in certain circumstances, such as distributors of general insurance products referred to above and timeshare scheme operators. Class orders are prefixed by (C) to distinguish them from other instruments such as policy statements (PS) and regulatory guides (RG), which replace previously issued documents including policy statements. The class order relating to general insurance distributors is CO 05/1070, with the numbers being an identifier.

4-090   Australian Competition and Consumer Commission

The Australian Competition and Consumer Commission (ACCC) was formed on 6 November 1995 by the merger of the Trade Practices Commission and the Prices Surveillance Authority. The Commission is an independent Commonwealth statutory authority that administers the C&C Act and fulfils additional responsibilities under other minor legislation.

The Commission's main responsibilities relate to anti-competitive behaviour and unfair market practices, mergers and acquisitions of companies, and product safety/liability. It has the power to take legal action if it discovers anti-competitive conduct. The Commission's consumer protection role complements that of the state and territory consumer affairs agencies that administer equivalent legislation in their separate jurisdictions.

The following release illustrates the kinds of investigations the Commission undertakes in order to prevent mergers that might result in the merged entity's gaining sufficient market share to adversely affect market pricing.

ACCC not to oppose merger between Suncorp Metway and Promina

The ACCC has indicated that it has conducted an investigation on personal insurance lines, particularly CTP and motor vehicle insurances in Queensland and home insurance nationally, as well as on suppliers of services to insurance companies. As a result, it is convinced that if Suncorp were to raise prices on these lines and in commercial lines, there are a large number of other competitors who would act to constrain prices.

The ACCC considers that the merged firm will not substantially lessen competition in any of the markets for various personal insurance lines, commercial insurance lines, or other financial products or services offered by Suncorp and Promina. It also considers that since a number of major banks have substantially increased their insurance distribution operations, they will be well placed to increase their market share in home and motor vehicle insurance if the larger players attempt to increase prices.

Source: ACCC media release 315/06, accc.gov.au.

At a glance

- The financial services sector in Australia is regulated by APRA and ASIC.

- APRA is the prudential regulator of both the life and the general insurance industries.

- ASIC is concerned with market integrity and consumer protection.

- Prudential regulation is about ensuring the insurance institutions are financially sound so they are capable of meeting their obligations to their policyholders.

- The ACCC in Australia is concerned with anti-competitive market practices.

IMPACT OF FSR ACT ON INSURANCE

4-100   Introduction

The *Financial Services Reform Act 2001* (Cth) (FSR Act) integrates the regulatory regimes for the distribution of insurance and other financial products such as investment products. Prior to the FSR Act the distribution of insurance products was regulated by the now-repealed IAB Act, referred to earlier. FSR Act provisions were incorporated under Ch 7, 'Financial Services and Markets', of the Corporations Act, replacing the former provisions in Ch 7 (Securities) and Ch 8 (The Futures Industry).

This section outlines the impact that the FSR Act has had on the insurance industry. All legislative references in this section, unless otherwise stated, are to the Corporations Act, which incorporates the provisions of the FSR Act. Financial products will also be examined as they relate to general insurance, life risk insurance and life investment products.

4-110   Financial products

A financial product in relation to general insurance is defined in s 763A of the Corporations Act as a 'facility' through which, or through the acquisition of which, a person manages financial risk. Section 763C states that a person manages financial risk if they:

"(a) manage the financial consequences to them of particular circumstances happening; or

(b) avoid or limit the financial consequences of fluctuations in or in the value of receipts or costs (including prices and interest rates)."

Examples of actions that constitute managing a financial risk are taking out insurance, or hedging a liability by acquiring a future contract or entering a currency rate swap. An example of what does not constitute managing a financial risk is employing a security firm. While this is a way of managing the risk that thefts will happen, it is not a way of managing the financial consequences if thefts do occur.

The term *facility* refers to a financial product that enables an individual to manage a financial risk, such as through the use of general and life insurance risk policies and life investment insurance policies. The specific provisions concerning the application of the definition and exceptions to general and life insurance are discussed below in the individual sections.

The following types of insurance products are defined in s 761A of the Corporations Act and are included as a financial product in s 764A:

- *general insurance product:* s 764A(1)(d) defines this as an insurance contract that is not a 'life policy' or a 'sinking fund policy' within the meaning of the *Life Insurance Act 1995.*

- *life risk insurance product:* s 764A(1)(e) defines this as an insurance contract that is a 'life policy' or a 'sinking fund policy' within the meaning of the *Life Insurance Act 1995.* This would include products issued by a friendly society.

- *investment life insurance product:* s 764A(1)(f) defines this as a product that is a 'life policy' or a 'sinking fund policy' within the meaning of the *Life Insurance Act 1995* that is not a contract of insurance. It would also include products issued by a friendly society.

Exclusions

The following general insurance and life insurance products will not be financial products as they are expressly excluded by s 765A of the Corporations Act:

- health insurance provided as part of a health insurance business as defined in s 67(4) of the *National Health Act 1953* (Cth) (s 765A(1)(d))

- general insurance and life insurance provided by the Commonwealth (s 765A(1)(c) and (d))

- general insurance and life insurance that is state or Northern Territory insurance, including general insurance entered into by a state or the Northern Territory and some other insurer as joint insurers (s 765A(1)(e))

- general insurance entered into by the Export Finance and Insurance Corporation (s 765A(1)(f))

- reinsurance (s 765A(1)(g))

- general insurance products or a life policy or sinking fund policy that is not a contract of insurance issued by an employer to one of its employees (s 765A(1)(v)).

A funeral benefit policy is not included within the definition of a general insurance product (s 765A(1)(w)). In addition, reg 7.1.07 of the Corporations Regulations 2001 provides that surety bonds are not financial products under s 764A of the Corporations Act. This exclusion is of particular interest to insurance companies because they are major providers of surety bonds in Australia.

4-120 Financial services

The definition of a financial service in the FSRA is important because if a person is providing a financial service, they are taken to be carrying on a 'financial services business', and they will require an Australian financial services licence (AFSL) in order to provide those services.

The two activities in Div 4, 'When does a person provide a financial service', that are most relevant to general and life insurance are:

- providing financial product advice (s 766B of the Corporations Act)
- dealing in a financial product (s 766C of the Corporations Act).

Insurers and insurance intermediaries need to know which of their staff are providing a financial service in order to identify their licensing, disclosure and training requirements. Section 766A(3) of the Corporations Act provides an exemption for 'clerks and cashiers' from the provisions of a financial service if the service is done in their ordinary course of work. This could involve receipting premiums or providing factual information such as when an insurance policy is due or the amount of a policy excess.

Financial product advice is defined in s 766B as a recommendation, statement of opinion or report that is intended to influence, or that could reasonably be regarded as being intended to influence, a person in making a decision in relation to a particular financial product, a class of financial products or an interest in such products. This section specifies two types of financial product advice: *personal advice* and *general advice*.

Personal advice to a retail client must be based on a consideration of one or more of a client's financial situation, objectives and needs (s 766B). An adviser giving personal advice to a retail client is required to determine the client's relevant personal circumstances and to conduct such investigations of the subject matter of the advice as is reasonable in the circumstances. This means that for a domestic insurance policy an adviser will need to establish such matters as the type of cover required (ie, indemnity or replacement value), the amount to be insured and the level of any policy excess. For life insurance, it would involve such activities as completing a needs analysis and valuing future income needs.

On the other hand, general advice may be given to a retail client without meeting the disclosure obligations that apply to personal advice. However, a retail client who receives general advice must be warned that the advice has been given without considering the client's objectives, financial situation or needs, and as such the client should consider the appropriateness of the advice (s 949A).

The provision of financial product advice does not include a statement made in response to an inquirer's question about the cost or likely cost of a financial product and the cost or estimate is worked out or to be calculated by reference to a valuation of an item (eg, a house or car) to which an insurance policy would relate, interpretation of relevant policy provisions, or estimates of loss or damage (s 766B(6)).

Other specific exemptions apply to lawyers, tax agents and others under s 766B when they simply give factual information in the normal course of their activities. Further, it would not be anticipated that handling or settling claims in relation to an insurance product will constitute the provision of financial product advice. An AFSL will not be required where the services provided fall within these exemptions.

4-130   Retail and wholesale clients

The distinction between retail and wholesale clients is important because licensing, disclosure and conduct requirements change considerably depending on which type they are.

In general insurance, s 761G(5) of the Corporations Act states that a person will be a "retail client" if the financial product or a financial service provided to the person relates to, a general insurance product, and if two tests are met:

- the individual or small business test; and

- the product type test

To qualify as a retail client both the person and the product must pass their respective tests. A client who does not qualify as a retail client will be a wholesale client.

The two tests are as follows:

Test 1 – either:

- the person is an *individual*; or

- the insurance product is or would be for the use in connection with a *small business*. A small business is defined in s 761G(12) to mean a business that employs fewer than 20 people. Categories of **small** businesses include: Non-employing businesses (sole proprietorships and partnerships without employees) ... Other **small** businesses (businesses that employ between 5 and 19 employees) or, if it is a manufacturing business, has less than 100, employees.

AND

Test 2 - an individual or small business will be defined as a retail client if they purchase one of the following general insurance products:

- motor vehicle insurance product
- home building insurance product
- home contents insurance product
- sickness and accident insurance product
- consumer credit insurance product
- travel insurance
- personal and domestic property insurance product

Where a financial product or service is provided in relation to a general insurance product that is not on the list, then the person acquires the product as a wholesale client (s 761(4)).

If a package of general insurance products and other kinds of financial products are provided to a client, then the client may be a retail client for the insurance products (e.g. they meet the individual test and product test), and a wholesale client for the others (e.g. they meet the individual test but not the product type test), or vice versa; that is, a distinction needs to be made between the two (s 761(11)).

Life insurance will be provided to a retail client if it is purchased under superannuation (s 761G(6)) and ordinary business (s 761G(7)) *unless* the financial product or financial service is a business that is not a small business, or a person who acquires the product or service provides a copy of a certificate given within the preceding six months by a qualified accountant that states that the person has net assets of at least $2.5 million or has a certified gross income for each of the last two financial years of at least $250,000, or is a professional investor (Reg 6D.2.03 & Reg 7.1.28).

4-140   Licensing issues

An AFSL is generally required where insurers or their agents or advisers carry on a business of providing financial services such as issuing or varying a policy or providing financial product advice in relation to insurance products. This means an insurer will require an AFSL in addition to their authorisation as a general insurer under the *General Insurance Reform Act 2001* or as a life insurer under the *Life Insurance Act 1995*. As discussed above, insurers authorised under these Acts are regulated by APRA, while AFSL licensees are regulated by ASIC.

Not all activities carried out by insurers require them to hold an AFSL, as there are a number of exemptions. These exceptions are separate to the activities that do not constitute 'financial services' generally, such as the services provided by clerks and cashiers and those that do not constitute a particular financial service such as the provision of certain insurance quotes.

Product issuers

Authorised insurers can act as pure 'product providers' without having to obtain an AFSL (s 911A(2)(g) Corporations Act). This exemption allows those insurance companies to 'manufacture' policies and distribute them through licensees. If an insurer operates in this way, it will not be able to market and sell directly to consumers or give financial product advice that is not within the scope of this exemption.

APRA-regulated wholesale

Under s 911A(2)(g) of the Corporations Act authorised insurers are able to provide services covered by their APRA authorisation to wholesale clients and do not need an AFSL for those activities. There are several types of products such as compulsory third party, workers compensation, professional indemnity and directors and officers insurance that will not require an AFSL for services provided under these policies.

4-150   Insurance intermediaries

Insurance intermediaries consist of agents and brokers. Each is discussed in turn.

Agents

Many financial services providers such as banks, credit unions, building societies, strata managers, real estate agents and car dealers sell insurance as agents of the relevant insurance companies. These agents have two choices: either they obtain their own AFSL or they become authorised representatives of one or a number of principal insurers who hold an AFSL. However, if they act for a number of insurers they will need to obtain cross-endorsement by all insurers for which they act. Although cross-endorsement is allowed under s 916Cof the Corporations Act, the reality is that insurers may be reluctant to cross-endorse because of problems associated with vicarious liability. Vicarious liability occurs when one person is liable for the negligent actions of another person, even though the first person was not directly responsible for the injury. For example, an insurance company will be responsible for the negligent acts of its agents. Therefore, if an agent holds proper authorities with insurance companies A and B, A will be equally liable for a negligent act committed by the agent with respect to a product issued by B.

A difficulty arises for banks that are a financial services provider and also hold their own AFSL for those activities. A licensee is prohibited from acting as an authorised representative of another licensee, other than under a binder. Therefore, banks either obtain their own AFSL to cover their insurance activities or form a subsidiary to obtain an AFSL covering insurance-related financial services or for the subsidiary to become an authorised representative of an AFSL holder such as an insurer or an insurance broker. For example, the Commonwealth Bank of Australia, through its subsidiary CommInsure, (at the time of publication) holds its own AFSL and has agencies with Colonial Mutual Life Assurance Ltd (although the life insurance may be sold to AIA Australia) for life insurance and with Allianz for general insurance where it operates under a binder.

Insurance brokers

As discussed above, insurance brokers, both general and life, act as principals and represent the client rather than the insurer, as an agent does. Under s 923B of the Corporations Act general insurance brokers and life insurance brokers are permitted to refer to themselves as brokers under their AFSL, provided they act on behalf of the client and their licence conditions authorise them to do so.

4-160   Disclosure

Anyone involved in the provision of a financial product or service to retail clients must abide by the disclosure provisions in the FSR Act, Pt 7.7. Disclosure is generally divided into three distinct stages:

- Financial Services Guide
- Statement of Advice
- Product Disclosure Statement.

Financial Services Guide

Financial services providers such as agents and insurance brokers must provide a Financial Services Guide (FSG) to retail clients before they provide the financial service. An FSG contains the basic information to enable any retail client to determine the terms under which the financial service will be provided and so decide whether or not to acquire the services. In a limited number of circumstances described in s 941C of the Corporations Act, an FSG does not have to be provided as it applies to insurance:

1. the client already has an FSG

2. the provider is a product issuer such as an insurance company dealing in its own product

3. the financial service is in the form of general advice provided in a public forum.

A public forum is defined as:

1. an event open to the public attended by more than 10 retail clients or an event where the number of retail clients could not be ascertained beforehand

2. a broadcast if any person may hear the broadcast

3. a flyer or other promotional material accessible to the public.

Section 942B of the Corporations Act provides that an FSG must contain the following information:

- the title 'Financial Services Guide' on the cover, or at or near the front, of the document (s942A)

- the date of the FSG (s942B(5) and 942C(5))

- the name and contact details of the providing entity (ss 942B(2)(a) and 942C(2)(a)) and, if the providing entity is an AFS licensee, its AFS licence number (s912F and reg 7.6.01C(1)(a))

- a statement of the purpose of the FSG and, if appropriate, information about other disclosure documents that the client may receive (i.e. an SOA or PDS), together with a description of the purpose of those documents (regs 7.7.03 and 7.7.06)

- details about the kinds of financial services that the provider is licensed to provide (ss 942B(2)(c) and 942C(2)(d)) or, will be or is likely to be providing to the client (regs 7.7.10AB and 7.7.10AC)

- details of anyone for whom the providing entity acts when providing the financial service

- details about how the provider is remunerated, including any commissions and other benefits that the providing entity (and other persons specified in ss 942B(2)(e) or 942C(2)(f)) will receive, or reasonably expects to receive, in respect of, or that is attributable to, the advice to be provided where this amount can be ascertained at the time the FSG is provided to the client (ss 942B(2)(e) and 942C(2)(f), and regs 7.7.04(3) and 7.7.07(3))

- where the providing entity reasonably believes that personal advice will be or is likely to be provided and the amount of the remuneration, commission or other benefits cannot be ascertained at the time the FSG is provided— either particulars or general information about the benefit (including ranges or rates of amounts) and a statement that the method of calculating the amount of the benefit will be disclosed at the time the advice is provided or as soon as practicable after that time (regs 7.7.04(4)(c), 7.7.04(4)(d), 7.7.07(4)(c) and 7.7.07(4)(d))

- where the providing entity reasonably believes that personal advice will not be provided and the amount of the remuneration, commission or other benefits cannot be ascertained at the time the FSG is provided— particulars of the remuneration, commission and other benefits (including ranges or rates of amounts) or general information about the remuneration, commission and other benefits with a statement that the client can request further particulars (regs 7.7.04(5)(c), 7.7.04(5)(d), 7.7.07(5)(c) and 7.7.07(5)(d))

- any associations that an adviser has with a product issuer that might reasonably be expected to affect the advice being provided (conflicts of interest) (ss 942B(2)(f) and 942C(2)(g))

- where the providing entity provides further advice or advice to which s 946B(7) applies—certain information about obtaining a record of the advice (ss 942B(2)(g) and 942C(2)(h), and regs 7.7.05, 7.7.08, 7.7.09 and 7.7.10AC– 7.7.10AE)

- where the providing entity (or authorising AFS licensee) is a participant in a licensed market or clearing and settlement facility—a statement to that effect (ss 942B(2)(j) and 942C(2)(k))

- where the providing entity is acting under a binder—certain information about the binder and its significance (ss 942B(2)(i) and 942C(2)(j))

- details of any internal and external dispute resolution procedures and how the client may access them (ss 942B(2)(h) and 942C(2)(i)).

- details about the kind of compensation arrangements the providing entity (or authorising AFS licensee) has in place (i.e. whether through professional indemnity insurance or otherwise) and whether these arrangements comply with s 912B:

Where the adviser is an insurance broker acting under a binder (see above) from an insurance company that authorises them to settle transactions on behalf of the insurer, the FSG must identify and explain the services provided under the binder.

The costs of providing the service are an important aspect of disclosure in the FSG and are covered in reg 7.7.02 of the Corporations Regulations. The purpose of disclosure of remuneration is to inform the client about how they will be paying for the financial service in general terms. This must consist of a written description of how the service provider is to be remunerated, including details of any upfront fee or hourly rate that will be charged. Further, details of any commissions that are anticipated to be payable and how they will be paid, including any non-financial benefits such as bonuses, must be stated.

The FSG is required to be provided to a retail client:

- after it becomes apparent that the financial services will be or is likely to be given, in which case the client is required to be provided with the FSG as soon as practicable and in any event before the service is provided s 941A, 941B and (s 941D(1)),

- however, in some cases an FSG may be given after a financial service has been provided (see RG 175.100–RG 175.103), and in other cases an FSG does not need to be given at all (see RG 175.104–RG 175.107)

The FSG must be given to a retail client personally or mailed, faxed or emailed.

Statement of Advice

A Statement of Advice (SoA) is required whenever personal advice is given to a retail client either as a means by which the advice is provided or as a record of the advice. The SoA must contain: the advice; the basis on which the advice is given; information about fees or commissions or both, or associations that influence the advice. Further, a warning must be given if the advice is based on incomplete information (s 947B). If the SoA is a separate record of the advice, the SoA must be provided as soon as practicable after the advice is given and before any further financial service is carried out in relation to the previous advice. The client must be given information about costs, commissions and associations at the time the advice is provided.

Soft dollar benefits

Section 35 of the IAB Act (now repealed) prohibited brokers from receiving gifts, gratuities or benefits other than as remuneration for services rendered in arranging contracts of insurance, dealing with or settling claims or other associated activities. Remuneration of this type is referred to as 'soft dollar' commission. While there is no restriction in Ch 7 of the Corporations Act on brokers from receiving these types of benefits, an insurance broker will be subject to the disclosure regime and must disclose these benefits to retail clients.

The level of information that is required to be contained in a SoA, like the FSG, should allow the client to be able to reasonably decide on whether to acquire a financial service from that entity as a retail client.

If the advice recommends that one product be replaced with another product, then additional information must be provided. The SoA must identify any charges that will be incurred by the client; any financial consequences to the client; or, if they are not known, a warning that they might arise (s 947D of the Corporations Act). Financial consequences may relate to where an income protection is being replaced by another income protection policy, as the client may incur a premium loading or policy exclusion that did not apply to the original policy if the health of the client has changed.

A failure to comply with the Corporations Act in terms of the provision and the content of the FSG and SoA exposes the financial service provider to criminal and civil penalties.

A SoA is not needed if there is an existing SoA that does not need updating or in relation to:

- a motor vehicle insurance product (reg 7.7.10)
- a home building insurance product (reg 7.7.10)
- a home contents insurance product (reg 7.7.10)
- a personal and domestic property insurance product (reg 7.7.10)
- a medical indemnity insurance product (reg 7.7.10)

If the client requires the financial advice urgently and there is no time to give the SoA beforehand, then the SoA must be given within five days of providing the service or sooner if practicable, or if a product is acquired before the end of the cooling-off period s 946C(3).

Key Facts Statement

Under section 33C of the IC Act insurers must provide consumers with a key facts statement when effecting policies for home buildings insurance and home contents insurance.

A Key Fact Sheet (KFS) is a one page document which summaries key information about a Home Building and Home Contents (combined and individual) (HBHC) insurance policy. It allows consumers to quickly and easily check the basic terms of the insurance policy, including the nature of cover and key exclusions. The KFS also helps consumers to compare the features of various insurance policies and select appropriate insurance products for their needs.

A KFS must be provided by the insurer when the consumer seeks information about a HBHC insurance product and when a consumer enters into a contract. It need not be provided where the customer is represented by an insurance broker.

Product Disclosure Statement

Under s 1012A of the Corporations Act, a Product Disclosure Statement (PDS) is required to be given to retail clients when personal advice is given to the client about acquiring a financial product. The PDS is to contain all the information necessary for a retail client to understand the product they are buying.

There are several types of person who are required to give a PDS, including:

- the issuer of the financial product
- any financial services licensee or their authorised representative
- a person who should, but does not, hold an AFSL.

In relation to general insurance, a PDS is not required to be provided when an interim contract of insurance is provided, but a PDS must be provided when a contract of insurance replaces the interim contract (s 1012D).

A PDS is to include the following information under s 1013D:

- name and contact details of the insurer
- information about the benefits the insured will or may become entitled to and when and how the benefits will be provided
- the cost of the policy
- any significant characteristics or features of the policy

- availability of dispute resolution services and how to access them
- information about the cooling-off period
- information about any significant risks associated with holding the product
- information that might have an influence on the decision of the retail client as to whether or not to acquire the product.

Further, the PDS must be dated (s 1013G).

Failure to comply with the Corporations Act in terms of the provision and content of the PDS exposes the financial services provider to criminal or civil penalties.

4-170 Staff training

The *Corporations Amendment (Professional Standards of Financial Advisers) Act 2017* commenced on 15 March 2017. It introduced several measures in the Corporations Act 2001 (Corporations Act) to raise the education, training and ethical standards of financial advisers providing personal advice to retail clients on more complex financial products.

The reforms apply to 'relevant providers'. A relevant provider is an individual who is:

- an Australian financial services (AFS) licensee, an authorised representative, employee or director of an AFS licensee, or an employee or director of a related body corporate of an AFS licensee, and
- authorised to provide personal advice to retail clients, as the AFS licensee or on behalf of the AFS licensee, in relation to relevant financial products.

'Relevant financial products' means financial products other than:

- basic banking products
- general insurance products
- consumer credit insurance
- a combination of any of those products.

The definition of 'relevant financial products' is broadly similar to the concept of Tier 1 financial products in Regulatory Guide 146 *Licensing: Training of financial product advisers* (RG 146), but the concepts differ slightly. Personal sickness and accident insurance products are not 'relevant financial products' (however, they are Tier 1 products).

The reforms do not apply to advisers who are not relevant providers. This means, for example, they do not affect advisers who only provide general advice or who only provide personal advice on products that are not relevant financial products, such as general insurance.

Obligations for relevant providers

Under the new requirements, all relevant providers must:

- have a relevant bachelor or higher degree, or equivalent qualification

- pass an exam

- meet continuing professional development (CPD) requirements each year (40 hours per year)

- complete a year of work and training (professional year) – although this will not apply for individuals who are already relevant providers before 1 January 2019

- comply with a code of ethics and be covered by a compliance scheme that monitors and enforces compliance with the code of ethics.

From 1 January 2019, only relevant providers who meet these standards can call themselves a 'financial adviser' or 'financial planner' or similar terms.

Application of RG 146

RG 146 will continue to apply to existing providers until the new requirements apply. Existing providers must pass the exam by 1 January 2021 (extended to 1 January 2022 – subject to legislation) and attain the required educational qualifications by 1 January 2024 (extended to 1 January 2026 – subject to legislation), otherwise they will no longer be able to provide personal advice to retail clients on relevant financial products.

For new entrants to the industry seeking to become a relevant provider from 1 January 2019 onwards, RG 146 will not apply and will need to hold an appropriate degree approved by the Financial Planning and Ethics Authority at Australian Quality Framework (AQF7) level Undergraduate Bachelor or higher degree, or equivalent qualification, complete a structured professional year, pass an exam, comply with Continuing Professional Development (CPD) requirements. Additionally, by 1 January 2020, comply with the Code of Ethics and be covered by a compliance scheme.

ASIC will be updating their guidance on training for financial advisers who are not relevant providers (e.g. advisers who provide general advice or who provide advice about products other than relevant financial products). RG 146 will be reviewed and updated as part of this process.

The Financial Adviser Standards and Ethics Authority

An independent standards body, the Financial Adviser Standards and Ethics Authority (FASEA), will:

- approve the relevant bachelor or higher degrees and equivalent qualifications that will satisfy the new requirement to have a relevant bachelor or higher degree, or equivalent qualification
- approve the exam that every relevant provider must pass
- set the CPD requirements
- develop the code of ethics that all relevant providers must comply with
- set the requirements for the year of work and training for new relevant providers (professional year)
- specify the words or expressions that can be used to refer to a 'provisional relevant provider' (i.e. those completing their professional year).

Compliance schemes for the code of ethics

Monitoring bodies will operate compliance schemes to monitor and enforce relevant providers' compliance with the code of ethics. Monitoring bodies may be professional associations but are not required to be. An AFS licensee, or an associate of an AFS licensee, cannot be a monitoring body.

A monitoring body for a compliance scheme applies to ASIC for approval of the compliance scheme. ASIC will only approve a compliance scheme if it is satisfied that:

- compliance with the code of ethics will be appropriately monitored and enforced, and
- the monitoring body has sufficient resources or expertise to carry out that monitoring and enforcement.

4-180   Confirming transactions

Retail insurance products are subject to the confirmation of transaction requirements under s 1017F of the Corporations Act. This effectively means that agents and brokers are required to issue a receipt where the premium is not paid by cheque payable to the insurer. Its purpose is to ensure that clients receive confirmation that payment has been made.

4-190   Cooling-off period

A 14-day cooling-off period applies to all risk insurance products, both general and life, as well as to investment life insurance products (s 1019A of the Corporations Act). However, there are some exceptions under s 1019B relating to a risk insurance product of less than 12 months' duration and a renewal of an existing product on the same terms and conditions as the product was issued in the preceding period. This section also applies to an interim contract of insurance within the meaning of s 11(2) of the IC Act.

A retail client has the right to return the product to the person who issued it within 14 days, which starts on the earlier of confirmation of cover or the end of the fifth day after the issue of the policy, and to demand a refund of the premium (s 1019B(3) and (4) of the Corporations Act). However, the client loses the ability to claim a refund if a claim is made on the policy within the 14-day period. Also, the client cannot claim a refund after the period of cover expires, such as when the cover was only for one week (s 1019B(5)).

4-200   Responsibilities of advisers

From 1 July 2012, the Australian Government's Future of Financial Advice (FOFA) legislation commenced with mandatory compliance from 1 July 2013. One of the core changes is the obligation to act in the client's best interests. The best interests duty requires financial advisers to place the interests of their clients ahead of their own in providing personal advice to retail clients. It is designed to build trust and confidence in the financial advice industry through an enhanced standard which aligns the interests of the adviser with their client, thereby reducing conflicts of interest.

On 13 December 2012 the Australian Securities and Investments Commission (ASIC) released long-awaited final guidance on the best interests duty in an update to Regulatory Guide 175 Licensing: Financial product advisers- conduct and disclosure (RG 175). The best interests duty and related obligations are contained in Division 2 of Part 7.7A of the Corporations Act 2001 (Cth), and require advice providers when providing personal advice to retail clients to:

- act in the best interests of their clients (section 961B)
- provide appropriate advice (section 961G)
- warn the client if advice is based on incomplete or inaccurate information (section 961H), and

- prioritise the client's interests (section 961J).

The best interests duty and related obligations generally apply to the "individual providing the personal advice" (RG 175.204) that is, the Australian Financial Services (AFS) licensee or authorised representative. However, the best interests duty does not apply to general advice (RG175.208). ASIC expects that advice providers themselves to have processes in place to ensure that they act in the best interests of their clients (RG 175.236).

But what does this mean?

These obligations meld the mechanics and motivation of providing advice and prescribe how an adviser should approach them. These obligations include:

- When providing the advice, the adviser must act in the client's best interests.
- There is a "safe harbour" – that is, a set of requirements that, once met, mean that the adviser has met their duty to act in the client's best interests. This introduces some mechanics to help prove the nobility of the adviser's motivation.
- The adviser's advice must be appropriate.
- The adviser must prioritise the client's interests if there is a conflict between those and the interests of the adviser or parties related to the adviser (such as the adviser's employer or the adviser's licensee).
- Conflicts cannot be managed simply by disclosing them. Nor can the adviser contract out of these obligations.
- Finally, all responsibility stops with the actual adviser with potential administrative action by ASIC (e.g. banning) or civil penalties.

What are the interests of the client

A client will potentially have a wide range of interests. The legislation acknowledges this by expressly referring to interests in plural. However, do all a client's interest then need to be identified? Most clients have an interest in improving their financial position or having a financially secure retirement but they may also have any number of other interests such as:

- access to particular product features
- providing for their relatives and dependents
- increasing their financial education and confidence levels
- managing risks and returns

- improving or maintaining their health
- involvement in sport, cultural activities and hobbies, and
- the advancement of particular causes

The potential range of interests is, therefore, huge and largely personal to the particular client. The courts have recognised this difficulty and have, in relation to a financial services context, narrowed down the range of interests that need to be considered. For example, in the case of Cowan v Scargill Sir Robert Megarry V-C (in relation to a superannuation fund) stated:

"When the purpose of the trust is to provide financial benefits for the beneficiaries…the best interests of the beneficiaries are normally their best financial interests."

Such a conclusion would appear to be equally applicable to a financial adviser so that the courts will normally confine their analysis to whether the provider has acted in the best financial interests of a client.

How to comply with the best interests duty

The term "best interests" is not defined in the Corporations Act or RG175. However, an adviser will comply with the best interests duty if they comply with the "safe harbour" provisions set out in the Corporations Act, which requires and adviser to:

a. identify the objectives, financial situation and needs of the client that were identified through instructions

b. identify the subject matter of the advice sought by the client (whether explicitly or implicitly)

c. identify the objectives, financial situation and needs of the client that would reasonably be considered relevant to the advice sought on that subject matter

d. if it is reasonably apparent that information relating to the client's relevant circumstances is incomplete or inaccurate, make reasonable enquiries to obtain complete and accurate information

e. assess whether you have the expertise to provide the advice sought and, if not, decline to give the advice

f. if it would be reasonable to consider recommending a financial product, conduct a reasonable investigation into the financial products that might achieve the objectives and meet the needs of the client that would reasonably be considered relevant to advice on the subject matter and assess the information gathered in the investigation

g. base all judgments on the client's relevant circumstances, and

h. take any other step that, at the time the advice is provided, would reasonably be regarded as being in the best interests of the client, given the client's relevant circumstances.

AFS licensees commonly require advisers (including authorised representatives) to provide advice only in relation to products on the Approved Product Lists (APL). The products which appear on the APL may be more profitable to the licensee and the adviser than alternative products and may not necessarily be the most appropriate product for the client.

The best interests duty requires a financial adviser to conduct a reasonable investigation into "classes of financial product and specific financial products commonly available" (RG175.263), ie, relevant financial products (including those not necessarily included on their licensee's APL) and base their advice on the client's relevant circumstances rather than the benefit that the adviser or the licensee will receive from the recommendation to invest in an "approved" product. However, the requirement to conduct a reasonable investigation advice is "scalable" (RG175.308). This means that less extensive enquiries are likely to be necessary when the advice is for a relatively simple purpose, such as when arranging motor vehicle insurance.

Advising on a product outside of the APL could arise where the client's existing products are not on the approved product list of the advice provider's licensee and these products might be able to meet the client's relevant circumstances (RG175.326(a). However, if the financial adviser is unable to provide advice on products that outside their licensee's APL then the financial adviser must not provide the advice (RG175. 329).

The best interests duty does not require that the advice is "perfect". The Australian Securities and Investments Commission (ASIC) has indicated that in assessing whether a financial adviser has complied with the best interests duty, they will consider whether a *reasonable* financial adviser would *believe* that the client is *likely* to be in a better position if the client follows the advice. The focus of ASIC will be on how the adviser acted in providing the advice rather than the outcome of the advice.

Financial advisers must ensure they can *demonstrate* that they have taken the necessary steps to comply with the best interests duty. This is particularly the case where:

- a client brings a formal complaint against the adviser at an external dispute resolution scheme, such as the Australian Financial Complaints Authority (AFCA), and

- the AFCA is required to determine the complaint on the documents held in the adviser's file

A failure to comply with the best interests duty may result in:

- a formal complaint being made to an external dispute resolution scheme, such as AFCA against the adviser's licensee

- a claim for compensation being brought against the adviser and/or their licensee

- a civil penalty being issued against the adviser and/or their licensee, or

- an administrative sanction being made, such as a ban from providing financial services for a period of time.

The FOFA reforms contain exemptions in relation to those advising about general insurance. For instance, general insurance brokers who are providing advice solely in relation to general insurance will satisfy their best interests duty if the broker takes the steps a) – (c) in the safe harbour provisions listed above.

Putting the best interests duty into practice

Consider whether the adviser in the following situation has complied with their best interests duty in the following illustrated example.

Illustrated example 4.1

Michael McCarthy comes to his adviser wanting to review his term life insurance. He has an existing death benefit of $500,000 and needs $800,000. His adviser's recommendation is to take out a new policy for $800,000, with terms that are otherwise very similar to the existing one. The adviser receives a commission on the $800,000 policy rather than commission on a $200,000 increase.

Question

1. Has the adviser acted in the client's best interests?

2. What possible issues could arise when a policy is replaced? (See discussion below)

Switching advice

When providing switching advice the financial advice must consider the benefits and disadvantages, including the costs and risks, of both the existing and new products (RG175.351). ASIC considers that the advice will generally only be appropriate if it would be reasonable to conclude that the net benefits that are likely to result from the product (or investment option) to be acquired, or into which further investment is to be made, are better than under the existing product (or investment option) which is to be disposed of or reduced (RG175.353).

This requirement to act in the client's best interests is illustrated in the case Commonwealth Financial Planning Ltd v Couper discussed in 5-050. In brief, Mr Stevens was advised to replace a long standing Westpac policy with a similar policy issued by CommInsure, an Insurer with whom the adviser was associated. The recommendation was accepted, the new policy issued and the old policy cancelled. A short time later Mr Stevens contracted pancreatic cancer and subsequently died. However, when the client was subsequently diagnosed with pancreatic cancer the Insurer voided the contract from inception on the basis of non-disclosure. It was revealed during the trial that Mr Couper was unaware of the three year rule. Although this case took place before FOFA, there is an important lesson to be learned.

Warnings

The purpose of the disclosures in the SoA is to assist clients to make an informed decision about the advice provided to them. Mr Couper failed to warn his client that commencing a new risk policy affords the new Insurer an opportunity to avoid the contract in the event of a claim. The right is not absolute, but, in this case, neither the adviser nor the client was aware of this risk.

The age of Mr Steven's policy meant that Westpac would have had no right to avoid the contract for non-disclosure in the event of a claim. However, by commencing a new policy with another insurer, Mr Stevens lost this significant benefit. Accordingly, the Court found that the adviser had negligently failed to comply with his "duty to ensure the plaintiff was adequately informed of the consequences of potential material non-disclosure of health and related matters, which an underwriter ... would regard as being material to the risk" (*Commonwealth Financial Planning Limited v Couper* [2013] NSWCA 444.

4-210   Advisers' due diligence

The above regulatory provisions impose considerable obligations on financial advisers. These regulatory obligations highlight the need for financial advisers to have a systematic due diligence (or, audit) process in place to check all documents and the advice before closing the client's file.

From a legal perspective, due diligence is defined as a:

> "*measure* of *prudence, responsibility, and diligence* that is expected from, and ordinarily exercised by, a *reasonable* and prudent *person* under the circumstances" (Business Dictionary, n.d.).

Therefore, in terms of reviewing financial advice, due diligence is the process of systematically verifying the accuracy of the information provided by the client/s, ensuring that the requirements of the C Act have been complied with and that full disclosure has been made by the adviser.

The types of matters that must be checked are outlined in the *Corporations Act 2001* (Cth) (C Act) and includes such obligations as: to provide a Financial Services Guide (FSG) (ss 941A and 941B) and met the FSG timing requirements (s 941D), additional requirements when the advice recommends replacement of one product with another (s 947D), to act in the client's best interests when providing financial advice to retail clients (s 961B), that the advice is appropriate (s 961G), to avoid conflicts of interest (s 961J), disclose any remuneration, commission and other benefits received (ss942B(2)(e) or 9423(B)(2)(f), to avoid conflicted remuneration that could reasonably be expected to influence the choice of the product recommended (ss 963E,963G,963H), warn clients if the advice is based on incomplete or inaccurate information (s 961H), warn a client about general advice (s949A), give an SoA (s 946A), meet the SoA timing requirement (s 946C) and keep client records for seven years (s 912(G)(4).

Failing to comply with these regulatory obligations can have severe legal repercussions for financial advisers. Recent legal actions brought against financial advisers provide guidance on the procedures that need to be followed by professional financial advisers. The Commonwealth Financial Planning Ltd v Couper case discussed in 5-050 illustrates the importance of ensuring advisers carryout appropriate due diligence both during and after the conclusion of the advice. This Couper case brought to light the following deficiencies in the advice process:

Dollar for dollar comparisons insufficient

In cases where an existing life insurance policy is switched on the basis that the proposed new policy is cheaper, have investigations been made to ensure that the new policy is cheaper on a like for like, dollar for dollar basis?

Policy comparisons

An adviser is expected to compare more than one alternative policy and have sound documented reasons as to why one policy is superior to another. The expectation of the Court was that at least three different policies would have been compared. This examination would rely on more than a comparison of price, but would include a comparison of policy terms and conditions, exclusions, stepped verses level premiums and special needs of the client.

Challenges for tied financial advisers.

Has a policy been recommended to cancel an existing policy that does not appear on the licensee's approved product list? If so has the licensee's permission been sought to advise on that policy? Would a better strategy be to recommend that the client consult another financial adviser who can advise on that policy?

Stepped verses level premiums.

The SoA on the Couper case recommended stepped premiums without clearly articulating the case for level premiums. This omission highlights the need for financial advisers to check that this comparison has been made at least to the date of cessation of cover. It is also necessary for financial advisers to check that they have fully explained the accumulated premium comparison over time.

The client's duty of disclosure.

Has the financial adviser fully explained the requirements of the client's duty to disclose all material facts? Has the financial adviser fully explained the ramifications of not fully disclosing all material facts? Has the financial adviser disclosed to the client the effect of any restrictive clauses, such as the re-freshening of the three-year non-disclosure period if a policy that has been in force for longer than three years is being abandoned as required by section 947D of the C Act?

A comprehensive SoA may be insufficient.

A wordy SoA full of caveats and disclaimers is insufficient in itself as a risk management tool. The risks need to be outlined in full to the client verbally and the financial adviser needs to ensure that the client fully understands the impact of the underlying risks. Therefore, a financial adviser must ensure that a comprehensive and comprehensible explanation of the risks is given and that these events are documented in a detailed and professionally prepared file note.

Providing financial advice to financially unsophisticated clients.

In these cases extra care needs to be exercised to ensure that there are no gaps in the client's knowledge. In the Couper case, the client was a construction site worker with below average reading and writing skills. The client's evidence was that the documents were passed over to him for signature without explanation. Therefore, has the financial adviser checked that they ensured that the client fully understands what they are signing?

Template dangers.

The SoA template used in the Couper case did not provide for the impact of the freshening of the three-year non-disclosure period, even though it envisaged a switch of policies. Therefore, the financial adviser must ensure that the SoA is relevant to the client's facts and circumstances before asking for the client's signature.

The Australian Securities and Investments Commission (ASIC) recently banned a financial adviser for five years for adopting a template approach to financial advice. ASIC found that the adviser failed to take into account his client's individual circumstances as he used a template for all clients.

The 'insurance needs calculation template' recommended his clients apply for levels of insurance which were higher than their needs. ASIC further stated that many cases were 'at complete odds' with clients' objectives and needs. The adviser also switched superannuation accounts from one provider to another without investigating their existing arrangements or demonstrating why the switch would be in their best interests. Finally, the adviser failed to provide advice on other areas requested by his clients such as debt reduction, instead focused solely on insurance and superannuation.

These cases illustrate that all clients are unique as they have their own objectives and needs that must be addressed in the advice process. It is clear that taking a template approach to providing advice will not sit well with the supervising authorities and the Courts.

The recent *Ravesi v National Australia Bank Ltd* [2014] FCA 99 (discussed below) should alert financial advisers to their further obligations when providing financial advice.

Post SoA follow up.

Financial advisers must follow up variances between the recommendations in the SoA and the insurance ultimately put in place. In the Ravesi case the bank's financial adviser, Mr Moore failed to implement the term life and TPD cover detailed in the SoA. The authority to proceed failed to contain the life and TPD cover specified although the other policies were put in place. Three years later, Mr Ravesi subsequently suffered an accident and the claim proceeds fell below expectations.

An action was brought against the adviser for failing to ensure that the cover articulated in the SoA was duly effected, or alternatively that the client was not alerted to the ramifications of effecting cover at the lower levels contained in the authority to proceed. Although Mr Moore claimed that his client, Mr Ravesi had decided not to continue with this cover there was no evidence to explain the reason for the differences between the cover originally advised and the cover eventually taken. The court held that the financial adviser was negligent for failure to address the consequences of the discrepancy between the cover in the SoA and the cover taken.

Key take outs from this case include.

Question client's actions. The Judge found that it was reasonable to expect that a financial adviser acting in the same situation as Mr Ravesi would have questioned why Mr Moore decided to reduce his cover. Simply accepting that it was 'the client's decision' was not, in the Judge's mind an appropriate course of action for a financial planner to take.

As noted in this case, financial advice clients look to their financial planner as an 'expert' in their field. Therefore, financial planners should be cautious when dealing with clients who request a departure from the original advice recommendation and be sure to document the reasons behind the client's decision.

Keep detailed documentation. Much of the evidence relied upon in this case was the documentation prepared by Mr Moore during the advice process. In nearly all cases, this documentation was incomplete, or unclear. In passing judgement, Judge Mansfield said there was no evidence to suggest the client had instructed the financial planner to remove an element of the cover originally recommended. Had the financial planner clearly documented this instruction, the client is unlikely to have been successful in their claim.

Importance of reviews. No annual review appointments appear to have occurred between Mr Moore and Mr Ravesi. The pro forma document completed at the start of the advice process included a section indicating the client's acknowledgement that the adviser had explained the need to review the insurance plan and for that review to occur either annually, at another regular period, or as notified to the adviser. None of these alternatives were marked as selected on the document. Had a meeting occurred in the intervening three year period, the gap in his cover is likely to have been identified prior to Mr Ravesi's accident.

The above due diligence actions and landmark cases cited indicate that the community and regulators require the financial planning industry to move to a higher level of professionalism.

At a glance

- The *Corporations Act 2001* regulates financial products including general and life insurance risk policies and investment insurance policies.

- The Corporations Act makes a distinction between retail and wholesale clients.

- Product providers do not require an AFSL when dealing with their own products. but they are restricted to giving factual information to their customers.

- Insurance intermediaries, such as agents and brokers must hold their own AFSL or be an authorised representative of an AFSL holder.

- The disclosure provision of the Corporations Act requires that a FSG, SoA and PDS be given to retail clients when providing financial product advice.

- Advisers must complete an approved training course appropriate to the level of advice they are authorised to provide (ie, Tier 1 or Tier 2).

- The FOFA reforms imposes a best interest duty on a financial adviser, which requires financial advisers to place the interests of their clients ahead of their own when providing personal advice to retail clients.

- The C Act imposes many obligations on financial planners so they need to have a comprehensive due diligence process to ensure these regulatory obligations have been complied with.

4-220　Study questions

4.1　Explain the importance of regulatory reform in Australia.

4.2　What are the differences between agents and brokers, and to whom do they owe their duty of care?

4.3　Explain the insurance brokers' obligations in Australia with respect to an insured's premiums.

4.4　Explain the regulatory control of intermediaries in Australia

4.5　Briefly explain the Australian Consumer Law (ACL) as it applies to insurance.

4.6　Explain the consumer protection laws as they apply to insurance in Australia

4.7　Explain the process for a person wishing to become a financial adviser in Australia.

4.8　What is the principle of utmost good faith and why is it important in insurance?

4.9　Explain the roles of APRA and ASIC in relation to insurance.

4.10　Explain the impact of the FSR Act on the insurance industry.

4-230　References and further reading

References

Business Directory (n.d.). http://www.businessdictionary.com/definition/due-diligence.html

Articles and Books

Axiss Australia 2007, *Executive Briefing: Insurance in Australia* p 18. Available at *www.axiss.com.au*

Macquarie Library Pty Ltd (1988) *The Macquarie Concise Dictionary*, 2nd edn, Sydney.

Reports

Australian Law Reform Commission (ALRC). *Report 20 — Insurance Contracts 1982*, AGPS, Canberra. Available at *www.austlii.edu.au*

Bailey, B 2003, *Report of the Royal Commission into HIH Insurance*, Research Note No 32 2002–03, 13 May, Department of the Parliamentary Library, Available at *www.aph.gov.au*

Campbell, K 1981, *Australian Financial System Enquiry — Final Report, Australian*

Corporate Law Economic Reform Program 1999, CLERP — Financial Products, Service Providers and Markets, Australian Government Treasury, Available at *www.treasury.gov.au*

Wallis Inquiry Report 1997. Available at *www.fsi.treasury.gov.au*

Releases

Australian Competition and Consumer Commission (ACCC) 2006, *ACCC not to oppose merger between Suncorp Metway and Promina*, Media release 315/06, Available at *www.accc.gov.au*

Australian Securities and Investments Commission (ASIC) Prudential Standard 124 *Investment advisory services: mixed advice on securities and life insurance products.* Available at *www.asic.gov.au*

Australian Securities and Investments Commission (ASIC) Regulatory Guide 146: *Training of financial product advisers*. Available at *www.asic.gov.au*

Australian Securities and Investments Commission (ASIC) Regulatory Guide 147: *Licensing: Discretionary Guide, p17*. Available at www.asic.gov.au

Australian Securities and Investments Commission (ASIC) Regulatory Guide 175: *Financial Product Advisers – Conduct and Disclosure.* Available at www.asic.gov.au

Australian Securities and Investments Commission (ASIC) 2005, Class Order 05/1070, *General insurance distributors*, ASIC. Available at www.asic.gov.au

Insurance Council of Australia (ICA), *General Insurance Code of Practice*. Available at *www.insurancecouncil.com.au*

Reserve Bank of Australia (RBA) 2007a, Council of Financial Regulators. Available at *www.rba.gov.au*

Reserve Bank of Australia (RBA) 2007b, Overview of functions and operations. Available at *www.rba.gov.au*

Legislation

Australian Prudential Regulation Authority Act 1998 (Cth)

Australian Securities and Investments Commission Act 2001 (Cth)

Corporations Act 2001 (Cth)

Corporations Amendment (Professional Standards of Financial Advisers) Bill 2015 (Cth)

Financial Services Reform Act 2001 (Cth)

Financial Services Providers (Registration and Dispute Resolutions) Act 2008 (NZ)

Insurance (Agents and Brokers) Act 1984 (Cth) (repealed)

Insurance Contracts Act 1984 (Cth)

Cases

Cowan v Scargill (1985) Ch. 270 at page 295

Further reading

International Monetary Fund (IMF) 2007, Financial Sector Assessment Program (FSAP). Available at *www.imf.org*

Websites

Australian Competition & Consumer Commission (ACCC): *www.accc.gov.au*

Australian Prudential Regulation Authority (APRA): *www.apra.gov.au*

Australian Securities and Investments Commission (ASIC): *www.asic.gov.au*

Australian Insurance Law Association (AILA): *www.aila.com.au*

Government Printing Service, Canberra: *http://fsi.treasury.gov.au*

Regulatory Guide (RG)175 Licensing: Financial product advisers- conduct and disclosure: *http://download.asic.gov.au/media/1240967/rg175-published-3-october-2013.pdf*

CHAPTER 5

CONCEPTS UNDERLYING INSURANCE LAW

5-000 *Insurance Contracts Act 1984*

The *Insurance Contracts Act 1984* (IC ACT) was not intended to codify the law, so state, territory and Commonwealth Acts, and the common law and equity, continue to apply to insurance unless expressly or by implication excluded by the IC ACT (s 7).

The legislation does not apply to the following insurance (s 9):

- reinsurance

- medical and hospital insurance written under the *National Health Act 1953* (Cth)

- insurance written by a friendly society or the Export Finance and Insurance Corporation

- marine insurance

- workers compensation insurance

- compulsory third party motor vehicle insurance

- state and Northern Territory insurance.

Any provision that may be inserted into an insurance contract that permits an insurer to vary the contract to the prejudice of any other person is void (s 53). It is not permissible to exclude the IC ACT unless expressly authorised by the Act (s 52). For example, an Australian policy that contains a clause making the contract subject to the laws of England would be overridden by s 52.

5-010 Key concepts

There are four key concepts that apply to insurance law:

- insurable interest

- indemnity

- utmost good faith

- subrogation.

5-020 Insurable interest

An insurable interest is the legal or equitable interest that is held by the insured in insured property or a life. In economic terms, it applies where an insured has suffered a pecuniary or economic loss through the damage to or destruction of the subject matter of the insurance. A pecuniary interest exists if a person is liable to pay or lose money in the event of a loss — that is, their loss can be measured in economic terms. An interest exists in transactions involving:

- the purchase of goods if they are at the purchaser's risk
- mortgagees and mortgagors
- landlords and tenants
- common carriers
- a creditor against a debtor's insolvency.

In the case of a creditor who insures property owned by a debtor, the insured will not have either a legal or an equitable interest in the property insured, but would stand to suffer a pecuniary or economic loss if the asset was damaged or destroyed.

In contrast, at common law, the insured must have an insurable interest when entering a contract of general insurance as well as at the time of the loss. The following case example illustrates the operation of common law in this regard.

Case example

Macaura v Northern Assurance Co Ltd

[1925] AC 619

Facts: The insured, Macaura, owned a timber plantation. The insurance policy with Northern Assurance Co Ltd (Northern), which covered the timber, was in his own name. Macaura sold the plantation to a company in which he was the only shareholder although he was not paid for the timber and stood as a creditor. Macaura did not take out a new policy on the timber and continued to insure the timber in Macaura's own name. The timber was later destroyed in a fire and when Macaura made a claim on the policy Northern refused to pay on the basis that Macaura did not have an insurable interest in the timber.

Issue: Did Macaura have an insurable interest in the timber at the time of the loss?

Decision: Macaura's claim failed. Although Macaura had an insurance policy on the timber, it was in his name and not the name of the company. Under common law, Macaura did not have an insurable interest in the assets owned by the company as a company is an entity in its own right separate from its shareholders. Also under common law, an unsecured creditor cannot insure the property of a debtor. Additionally, since shareholders do not own the assets of a company, they do not have a legal or equitable interest in the company assets.

The IC ACT changed all this and a contract of general insurance is no longer void if the insured did not have an interest in the subject matter of the contract at the time the contract was entered into (s 16). Further, legal or equitable interest is not required at the time of the loss; as long as the insured has suffered a pecuniary or economic loss through damage or destruction of the subject matter they will be able to claim (s 17), provided the loss was covered by the insurance contract. Therefore, under the IC Act, someone in Macaura's position would now be able to recover the loss from their insurer. Further, an insurer under a life or general contract of insurance is not relieved of liability just because the names of those who might benefit from the contract are not set out in the policy document (s 2 of the *Life Assurance Act 1774* (Imp) and equivalent state legislation) (s 20).

Change of insurable interest

Unless the policy clearly states that the insurer must be advised if the nature of the insured's interest changes, the validity of the contract will not change. Where no notification of a change is required, the principle of good faith and the duty of disclosure will operate on the renewal of the policy, since a renewal of a general insurance contract usually constitutes the creation of a new contract. Therefore, all material facts arising between the date of the original contract and the date of renewal must be disclosed before renewal of the policy.

Contracts of life insurance

As with policies of general insurance, s 18 of the IC ACT states that an insurable interest is not required in a contract of life insurance.

Section 18 of the IC ACT applies to a contract that provides for the payment of money on the death of a person by sickness or accident. A contract of sickness or accident is not void if the insured did not have an interest in the subject matter of the contract when it was entered into.

Extent of insurable interest

The principle of insurable interest is closely related to the principle of indemnity. This means that in the case of general insurance, the insured cannot recover more than the amount of the loss. This will generally be the amount of the insured's interest, which is usually specified in the contract.

Although an insured with a limited interest in the subject matter can insure for the full value, there is a presumption that the insured intends only to protect the insured's own interest. At common law, an insured with a limited interest can recover more than the value of the insured's interest if it can be shown that the insured intended to also insure the interests of others.

5-030   Indemnity

The objectives of insurance are to return the insured to the position they occupied prior to the occurrence of the loss. This is known as indemnity and enables an insured to purchase insurance to protect against loss to the extent of their insurable interest. Under the principle of indemnity, the insured cannot recover more than their loss. For example, if the owner of a house insured the house for $200,000 against fire and the house was subsequently destroyed by fire, the owner would be able to recover only up to a maximum of $200,000, even though the home at the time of the loss may have actually been worth $300,000. If the insured was able to claim $300,000 and so make a profit out of the insurance, this would constitute a wager and is against the true nature of insurance.

The value of the insured property is calculated at the time of the loss when determining the amount that can be recovered. This amount may be less than the replacement value of the property unless regular adjustments are made to the sum insured at renewal to allow for inflation. With reinstatement or replacement policies the insurer will provide 'new' for 'old', should the insured property be damaged or destroyed; that is, a building will be repaired to a new condition without any cost to the insured, subject to any policy excess.

The principle of indemnity is subject to a special rule relating to minimum premiums. Section 42 of the IC ACT states that an insured can recover the maximum cover for the premium paid. For example, if an insured insures some property for $8,000 for a premium of $150 and the insurer could have provided cover up to $10,000 for this premium, the insured can recover up to $10,000.

This objective does not apply to life and some accident and illness policies because they are contracts of contingency; that is, if the contingency of death occurs then the policy pays out the face value of the policy.

Double indemnity

Sometimes a property owner may inadvertently insure the property with two different insurance companies. In this instance, the total of the policies exceeds the value of the property. Section 76 of the IC ACT prohibits the property owner from recovering more than their loss, so the insured must decide which policy to claim under.

If one insurer does not provide full indemnity, the insured is able to claim the balance of the loss from the other insurer. Following the settlement of the claim, the insurer who has indemnified the insured is able to claim contribution from the other insurer so the loss is shared equally between both companies.

Valued policies

Valued policies are an exception to the indemnity principle. With these policies, the insurer and insured agree in advance on the value of the insured property, so that in the event of loss or damage this amount will be paid to the insured regardless of the actual value of the property at the time of the loss. For example, if a solid gold bracelet was valued at $2,000, and insured for this amount, two years ago and was subsequently lost, the current value of the bracelet could be as high as $4,000 because of the substantial appreciation in the value of gold over those two years. In this case, only the agreed value of $2,000 would be paid by the insurance company.

Life insurance

Life insurance and personal accident insurance are contracts of contingency and as such are exceptions to the indemnity principle, because the amount recovered under the policy is not usually measured in relation to the insured's loss.

5-040   Doctrine of utmost good faith

The doctrine of utmost good faith (Latin: *uberrimae fidae*) is an important concept in insurance law because it applies to intending insureds, insureds and insurers, and is linked to disclosure. Utmost good faith refers to "the greatest or highest degree of honesty of purpose or sincerity of declaration" (Macquarie Concise Dictionary 1988). The duty of good faith was originally an explanation of why the insured was required to disclose to the insurer all information relevant to the insured risk. This duty was also placed on the insurer so there was a mutual obligation to disclose prior to entering into a contract. Lord Mansfield stated in *Carter v Boehm* (1766) 3 Burr 1905 at 1909–1910:

"The policy would be equally void against the underwriter, if he concealed; as if he insured a ship on her voyage, which he privately knew to be arrived: and an action would lie to recover the premium. …Good faith forbids either party; by concealing what he privately knows, to draw the other into a bargain from his ignorance of the fact, and his believing the contrary".

The most common manifestation of the duty of good faith is the pre-contractual duty of disclosure. It goes without saying that the person with the greatest knowledge about the risk being proposed to the insurer is the insured. Therefore, the insured should be required to disclose all those facts that might influence an underwriter as to whether or not to accept the risk. This duty also applies to insurance brokers when disclosing facts to an insurer that relate to their client, as they act as agents for the insured.

The duty extends throughout the period of the policy; that is, it is also a post-contractual duty. It endures so long as the parties are in a contractual or continuing relationship with each other (*Boulton v Houlder Brothers & Co* [1904] 1 KB 784 at 791). The post-contract duty of good faith usually arises in relation to claims — either in the way the insured made the claim or in the way the insurer handled the claim.

This duty involves concepts of honesty and fairness, and as such it involves both objective and subjective components. The objective element of acting with 'fairness' is combined with the subjective element of 'honesty'. The determination of whether there has been a breach of duty equates to an objective test based on subjective facts. Put another way, would an objective person (a 'reasonable person'), knowing what the insurer knows, act in the same manner? An insurer would not be considered to have acted with due regard to the insured's interests if the insurer consciously delayed paying out a valid claim, speculating that the insured would not contest the delay and would give up pursuing the matter.

Simple mistakes are not breaches of the duty of good faith, and neither is negligence. 'Good faith' implies intention. Neither fraudulent claims nor an insurer's delay tactics, as noted above, represent 'good faith' (Shub 2001).

The duty of good faith is included in s 13 of the IC ACT, which states that each party must act in good faith towards the other and neither will be able to rely on any provision of the contract where this has not occurred. In short, the principle of good faith relies on each party making full disclosure to the other. Application of this provision is illustrated in the following case example.

Case example

Hobartville Stud Pty Ltd v Union Insurance Co Ltd

(1991) 25 NSWLR 358

Facts: A thoroughbred colt was insured under an insurance policy with United Insurance Co Ltd, which provided cover for accidental death, disease or destruction of the colt for humane reasons. Following veterinary advice, the owner had the colt destroyed for humane reasons, although the insurer's consent was not gained prior to this action. The owner made a claim on the policy, but it was denied on the grounds that the insurer's veterinary advice indicated that the colt's condition could improve with treatment and because of this the insurer had refused to give its consent to the colt's destruction, although the insurer offered to pay the associated veterinary costs.

The owner argued that the insurer was in breach of its obligation to act with the utmost good faith under ss 13 and 14 of the IC ACT because of its refusal to agree to the destruction of the colt. The insurer counter argued the insured was in breach of its good faith obligations under ss 13 and 14 through its destruction of the colt.

Issue: Was the insured entitled to compensation under the policy?

Decision: The action was settled in favour of the owner with the aid of an arbitrator's report. As a result the owner was entitled to a judgement of $500,000.

A breach may occur when information given is false or certain important material facts, which would have affected one party's view of the contract had they known about it, are withheld. The following tests can be used to determine whether an insurer has breached its duty of good faith:

- What are the relative bargaining positions of the insurer and insured?

- Was there anything unconscionable in the insurer's conditions and the fine print? Under the s 14(3) of the IC ACT an insurer is required to notify the insured of the contract provisions in 'clear, concise and effective' language, but was the insured able to understand the conditions as required by the *Competition and Consumer Act 2010* (Cth) (CC Act), Ch 2, or by the Australian Securities and Investments Commission Act 2001 (Cth) (ASIC ACT, ss 12CA-12CC?

Extra tests are imposed on insurers in the case of business versus business unconscionability (Ch 2, CC Act; s 12CC, ASIC ACT), such as:

- the insurer's track record in dealings involving similar transactions
- the insurer's willingness to negotiate with an insured and whether the insured was left uninsured.

The duty of good faith applies to insurers as well as insureds with regard to making and settling claims. This is confirmed by s 13 and reinforced by s 14 of the IC ACT, which provides that both insurer and insured are not to rely on any provision of the insurance contract if to do so would be to fail to act with the utmost good faith.

The duty of utmost good faith has been revised by the *Insurance Contracts Amendment Act 2013* (2013 Act), which received royal assent on 28 June 2013. The 2013 Act expands the existing provisions and makes a failure to act in the utmost good faith a breach of the IC ACT as well as a simple breach of contract.

In the case where an insurer fails to comply with the duty in relation to the handling or settlement of a claim, the IC Act now gives ASIC the power to vary, suspend or cancel an insurer's financial service licence and ban individuals from providing financial services.

The 2013 Act also extends the duty of the good faith provisions of the IC ACT to third party beneficiaries. A third party beneficiary is defined in section 48 of the IC ACT as a person who is not a party to the contract but is specified or referred to in it as a person to whom the benefit of the insurance extends. Third party beneficiaries are often referred to in general insurance parlance as "section 48 claimants". Some examples of third party beneficiaries include:

- A householder's policy which covers family members and perhaps a credit provider.
- A disability cover or income replacement cover issued for the benefit of a member of a superannuation fund under a group life policy affected by a trustee.
- Public liability cover extended to cover a principal, such as a local authority.
- Contract works cover extended to cover a subcontractor.
- Credit card covers affected by a bank for the benefit of cardholders.

5-050   Duty of disclosure

At common law, each party to the contract is under a duty to voluntarily disclose to the other during the negotiations leading up to the creation of the contract. The matters that must be disclosed are any facts the parties are aware of that might be material to the negotiations. A failure to disclose any material fact allows the innocent party to avoid the contract from the beginning.

The duty of disclosure is important from an insurer's perspective because the insurer needs accurate information about the risk being proposed so it will be able to calculate an appropriate premium and apply suitable conditions. Because the insured is in a special position of knowing all the facts of the risk, the duty falls more heavily on them. This duty will also apply to partners in a partnership and directors in a company. Therefore, if one partner signed a proposal for insurance and the other partners were not involved in the negotiations but were aware of facts that would have influenced the insurer's decision to accept the proposed risk, the non-disclosure of these facts will allow the insurer to avoid the policy. Under section 31A if the IC ACT this duty also applies to a life insured who is not the policyholder.

The consequences of non-disclosure are potentially very severe for the insured; however, there can be real difficulties for the insured in complying with this duty. There can be no defence for an insured who deliberately falsifies information in order to secure a cheaper premium or to secure insurance when a prudent insurer would not otherwise have taken on the risk, but an insurer may have a very different idea of what information is material from that of the insured. As we will see in the following sections, Australia has legislated under section 54 of the IC ACT to modify common law.

On the 4th February 2019, the final report of the Hayne royal commission was released. As noted above, the duty of disclosure falls heavily on intending insureds. In order to shift the burden to insurers to elicit information, the Hayne royal commission recommended that the Insurance Contracts Act 1984 be amended with 'a duty to take reasonable care not to make a misrepresentation to an insurer'. This proposed change may affect pricing, underwriting and claims assessment. No doubt more will be said about this subject in the future so readers should keep this in mind.

Length of duty of disclosure

The duty of disclosure of all *material facts* extends to all negotiations leading up to the making of the contract of insurance (ss 21, 25, IC ACT), which is usually when the insurer accepts the proposal. A material fact is defined as one that "had it been revealed, the insurer or reinsurer would either not have issued the policy or would have [done so] only at a higher premium" (Christiania General Insurance Corp. v Great American Insurance Co. (1990) WL 3231 at 278).

Any new facts that might arise between the completion of the proposal and before it is accepted, must be disclosed. If, for example, under the changed circumstances, a previously answered question would now produce a materially different answer, the insurer must be notified. However, s 54 reduces the insurer's recourse to decline a claim owing to nondisclosure. The insured is not required to disclose changed circumstances during the currency of the policy unless there is a specific provision in the policy for the insured to do so.

The duty of good faith also extends to the insurer, as under the IC ACT the insurer must inform the insured and any person who will be covered under a life insurance policy (whether or not they are the policyholder) in writing of the nature and effect of the duty of disclosure prior to their entry into the contract (s 22). The insurer must also include the fact that the duty applies until the proposed contract is entered into.

Furthermore, if the insurer accepts an application for insurance, or responds with a counter-offer, two months after the insured's most recent disclosure, then a reminder notice of the duty must be given. However, if an insurer has not complied with its duty to inform the client of their disclosure duty than the insurer can only rely on a failure by the insured to supply information if a failure to comply with the duty of disclosure was fraudulent (s 22(5)).

In general insurance, the renewal of a policy creates a new contract. Therefore, all material facts that may have arisen between the date of the original contract and the renewal date should be disclosed to the insurer before renewal, as they could affect the risk and, indeed, the insurer's decision to offer renewal on the same conditions as the expiring policy, if at all. For example, if an insured building was insured as a motor repair shop, and during the policy term the occupation changed to a fibreglass workshop (a high-risk business) this fact would need to be disclosed to the insurer before renewal.

Extent of insured's duty of disclosure

Section 21A of the IC ACT modifies the insured's obligation of disclosure with respect to eligible contracts of insurance when the contract was first entered into and on renewal (s 21(B)) — eg, home building and contents, motor vehicle, sickness and accident, consumer credit, and travel insurances. The insurer may request the insured to answer one or more specific questions that it considers necessary to evaluate the risk and the terms on which acceptance will be offered (s 21A(2)). If the insurer does not ask the relevant questions or the questions are incomplete, then the insurer is deemed to have waived compliance with the duty of disclosure (s 21A(3)).

If the insurer does ask specific questions before the contract is entered into and if the insurer asks the type of 'catch all' questions (eg. disclose to the insurer any other matter that would be covered by the duty of disclosure in relation to the contract) previously allowed under the IC Act, then the insurer is taken to have waived compliance with the duty of disclosure in relation to that other matter (s 21A(4)(b)).

If the insurer does ask specific questions and the insured answers each question specified in the proposal and discloses each matter that is known to them and a reasonable person in the circumstances could be expected to have disclosed in answer to that question, then the insured is taken to have complied with the duty of disclosure (s 21A(5)(b)).

The 2013 Act has also inserted a new section 21B to the IC ACT that applies to *renewals* of eligible contracts. This section allows the insurer, in addition to or instead of asking specific questions relating to disclosure, to give the insured a copy of its previous disclosure and ask if anything has changed. If the insured fails to disclosure any changes, it is taken to have informed the insurer that there have been no changes. Before the contract is renewed, the insurer must also clearly inform the insured in writing of the general nature and effect of the duty of disclosure (s 22(1)(a)).

These provisions of the IC ACT are a form of consumer protection and apply only to eligible contracts such as motor vehicle, home building and home contents. This protection has been provided to insureds because consumers frequently lack the knowledge or awareness to fully understand what is required of them in terms of compliance with their duty of disclosure. Conversely, the insurer is in a position to identify the information that it requires for underwriting purposes so must ask specific questions to obtain this information.

The above provisions apply only to prescribed contracts. What should be disclosed in other forms of insurance depends on the following considerations.

General insurance

Not all insureds have a clear understanding of the meaning of the questions being asked or the type of information being sought. Therefore, if the insured discloses each matter that a reasonable person in the circumstances could be expected to have disclosed in answer to that question then the insured is taken to have complied with the duty of disclosure in relation to the contract (s 21A). However, should the insured later claims to be unaware that a fact was material, there is a combination of two tests that the courts will apply. The first (subjective test) is the common law 'reasonable insured' test regarding matters the insured (or a reasonable person in the circumstances) would be expected to know to be relevant.

The second (objective) test directs a court to consider the nature and extent of the cover to be provided and the class of persons who would ordinarily take out such cover (s 21(1)(b)). For example, what might be expected of an insurance manager taking out contracts of work cover would differ greatly from the expectations on a boy racer insuring his WRX. In addition, an insurer's remedies for a misrepresentation are restricted under s 28, as discussed below. Therefore, a statement is only a misrepresentation if the person making it knew, or a reasonable person in the circumstances would have known, that it was material to the insurer's assessment of the risk (s 26(2)).

Section 28 of the IC ACT applies where a person fails to comply with the duty of disclosure or makes a misrepresentation to the insurer before the contract is entered into. However, the remedy does not apply if the insurer would enter into the contract for the same premium and on the same terms and conditions (s 28(1)). If the failure or misrepresentation is fraudulent, the insurer may avoid the contract (s 28(2)). If the insurer is not entitled to avoid the contract or elects not to under s 28(1), the insurer is able to reduce the liability to the amount that it would have been if the failure had not occurred (s 28(3)). The following case example illustrates the effect of non-disclosure prior to the completion of the policy.

Case example

Lindsay v CIC Insurance Ltd

1989) 5 ANZ Insurance Cases 60-913; 16 NSWLR 673

Facts: Lindsay owned a building which was managed by a real estate agent who insured the property with CIC Insurance Ltd (CIC) through a broker, describing its occupancy as 'office premises', when in fact, offices one and two were being used as a brothel. Both Lindsay and his agent were aware of this fact but did not disclose this to their broker.

Issue: Can an insured be liable for the non-disclosure of their agent, even if the agent commits this breach without their knowledge?

> *Decision:* Section 21(1)(b) of the IC ACT requires an insured to disclose "every matter that is known to the insured" or the insured's agent (s 21(1)). The fact that the tenant was using a part of the building as a brothel was a matter that should have been disclosed to CIC, because of the increased risk of damage to the property through threats of arson, fights and threats. As a result of this non-disclosure, CIC was able to reduce its liability on the claim to 'nil' under s 28(3) as they would not have insured the premises.

The courts have the power to disregard the contract's avoidance if it considers that the fraudulent misrepresentation did not prejudice the insurer or that the prejudice was minimal or insignificant and avoidance would be harsh and unfair on the insured (s 31(2)). In this case, the insured will be allowed to claim up to the full sum insured (s 31(1)).

An insurer can cancel a contract of general insurance, without affecting any prior claim, where there has been a non-disclosure or a misrepresentation (s 60).

Material facts

Facts that are material include:

- the name and occupation of the applicant. An insurer may be suspicious if the applicant is known by a different name than that disclosed. Occupation may be material particularly where the occupation is hazardous, eg, where a rigger applies for income protection insurance

- the health status of the applicant. Major illnesses and operations are important especially where life and income protection and personal accident insurance is being applied for. Minor ailments such as sore throats, chest pains while jogging and everyday ailments may not, in themselves, be material facts

- insurance and loss history of the applicant, including previous claims and whether the applicant has been refused insurance or had insurances cancelled

- criminal convictions (even if not directly related to the risk under consideration). Criminal convictions generally indicate that a convicted person poses an increase in moral hazard. However, convictions become stale over time and insurers should be careful not to breach the federal law on spent convictions, which generally expire after 10 years for adults and after five years for juveniles

- matters that indicate an increased risk for the insurer. The storage of inflammable liquid on the premises, and the type of materials used in the construction of a building (say, wood and fibro), are examples of material facts under common law and under the IC ACT.

Matters that need not be disclosed

The onus of establishing the non-disclosure of a fact and its materiality is on the insurer, and this applies both at common law and under the IC ACT. Gossip or rumours need not be disclosed because they are not 'facts'.

The duty of disclosure both at common law and under s 21 of the IC ACT extends only to what the insured knows. The insured cannot disclose what they do not know. In *Khoury v GIO of NSW* [1984] HCA 55; (1984) 3 ANZ Insurance Cases 60-581, it was held that the insured should have disclosed his belief that members of his household had stolen money from him, even if that belief was later shown to be wrong. 'Belief' in this case was held to be actual knowledge. Under s 21(2), matters that need not be disclosed are those:

- that diminish the risk

- that the insurer knows or in the ordinary course of the insurer's business as an insurer ought to know (common knowledge)

- where there has been a waiver of disclosure by the insurer, such as where an insurer fails to clarify an unanswered question in the proposal form.

Under common law, the innocent party to a contract may avoid the contract from the beginning for non-disclosure of a material fact. If an insurer avoids the contract, all premiums are refundable. However, under the IC ACT an insurer's remedy will depend on whether the non-disclosure was fraudulent or innocent. If it can be established that the non-disclosure was fraudulent then the insurer can avoid a general insurance contract (ss 28(2), or a life insurance contract 29(2)). In the case of life insurance, if the failure was not fraudulent or the misrepresentation was not fraudulent then an insurer is able to avoid the contract for up to three years after the contract was entered into (s 29(3)).

The court is able to disregard the avoidance if it considers that:

- the insurer's avoidance would be 'harsh and unfair' (s 31(1)), and

- the insurer has not been prejudiced by the insured's breach or the prejudice has been only minimal or insignificant (s 31(2)).

However, s 31 does not give the court the discretion to avoid a policy of insurance for non-disclosure by the insured after the contract is formed, such as when an insured breaches a general insurance warranty or condition of the contract, eg, the non-disclosure of the fitting of mag wheels to a car.

Where the insurer is not entitled to avoid the contract, such as where the insured has made an innocent misrepresentation in an application of general insurance, the insurer can reduce its liability to the amount that would place it in the same position as it would have been had the misrepresentation not been made (s 28(3)).

On the other hand, if the insurer has acted unconscionably in the events leading up to the formation of an insurance contract then it could infringe the Australian Consumer Law (set out in the CC Act) or equivalent state or territory fair trading legislation in Australia.

Importance of the three year period for financial planners

Financial planners need to be aware of the three year period as insurers are able to avoid an insurance policy for non-fraudulent non-disclosure during this period. This is especially the case when a financial planner is replacing or reducing the cover of an existing policy. Section 947D of the *Corporations Act 2001* ("the CA") stipulates that the client must be advised of any pecuniary or other benefits that may be lost by this action.

Section 947D is important as any health issues that have arisen during the currency of the old policy will need to be disclosed in the new policy and if not disclosed a resultant claim may be declined in the ensuing three year period. The results of non-disclosure for the client and adviser are illustrated in the following case example.

Case example

Commonwealth Financial Planning Limited v Couper

[2013]NSWCA 444

Facts: Mr Stevens had a life insurance policy with Westpac Life. An authorised representative of the appellant CFP (a subsidiary of the Commonwealth Bank of Australia) persuaded him to take out cover with another insurer, CommInsure, and cancel his existing policy. Mr Stevens' true medical history was not disclosed to CommInsure. When Mr Stevens was diagnosed with pancreatic cancer, CommInsure avoided the policy for non-disclosure pursuant to s 29(3) of the *Insurance Contracts Review Act* 1984 (Cth), which entitled an insurer to avoid a life insurance policy for non-fraudulent non-disclosure within three years from entry into the contract. That three year period had long since expired in relation to Mr Stevens' Westpac Life policy.

Issue: Was Mr Couper negligent and did he engage in misleading or deceptive conduct?

The trial judge found CommInsure validly avoided the policy, and no appeal was brought from that decision. The trial concluded that CFP's authorised representative was negligent and engaged in misleading or deceptive conduct, in that he was too hasty and failed to sufficiently impress upon Mr Stevens the risk he took replacing one policy for another.

This case illustrates that a client could be giving up a valuable asset particularly if the life insurance policy had remained in force beyond the three years period and under which the right to make a claim in the event of innocent non-disclosure being shown was safeguarded by statute.

The court established that the reason the Westpac life policy was replaced was to earn commission on the new product. Div 2 of Pt 7.7A of the CA stipulates that authorised representatives must exercise their fiduciary duty when providing personal advice to retail clients. This duty requires authorised representatives to place their clients' interests ahead of their own. Clearly, this duty was not exercised in this case.

Remedies for life insurers for non-disclosure and/or misrepresentation

Many life insurance contracts combine more than one type of cover for example, death, TPD, sickness, trauma and so on. Section 27A unbundles combined life policies so that each policy will be treated separately when applying the relevant remedies of non-disclosure and misrepresentation under s 29. Without this section a non-disclosure or misrepresentation in relation to one aspect to the cover could allow the insurer to avoid liability or cancel the whole contract.

Section 29 allows the insurer:

- where the non-disclosure or a misrepresentation was not fraudulent, the insurer can only avoid the policy in the first three years (s 29(3))

- can alter the sum insured at any time (unless the contract has a surrender value or provides a death benefit – in which case it can only do so within three years) (s 29(4))

- can choose not to avoid the policy or vary the sum insured. In these cases it can by giving written notice to the insured, retrospectively vary the contract in such a way as to place the insurer in the position it would have been in if the non-disclosure or misrepresentation had not occurred (s 29(6)). However, the following caveats apply:

  » the insurer can only do so to the extent that any variations are consistent with what other reasonable and prudent insurers would have done in similar circumstances

  » such variations are not applicable to a contract which has a surrender value or provides a death benefit.

Misstatement of an insured's age

Where there is non-disclosure in relation to an insured's age (such as where the date of birth is incorrectly stated), the policy cannot be avoided (s 30). This section provides that where the true age is understated, the insurer is able to reduce the sum insured on a proportionate basis. Where the true age is overstated, the insurer is able to either increase the sum insured on a proportionate basis or reduce premiums payable and repay the overpaid premiums.

Section 30 (3A) also gives the insurer the option of changing the contract expiry date to the date that would have applied if the correct date of birth had been disclosed in the first place.

Liability of co-insureds

The duty of disclosure also extends to co-insureds. Whether they are husband and wife in a household policy, partners in a partnership or directors in a company, they must disclose all matters that are material to the question of risk. A failure of one co-insured to disclose a material fact may result in the innocent co-insured losing their rights under a policy.

Waiver of information

An applicant does not have to disclose every material fact in minute detail. Both at common law and under the IC ACT (s 21(2)(d)), disclosure is not required if the insurer waives compliance with the duty of disclosure. The duty will be satisfied if the insured provides enough information to alert the insurer to make enquiries. If the insurer fails to pursue the matter, it will be deemed to have waived disclosure of the facts that would have been revealed. Further, an insurer is deemed to have waived compliance with the duty if, in response to a question in the proposal form, the insured failed to provide an answer, or gave an obviously incomplete or irrelevant answer, and the insurer failed to clarify the answers (s 21(3)). It will not amount to a misrepresentation (s 27).

Onus of proof

As mentioned earlier, the onus of proving the non-disclosure of a fact and its materiality is on the insurer and applies both at common law and under the IC ACT. The material date as to when full disclosure should be made is the moment when a binding contract is concluded. If the insured has not disclosed all the material facts, including any that may have arisen since the completion of the proposal, the insurer has the option of rescinding the contract on learning the true position.

Ambiguous questions

If a question asked on a proposal form is open to two meanings (ie, ambiguous), the approach taken by the court is to consider whether the answer given by the insured is true, based on a fair and reasonable construction of the question (s 23). At common law, an ambiguity in a question in a proposal is interpreted against the person who wrote it and if the court considers that the answer was true, based on a reasonable construction of the question, the insurer will not be able to rely on misrepresentation as grounds to avoid the policy.

Void and voidable

The terms *void* and *voidable* are sometimes incorrectly used interchangeably. Actually, to speak of a *void contract* is a contradiction in itself. A contract that is void is not a contract at all, but simply an agreement without legal effect. In essence, it lacks one of the requirements specified in law for a valid contract. A void contract cannot be enforced by either party and neither party to the contract can enforce it. For example, a contract having an illegal object is void, as neither party can enforce it.

A *voidable contract,* in contrast, is an agreement that, for a reason satisfactory to the court, may be set aside by one of the parties. It is binding unless the party with the right to void it decides to do so. Assume, for example, that the insured fails to comply with a condition of the agreement. The company may elect, if it chooses, to fulfil its part of the contract, or it may elect to avoid it and revoke coverage (unless relevant insurance legislation prohibits it from avoiding the contract). A contract may be voidable for any number of legal reasons. If one party was forced into the contract under duress, or if there was an element of fraud involved, the contract may be voidable.

Cancellation of contracts of life insurance

Life insurers are only allowed to cancel a contract of life insurance in accordance with either section 210 of the *Life Insurance Act 1995* (non-payment of the premium), or section 59A of the IC ACT (associated with fraudulent claims).

5-060   Subrogation

It was mentioned earlier that under the doctrine of indemnity, an insured is not permitted to make a profit from the insurance; otherwise the insurance is not a contract of insurance but a wager. When an insurer has indemnified an insured for a loss, the insurer is entitled to 'stand in the shoes' of the insured and take advantage of all the rights and remedies that the insured may have against any third party who may have been responsible for the damage that gave rise to the claim. Subrogation literally means the substitution of one person for another. This prevents the insured from making a profit on the loss by being indemnified under the policy and then bringing an action against a negligent third party or their insurer.

The effect of the doctrine is to make the negligent third party or, if insured, the third party's insurer, bear the responsibility for the loss caused by the third party. Figure 5.1 illustrates the principle of subrogation.

Figure 5.1: The principle of subrogation

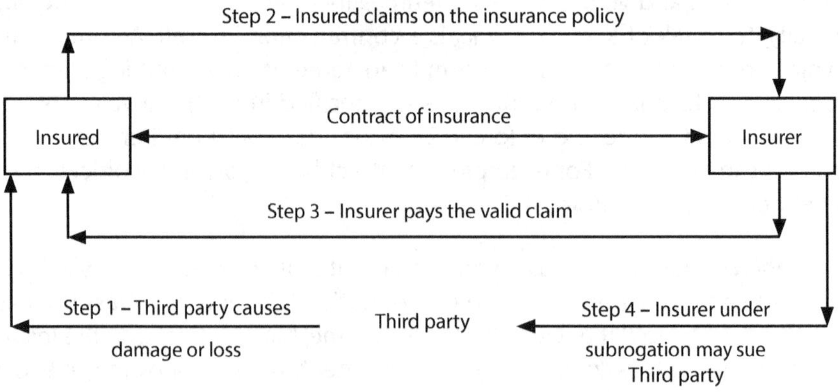

Source: Adapted from Gibson A, & Fraser, D 2005, *Business Law,* 2nd edn, Pearson Education Australia, Frenchs Forest.

Figure 5.1 shows that after the insurer pays the claim (step 3), the insurer 'steps into the shoes' of the insured (step 4) and exercises its right to recover from the negligent third party. On the other hand, if the insured has been fully indemnified but also receives a gift from another to mitigate the effects of the loss, the insurer is entitled to claim the amount of the gift unless the gift was paid under statute.

Although the IC ACT preserves the basic common law principle of subrogation (s 65), its application precludes or limits an insurer's rights of subrogation in relation to certain classes of potential defendants by ss 65–68:

Section 66 of the IC ACT states that an insurer has no right of subrogation against an insured's employee provided that the conduct of the employee which gave rise to the loss:

- occurred in the course of or arose out of the employment; and
- was not serious or wilful misconduct.

Accordingly, s66 of the IC ACT may defeat any purported subrogated action by an insurer against a co-insured who was also an employee.

Section 65 of the IC ACT limits an insurer's rights of subrogation against persons who the insured has not pursued and might reasonably be expected not to pursue because of:

- a family or other personal relationship between the insured and that person; or
- the insured having expressly or impliedly consented to that person's use of a road motor vehicle which is the subject matter of the insurance contract.

Section 65(2)(b) does not apply where the conduct of the third party giving rise to the loss:

- was serious or wilful misconduct; or
- occurred in the course of or arose out of the third party's employment by the insured.

 In such cases, the insurer's rights of subrogation are effectively limited to the extent that the third party has insurance in respect to his or her liability to the insured. For example, in the case of property damage insurance (ie no liability cover), s65 would prevent an insurer from bringing a subrogated action against a guilty co-insured, who has the requisite relationship with the indemnified co-insured, unless (and to the extent that) the guilty co-insured has other insurance which covers its liability to the indemnified co-insured.

The following common law case example shows how subrogation to recover a loss can arise out of employment.

Case example

Lister v Romford Ice & Cold Storage Co Ltd

[1957] AC 555

Facts: Both father and son Lister were employed by Romford Ice. Young Lister was reversing his truck into a loading bay under the direction of his father, when he lost sight of his father and accidentally ran over him. The father was successful in a claim for damages against Romford Ice on the basis that its employee, younger Lister, was negligent. The company's insurers exercised their right of subrogation by bringing an action against younger Lister on the grounds that he breached his duty to drive the truck carefully, thus causing his employer to suffer damage. The insurance company claimed that the young Lister should indemnify the employer (and ultimately the insurance company as any action is taken in the name of the insured-the employer) for the loss.

Issue: Can the insurer recover its loss against the son?

Decision: Younger Lister owed a duty of care to his employer to exercise care and competence as a truck driver. It was held that he operated the truck in a negligent fashion and because of this failed his duty of care by running over his father.

This decision has led to the Northern Territory, South Australia, Tasmania and New South Wales passing legislation to limit its effect at common law.

Section 67 of the IC ACT gives the insured the right to claim monies recovered by the insurer. This section shows how the proceeds of recovery actions are divided between an insurer and an insured:

- the party funding the recovery action is entitled to be reimbursed for the costs of doing so. If both parties contribute, both should be reimbursed fully if possible but if not then pro rata;

- any remaining sum after costs are paid is divided based on who funds the recovery. If an insurer funds the recovery, once it has recovered the amount paid to or on behalf the insured, anything left over must be paid to the insured up to the full amount of the loss. If the insured funds the recovery action, the order is reversed;
- if the action is funded jointly by both the insurer and the insured, then the recover funds will be shared on a pro rata basis if there are insufficient funds to reimburse them in full;
- any excess or windfall recovery is to be distributed to both parties in the same proportions as they contributed to the administrative and legal costs of the recovery action.

Finally, an insurer's right of subrogation can be prejudiced by the insured admitting liability to an injured third party. Therefore, it is not unusual for indemnity policies to contain a term prohibiting an insured from making an admission of liability, and if doing so, the admission may prejudice the insured's ability to claim under the policy.

At a glance

- There are four key concepts that apply to insurance law:
  - » insurable interest
  - » indemnity
  - » utmost good faith
  - » subrogation
- the duty of disclosure is linked to the doctrine of utmost good faith.

The duty applies to both insured and insurer

Material facts must be disclosed to insurers up to the completion of the contract and on renewal for a general insurance contract

Failure to fully disclose all material facts by an insured will allow the innocent party to avoid the contract under common law, but this right has been modified by the IC ACT

An insurer may waive its right to information under certain circumstances

5-070   Study questions

5.1   What is insurable interest? Explain how the *Insurance Contracts Act 1984* (Cth) modifies the common law principle of insurable interest, and give some examples.

5.2   Indemnity is the basis of all forms of insurance contracts. Discuss.

5.3   Discuss the length of an insured's duty of disclosure under a contract of insurance. Include in your answer the test that is used to determine what is material.

5.4   Discuss the principle of subrogation.

5.5   Mary McDonald holds a trauma policy with Dodgy Insurance Pty Ltd. She submitted a claim for a mild heart attack, which the insurer declined because she did not declare that her mother, who died while she was very young, also had a heart attack. Mary complained to you that she did not know about her mother's heart attack. Was the insurance company's action to decline the claim correct? Explain why you consider that it is correct or why you consider it is not correct.

5.6 Compare and contrast insurable interest as it applies to insurance contracts in common law and how it applies under the *Insurance Contracts Act*.

5.7   When does an insurer waive the right to enforce an insured's duty of disclosure.

5.8   List the types of information that an insured does not need to disclose.

5-080   References

Articles and Books

Gibson, A & Fraser, D 2005, *Business Law,* 2nd edn, Pearson Education Australia, Frenchs Forest.

Macquarie Library Pty Ltd (1988) *The Macquarie Concise Dictionary*, 2nd edn, Sydney.

Shub, O 2001, 'Focus: The duty of the utmost good faith -- May 2001', Allens Arthur Robinson. Available at *aar.com.au*

Legislation

Corporations Act 2001 (Cth)

Insurance Contracts Act 1984 (Cth)

Insurance Contracts Amendment Act 2013

Legal Authorities

Christiania General Insurance Corp. v Great American Insurance Co. (1990) WL 3231

CHAPTER 6

MAKING THE INSURANCE CONTRACT

MAKING THE INSURANCE CONTRACT

6-000   Common law

Common law is one of the two major legal systems of the modern Western world (the other is civil law), it originated in the UK and is now followed in most English speaking countries. Initially, common law was founded on common sense as reflected in the social customs. Over the centuries, it was supplanted by statute law (rules enacted by a legislative body such as a Parliament) and clarified by the judgments of the higher courts (that set a precedent for all courts to follow in similar cases). These precedents are recognized, affirmed, and enforced by subsequent court decisions, thus continually expanding the common law (Business Dictionary n.d).

Insurance transactions are formalised by way of a contract. Insurance policies are legal contracts that are governed by both common law and legislation such as the Insurance Contracts Act 1984 (Cth) (IC Act). There are five essential elements that must be present for an insurance contract to be legally enforceable. These are:

- *Intention to enter into legal relations.* Intention is evidenced by an individual completing and submitting a proposal for insurance to an insurance company.

- *Agreement — offer and acceptance.* The parties to the transaction agree on the terms and conditions and the payment for the transaction. For example, an insurance company or its representative makes an invitation to treat (ie invites the insured to make an offer) of life insurance to an individual. The individual then completes a proposal form, which the life underwriter assesses. An offer is then made to the insured and, if satisfied with the terms and conditions offered, the insured indicates acceptance by paying the premium stated in the offer.

- *Consideration.* Consideration means that something of value is given in exchange for a promise, a service or an item of value. In the case of insurance, consideration is usually made by the insured paying money.

- *Capacity to enter into a contract.* Both parties must have the legal capacity to enter into the contract. Certain classes of people have limited or no capacity under law. These include minors (those under 18 years of age), bankrupts and persons of unsound mind.

- *Legality of object or purpose.* The purpose of the contract must be legally valid. For example, a contract between two parties to supply illicit drugs would be considered illegal.

6-010   Parties to an insurance contract

In an insurance contract, the party taking out a contract of general insurance is known as the 'insured', while the party taking out a contract of life insurance is known as the 'assured'. However, in modern usage the distinction between the two terms has become blurred and the term 'insured' is generally used to describe both types of contracting party. The other party to the contract is the insurer, as shown in figure 6.1.

Figure 6.1 Parties to an insurance contract

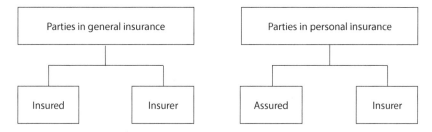

6-020   Steps in obtaining an insurance contract

The normal steps in the process of obtaining insurance cover through an insurance company or via an insurance broker are:

- securing an interim contract of insurance

- making an offer

- agreeing to the terms of the contract.

Securing an interim contract of insurance

Often the first step is to obtain a cover note, which is referred to in s 38 of the *Insurance Contracts Act 1984* (Cth) (IC Act) as an interim contract of insurance (or more commonly called a *cover note*). The purpose of a cover note is to provide temporary cover for the insured while the insurance company considers the proposal to determine whether to accept it and, if so, on what terms. A cover note is a contract in its own right and is regarded at law as being equivalent to the issue of an insurance policy and enforceable as such (s 11(2)(a) & (b) , IC Act). It should be noted that cover notes are not issued for life insurance because insurers will offer cover only after they have assessed the life proposed for insurance.

It is usual for a cover note or other forms of interim insurance to note that the contract is subject to the terms and conditions of the insurer's usual or standard form of policy. This standard policy referred to is the usual policy relevant to the particular risk(s) covered. An example of a policy condition that is inappropriate in a cover note is a condition requiring payment of the premium before the insurer comes on risk. If this condition was enforceable, it would make a farce of the issue of cover notes.

The definition of an interim contract in s 11(2) of the IC Act does not make it necessary for it to be issued in writing. Therefore, if an agent in the field represented to an insured that they 'are covered', this would fall within the definition provided the temporary cover is to be replaced or superseded by the issue of a standard form of policy.

Cover notes are generally issued for a period of one month. Insurers are able to reject the proposal and cancel the cover note at any time within that period (s 60(4), IC Act) by giving the insured three days' written notice if cancellation is to be effective (s 59, IC Act), or they may let the cover note expire without notifying the proposer. In either case, the insurer remains liable for valid claims that may occur until the cover note expires. The insurer remains liable until cover commences under another contract of insurance between the insured and the insurer or another insurer replaces the interim contract of insurance.

Making an offer

The next step is for the person applying for the insurance (applicant or proponent) to complete a proposal form sent to the person by the insurance company or provided by their agent or by an insurance broker. The proposal form contains enough information to allow the underwriter to assess the risk proposed for insurance. The proposal asks for information:

- about the property, risk or person to be covered
- regarding the insured, including details of past losses and claims and whether any other insurer has cancelled or refused to renew a policy or declined an application, and
- a description of anything that could make the risk greater than usual.

The offer does not come from the insurance company as sending out the proposal is an invitation to treat. An invitation to treat is a request to another person to make an offer. There is no offer by the insurance company as it retains the right to accept or reject the proposal, depending on what information is disclosed by the proponent. Usually an offer by the insured constitutes the submission of a completed proposal form, which may or may not be accepted by the insurer. However, in the case of interim cover, as discussed above, the insured's offer will usually be oral.

If an insurer rejects a proposal (offer), it must give the applicant, or in the case of life insurance the life insured, written reasons for its decision, if requested by the applicant or life insured (s 75, IC Act).

The offer usually contains the terms that limit the procedure by which it may be accepted and the period of time that the offer remains open. If the insurer wants to alter the terms of the proposal, its notification is a counter-offer, which the proponent may accept or reject. For example, an offer by a life insurance company may contain an exclusion for claims resulting from a previous injury to the lower back and may note that the offer will remain open for 30 days. Acceptance of the offer is indicated by signing the insurer's offer and, if necessary, paying any additional premium. In this case, the offer is considered accepted at the date of posting of the insurer's offer or, if faxed, on its receipt by the insurance company. The following case example confirms that acceptance of the offer made by the insurer is binding on the insurer.

Case example

Batty v Pearl

[1937] 1 AC 12

Facts: The insured's daughter (proponent) signed a proposal form on the life of her mother at a premium of 50p per week. She failed to enter a sum assured on the proposal form when it was signed but an amount of £250, the agreed sum, was entered later. However, the insurance company made a mistake and issued the policy for a sum assured of £1,000. The proponent paid the premium of 50p per week for more than eight years before the company found the mistake.

Issue: Was the insurance company bound by the mistake?

Decision: It was held that the company had made a counter-offer when it inserted £1,000 for 50p per week instead of £250 for 50p per week. This meant that the proponent was free to accept or reject the counter-offer. By paying 50p per week for the last eight years, she had clearly accepted the counter-offer. Therefore, a valid contract existed for the sum of £1,000 at a weekly premium of 50p.

Basis clause

The proposal may contain a basis clause specifying that the information provided by the proponent is correct and that it forms the basis of the contract between the insurer and the insured. The clause is considered by the insurer as a condition precedent to liability under the contract and appears at the end of the proposal form. Under common law, if any answers given by the proponent to questions in the proposal form were untrue, the insurer could avoid the contract. However, basis clauses are now rendered ineffective by various sections of the IC Act. In addition, state legislation such as s 25 of the *Instruments Act 1958* (Vic) or s 18A of the *Insurance Act 1902* (NSW) also prevents avoidance of a policy of general insurance unless the incorrect statement is fraudulent or material to the risk.

Similarly, in most jurisdictions legislation dealing with third party motor vehicle insurance and workers compensation insurance restricts an insurer's rights to avoid a policy or otherwise deny liability on the grounds of misrepresentation and non-disclosure.

Concluded contract and commencement of the risk

It is important for both the insured and the insurer to know when the insurance contract is concluded and when the insurer is on risk. Also, if a material misrepresentation is made, the insurer is entitled to avoid the policy even after the event insured against occurred. The question is judged at the time of making the contract, so that an answer to a question may be true in the proposal but untrue at the time when the policy is issued and the contract made. The insured's duty to disclose changes in their health after submission of a proposal is illustrated in the following case example.

Case example

Looker v Law Union & Rock Insurance Co Ltd

[1928] 1 KB 554

Facts: Looker affected life insurance with Rock Insurance Co Ltd. At the time of completing the proposal form he was free of any disease or ailment as specified in the proposal form. However, he contracted pneumonia between submitting the proposal and its acceptance, and failed to inform the company of his change in health. Shortly after the proposal was accepted by the insurance company, Looker died.

Issue: Was the insurer liable on the policy?

Decision: The court held that the insurance company was not liable because Looker had a duty to disclose any material changes in his health before the contract was completed.

Often the premium is forwarded to the insurer with the proposal, so that when the proposal is accepted the contract is concluded; the insurer will be on risk and the duty of disclosure ceases from that moment. The issue of the policy does not necessarily signal the completion of the contract unless this is indicated in the proposal or by some other means. A preliminary agreement does not give rise to a contract of insurance.

Under contract law, acceptance of an offer must be complete and unqualified. Therefore, where a proponent does not send in the premium with the proposal, the insurer will send notification of acceptance of the proposal and request payment of the premium. This is a counter-offer so the contract will be concluded on payment of the premium to the insurer. The insurer cannot refuse the premium if there has not been a change in the risk, but if there has been a material change in the risk, the payment of the premium would be regarded as a new offer for a new risk. The ramifications arising from a failure to pay the premium, and so conclude the contract, are illustrated in the following case example.

Case example

Canning v Farquhar

(1886) 16 QBD 727

Facts: Canning applied for life assurance and was told by the insurance company that no contract could take place until the first premium was paid. However, before the premium was paid, Canning fell off a cliff and died. The company refused to accept the premium from Canning's agent, even though Canning gave the premium to his agent before his death.

Issue: Did the change in risk between the time of the submission of the proposal and the payment of the premium cause the policy to lapse?

Decision: The company was under no obligation to pay the sum insured because the risk had substantially changed between the time of the original proposal and the agent's attempt to pay the premium.

A counter-offer could also apply where an insurer accepts a proposal subject to conditions such as the installation by the proponent of certain fire-fighting appliances. Acceptance of the offer is not usually effective until communicated to the proponent unless the offer is unilateral, such as with the issue of travel insurance offered at some airports, or under the terms of the contract where acceptance takes the form of the signing and sealing of a policy by the insurer.

Agreeing to the terms of the contract

Finally, the terms relating to the particular risk must be agreed to before there is a binding contract. In the case of life insurance, agreement would be evidenced by the insured signing an offer made by the insurer, which may contain a clause excluding cover for, say, claims arising from a previous injury. For standard risks, the terms that will apply are the insurer's usual terms and conditions regarding the type of insurance being sought. If,it is in relation to standard cover under the IC Act, then the particular terms set out in the regulations will apply, irrespective of the terms of the insurer's policy. Section 53 states that where a contract of insurance varies the terms of the contract to the prejudice of the insured, the contract and the provision is void.

Where the insurer offers cover to the insured on less advantageous terms than it would otherwise offer because of some particular risk, the insurer is required to give the applicant written reasons for the decision if the applicant makes a written application requesting these reasons (s 75, IC Act).

At a glance

- Under common law, there are five essential elements necessary for a legally enforceable insurance contract:
    » intention to enter into legal relations
    » agreement — offer and acceptance
    » consideration
    » capacity to enter into a contract
    » legality of object and purpose.
- Arranging an insurance policy generally involves the following steps:
    » issuing a cover note or interim contract of insurance
    » completing a proposal
    » agreeing on the terms of the contract before there can be a binding contract
    » concluding the contract
    » sending a renewal notice to the insured 21 days before the policy due date inviting renewal
    » payment by the insurer to the insured a proportionate return of premium if the insurance is cancelled during the term of the policy.

CONSTRUCTION OF THE INSURANCE POLICY

6-030   Introduction

Insurance policies are intended to represent the terms and conditions agreed to by the insurer and the insured, although the policies are invariably drafted by the insurer. Modern insurance policies generally include clauses and conditions that:

- define the risks covered (the insuring clause)

- set out exclusions to that cover (exclusion clauses)

- identify conditions that must be fulfilled, or occur, before the insurer will be liable

- define the terms of the insurance and the period of cover. These terms are generally found in the schedule attached to the policy.

A typical insurance policy begins with a general statement of the perils covered that, if they occur and cause loss or damage, will give the insured the right to claim indemnity up to the maximum amount stated in the attached schedule. For example, a typical householders insurance policy will either state that the insured property is covered for all accidental damage or provide a list of events, such as fire or storm and tempest, that defines the scope of the cover provided.

A list of defined exclusions follows. These exclusions indicate under what circumstances the policy will cease to provide cover. For example, motor vehicle policies contain exclusion clauses that relieve the insurer of liability while the vehicle is not in a roadworthy condition. They are also included in an attempt to restrict the expansion of the insurer's liability beyond what the risk originally proposed. The obligations of the insurer are further described by a statement of the conditions of the policy. In the past, those conditions that were designated as conditions precedent to any liability of the insurer were severely limited by s 54 of the IC Act, as described in the 'Exclusions' section at 6-090.

Thus, the typical insurance policy includes the policy document itself and the schedule or certificate that contains any endorsements, all of which are read together when determining the intention of the parties. The schedule or certificate of insurance identifies the insured and the various types of cover provided in the different sections of the policy, including the maximum amount of liability (sum insured) with respect to each section and any special conditions applicable to that particular cover.

In some of the older insurance law texts and cases, reference is made to the proposal forming the basis of the contract of insurance and its contents being incorporated in the policy. However, s 24 of the IC Act specifies that the statements made in the proposal form are pre-contractual statements only and cannot be incorporated into the policy.

6-040   Standard cover

Insurance policies have long been seen by the average insured as confusing, with complaints about the use of incomprehensible language even though the industry has adopted 'plain English' policies. To overcome this confusion among insureds, the regulators had a choice of imposing prescribed contracts or a standard cover. Prescribed contracts are compulsory standard policies containing prescribed terms. Standard cover allows an insurer to derogate (ie, deviate) from the standard prescribed, but only if it specifically draws the insured's attention to the relevant limits on the cover.

Sections 34 to 37 of the IC Act prescribe the contents of insurance policies in six areas of domestic insurance:

- motor vehicle (property damage only)
- home buildings
- home contents
- sickness and accident
- consumer credit
- travel insurance.

The regulations of the IC Act prescribe 'pre-printed standard cover' that specifies the events insured against, exclusions and the minimum amounts payable. However, an insurer does not have to follow these pre-printed standards and can offer less than the standard cover provided the insurer 'clearly informs' the insured in writing before or when the contract is made, or the insured knew, or a reasonable person could be expected to be aware of it (s 35(2)). Insurers have historically been unwilling to offer flood cover as part of their standard home building and contents insurance policies and excluded this cover however, following recent legislative changes this cover must be provided by all domestic insurance policies. Flood insurance is discussed further in Chapter 13 (see 13-030).

Insurers can fulfil their duty to 'clearly inform' the insured that a particular event is excluded from the policy by providing the insured with a notice that the event is not covered and by supplying a copy of the policy, or by providing a copy of the policy only where the terms and exclusions are not complex: *Marsh v CGU Insurance Limited t/as Commercial Union Insurance* [2004] NTCA 1; (2004) 13 ANZ Insurance Cases 61-594.

Standard terms are usually imposed under relevant state and territory legislation in compulsory insurance such as motor vehicle third party insurance and workers compensation insurance.

6-050 Unusual terms

The insurer is not entitled to rely on unusual terms in a contract of insurance unless it notifies the insured in writing of the effect of the limitation or has delivered a copy of the policy to the insured (s 37, IC Act). Examples of unusual terms most frequently encountered relate to time limits on bringing claims after rejection of liability by an insurer. Some policies have a claims notification period as short as six months, and under common law insurers are able to deny liability if the claim is not notified within this time limit. It is generally considered that any time period under two or three years may be unusual.

6-060 Instalment contracts

Section 11(8) of the IC Act defines an instalment contract of general insurance as a contract of general insurance "which is, by virtue of a provision of the contract, payable by 7 or more instalments in a year".

Insurers are not able to refuse claims made under instalment contracts or to cancel such contracts where an instalment of premium is outstanding. An insurer can refuse to pay a claim, in whole or part, only where at least one instalment of the premium has remained outstanding for at least 14 days and the insurer clearly informed the insured of the effect of this provision before the contract was entered into (s 39, IC Act).

Section 62(2) specifies that an instalment contract *can be cancelled* if at least one instalment of the premium remains unpaid for at least one month provided the insurer informed the insured in writing of the effect of the provision. Both ss 39 and 62 require the insurer to clearly inform the insured in writing of the effect of the provision before the contract is entered into.

6-070 Warranties and clauses

A warranty, in the insurance context, is a term of the insurance contract that, if breached, entitles the insurer to repudiate the contract. Under insurance law, warranties can be classified as:

- *Warranties of existing fact*; eg, the insured warrants that 'the vehicle has not been and will not be specially modified. Here, the insured is guaranteeing a fact or a set of circumstances, and where the insured modifies the vehicle without the insurer's consent before an accident occurs, the insurer would be entitled to terminate the contract.

- *Continuing or promissory warranties*, under which the insured promises to do, or refrain from doing, some act or series of acts. For example, the insured warrants that he or she will not drive the insured motor vehicle 'while there is present in his or her blood a concentration of 0.05 grams or more of alcohol in 100 millilitres of blood'.

Section 24 of the IC Act provides that a statement made by the insured regarding the existence of a state of affairs will not be treated as a warranty, but will be treated as if it were a statement made to the insurer by the insured during the negotiations for the contract but before it was entered into. Therefore, the insurer will not be able to avoid the contract automatically for breach by the insured. The remedies open to the insurer will be for innocent misrepresentation or fraudulent misrepresentation under s 28.

A breach of a continuing warranty is regulated by s 54 of the IC Act. This section applies to an act that occurred after the contract was entered into and prevents an insurer from refusing to pay a claim because of the breach. The insurer is able to reduce the claim by only the amount that fairly represents the actual prejudice suffered by the insurer.

Clauses are included in a policy in order to prevent an increase in risk by imposing an obligation on the insured. Again, the remedy for a breach of such an obligation is the same as for a warranty. For example, in a motor vehicle policy, 'the insured shall take reasonable precautions for the safety and protection of the vehicle'.

If the insured parks the vehicle on the side of a busy road with the keys in the ignition, the insurer may terminate the policy for failure to take reasonable care of the vehicle. Clauses are especially effective since they require the insured to take positive steps in preventing an increase in risk for the insurer. Again, the effect of clauses in an insurance contract is regulated by s 54, as described above.

6-080   Policy exclusions and excesses

A policy excess (or deductible) is a common feature of most general insurance policies. A policy excess provides that the insured will bear the first amount of any loss. An excess is used to eliminate small claims and the administrative expense of adjusting these claims. As a result, substantial premium savings are possible particularly on commercial policies where insureds are able to increase policy excesses in order to obtain premium discounts. Unfortunately, this facility is generally not available for household or private motor vehicle policies.

The policy excess on household, small business and other private insurance is stated as an amount of money. For example, if a householders policy carried an excess of $100 on all claims, and an insured lodged a valid claim for $1,000, the insurer would pay $900 ($1,000 less $100). Underwriters also apply policy excesses on policies that exhibit excessive claims as a method of preserving the underwriting pool.

6-090　Exclusions, conditions and endorsements

Exclusion or exception clauses are important and form a basic part of all insurance contracts. There are three major types of exclusions: excluded perils, excluded losses and excluded property.

Excluded perils

The policy may exclude certain perils, or causes of loss such as flood in a small business policy and subsidence in a household building policy. Motor vehicle policies insuring vehicles used for private purposes exclude physical damage caused while the vehicle is being used for business purposes such as by a commercial salesperson or real estate agent.

Excluded losses

Certain types of losses can be excluded such as the failure of the insured to protect the property from further damage in a household policy. In a private motor vehicle policy, damage caused while engaging in motor racing is excluded. The personal liability section of a household policy excludes liability arising from the use of a motor vehicle.

Excluded property

Policies may exclude or place limitations on the coverage of certain property. For example, in a householders policy certain types of personal property are excluded such as motor vehicles, aeroplanes, textile awnings and animals.

Reasons for exclusions

Exclusions are necessary for the following reasons:

- some perils are considered uninsurable

- presence of extraordinary hazards

- coverage provided by other contracts

- moral hazard problems

- attitudinal hazard problems

- coverage not needed by typical insureds

The peril may be considered uninsurable. A given peril may depart substantially from the ideal requirements of an insurable risk, as discussed in Chapter 3. For example, most property insurance contracts exclude losses for potential catastrophic events such as war or exposure to nuclear radiation. Predictable declines in the value of property such as wear and tear or damage caused by scorching are not insurable.

Presence of extraordinary hazards. Because of an extraordinary increase in hazard, a loss may be excluded. For example, the premium for liability insurance in a motor vehicle policy is based on the assumption that the vehicle is used for personal and recreational purposes and not as a taxi. The chance of an accident and a resulting lawsuit is much higher if the car is used as a taxi for hire. Therefore, to provide coverage for a taxi at the rate charged for a family motor vehicle could result in inadequate premiums for the insurer and unfair rate discrimination against other insureds who do not use their vehicle as a taxi.

Coverage can be provided by other contracts. Exclusions are used to avoid duplication of coverage and to limit coverage to the policy best designed to provide it. For example, motor vehicles are excluded from homeowners policies because of separate coverage under a motor vehicle policy. This prevents duplication of coverage.

Certain property is excluded because of moral hazard or difficulty in determining and measuring the amount of loss. For example, household insurance policies limit the coverage of money to a particular amount (such as to $500). If unlimited amounts of money were covered, fraudulent claims would increase. Also, loss-adjustment problems in determining the exact amount of the loss would also increase. Thus, because of moral hazard, exclusions are used.

Exclusions are also used to deal with attitudinal hazard (morale hazard). The exclusion forces individuals to bear losses that result from their own carelessness such as failure to protect property from a loss.

Coverage is not needed by the typical insured. For example, most homeowners do not own private aeroplanes. To cover aircraft as personal property under the householders policy would be grossly unfair to the vast majority of insureds who do not own aeroplanes because premiums would need to be increased substantially to cover this risk.

Conditions

Conditions are provisions that qualify or place limitations on the insurer's promise to perform. In effect, conditions impose certain duties on the insured. If the policy conditions are not met, the insurer can refuse to pay the claim. Common policy conditions include notifying the insurer if a loss occurs, not admitting liability following a motor vehicle accident and protecting property following a loss

Endorsements

An endorsement is a written provision that adds to, deletes from, or modifies the provisions in the original contract. For example, a small business policy may exclude flood, but a flood endorsement attached to the policy that extends the coverage to include damage by flood. An endorsement attached to a policy generally takes precedence over any conflicting terms in the policy.

6-100   Duration of the policy

Most non-life policies are in force for a period of 12 months, although insurers are willing to renew them indefinitely if the risk does not change. However, an insured has no legal right to have the policy renewed, unless the policy of general insurance provides otherwise.

An insurer is required to notify the insured at least 14 days before the expiry of a renewable general insurance policy whether the insurer is prepared to renew or negotiate to renew the cover (s 58, IC Act). However, if the insurer fails to provide the renewal notice within the prescribed time, then the cover is extended under a 'statutory policy' for a period equal to a period of cover provided under the original policy (s 58(3)). This means that if the expiring policy had been renewed for a period of 12 months, then the cover under the 'statutory policy' would be equal to 12 months. The insured is not liable for any premium under the 'statutory policy' (s 58(4)) unless a claim is made under the contract. If a claim is made, the premium payable is calculated by the following (s 58(6)):

$$\frac{\text{Period of claim x Hypothetical premium}}{\text{Period of original contract}}$$

where:

Period of claim means the number of days in the period that began on the day on which the contract came into force and ended on the day on which the claim was made.

Hypothetical premium means the premium that would have been charged if the original contract had been renewed.

Period of the original contract means the number of days in the period of the original contract.

If an insurer refuses to renew a contract of insurance or accept an offer to enter into a contract of insurance, it must give written reasons for its refusal if requested in writing by the insured (s. 75(1)). In the case of life insurance, the insurer will need to give the reasons for not accepting the offer, for cancelling the contract, for not renewing the cover or for offering life insurance cover on terms that are less advantageous to the insured than the terms that the insurer would otherwise offer (s. 75(5), IC Act).

Section 210(1) of the *Life Insurance Act 1995* (Cth) prevents an insurer from forfeiting a life insurance policy on which at least three years' premiums have been paid owing to non-payment of a premium, if the surrender value of the policy is greater than the overdue premium.

6-110   Cancellation

The IC Act restricts the rights of insurers to cancel insurance policies. Section 59, on cancellation procedures, requires an insurer who wishes to cancel a contract of insurance to give written notice of the proposed cancellation to the insured.

Section 60 of the IC Act allows an insurance company to cancel a general insurance contract only where the insured:

- fails to comply with the duty of good faith or the duty of disclosure
- made a misrepresentation during the negotiations but before the contract was entered into
- breaches a term of the contract, such as non-payment of the premium

- makes a fraudulent claim under the contract or some other contract of insurance.

Additionally, an insurer may cancel an interim contract of general insurance and a contract extended by s 58 at any time. However, if an insurer attempts to cancel a general insurance contract in breach of s 60, then the action is void (s 63). If an insured has had an insurance contract cancelled by any insurer, then this is a material fact and the insured must disclose this to any prospective insurers. The prior cancellation is such an important event that the insurer must provide the reasons for cancellation in writing if requested by the insured (s 75).

6-120   Renewal

The insurer invites the insured to renew the policy for the coming period by sending the insured a renewal notice. The insured indicates acceptance of this offer by paying the premium before the policy expires, which is generally at 4 pm (but may be another time as stipulated in the policy) on the date of renewal unless arrangements have been made with the insurer to 'hold the policy covered' (generally evidenced by the issue of a cover note) while the cover is being renegotiated or pending the receipt of the premium. On the other hand, life insurance policies are treated as ongoing contracts and are not subject to renewal, so any change in health of the insured (risk) does not have to be reported to the insurer. However, life insurance policies will generally lapse if the premium has not been paid for a period of 30 days after the payment date and if paid after that date a new health declaration will be required before cover recommences.

Because the renewal of a general insurance policy is a new contract, the insured must comply with the duty of disclosure and inform the insurer if the risk has altered (s 21, IC Act). This duty is generally printed on or attached to the renewal notice, and if the insurer does not advise the insured of their duty then the insurer may lose its rights in the event of non-disclosure by the insured, unless the non-disclosure was fraudulent (s 22, IC Act).

Acceptance of the insurer's offer generally takes place when the insured posts the renewal premium, not when it is received by the insurer. However, in order to overcome this restriction, insurers generally include a clause that specifies that they are not on risk until the premium is 'actually received'. Insurance brokers act as agents for the insured so if an insured notifies their broker of their intention to renew by paying the premium to the broker, this is not considered a notification to the insurer (s 14(2), IC Act), although there are generally limited 'held covered' clauses, such as up to 30, 60 or 90 days, in brokers' agreements to give brokers time to 'close' the business to the insurer, that is, advise the insurer that the premium has been paid and send the associated paperwork, such as proposal forms to the insurer. If a claim occurs before the insurer is paid in accordance with the credit terms allowed in the brokers' agreement, the broker is required to not only forward the premium before investigation can commence, they must also show that the premium was actually paid before the occurrence of the claim.

6-130   Return of premium

The insurer will have to pay a refund of their premium if the insured can establish that there was a total failure of consideration in the sense that the risk was never attached. This principle is illustrated in the following vignette.

Case example

Strickland v Turner

(1852) 155 ER 199

Facts: Strickland arranged a life assurance on the life of Turner, but, unknown to either Strickland or the insurance company, Turner was already dead.

Issue: Was Strickland entitled to a refund of premium?

Decision: The court held that Strickland was entitled to a return of premium as the contract was void because the purpose of the contract was absent at the time of making the contract.

If an insurance policy for example, on a home insurance policy, is cancelled before the expiry of the term, then the insurer will generally refund a proportion of the premium to the insured based on the number of days on risk, less an amount to cover administration charges.

At a glance

- Modern insurance policies generally include terms that:
    - » define the risks covered (insuring clause)
    - » set out the exclusions to the cover (exclusion clauses)
    - » identify the conditions of the cover
    - » define the terms of the insurance and the period of cover.
- The IC Act prescribes standard cover for domestic insurance, but insurers must advise insureds in writing if they offer less cover than the standard.
- Insurers are not permitted by the IC Act to incorporate unusual terms in a policy or rely on a technicality in order to limit their liability.
- Insurers use warranties and conditions in their policies to reduce the possibility of an increase in risk after the policy is issued.
- Insurers are permitted to cancel contracts of general insurance under prescribed circumstances
- The renewal of a general insurance policy creates a new contract and insureds must disclose any material change in the risk

6-140 Study questions

6.1 Discuss the purpose of a cover note in a contract of general insurance.

6.2 'When an insurer provides a proposal form to an intending insured, the insurer is making an offer to that person.' Is this statement correct? If so, why? If not, why not?

6.3 Explain the purpose of an insurance proposal.

6.4 Why is it important for both the insured and the insurer to know when a contract of insurance is concluded?

6.5   What is the purpose and effect of warranties and clauses contained in an insurance contract? Include any legislative provisions that might restrict their effectiveness.

6.6   'A contract of general insurance is regarded as "guaranteed" to be renewed by the insurer on the same terms as when the policy was issued.' Discuss this statement and include any obligations that the insured may have in relation to the renewal.

6.7   Explain the circumstances in which an insurer can cancel an insurance policy.

6.8   Lauren pays her broker the premium due on her home and contents insurance policy on the day that it is due. The renewal notice states that the cover expires at 12pm on that day and Lauren is concerned that her insurance policy will lapse since she has not paid the premium to the insurance company. Discuss Lauren's concern in relation to the broker's obligations for arranging renewal for her policy.

6.9   Margaret has obtained a cover note on 1 March 2013 from her agent of Reliable Insurance Company Pty Ltd on the contents her hair salon for $25,000, which includes public liability cover for $20 million. It is now 28 March and the building housing her salon is destroyed by fire resulting in a total loss of her contents. Margaret is concerned that she will not be covered for this loss. Discuss her concerns and give her advice on the position of her insurance coverage.

6.10   When Ralph completed an insurance proposal on his motor cycle dealership, he stated that a functioning back to base alarm system was installed on the premises. Eight months later, the business was burgled and he subsequently submitted a claim to his insurance company for $200 000. Discuss the options the insurance company has in relation to paying this claim.

6-150   References and further reading

References

Business Dictionary (n.d.). http://www.businessdictionary.com/definition/common-law.html#ixzz41B3zuU71.

CHAPTER 7

CLAIMS

CLAIMS

7-000   Introduction

The procedure for making a claim usually starts with the insured advising the insurer by telephone. This is followed by the submission of a claim form either directly by the insured or via their insurance broker. In many instances, the insurer will appoint an insurance assessor to 'adjust' the claim. This is done by the assessor investigating the circumstances of the loss or damage to ensure that the claim is covered by the policy.

Upon receipt of the assessor's report, the insurer either accepts or rejects the claim. If the insurer accepts the claim, a document called a 'release' is prepared for the insured to sign. This release contains the details of settlement; it releases both parties from further liability in respect of the claim. Section 13 of the *Insurance Contracts Act 1984* (Cth) (IC Act) requires that both parties act with the utmost good faith during the making and settlement of claims, and if one party deliberately conceals material information during the settlement negotiations, the settlement is unenforceable.

7-010   Claim notification

Insurance policies generally require that the insurer is notified of a loss within a specified time, such as 'promptly', 'immediately' or within a stipulated number of days. This notification is required to be made in writing and to contain the details of any proceedings being taken against the insured.

This notice of loss allows the insurer to begin investigating the loss and to commence proceedings to reduce their loss, such as bringing litigation against negligent third parties or arranging for salvage.

Under common law, insurers in the past have relied on the notice of loss clauses to deny otherwise legitimate claims. Section 54 of the IC Act allows insurers to reduce the amount of the claim by the amount of prejudice they have suffered, which will generally be the extra costs incurred because of any delay in notification of the claim, such as an increase in repair costs.

7-020   Proof of loss

In addition to the notice of loss clauses, most policies contain further clauses requiring insureds to provide 'satisfactory' proof of loss. A 'proof of loss' clause may be a condition precedent to the insured's right to recover under the policy. The object of these clauses is to enable the insurers to fully assess the claim by instructing an assessor and/or an investigator to fully investigate (adjust) the claim and decide on the appropriate action. What is considered 'satisfactory' is the type of proof that would be required by an insurer acting reasonably.

If an insured does not comply with an unreasonable request by an insurer for proof of loss, this will not prevent the insured from recovering under the policy. For example, if an insurer attempted to force an insured to provide more information than was required under the policy, therefore acting unreasonably, the courts should provide protection for the insured. Such an action might also be a breach of the insurer's duty to act with the utmost good faith implied in every contract of insurance by s 13 of the IC Act. In addition, s 54 of the IC Act may also protect the insured.

7-030   Onus of proof

Once the insured has established that the loss or damage has occurred — eg, in the case of liability insurance, that there is a liability in damages to a third party — it is then necessary to show that the loss, damage or liability is covered by the policy. Equally, it is a matter for the insurer to prove the operation of an exception, should it wish to dispute liability. Where an insured wishes to claim that only part of the loss falls within the exception, the burden of proof falls back on them.

The onus is on the insured to prove, on the balance of probabilities that the loss falls within the terms of the policy. The insured is required to show that the event in question caused the loss, or was a *proximate cause* of the loss. Proximate cause means the active, efficient motion that sets in motion a train of events, which brings about a result, without the intervention of any force started and working actively from a new and independent source (*Pawsey & Co v Scottish Union & National Insurance Co* (1908) (The Times, 17 October 1908, Privy Council)).

In order for an event to be the proximate cause, it must be the 'dominant', 'real' or 'effective' cause (*Wayne Tank & Pump Co Ltd v Employers' Liability Assurance Corporation Ltd* [1974] 1 QB 57). It need not be the first or the last cause, but it is the dominant cause (*Leyland Shipping Co Ltd v Norwich Union Fire Insurance Society Ltd* [1918] AC 350).

Frequently a chain of events or causes, rather than a single cause, leads to a loss. It is necessary to examine this chain to determine the proximate cause and whether it is excluded from cover or not. If an insured peril operates and directly gives rise to the loss, then it will be covered, provided there was no excepted peril that effectively or dominantly interrupted the chain of events.

On the other hand, the final loss need not be the consequence of an insured peril, provided the cause of loss was proximately initiated by an insured peril. For example, fire policies make no mention of water or smoke damage, but provided that the cause of the fire is not an excepted peril, all losses resulting from water or smoke that frequently follow the intervention of the fire services are deemed to be fire damage.

The perils that must be considered can be classified under three headings:

- *Insured perils:* those named in the policy as insured
- *Excepted perils:* those named in the policy as excluded, either as causes of insured perils or as results or consequences of insured perils
- *Other perils:* those that are not mentioned at all in the policy but may form part of a chain of events leading to the loss.

New cause

Sometimes a new cause (or remote cause) starts to operate independent of, and subsequent to, the peril insured against and it is difficult to say with certainty what were the relevant roles that each played in bringing about the loss. This is particularly so when a period of time elapses between the original cause and the new cause. The following two cases illustrate whether a new cause can be considered as the proximate cause of the loss:

In *Roth v South Easthope Farmers' Mutual Insurance Co* (1918) 44 OLR 186, lightning damaged a building and weakened a wall. Within a matter of hours the weakened wall was blown down by high winds. Lightning was considered to be the proximate cause.

In *Gaskarth v Law Union Insurance Co* (1876), fire damaged a gable wall and weakened it. Several days later a gale blew down the weakened wall. It was held that fire was not the proximate cause.

The crucial distinction between the two cases is the length of time that passed before the new cause occurred.

The loss claimed under an insurance policy must be caused by a risk insured against. Insurance law asks what was the proximate cause (ie the dominant , effective) (discussed below) of the loss:

- If there are two proximate causes of the damage both of which are covered by the policy then the insurer will be liable.

- If there are two proximate causes of the damage with one covered by the policy and one excluded by the policy then the insurer is able to rely on the exclusion.

Once the insured has proven that the cause of loss is covered by the policy, the onus is on the insurer to prove a breach of the policy by the insured. However, under s 54 of the IC Act, the onus is on the insured to prove that an act or omission that breaches the warranty or another term of the contract does not cause or contribute to the loss, whether wholly or partly.

Proximate cause application rules

The rules for the application of proximate cause include the following:

- The risk insured against must actually take place. The fear of losing goods by an insured peril is not loss by that peril (*Moore v Evans* [1918] AC 185).

- Further damage to the subject matter due to attempts to minimise a loss that has already taken place is covered. Therefore, water damage from sprinklers or fire hoses is covered (*Johnston v West of Scotland Insurance Co* (1828) 7 S 52).

- If a new cause intervenes, the resultant loss is not covered. Thus, if during a fire onlookers cause damage to surrounding property, the cause of the damage is the misdemeanour of the crowd and not the fire (*Marsden v City & County Assurance Co* (1865) LR 1 CP 232).

- In instances where the original peril has meant that loss was more or less inevitable, the original peril will be the proximate cause even though the last straw comes from another source ('last straw' cases) (*Leyland Shipping Co Ltd v Norwich Union* [1918] AC 350). The decision in the *Leyland Shipping* case settled the question in insurance law that the 'cause' is that which is the effective or dominant cause, as illustrated below.

Case example

Leyland Shipping Co Ltd v Norwich Union Fire Insurance Society Ltd

1918] AC 350

Facts: The *Ikaria* was insured against loss from perils of the sea, but not from war. During the First World War the ship was hit by a torpedo, which blew a hole in its side and damaged the bulkheads. The vessel was towed into a safe harbour where a gale subsequently caused the ship to bump against the harbour wall. The harbour authorities feared that the vessel would damage the harbour and ordered the ship's removal into the open sea, where it grounded at each low tide. After two days of this buffeting the bulkheads failed and the ship sank.

Issue: Were the owners of the *Ikaria* entitled to indemnity under their 'perils of the sea' policy?

Decision: The insurer was not liable, as the House of Lords took the view that the proximate cause of the loss was the torpedo, not the subsequent buffeting caused by the grounding. The impact of the torpedo meant that it was reasonably certain that sea water would flow into the ship and this is what happened, even if the extent of the damage caused might not have been expected.

(*Note*: If, on the other hand, as it was being towed out to sea, the *Ikaria* had sunk following a collision that had resulted from the negligence of the crew, then although the ship might not have been navigating out of the harbour had it not been for the torpedo, that event would no longer have been operating and the loss would have been proximately caused by the negligence.)

7-040   Liability insurance

Liability insurance policies provide cover for:

- events that occurred during the policy period, as documented in the 'occurrence wording'. These policies will allow a claim in respect of those events to be made after the insurance has expired. For example, public or personal liability policies may contain wording along the lines of '... the insurer will pay a claim for legal liability if the event that gives rise to the claim occurs during the period of insurance', or

- claims made against the insured only during the period of insurance, known as 'claims made wording', even though the events that gave rise to the claim occurred before the period of insurance. For example, professional indemnity insurance policies may contain wording along the lines of '... the insurer will pay for loss for which the insured is legally liable to pay on account of any claim made against the insured during the period of cover, *and which is notified to the insurer during the period of cover* (italic added)'.

Section 40(3) of the IC Act provides that where an insured advises the insurer in writing of the facts that might result in a claim, the insurer may be liable for the claim even though the actual claim on the policy by the insured was **not** made until after the policy expired.

In *Newcastle City Council v GIO General Ltd* [1997] HCA 53; (1997) 9 ANZ Insurance Cases 61-380, the insured advised its professional indemnity insurer in writing about facts that had occurred during the policy period and had the potential to result in claims before the policy expired as permitted by s 40(3). The High Court confirmed that s 40(3) applies to all 'claims made' policies and that the insured was able to make claims for fatalities, personal injuries and property damage outside the policy period.

A different situation would apply if a policy is a 'claims made and notified' policy. Under the terms of these policies, cover is limited to claims made and notified to the insurer during the period of insurance. The insured must not have had any prior knowledge of the fact, situation or circumstance before the period of insurance.

7-050   Exclusions

As noted in 6-090 exclusion or exception clauses are important in insurance policies, with some being common to most insurance policies for example, those excluding cover for claims arising from events, such as 'war, riots, civil commotion and radiation'. Other exclusion clauses will relate specifically to the type of cover provided by the policy.

The burden of proof that the loss falls within an exclusion clause lies with the insurer, although this can be modified by the express terms of the policy. The following case example illustrates how exclusion clauses contained in a professional indemnity policy can deny an insurance claim.

Case example

McCann v Switzerland Insurance Australia Ltd

[2000] HCA 65; (2001) 11 ANZ Insurance Cases 61-479

A law firm submitted a claim to their insurers under their professional indemnity policy. The claim was rejected on the grounds that one of the partners had committed fraud by accepting secret profits and commissions. These actions by the partner violated a policy exclusion stating that the insurer "shall not indemnify the Assured in respect of any liability ... brought about by the dishonest or fraudulent act or omission of the Assured". The other partners could not claim under the policy even though they did not know about the fraud.

Even where an exclusion clause does apply and a claim is defeated, as in *McCann*, the policy continues in force. In other instances, a policy may suspend indemnity if, for example, a house is left without an occupant for a period in excess of 60 days.

When deciding whether a claim can be rejected by reason of an exclusion, an insurer must be aware that the IC Act and other statutes now restrict the operation of exclusion clauses:

- If standard cover applies, the use of exclusions and limitations is limited if the insurer failed to draw the insured's attention to any unusual terms contained in the policy (ss 35; 37).

- If an exclusion states that the insurer will not be liable for some act or omission of the insured or third party, the insurer will not be able to refuse to pay a claim if this does not cause or contribute to the loss (s 54).

- If an insured fails to pay the premium on an instalment contract of general insurance, then the insurer cannot limit its liability under the policy through non-payment unless one instalment remains unpaid for at least 14 days and the insured was advised in writing of the effect of this provision before the contract was entered into (s 39).

- An insurer cannot rely on an exclusion relating to the existence of a pre-existing defect or imperfection in the insured property or a pre-existing sickness or disability of the insured, if the insured was not aware of this when the contract was entered into (ss 46; 47).

- The *Terrorism Insurance Act 2003* (Cth) prohibits an insurer from relying on a terrorism exclusion to avoid paying a claim for 'an eligible terrorism loss' caused by a terrorist act. A 'terrorist act' includes an act that causes serious physical harm to a person or serious damage to property (s 9(4)).

- Under the *Competition and Consumer Act 2010* (Cth) a claim made under a product liability or product recall insurance by a supplier of goods is not affected if the supplier provides information to the relevant authorities about goods supplied or proposed to be supplied.

- Most Australian states have insurance Acts that restrict the use of exclusion clauses. For example, in New South Wales, s 18B of the *Insurance Act 1902* (NSW) restricts an insurer from relying on a clause in an insurance contract that limits or excludes liability for losses caused or contributed to by factors not mentioned in that clause of the contract, unless it is not reasonable for the insurer to indemnify the insured.

While exclusion clauses are included in insurance contracts to restrict an expansion of an insurer's liability, s 54 of the IC Act prevents insurers from refusing to pay claims in certain circumstances. For example, a typical exclusion clause in a motor vehicle policy excludes cover for 'loss or damage caused by using the vehicle in either practising for or taking part in any race, time trial, rally, sprint or drag race, or similar motor sport event, demonstration, or test'. This clause excludes cover for loss whenever the insured uses the car in a drag race, even where the use of the car in that manner did not cause the loss. Even if the loss was caused by a gum nut falling from a tree and breaking the windscreen, the insurer would deny liability if the car was being used as described above. This exclusion provides protection for the insurer but is harsh on the insured.

Section 54 of the IC Act prevents an insurer from relying on a technicality to refuse to pay an otherwise valid claim. Under s 54 the insurer is able to reduce the claim by an amount that represents the extent to which the insurer's interests were prejudiced by the insured's breach (s 54(1)), or refuse to pay if the insured's breach caused or contributed to the loss (s 54(2)). Therefore, in the above example the use of the insured vehicle in a race did not contribute to the loss, so the insurer could not refuse the claim. However, if the car crashed during the race, the insurer could refuse a claim under s 54(2). The following case illustrates the application of s 54 of the IC Act.

Case example

Ferrcom Pty Ltd v Commercial Union Assurance Company of Australia Ltd

[1993] HCA 5; (1993) 7 ANZ Insurance Cases 61-156

The insured arranged insurance on a crane under an unregistered mobile machinery policy. The fact that the crane was registered was a breach of the policy condition requiring notice. Because the insurer was able to show that it would not have insured the crane if it had known it was registered, it was able to reduce the amount of its liability to the insured by the amount of the prejudice, which was 100 per cent, ie, the amount of the claim was reduced to nil.

7-060   Fraudulent claims

Insurance fraud is a major problem for insurers worldwide. KPMG's *2012 General Insurance Survey* reports on the degree of fraud in the insurance industry and has found that insurance companies are second only to banks as the main targets for fraud. KPMG labelled the insurance industry a "prime target for fraud" (p 16).

In the insurance industry, the term 'insurance fraud' is "most often associated with some form of manipulation of an insurance claim in order to obtain a financial advantage" (KPMG 2012, p.16), which in some instances, involves fabricating the entire claim including, or deliberately causing damage to the insured property. The KPMG report states that the most common form of fraud in Australia is "the aggregation of personal claims" (p16), rather than claims which have been entirely fabricated. Fraud costs the insurance industry $2 billion annually and it is estimated that this adds around $75 to each insurance policy.

The extent of insurance fraud can be shown in the following example given in the KPMG report.

> "A good example of how improved processes can lead to better fraud detection is a case involving a United Kingdom insurer, who introduced a Conversation Management process for claims under £1,500 for a 6 month trial. During the trial 49 per cent of claims were referred for further investigation, 27 per cent were withdrawn and 9 per cent were reduced significantly. Prior to this the insurer concerned paid almost 100 per cent of claims" (p 17).

It was established in Chapter 5 that the duty of good faith governs insurance contracts both at common law and under the IC Act. This duty is equally important in the making of a claim. The term 'fraud' is not defined in the IC Act but at common law it is defined as follows:

A false claim is fraudulent if it is made:

(a)   knowingly

(b)   without belief in its truth or recklessly, or

(c)   without care whether it be true or false.

In *Norton v Royal Fire & Life Assurance Co* (1885) 1 TLR 460, 461, Lord Coleridge LCJ judged a claim fraudulent if there was "... an intention to deceive and defraud the company by getting out of [it] money [the insured] knew [he/

she] had no right to". Thus, in *Engel v South British Insurance Co Ltd* (1983) 2 ANZ Insurances Cases 60-516, the insured falsely included items worth $1,437 in a claim worth $17,524; and the claim was fraudulent. Under common law, the insurer is entitled to avoid the entire claim even though only part of it was made fraudulently.

Section 56 of the IC Act denies an insurer the right to avoid a contract from inception as a result of a fraudulent claim, but the insurer is entitled not to pay the whole of the claim and to cancel the contract of insurance under s 60(1)(e). Section 56(2) limits the right of an insurer to refuse payment, as an insured can approach a court seeking an order that non-payment of the claim in whole would be harsh and unfair. The insured would be required to prove that 'only a minimal or insignificant part' of the claim was made fraudulently and non-payment of the remainder of the claim would be harsh and unfair, and seek an order that the insurer pay the claim having regard to any prejudice suffered by the insurer. The following case illustrates the operation of s 52(2) of the IC Act.

Case example

Tiep Thi To v Australian Associated Motor Insurers Ltd

[2001] VSCA 48; (2001) 11 ANZ Insurance Cases 61-490

Facts: Tiep Thi To's 15-year-old son damaged her car while driving it without her knowledge. To wrongly believed her insurance would not cover the claim, so she lied to the insurer about the cause of the damage, which she falsely claimed was damaged when her son was attacked by a gang of youths who stole the car.

Issue: Was the insurer entitled to deny liability under s 56 of the IC Act?

Decision: The insurer was entitled to reject the claim for fraud.

Insurance fraud hotline

Some individuals see nothing wrong with defrauding their insurance company and claim that it is a victimless crime. However, this is not the case because as mentioned above, insurance fraud is adding an additional $75 to every insurance policy. As many insureds hold multiple policies the cost can be substantial, so it is in the community's interest for its citizens to report instances of insurance fraud.

The Insurance Council of Australia established the Fraud Bureau of Australia to allow citizens to securely report instances of insurance fraud. Further information can be found on their website at *http://ifba.org.au/*.

7-070　Loss by own act

The basic purpose of insurance is to indemnify insureds for losses caused by fortuitous and unexpected events. Indeed, the very principle of the pooling of losses, the ability of losses to be calculable and the ability of an insurer to strike an economically viable premium, as discussed in Chapter 3, relies on the fortuitous presumption.

If an insured causes a loss with the intention of making a claim, then they will be denied the right to recover under common law and under the statutory duty of good faith imposed by s 13 of the IC Act. For example, if an insured deliberately sets fire to their house in order to recover from their insurance policy, such a claim will be fraudulent and will not be admissible under the policy. This principle does not arise from public policy of illegality, but simply from the construction of the contract.

In the case of life insurance, s 120 of the *Life Insurance Act 1995* (Cth) provides that a policy cannot be avoided if a person commits suicide. Most life insurance policies allow for payment in the event of death resulting from suicide if death occurs later than 12 months after the inception of the policy.

Fraud and the innocent co-insured

The principles surrounding the application of common law and the duty of good faith in relation to fraudulent claims raises an ethical dilemma when considering claims lodged by innocent co-insured policyholders. This arises where the husband and wife hold a joint policy and one party (frequently, the husband) commits a fraudulent act, such as burning down the family home following a relationship breakdown. The wife then makes a claim on the insurance policy. This begs the question – should she be indemnified either in full, or in part, under the policy? The traditional approach, for a joint insurance policy allows for the wrongdoing of a co-insured to preclude a claim by the innocent co-insured because the fraudulent act of one will taint the whole contract including the innocent party's interests. This approach argues that to allow a claim in relation to jointly held property to succeed would allow the party in default to indirectly benefit.

In contrast to the traditional approach, some jurisdictions are beginning to adopt a more modern approach where the Courts are more willing to sever joint insurance policies. This approach has been adopted by some states in the United States, Canada, New Zealand and Australia. In a 1998 Tasmanian case, (*Advance (NSW) Insurance Agencies Pty Ltd v Matthews* (1989) 5 ANZ Insurance Cases 60-910), the Court held that the insurance contract was composite (ie, a single contract that embodies insurance in favour of more than one insured, whose interests are different and each insured can have a separate and distinct claim) rather than a joint policy in accordance with the social reality of the situation. Although this decision does not bind all states, it is nevertheless persuasive.

7-080   Criminal and illegal acts

Under common law, no one is permitted to benefit from their own criminal act. However, a claim may still be successful if the loss was the unintentional outcome of the unlawful act. A court would consider whether it would be contrary to public policy to allow the insured to be indemnified for the consequences of their own act. Other factors that would be considered would be the duty of utmost good faith (s 13, IC Act), the seriousness of the offence and public interest.

7-090   Interest on claims

In some circumstances the insurer will be required to pay interest on claims from the day from which it was unreasonable for the insurer to have withheld payment (s 57, IC Act). There are often delays in paying claims, some of which occur because of inadvertence, administrative errors or "the general practice of the particular insurer", which can cause inconvenience and financial loss to insureds. The rate of interest (ALRC Report No 20 1982, p 197) payable by an insurer is the 10-year Treasury bond yield plus three per cent (reg 32, Insurance Contracts Regulations 1985).

7-100   Third party interests

The insurable interests of third parties who are not the insured named in the contract, such as lessees of premises or mortgagees who have a charge over a property as security for a loan are discussed above. In addition, there are other persons who can claim on an insurance policy because their interests are noted on a policy as an insured or because they are a class of persons who are entitled to claim a benefit under a policy, even though they are not a party to the contract. These may include persons driving an insured's vehicle with the consent of the insured, members of an insured's family who ordinarily reside with the insured (in respect of contents insurance) or a person who is nominated as a beneficiary under a disability or personal accident policy.

Under common law, only a contracting party can take action to enforce a contract. Therefore, persons who are not parties to a contract of insurance, but who may be entitled to the benefit under an insurance contract, would be precluded from forcing any entitlement against an insurer. Section 48 of the IC Act allows third parties who are not parties to a contract of general insurance the right to recover from the insurer, in accordance with the contract, the amount of any loss suffered by the third party beneficiary even though the third party beneficiary is not a party to the contract.

A similar provision applies to life insurance contracts under sections 48AA and 48A which grants this right for life insurance to the extent that the contract is expressed to be for the benefit of a third party beneficiary (who may be the life insured). Section 48A(1)(b) states that if the third party beneficiary is not the life insured, any money paid to the third party beneficiary under the contract does not form part of the estate of the life insured. When bringing a claim against the insurer, the third party beneficiary has the same obligations as the insured, which includes the principle of utmost good faith (s 48A(2)).

These obligations mean that an insurer may raise any defences to a general insurance or life insurance claim that relates to the conduct of the insured, which includes conduct that occurred before the contract was entered into (eg non-disclosure and/or misrepresentation).

A motor vehicle policy will often provide insurance cover for any person driving the insured's vehicle with the insured's consent. Likewise, contents insurance is usually extended to cover property owned by members of the insured's family who ordinarily reside with the insured or with whom the insured ordinarily resides. Such persons are not named as insureds, nor are their interests referred to by name.

70-110 Arbitration and complaints

Insurance policies generally contain clauses making the arbitration of disputes compulsory, although these clauses are rendered ineffective by s 43 of the IC Act. Section 43(2) allows the parties to agree after a dispute has arisen to submit the dispute to arbitration. In addition, it is possible to have a dispute heard by the Small Claims Tribunal.

It is a requirement of the *Corporations Act 2001* (Cth) for Australian financial services licensees that when services are provided to retail clients, they have an internal dispute resolution system (IDR) and are a member of one or more external dispute systems (s 912A(1)(g) and (2)). Complaints resolution schemes are discussed in later chapters.

At a glance

- Insureds must advise their insurer about their intention to claim as soon as practicable.

- The onus is on the insured to prove that the loss falls within the terms of the policy and for the insurer to prove that the claim fails because of the operation of a policy exclusion.

- The concept of proximate cause is used to determine the cause of the loss.

- Insurance policies contain exclusion clauses, which limit the insurer's liability under the policy.

- In order for a claim to be successful, insureds must comply with policy conditions such as not admitting liability following a motor vehicle accident.

- Insureds have access to internal dispute resolutions procedures.

MEASUREMENT OF LOSS

7-120   Introduction

Once it has been established that the loss in question is covered by the terms of the policy, the insured will be required to quantify their loss.

7-130   Quantifying the loss

The principle of indemnity requires the insured to be fully compensated for the loss within the maximum sum insured during the currency of the policy. This will restrict the company's maximum liability even if the value of the property or reinstatement costs is greater than the sum insured. The aim is to put the insured back in the position they occupied before the loss occurred. It is not intended that the insured make a profit from the loss. Establishing the loss is the cause of a large number of disputes between insurers and insureds (ALRC Report No 20 1982, Chapter 13). These disputes are often compounded by the absence of detailed records and by unrealistic valuations. In all cases, the outcome will depend upon the relevant policy wording and the circumstances of the loss.

Where the insured suffers a total loss of property or goods, the measurement of loss will be the market value of the property or goods at the time and place of the loss. For example, if a house is destroyed by a peril such as fire and the house was actually for sale at a price of $250,000, the current market value of the house for insurance purposes would be the sale price less the value of the land. Again, the true measure of the loss of a motor vehicle that was undergoing repairs is likely to be its value immediately before the loss less the value of the repairs already completed, as determined in *Dean v J Thomas & Son* (1980) 1 ANZ insurance Cases 60-402. The following case example illustrates the difficulty of determining the market value of machinery in a commercial claim.

Case example

Fire & All Risks Insurance Co Ltd v Rousianos

(1989) 19 ANZ Insurance Cases 60-909; 19 NSWLR 57

Facts: Rousianos owned a car washing pant and insured the machinery and plant with Fire & All Risks Insurance Co Ltd (FAI) against fire for $44,000. A fire damaged the machinery and plant and a claim was lodged with FAI, which included $35,000 for an automatic washer/dryer. However, FAI only valued this item at between $2,000 and $5,000.

Issue: What was the real value of the automatic washer/dryer?

Decision: The court applied the 'market value' test for an equivalent machine and allowed $15,000 for this item, plus $7,000 for freight and installation plus interest.

The principle of indemnity is contractual and is set out in the terms and conditions of the policy itself. Many policies provide the insurer with the option to reinstate, repair or replace the property damaged or destroyed instead of paying the insured the amount of the loss or damage. However, if the insurer does not reinstate, repair or replace, it must indemnify the insured (pay money).

Reinstatement means the replacement or restoration of property to its condition before the loss. In the event of a total loss, reinstatement would mean rebuilding the property as new, or if goods, replacing them with equivalent goods, or repairing them. Once an insurer elects to reinstate, it must do so within a reasonable time and cannot withdraw the election, because the policy becomes a contract to reinstate and not a fresh contract. The insurer must continue with the reinstatement even though the cost of reinstatement is more than expected at the time of the election. This could conceivably occur if the building is further damaged in the course of reinstatement, such as during a storm or by a second fire.

Extra costs could be incurred when the reinstatement becomes subject to changes in city council building codes, as occurred with the Newcastle City Council following an earthquake in December 1989. In *Lumley General Insurance Ltd v Vintix Pty Ltd* (1991) 6 ANZ Insurance Cases 61-087, the NSW Court of Appeal held that the sum of $231,000 was necessary to comply with the new Council earthquake code and should be borne by the insurer.

Generally, insurance policies require that the reinstatement be made on the same site as the property destroyed, while other policies allow insureds to rebuild at a different site.

Life and accident insurance policies

In the case of a life policy, the sum insured specified in the policy determines the amount payable by the policy. However, with accident policies the economic loss sustained by the insured is calculated by referring to lost income, medical bills, set amounts detailed in the policy for specified injuries or sickness and, in the case of residual injuries, the levels of damages awarded by the courts.

Legal liability policies

The amount that an insured can recover is the amount of their liability at law to the third party but restricted to the limit of liabiliheir liability at law, but restricted to njuries the levels of damages awarded by the courts.while other polty under the policy.

Valued policies

Valued policies are an exception to the indemnity principle and as discussed in chapter 5, the insured can recover the sum insured under a valued policy irrespective of the insured's loss at the time. In most cases, the calculation of agreed value will be based on the value declared by the insured in the proposal. This declaration often leads to disputes when motor vehicles are insured, and at common law a breach of a warranty of value will allow the insurer to void the policy if the stated value is inaccurate at the time. The following case example illustrates the importance of correctly valuing the property to be insured under common law.

Case example

Hajjar v. NRMA Insurance Limited

(1985) 3 ANZ Insurance Cases 60-647

Facts: The insured bought a car for $1,200 and spent an extra $1,300 on improvements. After the improvements were completed he filled out a proposal form declaring that the purchase price of the car was $2,500. The insurer issued a policy which stated that the purchase price was $2,500. Shortly afterwards, the car was stolen, but the insurer refused to meet the insured's claim under the policy, asserting that the policy was void because of the misrepresentation in the proposal as to the purchase price of the car. (*Note:* this case predated the IC Act.)

Issue: Is the policy void because of this misstatement of purchase price?

Decision: The New South Wales Court of Appeal found for the insurer. Priestley JA held the purchase price of the car determined the agreed value between the insurer and insured.

The ability of an insurer to void a policy on the basis of a misstatement is now modified by s 54 of the IC Act. If an insured breaches a warranty of value, the insurer is allowed to reduce the amount of the claim only by the amount by which their interests have been prejudiced. Therefore, in *Hajjar* above, under s 54 the amount of the claim would have been reduced to the actual purchase price of $1,200 and the insurer would not have been allowed to void the policy. However, if the misrepresentation as to value is wrong, it will not be held to be wrong if the insured reasonably believes it to be true (s 26(1), IC Act).

If there is only a partial loss, the amount recoverable will be worked out using the following formula (unless there is an average clause):

$$\frac{(\text{Value before the loss} - \text{Value after the loss}) \times \text{Value state in the policy}}{\text{Value before the loss}}$$

The following example shows the operation of this formula.

> The insured had a valued policy over certain buildings with an agreed value of £106,850. There was a partial loss and the insurer established that the market value of the damaged premises was £18,000 and that its value after the fire was £12,600. The court applied the above formula to give the insured £32,055.

7-140   Underinsurance

Some general insurance policies contain 'average' or 'co-insurance' clauses to protect insurers from the economic effects of underinsurance. Most domestic insurance no longer contains an average or co-insurance clause. However, the principles of averaging still need to be understood as this clause still appears in most small business insurance policies.

Under an average clause, only those insureds whose property has been totally destroyed will be fully indemnified. Where an insured has underinsured and the loss is partial, the insured bears a pro-rata proportion of any loss, which is calculated by using the following formula:

$$\frac{\text{Policy value}}{\text{Value of subject matter}} \times \text{Amount of loss}$$

Therefore, the insured becomes a self-insurer not only for the shortfall in the policy over the amount of the loss but also for an additional amount equalling the proportion that the shortfall bears to the total value. Where averaging applies, the insured will be paid less than the amount of the actual loss.

However, the insurer can rely on an average provision only if, before the contract was entered into, the insurer clearly informed the insured in writing of the nature and effect of the provision (s 44(1), IC Act). The following illustrated example shows the application of averaging in a commercial situation.

Illustrated example 7.1

Stock in a shop is insured for $200,000 and the policy is 'subject to average'. A fire breaks out and causes $50,000 worth of damage to the stock. On investigation, it is found that the actual value of the stock was $400,000. The amount that the insurer will pay is calculated as follows:

$$\frac{\$200,000}{\$400,000} \times \$50,000$$

$= \$25,000$ is payable by the insurer

In the case of homeowners, some relief is granted by s 44 of the IC Act, as it is difficult to accurately assess the true value of property, particularly as inflation and rising property values can lead to underinsurance. In the case of householders and houseowners insurance, where the building insured is used as a residence by the insured and/or persons with whom the insured has a family or personal relationship, an average clause will not apply if the sum insured is 80 per cent or more of the value of the insured property at the date of the contract (s 44(2); (4)).

If the sum insured is less than 80 per cent of the value, then the average clause will operate to allow the insurer to reduce the claim. The reduced amount is calculated by the following formula, as detailed in s 44(3) of the IC Act:

$$" \qquad \frac{AS}{P}$$

where:

A is the number of dollars equal to the amount of the loss or damage;

S is the amount of the sum insured under the contract in respect to the property; and

P is 80%of the number of dollars equal to the value of the property"

Section 44(4) of the IC Act specifies that the value of the property means that where a contract insures for the indemnity value of the property, or its reinstatement or replacement value of the property, the value to be adjusted is the value when the contract was entered into, rather than at the date of the commencement of the period of insurance or the date of the loss.

Application of averaging for a residence

The following illustrated examples show the application of the 80 per cent % rule.

Illustrated example 7.2

Insured value less than 80 per cent

If an insured house is valued at $300,000 but is insured for only $200,000, then the sum insured is less than 80 per cent of the full value. If the house is damaged by an insured peril to the value of $120,000 and the contract contained an average clause, then the insured would be able to recover:

Step 1
$$\frac{\$200,000}{80\% \text{ of } \$300,000} \quad X \quad \$120,000$$

Step 2
$$\frac{\$200,000}{\$240,000} \quad X \quad \$120,000$$

Step 3
$$\frac{10}{12} \quad X \quad \$120,000 = \$100,000$$

Insured value above 80 per cent

If the house is valued at $300,000 and is insured for $280,000 and the damage is

$30,000, even if the policy contained an averaging clause, the amount the insured would receive would be $30,000. The averaging clause would not apply because the house was insured within 20 per cent of the full value (in this case 93 per cent of full value).

7-150   Ex gratia payments

Ex gratia payments are voluntary payments made by the insurer in response to a loss for which it is not technically liable under the terms of its policy and are not an admission of liability. When an insurer makes an ex gratia payment, the insured must grant the insurer a release from all liability under the policy. The purpose of an ex gratia payment is to avoid expensive litigation and bad publicity or in some cases to preserve the business of a valued client.

7-160   'Double' or 'other' insurance

As discussed above, an insured may have more than one insurance policy covering the same subject matter. However, the insured cannot recover more than the amount of the actual loss, regardless of the number of policies held.

Some policies may contain a 'double' or 'other' insurance clause, which states that if the insured does not advise the insurer of all existing and later insurance on the same subject matter before any loss occurs, then all benefits under the policy are forfeited. However, s 45 provides that 'other insurance' clauses do not apply to excess policies or compulsory insurance such as workers compensation or third party motor vehicle insurance. An excess policy is a policy that pays benefits only when coverage under other applicable policies has been exhausted. For example, in some large businesses' insurance programs they may carry $50 million liability cover with their primary insurer and a further $50 million excess cover with a specialist liability insurer.

7-170   Contribution

Section 76 of the IC Act confirms the common law position that where one insurer indemnifies an insured in whole or in part, the insurer is entitled to recover a contribution at common law or in equity from any other insurer who insures the same property. Section 45 makes void such provisions that have the effect of limiting or excluding an insurer's liability if there is other insurance, except in an excess policy or if the other insurance is compulsory, such as workers compensation insurance or third party motor insurance.

> **At a glance**
>
> - The principle of indemnity applies to insured general insurance losses.
>
> - The amount paid by general and life insurance policies is generally limited to the sum insured.
>
> - Co-insurance applies to under insurance but generally only applies to business policies.
>
> - Contribution to a loss applies if more than one insurer insures the same risk.

7-180 Study questions

7.1 An insured must notify their insurer immediately after the happening of the event of their intention to make a claim. If the insured fails to comply with this condition of the contract, the insurer is able to decline their claim.'

Discuss the reasons why an insurer requires early notification of possible claims and any legislative provisions that may impact on the insurer's ability to decline a claim for late notification.

7.2 What is meant by the term *proximate cause*?

7.3 Explain the purpose of including exclusion clauses in an insurance policy. Include a discussion of *onus of proof* in your answer.

7.4 Explain how insurers measure their loss. Include a discussion of *market value* and *reinstatement* in your answer.

7.5 What is an 'averaging' clause and its impact on a general insurance claim? Include examples in your answer.

7.6 Explain the purpose of policy conditions and provide an example.

7.7 Insurance policies often contain endorsements. Explain the purpose of endorsements and provide an example.

7.8 Describe the claims settlement process.

7.9 Insurance fraud is a major problem for insurers in Australia. Discuss the common type of fraudulent claims, the common law remedies available to insurers and any legislative restrictions on their remedies.

7.10 Explain the reasons why losses deliberately caused by the actions of the insured are not covered by their insurance policy.

7-190 References

References

Australian Law Reform Commission (ALRC). *Report 20 — Insurance Contracts 1982*, AGPS, Canberra. Available at *www.austlii.edu.au*

KPMG (2012), 'Fraud in the General Insurance Industry', in *General Insurance Survey,* September, pp1-53. Available at *www.kpmg.com*

CHAPTER 8

INTRODUCTION TO LIFE INSURANCE

INTRODUCTION TO LIFE INSURANCE

8-000   What is life insurance?

The term life insurance is something of a misnomer as in reality people are insuring against the contingency of their untimely death. A life insurance policy is defined in the *Life Insurance Act 1985* (Cth) (LI Act) as an agreement to pay a stated amount of money on the death of the person insured (s 9(1)). This definition includes:

- a lifetime annuity

- a continuous disability policy

- a contract that provides for investment

- an investment-linked contract

Most new life insurance products have an optional risk component. However, a contract is not a life policy if the duration of the contract is not more than one year and the payment is to be made only in the event of death by accident or specified sickness (s 9(2)). This means that accident and sickness policies issued by general insurance companies are not life insurance policies, although they are defined as financial products under the *Corporations Act 2001* (Cth).

A life insurance company is a company that writes life insurance and shares the financial risk among its policyholders (s 11). Friendly societies that carry on life insurance business are required to be registered under the Act and are therefore considered life insurance companies. However, friendly societies also conduct 'non-life' business such as investment products, funeral policies and education policies, which will not be discussed in this text.

A policyholder (policy owner), who may be a different person from the life insured, pays a premium to the insurance company to conclude a valid contract. Fees and charges are then deducted and the remaining amount is invested by the life insurance company. It is this invested amount that enables the life insurance company to meet claims and make a profit. The owner of a life insurance policy has the right to:

- terminate the policy

- receive benefits arising from the policy unless a beneficiary is nominated

- transfer the ownership of the policy to someone else.

8-010   Purpose of life insurance

Life insurance was traditionally designed for the financial protection of families or dependent relatives or to extinguish debt. If a family head had life insurance and died, the insurance company would pay the beneficiaries a lump sum of money. Other life insurance policies, such as sickness or disability policies, provide payments in the form of an income stream for the duration of the impairment, or the benefit period specified in the policy.

Life insurance can be seen as a form of financial protection for the dependants of the insured, to provide for retirement or to protect one's estate or business interest. Its purpose is to provide for the needs of the living and to provide financial protection for the dependants of the deceased. Therefore, life insurance is designed to provide income at a future date or when a specified contingency occurs, such as on the death or disablement of the life insured. Life insurance is now commonly used as an investment product to which risk benefits can be attached.

8-020   General and life insurance compared

Traditional life insurance policies combine elements of both risk protection and savings. For example, whole-of-life policies guarantee the payment of the sum insured on death (the risk protection element) while also providing a share in the insurer's profits by allocating an annual reversionary bonus (the savings element). This inter-relationship between mortality and investment, as well as expenses, is complex, so actuaries are heavily involved in the operation of these policies. In contrast, the more modern investment-linked policies are used as a funds accumulation tool and do not require the same level of actuarial involvement.

As we saw in Chapter 7, general insurance has certain characteristics that distinguish it from life insurance. The principal differences are:

- a general insurer will issue a policy for a limited term, usually one year
- at the end of the term the policy comes due for renewal
- the insurer is not bound to renew, and if the risk is found to be unacceptable, the insurer can decline to renew
- on renewal the insurer can alter the premium and terms of cover
- risk is frequently covered for only the limited period of the policy.

8-030   Insurance or assurance

In the past, the life insurance industry used the term *assurance* when referring to life products because the benefit under the policy was 'assured' if the terms of the policy were complied with. This distinction has fallen into disuse and both 'insurance' and 'assurance' are now used to describe life insurance, although it is often suggested that 'assurance' be used to describe life insurance policies while 'insurance' be used to describe general insurance policies (*National Mutual Life Association of Australasia Ltd v Federal Commissioner of Taxation (1959)* 102 CLR 29).

The extent of financial protection secured through life insurance depends on the terms and conditions of the life policy held by the insured. The needs of insureds vary and insurers have a number of products to cater for these needs.

8-040   Life insurance policies

A life insurance policy is a policy issued on the life of a person (the insured) and owned by the proposer of the policy.

There are four main types of life insurance policies:

- traditional policies (eg, whole-of-life and endowment)
- investment policies (eg, capital-guaranteed and investment-linked)
- risk policies
- annuities.

These policies are explained in more detail later in the chapter.

Product classification

Until the 1980s the most common products offered by life insurance companies were the traditional whole-of-life and endowment policies. These are capital-guaranteed products that are invested in cash and near cash, so the returns tend to be quite low in comparison to modern investment products. The high inflation experienced in the 1970s led to a decline in these products as a far better return could be obtained in bank savings products. As a result, the life insurance industry was stimulated to develop more effective forms of savings vehicles. These traditional products are known as 'bundled' products; that is, they contain both a death benefit and a savings component. Consumers were demanding greater transparency in life products and products that unbundled, or split out, the various risk, savings and expenses components of a life insurance contract. As a result, several new products were developed:

- *Term insurance policy.* This policy covers only against death and has no savings element.

- *Trauma insurance policy.* This product provides cover against certain listed and defined trauma, such as diagnosis of a serious disease like cancer. There is no savings element with this product.

- *Investment account policies.* These products offer a savings vehicle in an accumulation, 'bank account' style format. They provide security to policyholders by giving capital guarantees for both accrued balance and declared interest. These were popular products during the 1980s, but the high capital costs of providing the guarantees resulted in a decline in their use.

- *Investment-linked policies.* These products were developed in the 1980s and provide a savings vehicle in which the policyholder shares in the fortunes of the asset pool. There are no guarantees of performance associated with these products, as all investment risk is borne by the policyholder rather than the insurance company. As a result, they require far less capital.

- *Allocated pensions and annuities.* These are retirement savings products that allow policyholders to draw down on their retirement savings for a defined period or throughout retirement.

Investment-linked superannuation policies have become very important for insurance companies as they derive a substantial percentage of their income from these products, mainly from the management fees that the companies charge.

Product characteristics

Life insurance policies can be categorised in a number of ways: by how proceeds are payable; by how premiums are payable; and according to rights to participate in bonus distributions. The following is a list of some types of policies to illustrate how this classification system works:

- Policies defined by how the proceeds are paid:

  » *whole-of-life* – the sum insured is payable only on the death of the life insured

  » *endowment insurance* – the sum insured is payable either on the death of the life insured or on his/her survival to a certain age or date

  » *temporary or term-life insurance* – the sum insured is payable only on the death of the life insured if it occurs before the expiry age is reached (usually in the range of 70 to 90 years)

> » *life annuity* – provides for payments at regular intervals during the annuitant's life

> » *disability insurance* – payment of an income benefit is based on a percentage of   the life insured's normal income in the event of his/her total or permanent disablement or in the event of a defined disability

> » *group life policies* – payment of benefits to the group members, their dependants or their estate on either death or disablement.

- Policies defined by how the premiums are payable:

> » single premium policies

> » policies with premiums payable for a limited term

> » policies with premiums payable throughout the term of the policy.

Policies are either single premium contracts or regular premium contracts. Regular premium payments are paid regularly on a fortnightly, monthly, half-yearly or yearly basis. The most common methods of payment are either regular yearly payments upon receipt of the insurer's premium notice or regular monthly payments made by direct debit to a nominated account.

- Policies defined by rights to participate in bonus distributions:

> » the company divides the profit, which is distributed as reversionary bonuses, among the policyholders. The amounts are not payable immediately, but are added to the sums insured and become payable on the death of the life insured or on the maturity of the policy.

In contrast, a non-participating policy has a level sum insured and does not include an entitlement to participate in any profit.

8-050   Pooled funds

Several life insurance products invest some part of a policyholder's premium in a pooled fund. The invested part of the policyholder's premium becomes part of a large pool of assets accrued from many similar policies. A common type of pooled fund is a unit trust. These pooled assets earn investment income and may experience capital gains and losses, which are distributed back to policyholders in proportion to the units they hold.

There are two types of pooled funds: *investment account* and *investment-linked*.

Investment account funds

An investment account fund is capital guaranteed as discussed above. At the end of the financial year, the insurer declares an interest rate for the pooled fund for the completed year, which is credited to each investment account. If a policy is cancelled part way through a financial year, its investment account is credited with an interim rate for that part of the year prior to cancellation.

The interest rate declared can never be negative, so the balance can never reduce as a result of negative investment performance. This is why the fund is described as capital guaranteed.

Declared interest rates have traditionally been fairly stable over the years, but since some pooled funds invest in volatile assets such as shares, the investment return may vary significantly from year to year. Therefore, the process of determining the declared rate usually involves some form of smoothing. This means that an insurer will declare a lower interest rate than the pooled fund earned in time of high earning rates and hold the excess investment earnings in an 'investment fluctuation reserve'. In years when the earned rate is low or even negative, the insurer is able to release funds from the investment fluctuation reserve and so declare a higher interest rate than the pooled fund earned.

While most investment account products give the insurer considerable discretion in determining the interest rate, with some the declared interest rate is calculated by a formula explicitly stated in the policy document. For example, the insurer may calculate the yield earned by the fund over each financial year, less management fees levied by the insurer. The declared rate for the year may be an average for that year and the two previous years. If this average is zero, the declared rate will be the minimum rate of zero, but the insurer may retain the right to recover any shortfall by reducing future declared rates.

Investment-linked policy

An investment-linked policy, where the fund is pooled in a manner similar to a unit trust, is also known as market linked or unit linked. The premium purchases units in a unitised fund, the unit price of which is recalculated each business day to reflect the investment performance of the assets in the fund. For example, if the investment return, which incorporates capital gains and losses on the assets as well as investment income earned by the assets, rises by two per cent over a particular day, then over that day the unit price will rise by two per cent. On the other hand, if the unit price were to fall, then the overall value of the investment would decline and the investor would lose money if they were to withdraw their invested funds at this point. The point is that investment-linked pooled funds are not capital guaranteed.

The operation of an investment linked policy is shown in the following illustrated example.

Illustrated example 8.1

If a policyholder placed a $100,000 single premium in an investment-linked pooled fund with a unit price of $1.25 per unit, they would have an investment containing 80,000 units. If the policyholder subsequently withdrew the investment when the unit price had fallen to $1, then they would receive only $80,000.

Investment-linked pooled funds provide the policyholder with a number of pooled funds to choose from, each having its own investment philosophy and its own unit price. A policyholder may invest in one or more of these funds and is able to switch between funds at any time by selling units in one fund and purchasing units in a different fund with the proceeds.

Pooled funds also include a range of sector pooled funds such as:

- government fixed interest securities
- commercial fixed interest securities
- overseas fixed interest securities
- Australian equities (shares in Australian companies)
- international equities
- domestic property
- overseas property.

Sector funds allow policyholders to control their investment strategy by specifying how their invested premium is to be allocated between the available funds and periodically adjusting their exposure to the various sectors by switching between funds. While the policyholders are able to control the spread of their investments between the sectors, they do not have any say in the selection of the assets within each sector. For example, the insurer selects the individual Australian equities to be invested in the Australian Equities Pooled Fund or in Asia–Pacific equities.

However, if policyholders do not want to be involved in their investment to the extent offered by the sector funds, they can leave the investment decisions to the investment experts employed by the insurer. They do this by investing in an array of managed funds (or diversified funds) available in the policy, which allows the policyholder to delegate the management of their investment to an investment company.

The difference between the managed funds is usually reflected in the risk assumed by the fund, which is characterised by the volatility of the return. Figure 8.1 illustrates volatility by showing the difference in volatility between various securities that are used in managed funds; eg, international shares exhibit the highest volatility with one-year returns of between approximately +56 per cent to –34 per cent, five-year returns between +24 per cent and –8 per cent, and 10-year returns from +19 per cent to +5 per cent.

Assets such as property and shares are more volatile over the short term, which means they are likely to produce negative returns more often than income-type investments but they have the potential of producing higher returns over longer terms. Therefore, the performance of managed funds, which invest in a range of asset classes, simply reflects the performance of the underlying funds.

Figure 8.1: Risk of major asset classes between 1 January 1986 and 31 December 2005

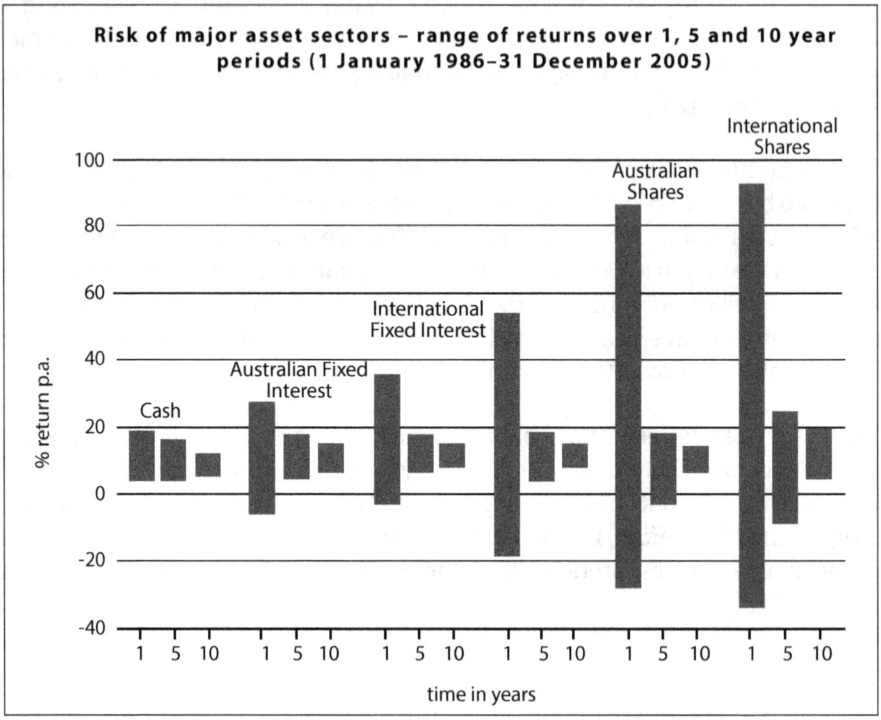

Risk of major asset sectors – range of returns over 1, 5 and 10 year periods (1 January 1986–31 December 2005)

Note: The graph does not reflect an investment in any Vanguard funds and past performance is not an indicator of future performance.

Source: Vanguard Investments Australia Ltd 2007, 'Managed funds', vanguard.com.au.

Examples of managed or diversified funds are:

- *capital stable funds* – referred to as conservative funds, these have a significant amount of their assets in fixed-interest securities and have less exposure to equities and other growth assets.

- *balance funds* – which funds seek to achieve higher returns than capital secure trusts and typically have 50 per cent to 70 per cent of the portfolio invested in growth assets and the remainder in fixed-interest (defensive) securities.

- *growth funds* – which are more volatile than capital stable and balanced trusts because exposure to defensive assets is kept intentionally low. These funds generally invest 95 to 98 per cent of the portfolio in Australian and international equities.

At a glance

- Life insurance:
    - » is a contract that insures against a contingency
    - » must be issued for a period longer than one year
    - » pays a stated amount on death
    - » includes annuities, disability and investment policies
    - » is owned by a policyholder.
- The purpose of life insurance is to:
    - » provide financial protection
    - » provide for retirement
    - » protect a deceased's estate
    - » protect business interests.
- The difference between general and life insurance is governed by:
    - » the term of the contract
    - » the interrelationship between mortality and investment
    - » the ability of the insurer to alter the terms and premium on renewal
    - » the ability to cease offering cover.
- Life insurance policies are issued on the life of a person and can be classified:
    - » as 'bundled' or 'unbundled'
    - » by product characteristics.
- Pooled funds are termed managed investments and are of two types:
    - » capital guaranteed
    - » investment linked.
- Managed funds are flexible investment vehicles because they allow:
    - » investment in different financial sectors
    - » a policyholder to manage investment risk

INSURANCE COMPANY OPERATIONS

8-060   Introduction

The most important operations of an insurance company are:

- rate making (pricing)
- underwriting
- claim settlement
- investments.

Insurers also engage in many other operations such as client services, accounting, legal services, data processing, relationship management with key stakeholders and data processing.

There are two basic functions in insurance: rate making and underwriting, which are closely associated with each other. Rate making deals with the pricing system applicable to the risk selected and underwriting deals with the selection of the risk. Each of these important operations is discussed in turn.

8-070   Rate making

Pricing life insurance products is different from pricing other products. With other products, the company knows in advance what its costs of production are and is able to set a price to give a profit. However, with life insurance the insurer does not know in advance what its actual costs are going to be. Therefore, when setting premiums the insurance company is faced with major risks, such as mortality risk, expenses risk and investment earnings risk.

Traditional policies tend to span a significant length of time so mortality, expenses and investment earnings can vary significantly from what was assumed when the policy was written. Therefore, there is a risk that the premium charged may be insufficient to cover all claims and expenses, particularly as the premium charged is fixed. In providing for this risk, the actuary will probably hedge on the conservative side and calculate a higher premium to allow for this uncertainty. If in a particular case the actuary was too conservative in the assumptions used, leading to premiums being levied too high, the excess can be returned as a bonus.

In some policies, such as whole-of-life, endowment, level premium term and level premium disability policies, the annual premium is fixed throughout the term of the contract. This means that in the earlier years in the life of the policy, the insurance company will be charging more than the actual risk and will accumulate this excess in order to be able to pay claims in later years when the premium will be less than the actual risk. In contrast, the premiums charged for renewable term insurance are lower for young ages and higher for older ages. This is because the premiums charged reflect the actual risk assumed in that year.

One of the major risks associated with setting a premium involves mortality. Actuaries base their estimates of future mortality on published studies of mortality rates based on past experience of groups of people. The outcome of these studies is the publication of mortality tables, which show the probability that a person of a particular age will die before their next birthday. These tables, compiled by life insurance companies and the Institute of Actuaries of Australia, relate to the mortality experience of specific sub-groups such as lives insured for death cover and annuitant lives (ie, individuals who receive a regular guaranteed income from their policy until they die).

Premiums for disability classes are calculated using morbidity tables, which show the number of individuals exposed to the risk of illness, sickness and disease and the number who actually incurred such ailments. Other mortality tables, such as the Australian Life Tables, which are produced every five years by the Australian Government Actuary, give the rates of mortality for the entire Australian population.

When setting a premium rate, the actuary will choose the mortality table that is most representative of the pool of lives that the insurance company will be insuring. For example, the Appendix contains the life mortality tables issued by the Australian Bureau of Statistics for each age for both males and females up to the age of 100. The figure 'qx' in these tables refers to the probability that someone at exact age 'x' will die before reaching exact age 'x + 1'. Therefore, a male aged 20 will have a 0.00062 per cent chance of dying before reaching age 21. Similarly, a female aged 20 will have a 0.00025 per cent chance of dying before reaching age 21. What becomes immediately apparent is that females have a lesser chance of dying than men (ie, overall they have a longer life expectancy than men) and therefore their life insurance premiums are lower than those for men. These probabilities are one of the major assumptions used by actuaries in the calculation of life insurance premium rates.

The premiums that a life insurance company receives from its policyholders are used to:

- create a pool of invested monies that will be sufficient to meet their future claim liabilities

- pay administrative expenses
- pay bonuses to policyholders
- make a profit.

The life insurance company will invest premiums in a wide range of investments both domestically and overseas.

8-080   Underwriting

Underwriting is a critical process where the underwriter decides whether or not to insure applicants, and at what rates and conditions, by following the company's underwriting standards. However, not all applicants are treated equally, as different underwriting rules apply to group insurance than to individual insurance.

Group insurance underwriting

In group underwriting, the group characteristics, demographics and past losses are taken into account. Since individual insurability is not taken into account, people who are sick or overweight with high blood pressure or people with AIDS can obtain life insurance through group policies. There are typically four criteria for automatic acceptance:

- *minimum acceptance rate.* The acceptance rate in group insurance is the proportion of people insured divided by the number of employees who were eligible to be insured. By specifying a minimum acceptance rate of at least, say, 75 per cent of eligible employees, the insurer is confident that the proportion of high-risk lives covered by the policy is not excessive and will not require more stringent underwriting requirements. In contrast, if the acceptance rate is only 15 per cent, the insurer will be concerned that it will be insuring only unhealthy lives among those eligible to join.

- *defined sum insured.* Group policies offer very little choice or no choice as to the level of sum insured. For example, the death and total and permanent disablement (TPD) sum insured may be limited to a maximum of twice annual salary, while disability income insurance may be limited to 75 per cent of annual salary. This removes the risk of unhealthy applicants choosing higher sums insured than healthy applicants.

- *defined risk commencement date.* People are given only a limited time span within which they can join the group insurance plan, eg, when the employee commences work with the employer. This minimises the risk of people joining only when they know they have a higher than average risk of claiming.

- *at-work certificate.* A condition of acceptance is that the employer certifies that the insured was at work on the day when he/she joined the plan. This allows the insurer to identify those staff members who are on sick leave and who may require more stringent underwriting.

Provided these four criteria are satisfied, the insurer will not separately underwrite each individual life, and this will result in significant cost savings that can be shared with clients in the form of a lower premium. However, if any of the criteria are not satisfied, then automatic acceptance is not available, and while the group insurance will still be available, a more stringent underwriting approach will be adopted. This will result in higher administrative expenses for the insurer, which will be passed on in higher premiums.

Because of the minimum underwriting employed, the insurer faces increased uncertainty when setting the premium scale, so the insurer incorporates a significant safety margin in the premium rates. Since the premium is conservative, there is usually a considerable profit, which is shared with the policy owners by crediting them with a rebate. The rebate is a return of a part of the premium that was previously paid and is based on the plan's claims experience. If the claims experience is better than expected (ie, fewer claims), a larger rebate applies. In contrast, if the claims experience is so poor that the safety margin is exhausted, no rebate will apply.

There are two methods of determining rebates, *self-experience* and *pool experience*:

- The self-experience approach uses the claims costs experience of the plan when calculating the rebate. This approach is usually used only for large plans where there are a large number of insured lives. These policies generally have a reasonably stable claims cost and thus receive a fairly stable yearly rebate.
- With the pool experience rebate approach, the insurer pools a number of group life policies into a single pool so the pool's claim costs determine the rebate. Under this approach, death and TPD are kept in a separate pool to the disability income insurance. Also, the policies receiving a self-experience rebate would be excluded from these pools.

Individual underwriting

For individual underwriting, the insured must provide evidence of insurability for life and health insurances. An individual applicant for life insurance must be approved by the company underwriter through a process that can be quite lengthy. First, the applicant must complete a questionnaire that includes questions about health, smoking, occupation, lifestyle habits (eg, participating in dangerous pursuits such as hang gliding), and medical history of the applicant and their close family members. Based on the results of the questionnaire, some applicants may be asked to undergo a medical examination or to provide further information. In other cases, once the amount applied for reaches a certain level, the applicant will be asked to undergo a medical examination and in some cases obtain a specialist's medical report.

Once the underwriter decides that the applicant is insurable, then the class premium rate that applies to that underwriting class is applied. It was discussed earlier how actuaries base their premiums on classes of insureds and it is the underwriter's task to decide which class is appropriate for a particular applicant (called class underwriting). The purpose of underwriting standards is to reduce the chance of adverse selection against the company.

Adverse selection may also occur when pricing categories are so broad as to allow both good and poor 'risks' to be lumped together and so pay the same price. Therefore, high-risk individuals will enjoy lower rates than their risk pool would require and low-risk individuals will be charged higher rates. The result will be that low-risk individuals will choose not to participate because they will realise that they are getting a bad deal. In order to prevent this market failure, insurers must charge low-risk insureds lower rates than high-risk insureds; that is, they must price discriminate in order to provide equity among policyholders.

Most applicants are accepted at standard premium rates, but some proposals are accepted at higher than normal rates; that is, the premiums are loaded or cover is offered with an exclusion, such as for disability claims resulting from lower back problems. For example, an applicant may be accepted at standard rates plus 150 per cent. In other cases, the application may be rejected because the health risk is too high, or rejected but subject to review in the future. For instance, an applicant who has suffered from certain cancers may be rejected for insurance cover but is able to reapply in five years' time for reassessment.

8-090   Claims management

There are various circumstances in which a policyowner or beneficiary will be entitled to make a claim under a policy. While the definition of death is fairly straightforward, definitions of disability and sickness are more problematic. The policyowner or personal legal representative will be asked to complete a claim form and to provide information to allow the insurer to evaluate the claim and determine if the policy covers the particular condition.

It is an insurer's business to pay genuine claims that satisfy the terms and conditions of the policy, based on medical and other evidence available. Insurers strive to deal with claims compassionately, efficiently and promptly, and keep the client informed throughout the process. Because of their ongoing nature, disability claims are of particular concern for insurers and where possible the insurer will work with the insured, their doctors and rehabilitation providers in order to help the insureds in their recovery and return to work.

If a claim cannot be accepted immediately, the reasons will be explained to the claimant. The insurer will advise what further information is required, eg, further medical reports or financial information relating to the insured's income may be requested. All this information is treated in the strictest confidence by the insurer.

There are instances where the claimant is not satisfied with the claim decision and requests a review of the claim. If they remain dissatisfied with the final decision, they must be able to access a dispute resolution procedure.

8-100   Dispute resolution

Many see complaints as negative, although the opposite can be the case. A complaint can often bring a weakness in a system to the attention of management, giving them the opportunity to provide a better service and develop a stronger client relationship by resolving the problem satisfactorily.

Sections 912A(2) or 1017G(1) of the Corporations Act and regs 7.6.02 and 7.9.77 of the Corporations Regulations 2001 require all licensees who provide a financial service to retail clients to have a dispute resolution scheme. The dispute resolution system consists of an internal dispute resolution (IDR) procedure that complies with standards and requirements made or approved by ASIC, and membership of one or more external dispute resolution (EDR) schemes approved by ASIC.

When considering whether to make or approve standards or requirements relating to internal dispute resolution, ASIC will consider Australian Standard (AS) 4269, 'Complaints handling', for internal complaints systems as specified in regs 7.6.02 and 7.9.77 of the Corporations Regulations. Regulatory Guide 165 (RG), 'Licensing: internal and external dispute resolution schemes', sets out in detail the current requirements established by ASIC for the IDR procedure. Since April 2006, Australian Financial Services licence holders must also comply with another standard on complaints handling, AS-ISC-10002-2006; ie, there are now two standards to comply with. EDR schemes and ASIC's requirements for approval are detailed in RG139, 'Approval of external complaints resolution such as the Australian Financial Complaints Authority Limited (AFCA).

AFCA is a core industry external dispute resolution body that is authorised to investigate, negotiate and conciliate over complaints concerning members of the financial services industry that fall within the AFCA's definition of a small business, i.e. having less than 100 employees. AFCA is able to investigate complaints involving: credit, finance and loans, insurance, banking deposits and payments, investments and financial advice and superannuation. AFCA is able to investigate legacy complaints back to 1 January 2008.

AFCA's role is to provide a free service to consumers and small businesses to reach agreements with financial firms about how to resolve their complaints. AFCA is impartial and independent, and do not act for either party to advocate their position. If a complaint does not resolve between the parties, AFCA will decide an appropriate outcome.

Decisions made can be binding on the financial firm involved in a complaint. AFCA can award compensation for losses suffered because of a financial firm's error or inappropriate conduct. There are other remedies that can also provide for superannuation complaints. AFCA's free service is offered as an alternative to tribunals and courts. AFCA do not, however, award compensation to punish financial firms or impose fines.

AFCA is not a government department or agency, and is not a regulator of the financial services industry. AFCA is a not-for-profit company, limited by guarantee that is governed by a Board of Directors, which includes equal numbers of industry and consumer representatives. AFCA's Chief Ombudsman is responsible for the management of the organisation.

The following jurisdictional limits apply to financial disputes.

Type of claim	AFCA Limits
Most non-superannuation disputes	Monetary limit $1 million
Dispute about a small business credit facility	Facility limit $5 million
Income stream product disputes	Compensation cap $13,400 per month
Uninsured third party motor vehicle claims	Compensation limit $15,000
General insurance broker disputes	Compensation cap $250,000
Superannuation disputes	No monetary limit
All other complaints	Six years from awareness of the loss. Two years from an IDR response.

AFCA (2019)

Time limits for lodging complaints apply. There are a variety of time limits depending on the type of claim being made. The following rules apply:

Total and Permanent Disability claims.

AFCA can only deal with a Superannuation Complaint about the decision of a superannuation trustee ('decision maker') relating to a total and permanent disablement (TPD) benefit provided through superannuation in the following circumstances:

If the fund member permanently ceased employment because of the physical or mental condition that gave rise to the TPD claim then:

1. The fund member must have submitted a TPD claim to the decision maker within two years of permanently ceasing employment.

2. The fund member must make a complaint to us about the decision to deny the claim within four years of the decision being made.

If the fund member did not permanently cease employment because of the physical or mental condition that gave rise to the TPD claim: That is, the fund member permanently ceased employment for reasons unrelated to their disability), the fund member must make a complaint to us about the decision to deny the claim within six years of the decision being made.

Death benefit complaints

The time limits for death benefit complaints are reflected in both the AFCA Rules and in section 1056 of the Corporations Act.

There are two 28-day periods that must be met: an interested person must object to the superannuation provider within 28 days of being notified of the proposed decision to pay the death benefit, and the interested person must complain to AFCA within 28 days of being notified of the final decision to pay the death benefit.

Who is an interested person?

To complain about a superannuation provider's decision, a person must have an interest in the death benefit. AFCA regards a person as having an interest in the death benefit (interested person) if the person is within the class of people eligible to receive all or part of the death benefit under the governing rules.

To be eligible to receive all or part of a superannuation death benefit, a person will usually need to be a dependant of the deceased member, or the legal personal representative of the deceased member. A dependant includes a spouse, a child, any person who had an interdependency relationship with the deceased member and any person who was financially dependent on the deceased member. However, if there are no dependants or legal personal representatives, other individuals (e.g. family members) may be eligible.

Variation of a credit contract

Where a complaint relates to a variation of a credit contract as a result of financial hardship, an unjust transaction or unconscionable interest and other charges under the National Credit Code, AFCA will generally not consider the complaint unless it was submitted to AFCA before the later of the following time limits:

a) within two years of the date when the credit contract is rescinded, discharged or otherwise comes to an end; or

b) where, prior to lodging the complaint with AFCA, the Complainant was given an Internal Dispute Resolution (IDR) response in relation to the complaint from the Financial Firm – within two years of the date of that IDR response.

Risk insurance in superannuation

Insureds who have their risk insurance contained in their superannuation scheme also have access to a company's internal dispute resolution facility. The

Superannuation Industry (Supervision) Act 1993 (the SIS Act) requires trustees of regulated superannuation schemes to have arrangements in place to allow beneficiaries to make enquiries and complaints about the management and operation of the scheme. The company must consider those enquiries and complaints and deal with them within 90 days.

If the beneficiary is dissatisfied with a trustee's decision, they have a statutory right of appeal to the Superannuation Complaints Tribunal. However, the Superannuation Complaints Tribunal can only deal with complaints about superannuation that have been received on or before 31 October 2018. New complaints must be made to AFCA.

8-110   Investments

As at 31 March 2019, Australian life insurers had total statutory assets of $231.9 billion (APRA 2019). The funds available for investment are derived from premium income, investment earnings and maturing investments that are being reinvested.

Life insurance investments have an important economic and social impact on the nation. Life insurance contracts are by nature long term, with the liabilities of insurance companies extending over periods such as 50 or 60 years. Most life insurance investments are also long term, with approximately 35 per cent being in equities, 33 per cent in unit trusts and 24 per cent in interest-bearing securities.

Investment income is extremely important for life insurance companies as it helps reduce the cost of insurance to policyholders and provides returns to those with participating policies. Also, it allows the insurance companies to pay dividends to their shareholders, who provide the risk capital for the companies.

At a glance

- Setting life insurance premiums is difficult because of:
  - » the fact that premiums are set for the duration of the contract
  - » the risk of mortality
  - » the expense risk
  - » the investment earnings risk.

- Underwriting is the process of applying the correct rate to classes of potential insureds and will differ depending on whether the application relates to:
  - » group insurance, because group history determines acceptance
  - » individual insurance, as individual and family histories and lifestyle affect premiums and acceptance.

- Claims handling procedures can vary depending on whether the claim is for:
  - » death, which is fairly straightforward, or
  - » disability, which can be protracted and involve several medical and rehabilitation services.

- Dispute resolution facilities are required by the Corporations Act and include:
  - » internal dispute resolution as the initial avenue for dissatisfied claimants
  - » external dispute resolution as the next avenue if the complaint cannot be resolved satisfactorily
  - » the Australian Financial Complaints Authority is the approved external authority that handles all life and superannuation complaints

- Investment earnings are important to life companies because they:
  - » support premium calculations
  - » provide returns for participating policies
  - » pay dividends to shareholders
  - » provide an economic benefit to the economy.

AUSTRALIAN KEY LEGISLATION

8-120   Introduction

While no regulatory regime can guarantee that failures will not occur, the success of the regulatory regime of life insurance in Australia can be evidenced by the fact that only three life insurers have failed since the establishment of the *Life Insurance Act 1945* (Cth) and none have failed since the reform of the legislative framework in 1995. This stability ensures strong public confidence in the life insurance industry.

8-130   Life Insurance Act 1995

The *Life Insurance Act 1995* (Cth) (LI Act) was assented to on 23 February 1995 and came into operation on 1 July 1995. The LI Act modernised the original legislation that was enacted in 1945. Its main regulatory aims concern:

- the financial strength of life insurance companies, which includes

    » the protection of policy owner funds and

    » fostering consumer confidence in the industry

- maintenance of a viable, competitive and innovative life insurance industry that ensures transparency to allow informed decisions to be made

- the promotion of fair dealing in an industry that has complex insurance products.

Section 3(1) of the LI Act states:

> "The principal object of this Act is to protect the interests of the owners and prospective owners of life insurance policies in a manner consistent with the continued development of a viable, competitive and innovative life insurance industry."

The major thrust of the LI Act is to ensure that life insurance companies that offer their products to the public are financially sound so that policyholders can be confident that their insurance company will be able to pay out a claim on their policy when it is made.

It is important that the industry be transparent so the public has sufficient information on which to make informed choices and for the market system to work effectively. Transparency involves making generally available information such as the financial performance of individual insurance companies and the features of particular products offered (especially fees and charges). This information must be made available in an understandable form so that the public can see through the detail and make well-informed decisions.

These objectives are achieved under the following parts of the LI Act.

Part 3: Registration of life companies and their non-operating holding companies (NOHCs)

The LI Act prohibits persons other than registered companies from carrying on a life business, which includes issuing a life policy or undertaking a liability under a life policy (s 17(1)). A registered company must "apply in writing to APRA for registration" (s 20(1)), and there are a number of grounds for refusal. Companies facing refusal are those which are unable to "or who are unlikely to meet their obligations, including obligations in respect of business other than life insurance business" (s 21(3)(d)); those "unlikely to be able to comply with the provisions of the Act" (s 21(3)(e)); and companies whose name "closely resembles the name of a company already registered under the Act as to be likely to deceive" (s 21(3)(f)).

Section 22(1) of the LI Act allows APRA to impose conditions on a registration at any time, while under s 22(4) APRA is able to revoke or vary the conditions by giving written notice if it thinks they are no longer required.

Part 4: Statutory funds of life companies

The statutory fund concept is integral to the LI Act as the mechanism for quarantining the life business of the company, and hence the entitlements of policyholders, from any other business of the company. A statutory fund is defined in s 29 as a fund that:

a. "is established in the records of a life company; and

b. relates solely to the life insurance business of the company or a particular part of that business."

Life insurance business must be conducted through statutory funds within a life insurer so that a separate accounting of the policyholder business and assets can be made from shareholder business and assets. Section 30 of the LI Act outlines the requirements regarding statutory funds, including requirements that the life company must credit all amounts such as premiums received from policyholders to a statutory fund (s 30(a)) and that the assets of a fund are available only for expenditure related to the conduct of the business of the fund (s 30(d)). Additionally, a life company must have at least one statutory fund at all times in respect of its life insurance business (s 31(a)). Section 37 allows capital payments to be made to the fund. Section 32 imposes a duty on companies in relation to assets in statutory funds in that they must give priority to current and prospective policy owners' interests.

Section 38 of the LI Act places restrictions on the application (expenditure) from a statutory fund by allowing funds to be applied only:

a. "to meet liabilities (including policy liabilities) or expenses incurred for the purposes of the business of the fund; or

b. for making investments in accordance with section 43 [such as depositing money with a bank, or other approved investments]; or

c. for the purposes of a distribution under Division 6 [such as the distribution of retained profits]." (s 38(2))

In a further attempt to ensure the security of policyholders' funds, s 39 of the LI Act prohibits any practice of reinsurance between statutory funds. Section 43 also places restrictions on the investment of statutory fund's assets such as limiting the investments in the ordinary voting shares of a related company to a maximum of 2.5 per cent. Otherwise, a life insurance company has wide powers to invest in a broad portfolio of assets including investments by way of loans. The investment income received from those assets flows back to the relevant statutory fund. Any operating profit or loss resulting from the operations of a statutory fund for a period must be allocated at the end of the period (s 59).

Shareholder capital is tracked and statutory fund profit allocated between participating policyholders and shareholders is determined annually, with a consequent tracking of each group's retained profits. Section 60 of the LI Act specifies that when allocating the operating profit from a statutory fund at least 80 per cent of the profit must be added to the "retained profits of the statutory fund".

Distribution of policyholder profits is subject to solvency requirements being met (s 62(3(a) & (3)(a)), while distribution of shareholders' profits is subject to capital adequacy requirements being met (s 63). In the investment, administration and management of the assets of a statutory fund, the life company must give priority to the interests of policyholders (s 48(2)(b)) and the directors must place policyholder interests before shareholder interests (s 48(3)). Conceptually, the life insurance company can be thought of as acting in a 'trustee' role for its policyholders.

Finally, there are rules about the types of business that can be conducted in the same statutory fund and there are investment restrictions on statutory fund assets, such as no borrowing and very limited investments in related companies.

Capital adequacy

It is obvious that capital adequacy is important for an insurer, as it is with any financial institution. Policyholders entrust their funds with a life insurance company to manage their funds for growth until they are needed at retirement (superannuation) and at other times (investment funds, death and disablement). These investors need to be confident that the insurance company is solvent and is a prudent manager. Ensuring that insurance companies are managed in a prudent manner is the responsibility of APRA. However, financial advisers should also have the tools to judge the solvency of the suppliers of financial products in the marketplace.

Up until the collapse of HIH, no trading bank, life or non-life insurance company had to close its doors in recent times. This was despite the share market crash in 1987, the Estate Mortgage Trust collapse and Pyramid Building Society closure, the collapse of the Bond and Skase financial empires, the Asian economic crisis in late 1997 and, more recently, the collapse of Westpoint and Australian Capital Reserve and the Global Financial Crisis (GFC) in 2008.

Section 230A(1)(a) of the LI Act gives APRA the power to set prudential standards for life insurance companies. In order to protect policyholders against such calamities, APRA has revised Prudential Standard 110 – *Capital Adequacy* (LPS 110) that applies from 1 January 2013 and establishes a three-pillar approach that measures assets and liabilities, demanding insurers maintain a certain level of minimum capital and transparency to be allowed to operate. This general approach to prudential regulation is based on risk management rather than compliance with a set of rules.

Three-pillar approach

APRA has adoption of three-pillar approach for life and general insurers, which is similar to that already in place for Authorised Deposit Taking Institutions (ADIs). Consistent with international trends, the approach is:

- Pillar I: the *quantitative requirements* – assessment of required capital, eligible capital and liability valuation to cover asset, asset concentration, insurance, insurance concentration and operational risk.

- Pillar II: the *supervisory review* process – as part of this process, APRA will be able to impose a supervisory adjustment to required capital where necessary following review of an insurer's risk management and capital management practices if APRA considers that an insurer's prescribed capital amount does not adequately account for all its risks, such as reputational or strategic risks. This will not be a formulaic calculation.

Pillar III: *disclosure requirements* designed to encourage market discipline.

The new single regulatory approach replaces the two-tier solvency and capital adequacy requirements that were in place until 31 December 2012. The regulatory focus is on a comparison of an insurer's required capital (termed the Prudential Capital Requirement (PCR)) against its eligible capital base. LPS110 also requires that a life company must ensure that its funds have a capital base, at all times, in excess of its PCR.

Prudential capital requirement

The PCR consists of the prescribed capital amount (under Pillar I) plus any supervisory adjustment applied by APRA (under Pillar II). The PCR is intended to take account of the full range of risks to which a fund or life company is exposed. Furthermore, a life company must ensure that the life company and each of its funds have a capital base that is at all times in excess of its PCR.

The PCR includes a prescribed capital amount that covers:

- asset risk
- asset concentration risk; and
- operational risk (based on exposure measures such as based on exposure measures premium, liabilities, and funds under management).

An aggregation benefit is then applied to produce the prescribed capital amount. A life company's prescribed capital amount cannot be less than $10 million.

Aggregation benefit is assessed in circumstances where the current requirements do not directly allow for diversification between risk types. There is an explicit allowance for diversification between asset and insurance risks only, which would reduce the required capital for insurers exposed to both risks.

Life companies are able to apply to APRA for transitional relief from any requirement of this Prudential Standard. If granted, this transitional relief will expire on 31 December 2014.

In order to ensure that life companies maintain adequate capital to guard against insurance risks associated with their activities, APRA has released Prudential Standard 115 – *Capital Adequacy: Insurance Risk Charge* (LPS115). The insurance risk charge is the minimum amount of capital required to be held against insurance risks. It relates to the risk of adverse impacts due to movements in future mortality, morbidity, longevity, servicing expenses and lapses.

LPS115 also requires life companies to develop stress margins for mortality and morbidity random stress, longevity, lapses and service expenses that reflect the risk that outcomes may be worse than the best estimate assumptions. The stress margins for random, future, event and longevity risks must be adjusted to allow for diversification between these risks.

The stress margins, before the adjustment for diversification, must be determined at a 99.5 per cent probability of sufficiency over a 12 month period. Therefore, there must be no more than a 0.5 per cent probability that the actual cost of claims will exceed the stressed estimate.

This Prudential Standard applies from 1 January 2013 with a transition period to 31 December 2014 by which time all life companies will be obliged to comply with this standard unless APRA has granted a life company transitional relief.

Part 6: Financial management of life companies

APRA has extensive powers to inspect records and request information of a life insurance company where the Commissioner forms the view that the insurer is unable, or is likely to be unable, to meet its liabilities. These powers extend to freezing assets, formally investigating an insurer, directing a company to take specific action such as to stop writing new business, and applying to the court to place the company under judicial management or have the company wound up.

The LI Act imposes an obligation on life insurance companies to keep such records of the income and outgoings of each statutory fund as will properly record the affairs and transactions of the company (s 75(1)). Section 113(1) requires the company to have its appointed actuary investigate the financial condition of the company as at the end of each financial year and to lodge a copy of this Financial Condition Report with APRA within three months after the close of the financial year (s 119(1)). The quarterly, half-yearly and annual returns and the board report on the financial condition of the company as prepared by the appointed actuary, as well as the financial statements and statistical returns, give the Commissioner the information to monitor the life insurance companies.

The adequacy of the assets to meet the policy liabilities is under the control of the appointed actuary, who will be guided by the minimum standards laid down by the Board. However, it should be appreciated that risk products are priced on the basis of certain assumptions and probability distributions, and it is not known with certainty whether these pricing parameters are appropriate until the risk has been run off for all policyholders. Therefore, it is wise for the actuary to be reasonably conservative in the assumptions made. The degree of conservatism will be reflected in the actuarial valuation contained in the Financial Condition Report. The Financial Condition Report is an important regulatory document that can be used by APRA to instigate and carry out an official investigation (s 115, LI Act).

The auditor's role is more traditional and involves certifying the revenue account and balance sheet on the basis of physical verification of assets, testing internal controls and checking to confirm that the policy of the insurer's board has been properly implemented, given the responsibilities of the board of directors under the Act. Section 88(1) of the LI Act places an obligation on the auditor to draw to the attention of the company or the directors or an officer of the company any action that needs to be taken to avoid: (a) a contravention of the Act; and (b) prejudice to the interests of the owners of policies issued by the company. It is also necessary to have an internal audit committee under the control of the Board (s 90), to assist the directors in ensuring that the financial statements are prepared according to s 82. An additional function of the audit committee is to ensure that the company has a proper system of management and financial controls (s 92).

Finally, the LI Act requires that before a life insurance company issues policies it must obtain actuarial advice regarding the proposed terms and conditions of new policies, the proposed basis on which surrender values of policies is to be determined and the means by which unit values in a unit trust will be determined (s 116).

Part 7: Monitoring and investigation of life companies

This part of the LI Act allows APRA or ASIC (the regulators) to monitor the performance of life insurers and their compliance with the provisions of the LI Act, and to carry out certain investigations. In particular, life insurance companies are required to provide information, produce records and provide access to premises to the regulator (s 132). APRA exercises post-registration supervision through:

- regular quarterly returns under the prudential rules that focus on certain exception issues such as derivative usage and large asset exposures (s 252)

- half-yearly returns that include statistical and financial information
- the financial statements (s 82)
- the financial condition report
- the auditor's report
- formal investigations under Div 3 of the LI Act
- consultation with the principal officer (s 246).

The overriding objective of the regulator is to ensure that the statutory funds remain solvent, and the above returns/reports are the manner in which this objective is achieved. Within the revenue account and balance sheet, APRA will examine the various expense and return on asset ratios. However, financial ratios need to be considered carefully and interpreted in conjunction with the notes attaching to the financial statements and the operations of the company. For example, insurers with increasing market share will usually show a higher expense ratio than insurers with a steady or declining overall market share, as most of the expense of writing new business is 'up-front' and profit may not be earned for several years. APRA will seek explanations in appropriate circumstances.

The preparation of the balance sheet requires that the directors certify that both assets and liabilities are fairly stated. They must also certify that "each statutory fund … has complied with the solvency standard and capital adequacy standard…", as required under s 113(1). Section 82(6) of the LI Act requires that the financial statements be prepared in accordance with accounting standards issued by the Australian Accounting Standards Board (AASB) or actuarial standards issued by the Life Insurance Actuarial Standards Board (LIASB), or both, as in force or existing from time to time.

Part 8: Judicial management and winding-up

Section 157 of the LI Act allows APRA to apply to the court for an order that a life company, or part of the business of a life company, be placed under judicial management. The court will make such an order:

- if it is satisfied that the company is, or is likely to become, unable to meet its policy or other liabilities as they become due
- if the company has failed to comply with the solvency standard
- with a direction under s 68, or

- if there are reasonable grounds for believing that the financial position or management may be unsatisfactory (s 159).

The arrangement of judicial management rather than receivership or winding-up is a regime that seeks to limit prejudice to the interests of policyholders of the company. In this way, policies are given the best chance of providing the protection originally intended.

Part 9: Transfers or amalgamation of life insurance business

Part 9 of the LI Act gives the court power to confirm or otherwise the transfer and amalgamation of life insurance business. Certain steps need to be taken before an application is made to the court for confirmation (s 191). APRA may arrange for an independent written report on the scheme (s 192(1)) and is entitled to be heard on an application before the court (s 193(3)). Given the substantial nature of the business propositions involved and the accompanying actuarial calculations, it should be anticipated that few schemes of this nature come before the courts. However, all parties may benefit from a court-confirmed transfer/amalgamation rather than resorting to judicial management.

Part 10: Provisions relating to policies

Part 10 of the LI Act mandates the arrangements pertaining to a raft of issues concerned with the operation of insurance policies. These include:

Alteration of proposal and policy forms

ASIC is given the power under s 198 of the LI Act to require a life company to submit a proposal or policy document for inspection. If ASIC considers that the form does not comply with the LI Act or is likely to mislead, ASIC may give written notice to the life company setting out the way in which the form fails to comply with the LI Act or is likely to mislead. The life company must make a submission within 14 days to ASIC setting out how they will make the forms comply. If the life company does not respond within 14 days, ASIC may give the life company a written direction to change the form in the way specified in the direction.

Capacity of young persons to insure

Section 199(1) of the LI Act allows any child who has reached age 10, but not age 16, with the written permission of a parent or a personal representative, to enter into or take an assignment of a life policy. Once a child reaches the age of 18 years he or she will have full legal rights to enter into a life policy.

A person who has reached 16 but has not reached 18 has the same capacity to exercise rights or powers in relation to a policy of which he or she is the owner as a person who has reached 18.

The law relating to minors' contracts has two main aims:

3. to protect people under 18 ("minors") from entering bad contracts because of their lack of understanding or their experience

4. to protect adults who deal with minors otherwise, they would not deal with minors and minors would not be able to get goods and services.

Except for certain exceptions, contracts are not enforceable against minors, but minors can enforce their contracts against the other party.

Assignment of policies

Sections 200 and 201 of the LI Act allow the owners of a life policy to assign the policy. To be effective, the assignment must be by a memorandum of transfer endorsed on the policy or on an annexure to the policy. The assignment must be signed by the transferor and the transferee, dated and signed by the principal executive officer authorised to sign such memoranda. The assignment must be registered in a register of assignments kept by the life company concerned.

Protection of policies from creditors

Section 204 of the LI Act provides protection of life policies against creditors. A life policy on a person's life or the life of the person's spouse or de facto partner cannot be made available by a court to discharge a debt owed by the person. Similarly, s 205 provides protection when the proceeds of a life policy are paid into an estate. However, the money may be applied to pay a debt if the person entered into a contract expressly for the money to be applied to the debt, the person had charged the money with the payment of the debt; or the person gave an express direction, in his or her will or other testamentary document signed by the person, that the money be so applied.

Surrender of policies

Traditional whole-of-life and endowment policies generally acquire value after three years premiums have been paid. Section 207 gives the owner of the policy the right to make written application to the life company to surrender the policy. Subject to the terms of the policy, the owner of the policy is able to access part of its accumulated value in the form of a loan. On the surrender of the policy, the life company is allowed to deduct the amount of the loan from the surrender value.

Paid-up policies

Section 209 provides that if the owner of a life policy has paid at least three years premiums, he/she may make written application to the company to vary the policy so no further premiums are payable and to treat the policy as paid-up.

Non-forfeiture of policies

Protection against the forfeiture of policies because of the non-payment of a premium (the overdue premium) is provided by s 210 of the LI Act. Protection is provided when at least three years' premiums have been paid on the policy and the surrender value exceeds the value of the overdue premium and any other amounts owed to the company or secured by the policy.

This section also prevents the forfeiture of a policy unless the premium remains outstanding longer than 28 days. The life company is required to send the policy owner a written notice setting out the amount of the premium, the due date and stating that the policy will be forfeited at the end of 28 days if the premium is not paid.

Register of life policies

Under s 226 of the LI Act, a life company must have a register of life policies for each state or territory in which it carries on life insurance business. Also, a life company must register each life policy issued by the company in the register for the state or territory in which the policy owner lives or in a register chosen by the policyholder (s 227).

Part 11: Miscellaneous

Section 234 of the LI Act prohibits a life company from intentionally carrying on any business other than a life insurance business, eg, a general insurance business.

Part 12: How this Act affects existing life companies

This is an administrative part dealing with continuance arrangements from the 1945 Act, which was repealed. In effect, life companies registered under the 1945 Act are subject to the provisions of the LI Act.

At a glance

- The life insurance industry is governed by the *Life Insurance Act 1995* (Cth) (LI Act), which is concerned with the financial strength of life companies, maintaining a viable, competitive and innovative industry, and the promotion of fair dealing. It does this by:

  » controlling who can start up a life company and how policyholder premiums are protected

  » specifying required capital standards

  » allowing APRA to inspect records and, with ASIC, to monitor performance and compliance with the LI Act

  » giving APRA the power to place a life company in judicial management or wind it up

  » allowing the transfer or amalgamation of life business

  » mandating a raft of protective issues relating to life policies

  » allowing APRA to collect statistics and issue prudential rules.

- Protection is given to policyholders' funds contained in superannuation from creditors.

LIFE INSURANCE INDUSTRY STRUCTURE

8-140   Australian life insurance industry

Consolidation

The history of the Australian life insurance industry over the last 20 years has been dominated by rationalisation. In 1990 the two largest life insurers (excluding friendly societies) together held over 50 per cent of the life insurance market, whether measured by assets or premiums. The next largest life insurer held eight per cent of the market by assets or five per cent by premiums. There were five State government insurers that held 6 per cent of industry assets and two per cent of premiums.

The largest life insurers were predominately mutual companies and dominated the market. The seven mutual companies held 43 per cent of industry assets and premiums. The four major banks had only just entered the market either through acquisition or start-up operations.

Today, the landscape is very different. The number of life insurance licences (excluding friendly societies) has reduced from 55 in 1992 to 29 as at September 2017 (APRA 2018). The formal conclusion of AMP's acquisition of National Mutual Life Association in early 2011 represented the largest of the acquisitions over this 20 year period. Many foreign owned insurers principally based in the United Kingdom or the United States exited the market. The big four banks each owned life insurance businesses until 2017, after some of those life insurance businesses were either completely or partially sold.

The life insurance industry is undergoing significant structural changes. Until recently, the major banks dominated the life insurance industry holding 50-60 per cent of policyholder assets and premium income. However, following several scandals involving the banks' wealth management divisions, increased regulatory intervention, low customer trust, increasing competition from non-traditional players, high policy lapse rates and declining profits, some of the banking sector are divesting their life insurance portfolios for example, the sale of: ANZ life to Zurich for $2.85 billion, Commonwealth sold its troubled insurance business CommInsure Life to a Hong Kong-listed group for $3.8 billion and the expected sale of NAB's life portfolio.

In addition, some non-bank life insurance companies are also exiting the market with AMP having recently sold its Life business to Resolution Life for $3.3 billion and Suncorp has sold its life insurance division to Japanese insurer Dai-ichi

Life Holdings (TAL) for $725 million. The future of structure of life insurance distribution will be significantly different from the past.

As at year ended September 2018, life insurance risk market inflows were up 1.7 per cent over the year from $16.2 billion to $16.5 billion. The state of the life insurance risk market by total premium inflows and market share as at September 2018 is shown in table 8.1.

Table 8.1 The Life insurance risk Market by total risk premium inflows and market share

$millions	Year Ended Sept-18 2018	Market Share
TAL group	2,942.0	17.8%
AIA Australia	2,575.2	15.6%
MLC Life Insurance	1,929.1	11/7%
AMP Group	1,808.8	11.0%
OnePath Australia Group	1,644.8	10.0%
Comminsure Group	1,300.6	7.9%
BT/Westpac Group	1,279.2	7.8%
Suncorp Group	822.1	5.0%
MetLife Insurance	749.5	4.5%
Zurich Group	699.2	4.2%
Others	738.0	4.5%
Total	16,488.3	100.0%

Source: Strategic insight, 2019

Note: With the exit of many banks and others from the life insurance risk business the premium income flows and ranking shown in table 8.1 will change and so are a guide only.

Financial position

As at 31 March 2019 (the most recent statistics), the life insurance industry held statutory funds of approximately $226.9 billion. Investment linked revenues were $15.4 billion during 2018/19 compared 12.3 billion in 2017/18. (APRA 2019). The APRA report also shows that total net profit fell to $ 0.8 billion in 2018/19 down from $ 2.2 billion in 2017/18.

Industry dynamics

Life insurance plays a vital role in Australia's social construct, and in providing financial protection to those policyholders in need. As an industry that pays more than $7.5 billion (APRA 2019) in claims annually, the life insurance industry is facing unprecedented challenges.

The public trust that is vital to the insurance model is a key issue on which the industry has found itself under pressure. The industry is also seen as being one of the ripest for disruption. Non-traditional players are looking for ways to use technological advances to create more valuable customer propositions and greater efficiency across the life insurance value chain. This is also a sector where legislative and regulatory parameters have prescribed the extent of the customer offer and where innovation has focussed around the edges of benefit design and distribution enhancements. Life products are typically long term contracts and yet the increased competition for customers is bringing a shorter term dynamic to life insurance business. Competition and the risks of first mover disadvantage around pricing on products which customers find hard to differentiate mean that the continued pressure on pricing and return of capital is unlikely to abate.

The customer base for the Australian life insurance industry is heavily influenced by two distinct trends – an increase in the number of older customers as well as tech savvy customers, particularly millennials (i.e., those born after 1982).

Changing customer profile

The number of Australians over 65 is growing rapidly – between 2012 and 2025, it is expected to increase from 3.2 million to 4.9 million people. By 2050, more than 50 per cent of the Australian population will be over 40 years old, and a further 20 per cent will be 65 or older (ABS 2019). In contrast the expectation is that China's population will be 400 million people with 30 per cent of the population over the age of 65 by 2050 (UN probabilistic Projections (2015).

While the importance of its role in Australian society remains, and could well increase, the future delivery of Australian life insurance will be shaped by changes to customer profiles, trust, regulation, technology, gradual integration with Asian economies and rebase lined economic expectations.

Australia's demographics is changing and this will have a profound impact on life insurance risk companies. Millennials are growing in importance. They are already one of the largest demographic groups in the workforce and by 2025, will represent 75 per cent of the global workforce (Forbes 2016). Millennials are highly educated, care deeply about social impact, are accustomed to transacting online, and expect most transactions to be high quality digital experiences.

This demographic division is profound and will impact on how insurers position their brand in the market, their core value proposition and how they engage with customers to remain competitive. In order to be competitive, insurers will need to be deliberate about which customers they target – focusing on the over 65 segment, for instance, will require tailored products to meet the needs of an ageing population, with their unique longevity and financial challenges. On the other hand, high quality digital experiences aimed at millennials require significant upfront investments to build infrastructure and a complete rethink of the current customer experience, but may have lower ongoing operating costs in the long run.

Issue of Trust

A recent PwC survey demonstrated that Australian customers have high confidence in their ability to self-manage their finances. The same survey found that Australians generally understand the need for life insurance, and believe they have adequate coverage. However, as a population, Australians are in fact underinsured – a life insurance premium as a proportion of GDP is much smaller than in comparable developed countries (e.g., 1.5 times smaller than in Sweden, and 2 times smaller than in Japan). The survey suggests that the underinsurance gap could be due in part to the perception by consumers that life insurance is a low engagement purchase, but it may also be a consequence of a lack of trust and product complexity (PwC 2016).

It is easy to see why a natural human scepticism might affect trust in life insurance – for example, "why pay premiums for a low likelihood event in the future, and even if it occurs will they pay?" Exacerbating this sentiment, media investigations have led to perception of serious cultural problems, and regulatory pressures have increased. Trust in life insurance remains an issue no one has addressed – the same survey found that while 78 percent of Australians view life insurance as important, only 42 percent believe their life insurer will be there for them in their time of need. Several recent high profile reputational scandals have only widened the gap between insurers and customers when it comes to trust and responding to these concerns remains a near term focus for several insurers.

The challenge is exacerbated by customer centric businesses in other sectors that have their customers' trust. Life insurance, which lacks the supply chain complexity of general insurance, might be easier to disrupt, if one has the capital. The imperative for life insurers to claim back the mantle of trust has never been stronger.

As can be seen the issues facing the life insurance risk industry re profound and readers will need to be aware of changes as they develop.

At a glance

- The life insurance industry in Australia is governed by the *Life Insurance Act 1995* (Cth) (LI Act), which is concerned with the financial strength of life companies, maintaining a viable, competitive and innovative industry, and the promotion of fair dealing. It does this by:

  » controlling who can start up a life company and how policyholder premiums are protected

  » specifying required capital standards

  » allowing APRA to inspect records and, with ASIC, to monitor performance and compliance with the LI Act

  » giving APRA the power to place a life company in judicial management or wind it up

  » allowing the transfer or amalgamation of life business

  » mandating a raft of protective issues relating to life policies

  » allowing APRA to collect statistics and issue prudential rules

  » the life insurance risk industry is undergoing profound changes and subject to unpresented challenges.

8-150   Study questions

8.1   Explain the difference between life insurance and general insurance.

8.2   What is meant by the term *policyholder* and describe the rights of a policyholder under a life insurance policy.

8.3   Compare and contrast *investment account policies* and *investment-linked policies*.

8.4   Explain the functions of *rate making* and *underwriting* in life insurance.

8.5   Discuss the terms, mortality and morbidity.

8.6   Explain how group and individual underwriting differ.

8.7   Discuss *solvency* and *capital adequacy*.

8-160   References

References

Australian Bureau of Statistics (ABS) 2019, *Population Projections, Series B.* Available at ABS.gov.au

Australian Prudential Regulation Authority (APRA) 2019, *Life Insurance Claims and Disputes Statistics*. Available at apra.com.au

Australian Prudential Regulation Authority (APRA) 2018, *Insight*. Available at apra.gov.au

Australian Prudential Regulation Authority (APRA) 2019, *Statistics*. Available at apra.gov.au

Australian Securities and Investments Commission, *Submission 45*, pp. 30–31. Available at https://download.asic.gov.au/media/4537030/pjc-inquiry-life-insurance-industry.pdf

Australian Securities and Investments Commission (ASIC) Regulatory Guide 165 (RG): *Licensing: internal and external dispute resolution schemes*. Available at asic.gov.au

Forbes Workforce 2020: *What You Need to Know*, May 2015. Available at forbes.com/sites/workday/2016/05/05/workforce-2020-what-you-need-to-know-now/#23e743722d63

PwC survey (PwC) 2016. Available at PwC.com.au

Strategic insight 2019. Available atwww.strategic-i.com.au

UN Probabilistic Projections based on World Population Prospects: *The 2015 Revision, 2015*. Available at un.org/en/development/desa/publications/world-population-prospects-2015-revision.html

Legislation

Life Insurance Act 1995 (Cth)

Life Insurance Regulations 1995 (Cth)

Websites

Australian Bureau of Statistics (ABS): *abs.gov.au*

Australian Prudential Regulation Authority (APRA): *apra.gov.au*

Superannuation Complaints Service (SCS): *sct.gov.au*

CHAPTER 9

INTRODUCTION TO GENERAL INSURANCE

LEGISLATION AND REGULATION

9-000   *Insurance Act 1973*

The structure of the general insurance industry in Australia is influenced by the *Insurance Act 1973* (Cth) as amended. The Australian Prudential Regulatory Authority (APRA) is charged with administering the Act (with the exception of s 113) and monitoring the day-to-day affairs of authorised insurers. The Australian Securities and Investments Commission (ASIC) is also involved in the regulation of the general insurance industry as it has the power to approve the codes of practice, a power originally granted under se 113 of the Insurance Act. However, s 113 was repealed by the *Financial Services Reform (Consequential Provisions) Act 2001*, and this authority is now contained in s 1101A of the *Corporations Act 2001* (Cth).

APRA had been consulting with the general insurance industry since its inception to modernise the Insurance Act, as well as generating a set of prudential standards for the industry designed to be responsive to changing circumstances. The repercussions of the collapse of HIH hastened the introduction of the *General Insurance Reform Act 2001* (Cth) (GIR Act), which amended the Insurance Act and introduced a more stringent supervisory regime for the general insurance industry. This GIR Act was assented to on 19 September 2001 with the important Sch 1 and 3 taken to commence on 2 July 2002. The GIR Act totally repealed Pt III, IV and IVA of the Insurance Act and amended many other individual sections.

Part III: Authorisation to carry on insurance business

Section 2A(1) of the Insurance Act (as amended by the GIR Act) states that its main object is:

> "to protect the interests of policyholders and prospective policyholders under insurance policies (issued by general insurers and Lloyd's underwriters) in ways that are consistent with the continued development of a viable, competitive and innovative insurance industry."

It does this mainly by:

- requiring general insurers, and directors and senior managers, to meet certain suitability requirements

- making directors and senior managers responsible for the protection of policyholders' interests

- imposing requirements to promote prudent management
- providing for the prudential supervision of general insurers by APRA (s 2A(2), Insurance Act).

The Insurance Act applies to general insurers, with special provisions applying to Lloyd's underwriters.

The Insurance Act specifies the need for authorisation to carry on insurance business (s 9), that this authorisation is granted in writing by APRA (s 12) and that it may be issued subject to conditions (s 13). Section 15 lists a number of instances in which APRA may revoke an authorisation, such as where an insurer fails to have adequate capital and is unlikely to have adequate capital within a reasonable time.

A non-operating holding company (NOHC) is defined in s 2A(3) of the Insurance Act. Division 4 applies to the authorisation of such a body corporate and the conditions that may be imposed in relation to its authorisation. APRA can revoke such an authorisation and must do so in appropriate circumstances.

Section 17B prohibits the transfer of the business of a general insurer to another insurer or its amalgamation with another insurer unless a copy of the scheme, accompanied by an actuarial report, has been submitted to, and approved by, APRA (s 17C(2)).

The Insurance Act also ensures the integrity of the industry by prohibiting disqualified persons from acting as a director or senior manager of a general insurer (s 24(1)(a)), or a senior manager (s 24(1)(b)) or agent of a foreign insurer (s 24(1)(c)). Section 25 defines a disqualified person as:

- a person who has committed an offence under:
  - » this Act
  - » the *Financial Sector (Collection of Data) Act 2001*
  - » the Corporations Act, or a law in a foreign country that corresponds with the Corporations Act
- or a person who has been:
  - » convicted of dishonest conduct in Australia or in a foreign country
  - » a bankrupt (or becomes one)
  - » disqualified by APRA
  - » convicted under s 19B of the *Crimes Act 1914* (Cth).

In addition, APRA may disqualify a person if it is satisfied that the person is not a fit and proper person (s 25A, Insurance Act).

Finally, a general insurer must hold assets in Australia of a value equal to or greater than the amount of its liabilities in Australia (s 28), and if it wishes to change its name it must place a notice in a daily newspaper that circulates in each state or territory in which the insurer carries on insurance business (s 29).

Part IIIA: Prudential standards and monitoring of general insurers, authorised NOHC and their subsidiaries

Section 32 of the Insurance Act gives APRA the authority to determine and modify prudential standards, which are disallowable instruments for the purpose of s 46A of the *Acts Interpretation Act 1901* (Cth). A disallowable instrument is a type of delegated legislation (to APRA in this case) that must be tabled in both houses of Parliament shortly after having been made. If either house passes a motion to disallow the instrument, it will cease to have effect. In addition, all disallowable instruments are referred to the Senate Standing Committee on Regulations and Ordinances for scrutiny. The purpose of making a piece of delegated legislation a disallowable instrument is to allow for parliamentary scrutiny of rules made by non-parliamentary bodies.

General insurers have an obligation to comply with prudential standards (s 35, Insurance Act).

Part IV: Auditors, actuaries and accounts

Under the Insurance Act, a general insurer must have an auditor and an actuary (s 39), and if APRA requires, a specified auditor approved by APRA (s. 40) who must comply with the prudential standards in performing their duties (s 41). Under s 44, APRA may disqualify a person from holding any appointment as an auditor or actuary of a general insurer.

Section 49J sets out the role of an auditor of a general insurance company, while section 49K sets out the role of an actuary. In addition, s 49 provides that auditors and actuaries of a general insurance company must give APRA accurate information or produce books, accounts or documents about the insurer. If the information is given to APRA in good faith and without negligence, the auditor will not be subject any action, claim or demand in respect of the information given (s 49C). APRA also has the power to conduct an actuarial investigation of a general insurer's liabilities to be prepared by an independent actuary (s 49E). Finally, section 49Q requires a general insurer to keep its accounting records in Australia, in English or in a form readily convertible into English (s 49Q(1)).

Part V: Investigations

Part V of the Insurance Act concerns the powers given to APRA to conduct investigations into a general insurance company where the company is unlikely to meet its liabilities or has contravened or failed to comply with a provision of the Act, or where there appears to be a risk to the security of its assets or financial condition (s 51).

APRA is able to enter the premises of the general insurer, examine the books, take possession of the books and make copies of or take extracts from the books (s 54) and require a prescribed person to produce these books and provide reasonable assistance or appear before a specified authorised person or inspector for examination in relation to the investigation (s 55). It is an offence to conceal, destroy or alter a book in relation to the matter being investigated and a breach of this requirement is subject to a term of three months' imprisonment or a fine under the *Crimes Act 1914*.

Part VI: Review of decisions

Part VI of the Insurance Act gives a person affected by a reviewable decision the right to make a written request to the Treasurer or APRA to reconsider the decision (s 63). This request must be made within 21 days after the decision comes to the notice of the person (s 63(2)).

Part VII: Lloyd's

Part VII of the Insurance Act deals with Lloyd's underwriters and the legal personal representative of a Lloyd's underwriter, and specifies that Lloyd's must establish a security trust fund called a 'designated security trust fund' to satisfy final judgements in respect of a class of insurance liabilities specified in the deed (s 67). Section 70 gives APRA the power to make rules in relation to designated security trust funds.

Section 74 gives APRA considerable powers over the operations of Lloyd's underwriters; eg, APRA can direct that Lloyd's underwriters must not issue or renew policies, and rule when APRA can exercise these powers. Section 75 allows APRA to require Lloyd's to conduct an actuarial investigation by an independent auditor into the adequacy of the security provided by the designated security trust funds.

APRA is also empowered to make enquiries into the affairs of a designated security trust fund (s 77) and to direct the trustees of the fund not to deal with certain assets (s 78). APRA or its inspector is allowed to enter premises (s 80), and a person must not intentionally or recklessly contravene a requirement of APRA or the inspector (s 82).

Division 5 of the Act allows APRA to apply to the Federal Court for an order that a designated security trust fund be placed under judicial trusteeship (s 88) and the grounds on which such an order can be made, such as that Lloyd's have contravened the security trust fund arrangements as specified in s 68 (s 89). The judicial trustee is empowered to formulate a written scheme for the winding up or dissolution, or both, of the fund (s 92M).

Division 6 enables APRA to require Lloyd's to show cause why their underwriting authorisation should not be withdrawn (s 93), which must be answered within three months after service of APRA's notice (s 93(3)). However, Lloyd's do have a right of appeal by making application to the court (ss 93(6)(e); (7)).

Finally, Division 7 deals with miscellaneous matters including injunctions (s 94A), Lloyd's agents (s 95), address for service of notices (s 96) and other matters.

Part X: Miscellaneous

Part X of the Insurance Act deals with administrative matters such as the requirement of a general insurer to produce information, documents, books, etc, when requested by APRA (s 115); access to premises (s 115A); the requirement that a general insurer not trade after the start of winding up (s 116); a definition of what constitutes 'assets' in Australia in relation to s 28 (s 116A), address for service of notices in Australia (s 117) and the requirement of a foreign insurer to have a resident agent in Australia (s 118).

At a glance

The operations of the general insurance industry in Australia are governed by the Insurance Act 1973 (Cth) as amended. This Act contains provisions:

- appointing APRA as the principal supervisory body to monitor the operations of authorised insurers, including Lloyd's underwriters
- requiring that general insurers, including Lloyd's underwriters, are authorised in writing by APRA to conduct business in Australia
- empowering APRA to revoke an authorisation to carry on business
- giving APRA the authority to determine prudential standards, which are disallowable instruments
- governing the operations of Lloyd's underwriters
- requiring Lloyd's underwriters to maintain a security trust fund.

GENERAL INSURANCE MARKET DYNAMICS

9-010   Introduction

In Chapter 1 the various methods of dealing with risk were discussed. If risks cannot be totally eliminated through risk avoidance, losses that might occur have to be financed in some other way. The methods of financing these losses, which are discussed in Chapter 2, are risk retention and risk transfer (see 2-040). Retained losses must be paid out of current earnings or loss reserves, by borrowing or by a captive insurance company. Risk transfer shifts the liability to pay losses to an insurance company, but the decision to transfer or retain risks is influenced by two important factors:

*   the underwriting cycle

*   consolidation in the insurance industry.

9-020   Underwriting cycle

The general insurance industry is characterised by cyclical market behaviour with alternating periods of hard and soft market conditions. This characteristic is referred to as the underwriting cycle and is depicted in figure 9.1.

Figure 9.1: The underwriting cycle

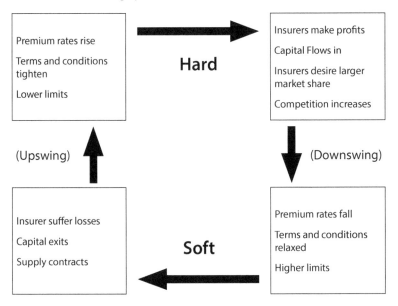

267

The downswing of the cycle can be described as the starting point from which underwriting profits peak, giving rise to capacity increases, leading to an increase in competition. This is followed by a deterioration in premium rates, relaxed wordings as the combined ratio increases, and finally major underwriting losses and falling profits — this is known as a 'soft' insurance market. On the upswing, capacity (ie, the maximum amount of insurance that an insurer will write) exits the industry, premium rates rise, wordings are tightened and the combined ratio improves, which leads to a completion of the cycle, with underwriting profits once again peaking — this is called a 'hard' insurance market.

The time period used in figure 9.2 illustrates the typical underwriting cycle that exists worldwide in general insurance. These figures show that underwriting results (ie, premiums less reinsurance, claims and other underwriting expenses, but excluding investment and other earnings) have improved since 1999 as the insurance market hardened. It also shows that the last soft market in Australia in the period illustrated occurred between 1995 and 1999, after which premium rates began to increase, but the industry did not make underwriting profits until 2003. This indicates a time lag between increasing rates and making profits.

Figure 9.2: General insurance revenue and profitability (1995–2005), year ended 30 June

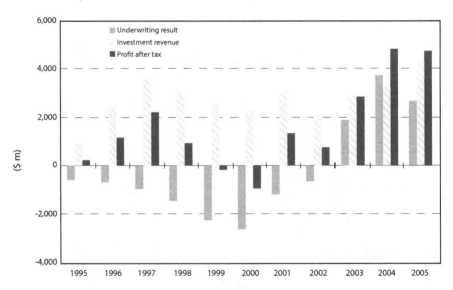

Source: APRA 2006a.

As a result of underwriting initiatives taken after 1999 and improving returns from investments, industry profitability improved further in 2006, with the underwriting result rising to $3.5 billion and profitability increasing to $5.4 billion (APRA 2006b).

One of the measures of financial year underwriting profitability that can be used to ascertain the status of the underwriting cycle is to examine the combined ratio for the industry. The combined ratio is a percentage calculated by applying the net claims and underwriting expenses to net premiums. If the combined ratio is greater than 100 per cent, the underwriting is unprofitable; if the combined ratio is less than 100 per cent, the underwriting is profitable. The ratio does not include income from investments, so a high number does not necessarily mean a company is unprofitable. Because of investment income, an insurer may be profitable even if the combined ratio is over 100 per cent. This is illustrated by the years 1995 to 1998 in figure 9.2, when, despite underwriting losses, the industry made profits after allowing for investments and tax. Table 9.2 shows the combined ratios for the period 2010 to 2015.

Table 9.2: Combined ratios for the period year end December 2013–2018

Year	2013	2014	2015	2016	2017	2018
Combined ratio (%)	93	87	94	92	88	87

Source: APRA 2018.

The combined ratio of 88 per cent in 2017 resulted in an underwriting result of $3,536 million which increased to $3,912 million as at 30 September 2018 when the combined ratio fell to 87 per cent. This increased performance was mainly the result of benign catastrophe claims experience and higher reserve/ risk margin releases and an improvement in the expense ratio of one per cent. Consequently the industry's loss ratio fell from 68.5 per cent in 2017 to 62.7 per cent in 2018.

When combined ratios are high, as shown in table 9.2 the industry tends to raise its underwriting standards and increase premiums and deductibles to offset claims. It is not always possible to raise insurance premiums across all classes of business when companies are attempting to retain good accounts particularly in the commercial insurance area. The industry is currently in a hard phase of the underwriting cycle with increasing premium rates and tighter underwriting standards.

The underwriting cycle has a significant effect on insureds, as a hardening market can make insurance premiums unaffordable, as seen by the massive increases in flood insurance premiums for households in flood areas, or make insurance coverage for some risks unavailable.

The cause of these price fluctuations can generally be traced to the competitive environment.

Competitive environment

Competition is prompted by two key factors:

- the desire to compete
- the means to compete.

The desire to compete is driven by the returns generated by the industry. If the returns are high, underwriters will be willing to compete for business, as any resulting growth is likely to be profitable at the margin. The ability to compete is driven by the capital position of the industry. If there is surplus capital in the industry, underwriters are able to finance a reduction in premiums.

Industry profitability

For the year ended 30 September 2018 APRA reported an industry net profit after tax of $ 3.9 billion up from $ 3.0 billion in the previous year. This resulted in a return on net assets of 9.6 per cent (March 2019) up from 7.0 per cent (March 2018).

Investment income allocated to insurance funds was $1,117 million down from $1,320 million in 2016/17 on the back of the continued depressed interest rate environment and conservative investment portfolios. With these ongoing low returns, some insurers have looked to diversify investment portfolios.

While a strong equity market will influence these results, a key component of profitability is the state of the combined ratio. As reflected in table 9.2, the combined ratio as at December 2018 stood at 87 per cent, an improvement on the previous year's result of 88 per cent. With these high combined ratios and the nervous outlook for the global economy, underwriters are more concerned about improving their underwriting result by raising premiums on existing business particularly in those areas of high risk as mentioned above in relation to flood coverage in domestic lines.

Surplus capital

When the industry is in a strong capital position, underwriters are able to reduce premiums and lower underwriting standards because they have a reserve to draw on if underwriting results prove unfavourable. The capital position is indicated by the strength of the industry's average minimum capital requirement. As at September 2018, the industry's average coverage of the prescribed capital requirement stood at 1.82 times, down from the 1.85 times recorded in 2017. This means there is not plenty of capital in the industry to fuel competition (APRA 2018).

However, the average coverage could change if premiums are lowered too far in times of high coverage ratios and underwriting losses start to accumulate. When this happens, one prudent remedy would be to increase premiums to reverse the cycle. However, this is a simplistic solution as the frequency and severity of claims, claims handling costs, commissions and the effect of legislative and environmental developments as well as social issues, must also be managed. To manage underwriting profitability effectively, overall expenses must be actively managed. Perhaps the easiest way to explain the operation of the insurance market and its problems is to examine the economic laws of supply and demand.

Supply and demand

Economists have long held that the most efficient distribution of society's scarce resources would occur if prices were set in a perfectly competitive market. 'Efficient' means that no-one's welfare would be increased without decreasing somebody else's welfare. Unfortunately, these requirements of perfect competition do not currently exist. These requirements include:

- numerous independent sellers, each holding a market share too small to influence price
- numerous well-informed consumers
- a homogeneous, perfectly substitutable product
- freedom of entry and exit from the market.

In a perfectly competitive world, one equilibrium price would prevail that satisfies both consumers and producers of the product or service. This point occurs at price P_1 and quantity Q_1 in figure 9.3.

Figure 9.3: Law of supply and demand

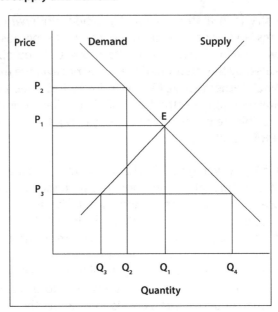

The demand curve in figure 9.3 is backward sloping, indicating that utility-maximising consumers will purchase less insurance as prices rise. Less insurance may result from a lower quantity purchased, higher deductibles or a reduction in coverage.

In the insurance context, the supply curve slopes forward, showing that insurers will provide more insurance as prices increase. Economic theory suggests that if any price other than the equilibrium price P_1 was tried by producers or consumers, dynamic forces would move the price up or down to P_1. A freely competitive market for insurance serves as a screening device. People who are most willing or able to pay obtain what is sold and firms providing insurance supply insurance at the least cost.

If prices are raised above those freely determined by the forces of supply and demand, the economic model predicts lower total welfare or total utility (or, amount of satisfaction). If prices were to be increased to P_2 and quantity demanded would fall to Q_2 in figure 9.3, then consumers would be hurt in two ways. First, some consumers would purchase insurance, but they would have to pay a higher price, thus reducing their welfare. Second, some consumers who would have purchased the insurance at the freely set price will not make the purchase at the higher price because they cannot afford to pay the higher price. Thus, forgone consumption reduces their utility.

Therefore, when premiums are too high (or excessive), policyholders will not renew their policies as they see more value in using the savings for immediate consumption. The result will be a reduction in the policyholder base and an increase in risk concentration. The outcome of risk concentration will be earnings volatility and lower profitability.

Consider the alternative where price is artificially lowered from the freely determined price, perhaps by regulation or bad underwriting (which contributed to the HIH collapse in 2001), so that the price for insurance is set at P_3 with quantity demanded at point Q_4. In this case, the total welfare would be lowered because although demand would increase beyond the equilibrium point E, supply, especially in the long term, would fall to Q_3, as firms would not be able to supply insurance at that price. In this situation, suppliers would attempt to cut back on services and other costs or move out of unprofitable areas (eg, private motor vehicle insurance) in order to maintain profits.

Additionally, if premium levels are too low, insurers are reliant on investment income to provide profitability, as shown in figure 9.2 for the years 1992 to 1998. In this situation, insurers are subject to the fluctuation of the share market, so if there is an underwriting loss combined with negative share market returns, the overall loss situation for insurers would be disastrous. As a result, capital reserves would be reduced, making them vulnerable if catastrophic losses were to occur. Inadequate premiums result in high underwriting vulnerability, an overexposure of capital and a risk of reduced profitability.

9-030   General insurance industry structure

The Australian insurance industry is highly concentrated, particularly with respect to personal lines, which includes comprehensive and compulsory third party (CTP) motor vehicle insurance, household building/contents and personal liability insurance, together with pleasure craft coupled with liability insurance. Table 9.3 shows that the increase in concentration from 1993 to 2011 has been significant.

Table 9.3: Industry structure by gross written premiums

Year	Top six companies (%)	Rest of companies (%)
1993	38	62
2018	78	22

Source: Information derived from KPMG, *General Insurance Industry Survey 2018*

Table 9.3 shows that the top six general insurance groups accounted for 38 per cent of gross written premiums in 1993, increasing to approximately 78 per cent in 2018. Significantly, in 1993 the rest of the companies held 62 per cent of gross written premiums, but in 2018, 90 companies out of a total of 97 held only 22 per cent of gross written premiums, which indicates a very long tail of smaller insurers and a dramatic change in the competitive landscape.

As at March 2019 , the APRA *Quarterly General Insurance Performance* report indicated that there are 96 licensed general insurance companies authorised by APRA to operate in Australia, down from 115 in 2011. Table 9.4 shows the gross written premiums of the top 10 companies for 2018. (Note: Some companies have a balance date of 31 December, while others have a balance date of 30 June.)

Table 9.4: Top ten general insurers in 2018

Company	Gross written premiums ($ million)
QBE Insurance Group	$13,657
Insurance Australia Group	$8,128
Suncorp Insurance Group	$8,001
Allianz Australia Group	$4,500
Zurich Australian Insurance	$1,029
RACQ Insurance	$852
CommInsure	$768
AIG Australia Limited	$736
Auto & General Insurance Co. Ltd	$690
Youi Pty Ltd	$736
Westpac Insurance	$507
Total	**$39,604**

Source: KPMG General Insurance Industry Survey 2018

The total reported general insurance gross premium revenue for the year ended September 2018 was $ 4.275 billion (KPMG 2018). Industry concentration is illustrated by six companies writing 78 per cent of the gross written premium by these 10 companies. Of significance is the appearance of two bank insurance companies in the top 10, which illustrates their penetration of their customer base.

This concentration would indicate only a limited scope for further consolidation mainly because of the current high valuations of general insurers in Australia relative (as discussed below) to international comparators. This would suggest that further mergers and acquisitions may be concentrated on mid- and small-sized insurers, including specialist insurers such as mortgage insurers, other foreign-owned insurers and bank-owned insurers (JP Morgan and Deloitte 2006).

The KPMG General Insurance Industry Survey 2015 indicates that despite the increased industry concentration, the level of competition remains strong with ever increasing transparency and policy features due to both financial service reform and greater information availability. Importantly, there have been no failures of insurers since HIH a decade ago.

In addition to private sector insurers, there are 14 public sector insurers that are not subject to the Insurance Act. These insurers are the remaining federal and state government insurance offices, which were set up in times past, when state socialism was seen as the way to combat the excesses of private capitalism in many markets. These insurers comprise workers compensation authorities such as WorkCover Queensland and WorkCover Authority of NSW, compulsory motor vehicle third party insurers such as the Transport Accident Commission and the Motor Accident Commission, and export insurance authorities such as the Export Finance and Insurance Corporation. In addition to these insurers, the Defence Service Homes Insurance Scheme (effectively a self-insurer) provides home insurance to eligible veterans and defence force personnel.

9-040   Market structure

The total number of insurers authorised to conduct business in Australia as at September 2018 was 91, down from 115 in 2011(APRA 2019). This decline can be explained in part by the introduction by APRA of a minimum capital requirement of $5 million in 2002, plus further capital adequacy requirements, mergers and acquisitions. Further reasons include that companies in a run-off situation have withdrawn from the market, while others have been taken over by bigger insurance groups. The general insurance industry can be classified according to the type of business written and the participants, as illustrated in figure 9.4.

Figure 9.4: Structure of the general insurance industry

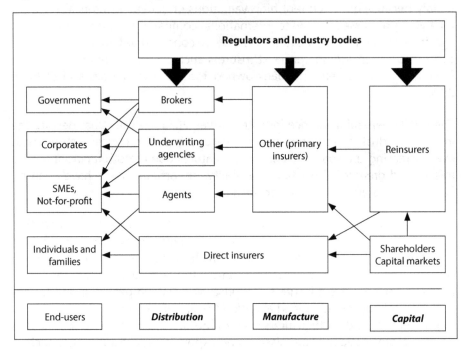

Source: Based on D Minty 2002, *General Insurance in Australia.*
Presentation to UNSW actuarial students, 27 August 2002

Figure 9.4 illustrates an industry structure based on:

- *direct and primary insurers:* may underwrite (ie, manufacture) and/or directly distribute
- *brokers, agents and underwriting agencies:* distribute to particular markets or channels
- *reinsurers:* provide catastrophe and large loss protection for insurers
- *capital:* provided by the owners of a business and by financiers
- *regulators and industry bodies:*
  - » Australian Prudential Regulation Authority (APRA)
  - » Australian Securities and Investments Commission (ASIC)
  - » Australian Competition and Consumer Commission (ACCC)
  - » Insurance Council of Australia Limited (ICA)
  - » National Insurance Brokers' Association (NIBA)

» Institute of Actuaries of Australia (Actuaries Institute)

» Australian and New Zealand Institute of Insurance and Finance (ANZIIF).

While insurance business can be classified according to type, as mentioned above, it can also be thought of in terms of personal and commercial lines. Personal lines are defined in 9-030. Commercial lines embraces physical damage to property and stock covered by fire and industrial special risks (ISR) policies, which may include injury to third parties and staff, professional indemnity, workers compensation, theft, public and products liability, and a number of additional policies, all of which are discussed in detail in Chapter 13.

Intermediaries facilitate the flow of insurance from suppliers/manufacturers to end-users. They also provide advice on levels of protection, policy terms and assistance with claims. Individuals, partnerships or small businesses are authorised under agency or broker agreements to sell insurance on behalf of one or more (in the case of multi-agents) insurance companies. Agents are generally paid a commission, which is calculated as a percentage of the base premium charged by the underwriter for a particular risk. The relationship between the agent and the insured, and his or her legal responsibility, is discussed in detail in Chapter 4.

An *insurance broker* is appointed as a professional adviser. The broker's role is not just to purchase insurance cover, but also to analyse the insured's business and find a satisfactory solution to the client's risk and insurance needs. Some large brokers have dedicated risk management businesses that provide an important service to large businesses. The regulation of brokers and their legal responsibilities is discussed in detail in Chapter 4. Brokers act for and have a legal responsibility to their clients; therefore, professional indemnity insurance can at times be difficult and expensive to obtain.

Brokers can be divided into local brokers, who tend to concentrate their efforts on the small business, farm and household markets, and international brokers, who have branches in many countries and generally arrange insurance for major companies as well as specialised risks such as floating oil rigs and super oil tankers. Major brokers include are Aon Corporation Australia Limited, Marsh Australia, Jardine Lloyd Thompson Australia Pty Limited and Willis Australia Limited.

Underwriting agencies are wholesalers of insurance capacity provided by general insurers. They are generally established and supported by a group of insurers on the principle of sharing high-risk or specialist exposures such as childcare centres, accessing the expertise of specialist individuals and/or providing a more cost-effective method of distribution. These agencies generally only accept risks placed by brokers or particular organisations, such as the National Rugby League. Underwriting agencies include the Australian Aviation Underwriting Pool Pty Limited, Dexta Corporation Limited, Over Fifty Insurance Pty Limited, SLE Worldwide Australia Pty Limited and Triton Insurance Agency Pty Limited.

Reinsurers are in effect the insurers' insurers. Reinsurers wield significant power and influence in the market, and it is often their perceptions of risk and premium rating that dictate the final terms of cover. Although an insurer may issue a policy for a $40 million public liability cover or a $100 million property insurance cover, in reality, most of this risk is not retained by that insurer but passes on to a reinsurer.

Reinsurance allows an insurer to stabilise its underwriting results by spreading the effects of any potential losses and to increase its capacity to underwrite larger risks. In simple terms, reinsurance is available to insurers under either *facultative* or *treaty* placements or a combination of both. Reinsurance is discussed at 10-050.

Other participants in the general insurance industry include mortgage insurers, captive insurers and section 37 exempt insurers.

Mortgage insurers provide mortgage protection for property loans, which is a condition of many property finance contracts, especially where the loan-to-value ratio is high (eg, greater than 80 per cent). Mortgage insurance reduces the risk of loss for the lender if the borrower defaults and when the property is sold the realised value is less than the valuation used to structure the loan.

Captive insurers are companies that underwrite some or all of the risks of a company and its subsidiaries within the group of related companies and are usually established as a subsidiary of the organisation. These subsidiaries pay insurance premiums to the captive or to an insurer (called a fronting insurer) who issues a policy on behalf of the captive and looks to the captive to pay any losses incurred.

Captives are the most sophisticated self-insurance mechanism. They are used by larger organisations internationally to maximise the benefits of their self-insured retentions. Many of the top 100 companies as well as some mutual and cooperative organisations, use captives to varying degrees.

Section 37 exempt insurers who write a limited amount of insurance for associations only and do not write contracts of insurance for any other persons.

Exempt insurers include the Dentists' Sickness and Accidents Insurance and the Taxi Insurance Co-Operative.

1-050   Reinsurance

Reinsurance, at least in the eyes of the regulators, and in many people's eyes, connotes property and casualty reinsurance. It's a huge industry. In contrast, life reinsurance, in many ways, is smaller. There are very fundamental differences between life and property and casualty. For example, the risk concentration issue in life reinsurance is fairly small. However, Hurricanes Harvey (2017) and Katrina (2005) was not a very big deal in the life insurance business, but damage from wind and floods cost US$125 billion and US$161 billion respectively. If you were a property and casualty insurer doing business in southern Florida, and if you weren't properly reinsured, these hurricanes may have put you out of business because of the high concentration of loss in one area.

The term of *risk* is a fundamental difference. Life insurance risks are typically very long as they are lifetime risks whereas property and casualty risk can be very short. There are one-year agreements, or they can be very long in what are often called long-tail agreements. A perfect example is asbestos and pollution risks. There are risks that were written in the 1950s that nobody really believed would be coming to claim in the 1990s and 2000s, but they are.

The claim amount is what makes the mathematics of reinsurance very different. If you have a $100,000 life insurance policy, and the individual dies, the odds are overwhelming that the beneficiary is going to get $100,000. If you have a property and casualty risk, as in automobile insurance, and you damage your Mercedes, you don't know how much you are going to get. It depends on how big the crash was. Did you total the car? Was it a fender bender? The point is the claim amount isn't known until the event takes place. That makes the mathematics of it completely different. It makes the entire approach to the risk completely different.

There are further differences. The premium rates in life are typically fixed. For term or income protection policies, there's a single premium rate that is paid for the life of the contracts. In contrast, for property and casualty insurance, rates are typically changed every year. Reinsurance policies are written for a single year when premium rates are renegotiated with the policies renewed and replaced at the end of the year. The balance sheet focus for life used to be liabilities, but with the whole notion of immunization theory and asset/liability matching, the focus is now more often on the asset side of the risk. In the property and casualty business, the primary focus is on the liability side because that's where insurance companies really take their serious losses. For example, the 2019 category 5 hurricane Dorian, which devastated northwestern Bahamas.

The process of reinsurance

Reinsurance involves an agreement between two or more insurance companies to share proportionally in the risk of loss; thus the risk of loss is spread and a disproportionately large loss under a single policy does not fall on one company. Another insurer, called a reinsurer, accepts all or part of the risk of loss from the insurer; an insurer who issues a liability policy for $100,000 per accident, for example, may reinsure its liability in excess of $10,000.

There are two types of reinsurance: contributing or proportional reinsurance; and non-contributory or non-proportional reinsurance. With contributing or proportional reinsurance, the reassured passes on a proportion of the liability on an individual risk or a number of risks, and pays the same proportion of the individual premium to the reinsurer, who will reimburse the reassured for the same proportion for any claims. These two types of reinsurance are shown in the following illustrated example.

Illustrated example 9.1

Prudent Insurance Pty Ltd accepts an insurance for $100,000 on a shop and passes on, or cedes, to Greater Pacific Re $70,000 or 70 per cent of the $100,000. Greater Pacific Re accepts 70 per cent of the liability and 70 per cent of the original premium. If a claim for $1,000 arises, Greater Pacific Re will pay to Prudent Insurance Pty Ltd its 70 per cent share, or $700.

In contrast, with non-proportional reinsurance the reassured will retain a certain percentage of the risk and cede the remainder. Prudent Insurance takes out a non-proportional reinsurance with Greater Pacific Re to reinsure should the shop suffer a loss exceeding $30,000 up to the value of the shop of $100,000. Greater Pacific Re assumes the liability of up to $70,000 in excess of $30,000 on any one loss in respect of that shop. In the event of a claim of $30,000 or less, Greater Pacific Re makes no contribution to that loss. Should the claim exceed $30,000, Greater Pacific Re reimburses Prudent Insurance for the amount of loss in excess of $30,000 up to a further $70,000.

Although Greater Pacific Re takes on 70 per cent of the total policy liability, it does not contribute proportionally to all losses, and therefore does not receive a proportionate share of the premium. Such a non-proportional reinsurance is called an excess of loss contract, because Greater Pacific Re's liability only commences in excess of a certain defined amount.

There are three ways of effecting reinsurance: facultative, obligatory treaty and by contract or policy of indemnity.

Facultative reinsurance

Facultative reinsurance was the earliest method of reinsurance used and simply offers another insurer a portion of an individual risk where the amount accepted is too large for the company's own requirements. If the offer is accepted, a simple reinsurance policy is issued between the two parties. The essential element of the facultative method is the offer of part of the risk and its acceptance or rejection. There is no obligation to make the offer and no obligation to accept it. As each reinsurance is offered and accepted or rejected individually, the accepting or rejecting reinsurer must make its own judgement of each risk in much the same way that it would if offered the same risk as a direct insurer. Both of the above examples of a shop insured for $100,000 are examples of facultative reinsurance.

Obligatory treaty reinsurance

Obligatory treaty reinsurance refers to agreements between the reassured and reinsurer that allows the insurer to automatically accept a risk offered by a client or broker within formally agreed limits and parameters. The formal agreement, or obligatory treaty, will stipulate the type of business to be ceded, the amounts to be ceded, and the terms and conditions under which cessions are to be made. In illustrated example 9.1, suppose Prudent Insurance is insuring shops and instead of insuring each one facultatively, it enters into an obligatory treaty with Greater Pacific Re under which Prudent Insurance agrees to cede (ie, pass on) to Greater Pacific Re 70 per cent of liability on *all* the shops insured for $100,000 or less that Prudent Insurance underwrites, and to pass on 70 per cent of all premiums received. Greater Pacific Re agrees to accept 70 per cent of the liability and to pay 70 per cent of all claims that may arise. This type of treaty is known as a quota share treaty.

Policy of indemnity

The third main method of reinsurance is by a non-contributing contract or policy of indemnity. This method of reinsurance is clarified in the following illustrated example.

Illustrated example 9.2

Prudent Insurance Pty Ltd has entered into an obligatory quota share treaty with Liverpool Insurance Pty Ltd to reinsure 70 per cent of all insured shops up to a maximum of 70 per cent of $100,000 on any one shop. Prudent Insurance will retain 30 per cent of all shops up to a maximum of $30,000 on any one shop. On a small shop valued at $20,000 the line retained by Prudent Insurance will be $6,000 (ie, 30 per cent of $20,000). As a result of the number of shops that Prudent Insurance has insured, it is concerned that a large fire, or some similar disaster, could occur that might destroy a number of shops and that the retained lines of 30 per cent might be considerable. As a precaution, Prudent Insurance decides to limit the possible loss from such an event to $50,000, leaving a net loss of $50,000 in any such disaster. Prudent Insurance buys reinsurance from Guardian Re to reinsure any loss in excess of $50,000 in any one disaster involving more than one shop. Such a contract is a contract of indemnity for which Prudent Insurance will pay a premium to Guardian Re to be indemnified against a disaster costing Prudent Insurance more than $50,000. This is an example of an excess of loss contract.

Let's take the example one step further. Prudent Insurance finds that shops are being consistently proposed for insurance valued between $100,000 and $200,000. While there are other options, let's simply assume that Prudent Insurance arranges another obligatory contributing treaty in addition to the 70 per cent quota share treaty. This treaty would be an agreement under which Prudent Insurance can cede to another reinsurer or the same reinsurer, but for this explanation it is assumed that a different reinsurer, London Re, is used to accept all amounts surplus to $100,000 up to a further $100,000 on any one shop, and London Re agrees to automatically accept all such surplus amounts up to a further $100,000 for any one shop. Thus, Prudent Insurance knows that London Re's liability attaches automatically with Prudent Insurance, and it can accept insurance up to $200,000 on a shop knowing that its liability is automatically ceded to London Re.

Such an obligatory contributing treaty is known as a surplus treaty. The quota share treaty and the surplus treaty are the two types of contributing treaties.

Prudent Insurance is now asked to insure a shop valued at $250,000. Prudent Insurance may enter into a facultative contributing reinsurance for $50,000, part of $250,000 on this shop, then cede $100,000, part of

$250,000, to the surplus treaty and then cede 70 per cent of $100,000 to the 70 per cent quota share treaty. Prudent Insurance's retained line on the shop would be $30,000, part of $250,000. In the event of any loss on the risk, all would contribute proportionally to that loss.

How this reinsurance arrangement would work in the event of a claim is discussed in the following illustrated example.

Illustrated example 9.3

A loss of $100,000 would be apportioned as follows:

Facultative reinsurance contributes	$20,000 – 20% ($50,000 of $250,000)
Surplus treaty contributes	$40,000 – 40% ($100,000 of $250,000)
Quota share treaty contributes	$28,000 – 28% ($70,000 of $250,000)
Prudent Insurance retained loss is	$12,000 – 12% ($30,000 of $250,000)

Let's continue the example by assuming that Prudent Insurance, the reassured, has built up a sizeable book of shop business, which represents a sizeable book of premium income. (The term *book* is used to describe all the business of a particular type held by a company. Therefore, all domestic insurance held by a company would be referred to as the company's domestic book of business.) However, Prudent Insurance is worried that a bad claims year would upset the whole balance of profit and loss on its insurance account. In order to protect the book of business, Prudent Insurance seeks a contract of indemnity to reimburse the underwriter if in any one year's operation the losses on the net retained account are excessive, ie, if Prudent Insurance's aggregation of losses after collecting from the reinsurances, the surplus treaty, the quota share treaty and the catastrophe excess of loss exceed a certain figure. Such a contract would stop Prudent Insurance's annual net losses at a certain predetermined amount. This is a contract of indemnity known as a stop loss or excess aggregate reinsurance.

The amount at which Prudent Insurance's losses are stopped can be a monetary figure; more often it is expressed as a ratio of the annual retained premium income from the shop account. The retained premium income is Prudent Insurance's gross premium income after deduction of premiums ceded to their facultative reinsurances, the surplus treaty, the quota share treaty and premiums paid for the catastrophe or disaster excess of loss contract. How a stop loss treaty works is shown in the following illustrated example.

Illustrated example 9.4

Suppose Prudent Insurance anticipates a retained premium income of $100,000 per annum and wishes to limit the aggregation of losses in any one year to $150,000. Prudent Insurance could buy a stop loss excess of $150,000 in the aggregate per annum or excess of 150 per cent of their annual retained premium income.

Prudent Insurance has now used all types of reinsurance and all methods. All reinsurance is based on these principles, which can be summarised as follows:

- Facultative reinsurance reinsures individual large risks or exposures.

- A contributing surplus treaty automatically takes all risks over a certain size.

- A contributing quota share treaty takes a fixed proportion of all risks.

- An excess of loss contract protects against an unfortunate disaster.

A stop loss contract protects against an unfortunate aggregation of losses during a period of time.

However, reinsurance needs to be considered in the order in which they operate:

1. Facultative reinsurance reduces a peak exposure.
2. First surplus further reduces individual exposures.
3. The quota share further reduces all exposures.
4. The excess of loss protects the remaining accumulations.
5. The stop loss protects the residual net exposures against an adverse experience.

In other words, the stop loss has the benefit of all the other reinsurances; ie, any losses collected under points 1 to 4 are deducted before calculating the loss under the stop loss.

9-060 Investments

Figure 9.2 illustrates how important investment income is to the general insurance industry, because in the years 1995 to 2002, when the industry was making underwriting losses, it was achieving substantial returns on its investments, which counteracted these losses (with the exception of years 1999 and 2000) (see figure 9.2). It is arguable that these high investment returns from insurers' investment portfolios were a major factor contributing to the prolonged soft market from 1995 to 2002.

The aggregate balance sheet for the general insurance industry comprises mainly investments and unpaid premiums as assets and, largely, underwriting and other provisions among the liabilities. Because liabilities consist mainly of provisions, there is an evident time lag between the requirement to pay out liabilities and the time they are recognised. Hence, companies have a considerable value in their investments, so they are able to pay when required.

About half of total investments held by general insurers within Australia are held in debt securities such as government bonds, floating rate notes, short-term notes (30, 60, 90 and 180 days), and so on. The advantage of this form of investment is that maturities can be scheduled to meet expected payment obligations. Further investments are held in deposits, which are readily available to meet liabilities, listed and unlisted equities, indirect investments, property, managed investments and s 30 (Insurance Act) loans to directors and employees.

Investment in unlisted equity deserves comment because these investments suffer from liquidity problems. One could surmise that the reason for their inclusion in the investment mix is because the companies expect to make superior returns from holding (probably large) direct stakes in other firms. These may include so-called private equity and venture capital propositions.

In recent times, insurers have concentrated on backing their technical reserves with interest-earning and cash investments, as suggested above, with shareholder funds and surplus capital being invested in equity markets. Thus, any increases in equity exposure can be linked to the increases in capital.

At a glance

- The dynamics of the general insurance industry are influenced by the underwriting cycle and concentration of business to the top six companies.

- The underwriting cycle reflects how general insurance premiums alternate between hard and soft, which influences underwriting profits.

- The combined ratio indicates the status of the underwriting cycle.

- Companies need both the desire and the means to compete for market share.

- The means to compete is provided by a strong combined ratio and surplus capital.

- The top six companies, which control 92 per cent of the market, dominate the general industry in Australia.

- Australia has 14 public sector insurers, which are not subject to the Insurance Act.

- The stakeholders in the general insurance industry can be classified as end-users, distributors, manufacturers and suppliers of capital.

- Reinsurance contracts can be classified as either contributing/proportional or non-contributing/non-proportional.

- General insurance companies hold about 50 per cent of their investments in debt securities so as to have funds readily available to meet policy liabilities.

- Shareholder funds and surplus capital are invested in equity markets.

PRUDENTIAL STANDARDS AND SOLVENCY

9-070   Background

Financial institutions such as general insurance companies have a large number of retail customers many of whom are unable to make informed and sufficiently accurate judgements about the financial strength of a general insurer and the capacity of an insurer to meet its promises, now and in the future. The consequences of failing to meet promises may be considerable.

The financial system is prone to external events as was seen in 2008 when the global financial crisis (GFC) shook the financial world by triggering a contagion event that lead to the insolvency of many financial institutions. Several overseas insurers would have failed but for a timely government bailout. The financial regulators are concerned that the failure of an individual firm could cause a contagion effect where this failure could spread to other institutions or sectors.

The GFC illustrated how events in the financial world tend to move rapidly and the regulators must have the ability to introduce regulations in an attempt to reduce the likelihood of insolvency resulting in financial loss to policyholders. Prudential supervision helps to preserve stability across the financial system and the broader economy.

The prudential framework for general insurance is established by the Insurance Act and related instruments. Section 32 of the Insurance Act (as amended by the General Insurance Reform Act 2001) gives APRA the authority to determine (in writing) standards relating to prudential matters (prudential standards) that must be complied with by general insurers or authorised non-operating holding companies that engage in general insurance business or their subsidiaries or a specified class of any of the foregoing.

APRA's prudential standards address:

- capital adequacy
- corporate governance
- fitness and propriety of responsible persons
- asset quality and concentration
- liability valuations
- liquidity
- credit risk

- operational risk

- market risk

- insurance and reinsurance risks

- contagion risk from related entities

- outsourcing, and

- business continuity.

9-080   Solvency and capital adequacy

The financial strength of a general insurance company is determined by the quality of its capital management. Having adequate capital is vital for a company's operations by providing a buffer to absorb unanticipated losses from its insurance operations. Should such losses eventuate, having adequate capital enables the company to meet its obligations to its policyholders and remain solvent.

It is the company's Board that is responsible for ensuring that the company has capital that is adequate for the scale, nature and complexity of its business and risk profile so that it can meet its obligations under a wide range of circumstances.

A general insurer must have a documented Internal Capital Adequacy Assessment Process (ICAAP) to manage the company's capital base. The ICAAP must be appropriate for the company's size, business mix and complexity of its operations and group structure (if applicable). The capital must provide a permanent and unrestricted commitment of funds that are freely available to absorb losses.

Prudential Standard GPS 110 – *Capital Adequacy* (GPS 110) specifies that the level of capital required for regulatory purposes be referred to as the Prescribed Capital Requirement (PCR). An insurer must at all times hold eligible capital, which comprises Tier 1 and Tier 2 capital (after deducting items such as goodwill and deferred tax), in excess of its PCR and must seek approval from APRA if it proposes any reduction in its capital base. Tier 1 capital comprises the highest quality capital elements that are freely available to absorb losses and includes paid-up ordinary shares, reserves, retained earnings and current year's earnings net of expected dividends and tax expenses. The company must hold Tier 1 capital to exceed 80 per cent of the Prescribed Capital Amount (GPS112 – *Capital Adequacy: Measurement of Capital*, cl 9).

Tier 2 capital includes elements that fall short of Tier 1 capital, such as perpetual cumulative preference shares, perpetual cumulative mandatory convertible notes, perpetual cumulative subordinated debt, permanent hybrid capital instruments and 45 per cent of pre-tax revaluation reserve of property, investments held in subsidiaries and readily marketable securities available for sale in the insurance company, all of which are held at fair value (APS111, p 10). An insurance company's PCR can be determined by using one of three models:

a.   the standard framework detailed in the prudential standard — the Prescribed Method

b.   an internal model developed by the insurer to reflect the circumstances of its business — the Internal Model Based (IMB) Method, or

c.   a combination of the methods specified in (a) and (b). (GPS110, cl 22)

In all cases, insurers must have in place capital management processes, which must be set out in the insurer's Risk Management Strategy (RMS), as specified in Prudential Standard GPS 220 – *Risk Management*.

When using the Prescribed Method the prescribed capital amount will be determined as the sum of the capital charges for:

- insurance risk

- asset risk

- operational risk.

Regardless of the outcome of the method used for determining the PCR, an insurer's PCR cannot be less than $5 million. Each capital charge is briefly discussed in turn.

The insurance risk capital charge is the minimum amount of capital required to be held against insurance risks. It relates to the risk that the actual value of net insurance liabilities reported to APRA will prove to be understated. Investment risk has two components: outstanding claims risk, which relates to the risk that the net outstanding claims liabilities are greater than reported; and a charge in respect of premiums liability risk, which relates to the risk that premiums are insufficient to fund business liabilities.

The insurance risk capital charge is calculated by multiplying the net outstanding claim liabilities by the relevant outstanding claims risk factor. Prudential Standard GPS115 – *Capital Adequacy: Asset Risk Charge* Attachment B specifies the percentage factors that must be used when calculating the insurance risk charge. For example, a risk factor of 9 per cent is to be used for householders insurance business, 11 per cent for fire insurance, and 14 per cent for CTP insurance.

The asset risk capital charge relates to the risk of adverse movements in the value of an insurer's assets and off-balance sheet exposures or both (GPS 110, cl 28). Investment risk can arise from large exposures to individual assets and can be derived from risks arising from investments and from reinsurance assets. The capital charge for asset risks should reflect the potential losses arising from such risks, including asset/liability mismatch, and encourage insurers to adopt an investment policy that has regard to the term and nature of their liabilities.

Finally, the insurance concentration risk capital charge is the minimum amount of capital required to be held against insurance concentration risks. This charge represents the net financial impact on the insurance company from either a single large event, or a series of smaller events, within a one year period (GPS 110, cl 27) and is calculated by using the formulae set out in Prudential Standard GPS116 – *Capital Adequacy: Insurance Concentration Risk Charge*.

Supervisory review and assessment

Capital adequacy also depends heavily on the way an insurer monitors and manages its capital position and its risks. APRA therefore considers its supervisory processes in regard to an insurer's capital management and risk management to be of utmost importance. APRA's capital adequacy framework is based on a three pillar approach that is intended to be mutually supporting and consists of:

- Pillar I – the required capital of an insurer is the prescribed capital amount determined as the sum of the various components of prescribed capital as discussed above

- Pillar 2 – as part of the supervisory process, APRA may require an insurer to hold capital in addition to the prescribed capital amount, ie, APRA may apply a supervisory or Pillar 2 adjustment, and

- Pillar 3 relates to disclosure rather than assessment of capital.

If APRA considers that an insurer's prescribed capital amount or its capital base is inadequate in quantity or quality, APRA will make a Pillar 2 supervisory adjustment, requiring the insurer to hold additional capital and/or a greater proportion of higher quality capital.

Capital base

An insurer must hold admissible assets that exceed the sum of its liabilities and its required capital (ie, it's PCA). In addition, an insurer is expected to hold surplus capital in excess of its required capital. Therefore, an insurer's capital base is the sum of its required capital and its surplus capital. Insurers are expected to set appropriate target surplus levels and falling below such levels could be a trigger for supervisory attention.

Minimum capital requirement

An insurer's total required capital is the sum of the prescribed capital and any supervisory adjustment which is equal to its minimum capital requirement (MCR). When the MCR is applied to a company's capital base, the result is the company's solvency coverage. APRA publishes half-yearly industry statistics, which include the industry and individual company MCR and solvency ratios. Table 9.5 shows the general insurance industries capital position for the 12 months ended December 2018 and 2019.

Table 9.5: Insurers' capital position for the 12 months ended March

All insurers	Prescribed capital Requirements ($ million)	Capital base ($ million)	Prescribed Capital Amount coverage Ratio (%)
2018	15,531	27,490	177
2019	15,674	27,587	176

Source: APRA, *Quarterly, March 2019*

Table 9.5 indicates that the Australian general insurance industry is in a very strong capital position, with a prescribed capital amount coverage ratio of 176 per cent, which is a slight drop from the solvency coverage of 177per cent in 2018. There are a number of reasons why the solvency coverage has declined. These include:

- Low growth in premiums owing to competitive pressures in a benign catastrophe environment, and

- Continued weak investment returns reflecting the low interest rate environment.

9-090   Assets in Australia

Section 28 of the Insurance Act requires all general insurers to maintain assets in Australia of a value that equals or exceeds the total amount of the general insurer's liabilities in Australia. Prudential Standard GPS 120 – *Assets in Australia* specifies assets that are excluded as assets in Australia for the purpose of s 28. APRA specifies assets that it considers will be of little value to policyholders in Australia should a general insurer become insolvent.

These specified assets include items such as goodwill, chattels and real property held outside of Australia, and other amounts excluded by this prudential standard. These specified assets are deducted from a company's capital base when determining its ability to meet its MCR.

9-100   Risk management

An insurer's risk management is regulated by Prudential Standard GPS 220 – *Risk Management* (GPS 220). This Prudential Standard sets out the requirements for a general insurer to maintain a risk management framework and strategy that is appropriate to the nature and scale of its operations.

The risk management framework refers to a general insurer's and insurance group's "processes, structures, policies and people for identifying, assessing, mitigating and monitoring risks" (GPS 220, Objective and key requirements) that may affect its ability to meet its obligations to policyholders.

To meet the key requirements of this prudential standard, a general insurer must:

- have in its risk management framework a documented Risk Management Strategy, and also include sound risk management policies and procedures and clearly defined managerial responsibilities and controls;

- submit its Risk Management Strategy to APRA on an annual basis and resubmit when any material changes are made;

- have a dedicated risk management function (or role) responsible for assisting in the development and maintenance of the risk management framework;

- submit a three-year Business Plan to APRA and re-submit after each annual review or when any material changes are made;

- submit a Risk Management Declaration to APRA on an annual basis; and

- submit a Financial Information Declaration to APRA on an annual basis." (GPS 220, Objective and key requirements)

9-110   Reinsurance management

Prudential Standard GPS 230 – *Reinsurance Management* obliges:

"a general insurer ... to maintain, as part of its overall risk management framework, a specific reinsurance management framework to manage the risks arising from its reinsurance arrangements" (GPS 230, Objective and key requirements).

This Prudential Standard requires a reasonable assurance on the part of the insurer that its reinsurance arrangements are being prudently and soundly managed, but takes into account such factors as the size, business classes and complexity of the insurer's operations and risk appetite.

9-120   Outsourcing

Prudential Standard CPS 231 – *Outsourcing* aims to ensure that all outsourcing arrangements involving material business activities entered into by a general insurer are subject to due diligence, approval and ongoing monitoring. All risks arising from outsourcing material business activities must be appropriately managed to ensure that the general insurer is able to meet its policyholder liabilities.

9-130   Audit and related matters

Prudential Standard GPS 310 – *Audit and Related Matters* outlines the roles and responsibilities of a general insurer's appointed auditor and group auditor. It also outlines the obligations of a general insurer or insurance group to make arrangements to enable its auditor to fulfil their responsibilities. In addition, a set of principles and practices for the consistent measurement and reporting of insurance liabilities is specified.

The aim of this prudential standard is to ensure that the Board and senior management are provided with impartial advice in relation to the insurer's operations, financial condition and insurance liabilities.

9-140   Transfer and amalgamation of insurance business

Prudential Standard GPS 410 – *Transfer and Amalgamation of Insurance Business for General Insurers* specifies that insurers transferring or amalgamating insurance business in accordance with the Insurance Act are subject to procedural requirements set out in the Act and this standard.

These requirements are designed to ensure that affected policyholders and other interested members of the public are kept fully informed, given accurate information and provided with the opportunity to obtain more detailed particulars.

9-150 Governance

Prudential Standard CPS 510 – *Governance* sets the minimum requirements for good governance of regulated institutions. It aims to ensure that regulated institutions are managed in a sound and prudent manner by a competent board of directors that is capable of making reasonable and impartial business judgements and that gives due consideration to the impact of its decisions on policyholders.

This standard emphasises that a culture that promotes good governance is beneficial to all an organisation's stakeholders and helps to promote and maintain public confidence in the institution.

9-160 Fit and proper

Prudential Standard CPS 520 – *Fit and proper* specifies that its objective is to ensure that a regulated institution is managed soundly and prudently by a competent Board (or equivalent), which can make reasonable and impartial business judgements in the best interests of the institution and which duly considers the impact of its decisions on depositors and/or policyholders (CPS 520, Objective and key requirements).

This standard sets out the minimum requirements for general insurers and authorised non-operating holding companies in determining the fitness and propriety of individuals to hold positions of responsibility.

At a glance

- APRA provides prudential supervision of the general insurance industry by setting prudential standards.
- General insurance companies must comply will all prudential standards.
- The aim of prudential standards is to ensure that general insurance companies have the capacity to pay claims.
- It is the general insurance company's Board that is responsible for the sound management of the company's capital.
- Solvency and capital adequacy are two important prudential standards.
- Other prudential standards set standards for the sound operation of a general insurance business.

9-170 Study questions

9.1 Compare the number of general insurance companies to life insurance companies. What does this tell about the state of these industries?

9.2 If an underwriter is experiencing underwriting losses, what effects will continuously increasing premiums have on policy retention and risk concentration?

9.3 How do insurance companies seek to maximise underwriting profitability?

9.4 Give two specific reasons for reinsurance. Distinguish between facultative and treaty reinsurance.

9.5 Distinguish between the different types of reinsurance and give an example of each. What are the advantages of reinsuring?

9.6 Explain the underwriting cycle. What causes the underwriting cycle? When would there be a hard market or a soft market?

9.7 What is meant by solvency? Why is solvency important to current and intending insureds?

9.8 What reasons can you give for the world reinsurance markets becoming hard in 2001?

9.9 Explain the major differences between general insurance company investments and life insurance company investments.

9-180 References and further reading

References

Articles and Books

KPMG (2018), *General insurance industry survey*. Available at *kpmg.com.au*

Reports

Australian Prudential Regulatory Authority (APRA) 2018, *Quarterly General Insurance Performance*, September. Available at *apra.gov.au*

Australian Prudential Regulatory Authority (APRA) 2019, *Statistics — Half Yearly General Insurance Bulletin*. Available at *apra.gov.au*

Australian Prudential Regulatory Authority (APRA) 2005, *Statistics — Half Yearly General Insurance Bulletin*. Available at *apra.gov.au*

Releases

Australian Prudential Regulatory Authority (APRA) 2013, *Prudential Standard GPS 110 – Capital Adequacy*. Available at *apra.gov.au*

Australian Prudential Regulatory Authority (APRA) 2013, *Prudential Standard GPS 112 – Capital Adequacy: Measurement of Capital*. Available at *apra.gov.au*

Australian Prudential Regulatory Authority (APRA) 2013, *Prudential Standard GPS 115 – Capital Adequacy: Insurance Risk Charge*. Available at *apra.gov.au*

Australian Prudential Regulatory Authority (APRA) 2013, *Prudential Standard GPS 120 – Assets in Australia*. Available at *apra.gov.au*

Australian Prudential Regulatory Authority (APRA) 2013, *Prudential Standard GPS 220 – Risk Management*. Available at *apra.gov.au*

APRA, Australian Prudential Regulatory Authority (APRA) 2013, *Prudential Standard GPS 230 – Reinsurance Management*. Available at *apra.gov.au*

Australian Prudential Regulatory Authority (APRA) 2013, *Prudential Standard CPS 232 – Business Continuity Management*. Available at *apra.gov.au*

Australian Prudential Regulatory Authority (APRA) 2013, *Prudential Standard CPS 231 – Outsourcing*. Available at *apra.gov.au*

Australian Prudential Regulatory Authority (APRA) 2013, *Prudential Standard GPS 310 – Audit and Related Matters*. Available at *apra.gov.au*

Australian Prudential Regulatory Authority (APRA) 2013, *Prudential Management GPS 410 — Transfer and Amalgamation of Insurance Business for General Insurers*. Available at *apra.gov.au*

Australian Prudential Regulatory Authority (APRA) 2013, *Prudential Standard CPS 510- Governance*. Available at *apra.gov.au*

Australian Prudential Regulatory Authority (APRA) 2013, *Prudential Standard CPS 520 – Fit and Proper*. Available at *apra.gov.au*

Legislation

General Insurance Reform Act 2001 (Cth)

Insurance Act 1973 (Cth)

Further reading

Websites

Australian & New Zealand Institute of Insurance and Finance (ANZIIF): *theinstitute.com.au*

APRA Statistics and Insight: *apra.gov.au*

Insurance Council of Australia (ICA): *insurancecouncil.com.au*

Institute of Actuaries of Australia (Actuaries Institute): *actuaries.asn.au*

National Insurance Brokers of Australia (NIBA): *niba.com.au*

Standard & Poor's (S&P): *standardandpoors.com*

CHAPTER 10

TAXATION

TAXATION OF LIFE AND GENERAL INSURANCE COMPANIES

10-000 Introduction

In order to effectively advise clients on insurance, advisers must understand the fundamentals of how the life and general insurance industries are taxed. This section gives a basic understanding of the complexities of how assessable income is derived for these industries in Australia. Those wishing to learn more about the taxation of life and general insurance companies can do so by exploring the 'Further reading' section at the end of this chapter.

10-010 Australian life insurance companies

Section 995(1) of the *Income Tax Assessment Act 1997* (Cth) (ITAA97) defines a life insurance company as a company registered under the *Life Insurance Act 1995* (the LI Act). Companies registered under the LI Act include life insurance companies, life reinsurance companies and friendly societies that carry on life insurance business.

A life insurance business is defined in s 995(1) of the ITAA97 as a business that consists of or relates to the issuing of life insurance policies. The LI Act also states that a life insurance policy consists of the following:

- whole-of-life policies, endowment policies (excluding pure endowment policies), term and life annuities, continuous disability policies, investment account contracts and investment-linked contracts (s 9)

- fixed-term annuities that have a term of less than 10 years and income bonds and scholarship plans issued by friendly societies (ss 12A; 12B)

- sinking fund policies — contracts under which an amount of money is paid on one or more specified dates, irrespective of the death or survival of the person to whom the policy is issued or of any other person.

Life insurance companies are taxed under Div 320 of the ITAA97, which means they are taxed on all their profits including management fees, underwriting profit and profits on any immediate annuity business. Taxable income of life insurance companies is divided into two classes:

- complying superannuation class, which is taxed at 15 per cent

- ordinary class, which is taxed at the company tax rate of 30 per cent.

Any tax losses incurred within each class can only be deducted from the income generated from the class (s 320-134, ITAA97).

Assessable income

The assessable income of life insurance companies includes amounts that are assessable under the general provisions of the income tax law, such as the ordinary income provisions and the capital gains tax (CGT) provisions, and a number of additional items as specified in s 320-15 of the ITAA97, such as:

- life insurance premiums paid to the company in the income year
- amounts received under a reinsurance contract that relate to the risk components of claims paid under a life insurance contract
- refunds of reinsurance premiums paid under a contract of reinsurance
- reinsurance commissions received
- amounts received under a profit-sharing agreement under a contract of reinsurance
- transfers of taxable contributions from complying superannuation funds or Australian Defence Force members (ADFs)
- the untaxed element of the post–June 1983 component of an employment termination payment (ETP) roll-over.
- fees and charges imposed by the company on life insurance policies
- taxable contributions made to any retirement savings account (RSA) provided by the company
- net investment income, which includes realised gains and losses.

The assessable income of life insurance companies also includes amounts of ordinary and statutory income that are assessable under other provisions of the ITAA97 and amounts assessable under the capital gains tax provisions.

Specific deductions

In addition to some exempt and non-assessable non-exempt income, life insurance companies are entitled to the following specific deductions:

- certain components of life insurance premiums (ss 320-55 to 320-75, ITAA97)
- the risk component of claims paid under life insurance policies (s 320-80, ITAA97)

- an increase in the value of the net risk components of risk policy liabilities (ie, the policy's risk component less reinsurance) (s 320-85, ITAA97)

- reinsurance premiums paid (s 320-100, ITAA97)

- amounts relating to assets (other than money) that are transferred to or from a virtual pooled superannuation trust in certain circumstances (s 320-87, ITAA97)

- the transfer value of assets that are transferred to segregated exempt assets in certain circumstances (s 320-105, ITAA97)

- general and administrative expenses (fully deductible)

- interest credited by friendly societies to holders of income bonds issued after 31 December 2002; to nominated students under scholarship plans issued after that date; and to beneficiaries of funeral policies issued after that date (ss 320-110 to 320-112, ITAA97).

However, life insurance companies cannot deduct any part of life insurance premiums received in respect of life policies that make provision for benefits to be paid only on the death or disability of a person, except where those policies provide participating benefits or discretionary benefits, ie, investment account benefits that are regarded as non-participating benefits under s 995-1 of the ITAA97 (s 320-70, ITAA97). A life company that is an RSA provider cannot deduct amounts credited to retirement saving accounts (s 320-115, ITAA97).

Establishment of virtual pooled superannuation trust

Life insurance companies can segregate assets to be used for the sole purpose of discharging their complying superannuation liabilities (s 320-170, ITAA97). The segregated assets are known as a virtual pooled superannuation trust (PST) ts (as defined in s 995-1): s 320-70. A life company that is and are effectively treated as an entity within a life insurance company. The taxable income of a virtual PST is calculated in a way consistent with the calculation of the taxable income of a PST and taxed at the same rate (15 per cent).

The company can hold only sufficient virtual PST assets to cover its complying superannuation liabilities, and if the value of these assets exceeds their liabilities the company must (within 30 days after completing the valuation) transfer out the excess assets (s 320-180, ITAA97). The transfer is taken to occur at the valuation time.

Segregated exempt assets

Life insurance companies may maintain a pool of segregated assets (known as segregated exempt (i.e. Tax exempt) assets) to be used for the sole purpose of discharging their liabilities under exempt life insurance policies, eg, a complying superannuation income stream such as an annuity or allocated pension (s 320-225, ITAA97). This purpose includes the payment of fees and expenses in respect of the policies or the segregated exempt assets.

An exempt life insurance policy is a life insurance policy (s 320-246, ITAA97):

- held by the trustee of a complying superannuation fund and is a segregated current pension within the meaning of Pt IX of the *Income Tax Assessment Act 1936* (Cth) (ITAA36)

- held by the trustees of a PST as a segregated exempt asset of the PST within the meaning of Pt IX of the ITAA36

- held by the trustee of a constitutionally protected superannuation fund that provides for an eligible immediate annuity

- held by another life insurance company where the policy is a segregated exempt asset of that other company that provides for a personal injury annuity and/or a personal injury lump sum, payments of which are exempt under Div 54 of the ITAA97.

Allocation of income

Because of the two distinct aspects of the life insurance business (ie, non-mutual and mutual companies), special imputation rules apply. Non-mutual life insurance companies operate the business for the benefit of their shareholders and attempt to maximise the return to these shareholders. This is achieved via an increase in the share price through profitable trading and distribution of profits by the payment of franked dividends from non-participating business profits. Insurance companies also invest funds on behalf of policyholders, with profits from participating policies being split at least 80:20 between policyholders and shareholders. On the other hand, mutual life insurance companies operate their businesses on behalf of their policyholders, and so are not franking entities and cannot frank a distribution.

Life insurers receive dividend income, which is taxable. However, where the dividends are received from New Zealand companies and carry an imputation credit, this credit can be offset against the life insurer's tax liability.

Where life insurers declare bonuses on life investment policies, these form part of policyholder liabilities. The insurer is not allowed a tax deduction on the life insurer base for these bonuses, which are included in the policyholder income calculation as part of an increase in the actuarial reserves.

10-020 General insurance

A general insurer is defined both in the *Insurance Act 1973* (Cth) and for taxation purposes, as a body corporate that is authorised by APRA to carry on insurance business in Australia (ss 11; 12). The definition of a general insurer includes a foreign general insurer. The corporate tax rate applicable to all Australian companies is 30 per cent.

Income

As for life insurers, general insurers' income is derived during a particular period when the right to receive it arises (s 6-5; ITAA 97). However, if a general insurance contract extends beyond the income year, the income is not considered to be derived wholly in that year. Therefore, if a premium is paid for a period of two years, the second half of the premium is derived for tax purposes in that later year. Premiums are generally apportioned on a day's basis, except where the risk exposure is not spread evenly over time (*Taxation Ruling* IT 2663). In other words, premium revenue is recognised only when it has been earned.

In a similar context, if the term of an insurance policy extends beyond the insurance company's accounting period, then only that part of the gross premium that falls within the accounting period is considered 'earned' and included in the company's accounts as revenue. That part of the gross premium that extends beyond the accounting period is called unearned premium and will be included as revenue in the later accounting period. Unearned premiums represent a liability in the form of an obligation to provide insurance cover over a future period of risk. These premiums are allocated to an account called the unearned premium reserve (UPR), and the taxation of that part of the gross premiums is deferred under s 321A of the ITAA97.

For income tax purposes, the UPR is brought to account at year end through a process of comparing the value of the UPR at the end of the income year with the value at the end of the previous year. Any decreases in the value of the UPR over the income year are included in assessable income, which ensures that net premiums relating to risk exposure in the current year are included in assessable income.

Investments

When insurance companies realise or 'switch' investments, any realised profits will be assessable as income, even where the investments have stood for some considerable time. Where gains are not assessable as ordinary income, CGT may apply if the property was purchased after 20 September 1985. However, interest is included as income on a due and receivable basis, and domestic dividends are grossed up by the franking credits.

Deductions

In addition to the normal business deductions allowable to all trading companies, general insurance companies have some unique allowable deductions. At the end of the income period, insurance companies will have outstanding claims that have not been paid in full and claims that have been incurred but not reported (IBNR). These claims will be subject to revision and a deduction will be allowed for any increase in them. This provision is also applied to reinsurers' outstanding claims provisions (*Taxation Ruling* TR 95/5) and to self-insurers in relation to their estimated workers compensation liabilities (*Taxation Determination* TD 97/14).

The deduction is calculated by making a statistical estimate of both unreported claims and IBNRs and discounted on a 'present value' basis. This means that the deduction is equal to the annual increase in the amount that the company reasonably estimates is appropriate to set aside and invest in order to provide sufficient funds to pay the liabilities.

Insurance companies reinsure much of their risks, and the premiums paid or payable to both local and non-resident reinsurance companies are deducted from the gross premiums. Hence any recoveries from the reinsurers are treated as assessable income.

In addition, any increases in the value of a company's UPR over the income year are allowed as a deduction. This ensures that net premiums that relate to exposure in subsequent years are appropriately deferred.

Other taxes

Insurance premiums are subject to state premium taxes (stamp duty) that range between two per cent and 11 per cent, depending on the state and on the type of insurance. No goods and service tax (GST) is payable on the stamp duty component of insurance premiums, but it is applied to the fire services levy (FSL) in those states where the FSL applies.

From 1 July 2000, a 10 per cent GST was imposed on premiums charged by insurance companies. However, where insureds are registered for GST, they are generally able to claim a credit for the GST included in the premiums against their own GST liability.

At a glance

- Like any other enterprise, Australian life insurance companies are subject to the ITAA36 and the ITAA97.

- Life insurance companies are able to segregate assets that are required to cover superannuation assets and income stream payments.

- Australian general insurance companies are taxed on earned premiums.

- Unearned premiums are assigned to a UPR account.

- General insurance companies are allowed a tax deduction for any increase in current claims and IBNRs.

TAXATION OF LIFE PREMIUMS

10-030 Introduction

A number of taxes may affect the cash flows related to life products, including:

- income tax
- capital gains tax (CGT)
- goods and services tax (GST)
- fringe benefits tax (FBT)
- stamp duty.

These taxes, as they relate to insurance products, are examined below.

10-040 Life insurance in general

For private individuals, the premiums paid for whole-of-life, endowment, yearly renewable term (YRT), and total and permanent disablement covers are not deductible or rebateable, as the proceeds received under these policies are regarded as capital sums (which are not treated as assessable income). However, this may not apply where the policy was taken out by a business for a revenue purpose, or in certain circumstances such as where the cover is taken out through a superannuation fund. Where a business takes out a life policy for a capital purpose, such as to give substance to a buy/sell agreement, the premiums are not an allowable deduction and the benefit is not assessable, provided the policy is taken out on the life of a taxpayer or their spouse.

Lump-sum payments received under an endowment policy are regarded as capital and are not assessable; however, if the policy provides for the payment of a pension or annuity these payments will be assessable. The taxation treatment of bonuses received under a life policy depends on the nature of the bonus and the date of commencement of the risk (rather than the date on which the policy is taken out). This same taxation treatment generally applies to insurance bonds under the 10-year rule.

If the risk commenced before 28 August 1982, bonuses received are generally tax free to the recipient. If the risk commenced after 7 December 1983, reversionary bonuses are assessable in full if they are received within eight years of the commencement of the risk (s 26AH(6), ITAA36). Amounts received in the ninth year are assessable as to two-thirds and amounts received in the tenth year are assessable as to one-third. After the tenth year, the gains are tax free to the recipient. As insurance companies have paid tax at the rate of 30 per cent (as from 1 July 2001) on their investment earnings, policyholders are allowed a rebate to offset tax payable. Thus, a person on the highest marginal tax rate who cashes in an insurance bond after seven years will be liable for 15 per cent tax on the insurance gain (45% – 30%). Any excess rebate accruing to taxpayers on less than 30 per cent marginal tax rate may be applied to offset other tax payable.

Premium increases to an insurance bond may result in the commencement of a new bond subject to the 10-year rule; however, a provision exists that allows the premium to be increased by up to 125 per cent of the previous year's premium without triggering the 10-year rule, provided the investor does not make any withdrawals. These additional contributions are treated as if they were made at the commencement of the bond and so will achieve full tax-free status after 10 years. However, there can be a catch, because if a contribution is not made in any one year, any further contribution will start the 10-year period again for the whole invested amount.

The proceeds from life insurance policies are generally exempt from capital gains tax (CGT). For private individuals, the beneficial ownership of policies may be transferred as securities for loans or as gifts. Such transfers may not alter the CGT-exempt status of policies if no consideration is charged on the transfer. However, CGT may apply where any benefits are paid other than to the insured person, their spouse, and children and other dependants. State stamp duty applies to transfers and the registration of loans and caveats. The effects of such taxes must be factored into any strategy to ensure that the course of action still makes good financial sense. Centrelink does not apply an income test to whole-of-life or endowment policies, but their surrender value is included as an asset under the assets test.

Where an employer provides, as part of an employee's salary package, a non-cash fringe benefit in the form of the payment of life insurance premiums (non-superannuation contracts) on a policy owned by the employee, fringe benefit tax (FBT) is payable. The premium is an allowable deduction for the employer, but it is not included as assessable income for the employee.

10-050 Trauma (recovery) insurance

Premiums paid on a trauma insurance policy, which provides a capital sum on the suffering of a specified medical condition, are not deductible by an employee or a self-employed person. If an employer owns such a policy on an employee as part of a key-person arrangement and the purpose is to replace a loss of revenue, the employer is allowed a deduction. Any proceeds paid under the policy are assessable. However, if the policy is taken out by a family business for a capital purpose, then there is no deduction and the benefits will be tax free provided the policy is taken out on the life of the partner or spouse (*Taxation Determinations* TD 95/41 and TD 95/42).

Claim payments made under a trauma policy do not replace a loss of earnings and are therefore not deemed to be assessable income for an employee or self-employed person. The amount received is generally exempt from CGT if the owner of the policy is the insured or the spouse of the insured (*Taxation Determination* TD 95/43). In other cases, such as where the owner is a company or insurance trust or in cross ownership situations, CGT may be payable on the claim proceeds. Also, a liability for CGT may arise where there has been a change in ownership of the policy.

10-060 Key-person insurance

Key-person insurance refers to a policy is taken out by a business on the life of an employee or some other key person who contributes significantly to the organisation and who would be difficult to replace in the event of their premature death or permanent disablement, the taxation treatment of the premiums depends on two factors:

* the type of policy
* the purpose for which the insurance is effected and maintained.

Premiums paid on key-person life and endowment policies are non-deductible (s. 8-1, ITAA97). Where key-person accident or term policies are taken out, the premiums are deductible if the purpose of the insurance is to replace a revenue item (*Taxation Ruling* IT 155). However, the sums insured must be reasonable within the context of the business; that is, they must be in proportion to the revenue need and not be excessive. If the purpose is to insure against the possibility of a capital loss, such as to allow the estate of a director to repay a debt owed by them, then the premium would be non-deductible and the proceeds not assessable.

A deduction may be allowed for the premium paid on a policy where there is a split purpose, such as where an accident and/or sickness rider is added to a term life policy. In this instance, the premium may be allowed as a deduction where the premium that applies to the revenue purpose can be readily identified. If the premiums cannot be split, the Commissioner treats the premiums as being wholly for life insurance and not deductible.

10-070 Partnership insurance

Partners may claim a deduction for insurance premiums paid on life policies where the proceeds are to be used to replace a revenue item (*Taxation Ruling* IT 155). This would apply where a partner takes out a policy to insure against the sickness or disability of one or more co-partners.

Where the purpose of the life insurance is to guard against capital loss, such as to meet any liabilities on the death of the partner or to provide funds to allow the partner's interest in the partnership to be acquired, then the premiums will not be deductible and the proceeds will not be assessable. A self-employed business owner can claim a deduction for premiums on a policy that pays income during a period they are disabled. Normally, a policy that includes a component to pay a sum on the death or disability, the component relating to death will not be deductible. However, it may be deductible if the following four criteria are met: the premium is paid for a revenue purpose, the policy's purpose is to advance the business, the policy is owned by the employer, the employer is the beneficiary of the policy.

Partnership is funded by a buy/sell agreement (discussed in 11-030). As the buy/sell agreement results in the sale of the business, a CGT liability will arise to the vendor. The small business CGT concessions may operate to reduce this CGT liability. A trauma or total and permanent disability insurance (TPD) policy is subject to CGT if it is owned by the business. However, no CGT liability would arise if the proceeds are paid to the original beneficial owner of the policy, ie, if the policy has not been assigned to another party or paid to a person who did not acquire the rights under the policy for money or other consideration (s 118-300, ITAA97).

10-080 Total and permanent disablement in superannuation

Total and permanent disablement (TPD) insurance is quite often held within superannuation because the premiums can be tax deductible for eligible individuals. However, the deductibility of the premiums for tax purposes is governed by several factors.

Since 1 July 2011, premiums for TPD insurance are only wholly or partially deductible if paid to a complying superannuation fund and the payment relates to a current or contingent liability by the fund to provide a 'disability superannuation benefit' (s 295-460(B), ITAA97). A disability superannuation benefit will arise if the person suffers physical or mental ill-health and two legally qualified medical practitioners certify that it is unlikely the person will ever be able to perform the duties of any occupation, business, profession or employment for which the person is reasonably suited by education, training or experience.

The extent of the allowable deduction will depend on the definition of 'occupation' contained in the TPD cover and whether the TPD cover is combined with life insurance. The deductible proportion for premiums for certain types of TPD policies are set out in reg 295-465.01(1) of the Income Tax Assessment Regulations 1997 (ITAR) and are detailed in table 10.1. The terms used in Table 10.1 are defined in reg 295-465.01(5).

Table 10.1: Tax deductibility of TPD premiums in superannuation

INSURANCE POLICY	SPECIFIED PROPORTION %
TPD any occupation	100
TPD any occupation with one or more of the following inclusions: (a) activities of daily living; (b) cognitive loss; (c) loss of limb; (d) domestic (home) duties	100
TPD own occupation	67
TPD own occupation with one or more of the following inclusions: (a) activities of daily living; (b) cognitive loss; (c) loss of limb; (d) domestic (home) duties	67
TPD own occupation bundled with death (life) cover	80
TPD own occupation bundled with death (life) cover with one or more of the following inclusions: (a) activities of daily living; (b) cognitive loss; (c) loss of limb; (d) domestic (home) duties	80

Source: ATO (2012)

As shown in table 11.1, full deductibility will only apply to *any occupation* cover where the policy definition is more restrictive than or has substantially the same meaning as the definition of TPD as mentioned above. Premiums for stand-alone *own occupation* TPD in super attract a 67 per cent tax deduction; however, if bundled with life cover, this rises to 80 per cent. Superannuation funds have the option to use these prescribed percentages or obtain an actuarial certificate to determine the deductible portion.

10-090 Goods and services tax — life products

Goods and services tax (GST) is governed principally by the *New Tax System (Goods and Services Tax) Act 1999* (the GST Act). Under the GST Act, life insurance is treated as a financial supply and is input taxed; that is, the inputs of life insurers, such as office space, computing supplies and stationery, are taxed but their sales are not. As a result, premiums paid on life, trauma and disability policies are GST free.

At a glance

- The deductibility of life insurance premiums depends on whether they were incurred for revenue or capital purposes.

- Premiums paid for revenue purposes are tax deductible and benefits are assessable income.

- Premiums paid for capital purposes are not deductible and benefits are not assessable.

- Bonuses paid on life policies are fully assessable if received within eight years of the commencement of the policy.

- Life insurance premiums are exempt from GST.

- Life insurance premiums paid by employees whether ordinary or as part of a superannuation plan are not tax deductible, nor are the policy benefits subject to tax.

TAX IMPLICATIONS OF LIFE INSURANCE CLAIM PROCEEDS

10-100 Life insurance in superannuation

It has been a common practice in Australia to include life insurance in superannuation for self-employed persons mainly because of the tax deduction available up to the person's maximum deductible contribution (MDC), which varies depending on the person's age. Currently (2019/20) under the ITAA97, the MDC will allow a tax deduction of $25,000 per person per annum up to age 74 when the ability to contribute ceases. Any contributions claimed as a tax deduction above this amount will be effectively taxed at the top marginal rate and count towards a person's non-concessional limit. Readers should be aware that these caps may change in the future.

The payment of death benefits from a superannuation fund is governed by whether the beneficiary is classified as taxation dependent or non-dependent. If the benefit is paid to a taxation-dependent beneficiary, the entire death benefit will be tax free. Taxation dependents under s 159J of the ITAA36 fall into the following categories: spouse (married or de facto), child-housekeeper, a child who is under 21 and not a student, invalid relative (ie, a child, brother or sister) aged 16 or older, parent or parent in law, all of whom must be an Australian resident for tax purposes. Those aged 18 or more are not dependants unless they can prove financial dependency (s 27A(1), ITAA36).

For non-tax-dependent beneficiaries, the taxation position is entirely different. From 1 July 2007 lump-sum payments made to non-dependants (irrespective of age) resulting from death have the fund balance, including any term life insurance, divided into taxable and tax-free components. For the majority of superannuants, the tax-free component consists only of personal non-tax-deductible contributions, while for others it also includes the pre–July 1983 component and contributions derived from small business concessions.

For 2019/20, a superannuation death benefit paid to a non-dependent is taxed as follows:

- the tax free component paid to a non-tax dependant is free of tax, and
- the taxable component is included in the beneficiary's assessable income with a tax offset to ensure that:
  » the rate of tax on the taxable component does not exceed 15 per cent,

» and the element untaxed in the fund (eg, paid from a government defined benefit superannuation scheme) does not exceed 30 per cent.

A Medicarecare levy of 2 per cent applies to tax payers' taxable income.

How the operation of the new tax laws effects lump-sum death benefits paid to a non-dependant from a superannuation fund is shown in the following illustrated example.

Illustrated example 10.1

Harold, aged 55, dies in a car accident and has a $600,000 death benefit, which does not have a tax-exempt component. This death benefit is made up of $250,000 in term life insurance and a $350,000 superannuation balance. His 30-year-old non-dependent son is his sole beneficiary and will receive a payout of $508,650, after the payment of $91,350 in tax (including 2% Medicare levy).

10-110 Death benefits paid from employer-sponsored group insurance

Many employers have arranged employer-sponsored group insurance outside of superannuation for their staff members in order to meet their insurance obligations. In most instances, the employer owns the life insurance policy, with the employee being the life insured, and the employer receives the benefits on the employee's death. This ensures that the employee does not have absolute entitlement to the death benefits, which allows the employer to pay the premiums without attracting FBT.

Until 30 June 2007, the employer was able to forward the life insurance benefits to the employee (or beneficiary) as an eligible termination payment, which could be rolled into superannuation for the purpose of deferring lump-sum tax. However, this changed with the introduction of Simplified Super.

From 1 July 2007, traditional employer-eligible termination payments became known as employment termination payments may no longer be rolled over into superannuation for the purpose of deferring lump-sum tax. An employment termination payment (ETP) is a lump sum paid to an individual for the termination of employment and must occur within 12 months of the termination. There are two components to the employment termination payments:

• *life benefit termination payment*, which is paid other than for reason of death

- *death benefit termination payment*, which is paid as a result of death.

If the employer provides death benefits to a dependant, the pre–1 July 1983 component, discussed above, is exempt and not assessable (tax-free component). The taxable component within the employment termination payments cap for 2018/19 ($0–$205,000) is not subject to tax. The part of the taxable component that exceeds this cap ($205,000 plus) is taxed at the top marginal rate (45%) plus Medicare levy (2%). The ETP cap amount is indexed in line with average weekly ordinary time earnings (AWOTE), in increments of $5,000 (rounded down) (s 960-285, ITAA97). The current applicable cap amount can be obtained from http://www.ato.gov.au.

If the employer provides death benefits to a non-dependant of the former employee, the pre–1 July 1983 component is exempt and not assessable. The remaining portion of a death benefit employment termination payment (the taxable component), where it is below the employment termination payments cap of $205,000 (2018/19), is included in the beneficiary's assessable income and an offset applies to ensure that the tax rate does not exceed 30 per cent tax plus Medicare levy.

The part of the taxable component that exceeds this cap ($205,000 plus) is taxed at the top marginal rate (45%) plus Medicare levy. Therefore, beneficiaries of payouts in excess of $205,000 are likely to lose almost half of the death benefits in taxes over this threshold (s 82-70, ITAA97). As can be seen, this provision poses significant estate planning issues for the insured.

In many employment situations, the employer pays the premiums, but the employee is the life insured and the beneficiary of the policy with an absolute entitlement to the death benefits. In this case, the death benefits will be CGT free (s 118-300, ITAA97). The only problem is that since the employer is providing a fringe benefit to the employee, the premiums the employer pays attract FBT.

10-120 Disability (income protection) insurance

The premiums for income protection policies are deductible for self-employed taxpayers under s 8-1 of the ITAA97, provided the benefits are used as income to replace lost earnings during a period of disablement. A similar deduction is also available to employees, who can claim a deduction for premiums paid for disability cover as part of a mortgage protection policy (*Interpretative Decision* ID 2004/661). Any income payments received in compensation for lost earnings are treated as assessable income in the hands of the recipient.

Where the benefits under the policy are solely of a capital nature, eg, a lump-sum payment for death, trauma or loss of a limb, no part of the premium is deductible. Where the policy provides for both income and capital payments, that part of the premium that relates to the income benefits is deductible while the premium relating to the capital benefits is not deductible.

Superannuation funds generally offer their members death and disability income benefits. The premiums for these group policies are usually very competitive and are paid for out of the compulsory employer contributions where the policy automatically provides a certain level of cover without each person having to provide evidence of health. The premiums for death coverage are an allowable deduction for the employer, as are the premiums for the disability income benefits.

There is very little difference in the taxation treatment of benefits paid from within a superannuation fund and those paid outside of superannuation. In each case, the benefits to replace lost income are fully assessable in the hands of the recipient. The benefits of disability insurance within the superannuation system relate more to competitive premiums and lower medical disclosure than to tax effectiveness.

At a glance

- Life insurance premiums paid as part of a superannuation scheme are tax deductible for self-employed persons.

- Death benefit proceeds are assessable if paid to a non-dependant.

- Death benefits paid from employer-sponsored group insurance will be subject to varying rates of tax depending on whether the recipient is a dependant or a non-dependant.

- Disability insurance premiums for policies to replace income are deductible for all taxpayers and the benefits assessable.

- Premiums in relation to capital benefits are not deductible.

TAXATION OF INSURANCE PRODUCTS USED FOR BUSINESS PURPOSES

10-130 Introduction

Insurance products used for business purposes in Australia and New Zealand are subject to a variety of taxes and deductibility rules. How these rules apply in both jurisdictions is considered below.

10-140 General insurance

Premiums paid by a business for fire, burglary, professional indemnity, public risk, motor vehicle or loss of profits insurance are deductible, even where the loss insured against is a capital loss. Any claim proceeds are not subject to tax, but special provisions exist with respect to:

- *assessable recoupment* of a loss or outgoing that can be deducted or has been deducted under any provision of the Act (s 20-20(2), ITAA97) that is not ordinary or statutory income (s 20-20(1), ITAA97)

- *balancing charges* in a situation where depreciated assets are destroyed and insurance claims on them are paid. Balancing charges need to be made in the books to satisfy both accounting and taxation considerations.

Insurance premiums paid by private individuals on insurance policies to cover assets and to provide protection under a public liability policy against being held legally liable for negligence are not income tax deductible. On the other hand, claim proceeds are generally not income tax assessable.

Allowable deductions for business

Business insurance premiums are deductible under s 8-1 if the ITAA97, if they are incurred in connection with the operation of a business for the purposes of earning assessable income. Allowable deductions include premiums for fire, burglary, professional indemnity, public liability, motor vehicle insurance or loss of profits even though the policies relate to the protection of capital assets (eg, buildings and motor vehicles). Capital outlays such as premiums payable on savings investment, endowment and whole-of-life policies, including 'split purpose' insurance arrangements, are non-deductible (*Taxation Ruling* TD 94/40 and *Taxation Ruling* IT 2434).

Premiums paid on recovery (trauma) insurance policies that pay a capital amount of the diagnosis of a specified medical condition are generally not deductible (*Taxation Determination* TD 95/41). However, these premiums may be deductible if the premium is paid for a revenue purpose, the purpose of the policy is to advance the business ends of the employer, and the employer is both owner and beneficiary of the policy (*Taxation Determination* TD 95/42).

Premiums paid by an employer for workers compensation insurance and premiums paid on employees' accident policies to compensate the employer for the employees' death or disablement through accident are usually deductible. The premiums paid on income protection policies to replace lost income during a period of disablement are deductible.

The deductibility of life insurance premiums is more complicated, as this depends on whether the insurance is to replace income or to protect capital. Life insurance is used in key-person and partnership insurances, and the premiums are deductible if the intention is to protect against the loss of a revenue item. However, if a premium is paid to protect a capital loss, then the premium is not deductible. Key-person and partnership insurances are discussed at 10-060 and 10-070 respectively.

In summary, the general principle is that in most cases deductions are allowable for premiums related to the protection of revenue streams and the loss of physical assets. However, in the case of directors and employees, the Commissioner is keen to ensure that the premium is directly related to the protection of net revenue and not to the loss of human capital.

Assessable income for business

Receipts from insurance claims are treated as assessable income under a number of sections of ITAA36 and ITAA97. Generally, periodical and lump-sum payments received by an employer or self-employed person under a personal accident, income protection or disability insurance policy and workers compensation insurance in compensation for loss of earnings are assessable.

Where amounts are received by an employer under an accident or term insurance policy taken out on the lives of directors or other employees, they are assessable as ordinary income if the purpose of the insurance is to replace revenue, such as to replace profits lost through the loss of the employee's services.

The same rules apply to the deductibility of premiums paid on policies taken out to replace capital, so that amounts received under these policies are not treated as assessable income. Therefore, the proceeds of a life, endowment or accident policy taken out on the life of a director to provide funds to be paid to the director's estate for the repayment of a loan would not be assessable. Similarly, the proceeds of a life or endowment policy taken out on the life of an employee or director by an employer are not treated as assessable income (*Taxation Ruling* IT 155). The same rules apply for partnership insurance where one partner takes out insurance on the life of another partner, or on the life of a 'key' business associate.

Goods and services tax

Under the GST Ac), general insurance premiums are subject to GST. The insurer is making a taxable supply and therefore incurs a GST liability to the extent of 10 per cent of the pre-tax selling price, which includes a fire services levy, but excludes stamp duty. GST is essentially a tax on final consumption so that tax is effectively collected on the value added to goods and services provided to consumers.

Where the insurance cover can be regarded as a business input and the entity is registered for GST purposes, the insured is entitled to an input tax credit of one-eleventh of the post-tax price and the insurer remits the collected GST to the Australian Taxation Office (ATO). Additionally, the insured claims an offsetting input tax credit, so the net effect is that the GST will be zero. In this case, no GST liability is generally incurred by the insured on an insurance settlement (s 78-45, GST Act) and the insurance company will not claim an input tax credit, as GST will not apply (s 78-80, GST Act).

However, where the insured is the final consumer, the GST position is different. How GST is calculated in this situation is shown in the following illustrated example.

Illustrated example 10.2

Michelle pays an insurance premium of $112, which includes GST. The insurer will remit $10.20 (1/11th of $112) to the ATO at the time the policy is issued. If the insurer pays a claim of $90, the insurer is granted a decreasing adjustment of $8.20 (1/11th of the $90 payout) on its net GST liability. In this case, the ATO collects a net GST of $2 ($10.20 – $8.20).

Capital gains tax

Where an asset or part of an asset is lost or destroyed, any insurance proceeds received by an insured are taken to relate to the asset and not to the policy for CGT purposes (*Taxation Determination* TD 2000/31). Hence, the insurance policy is not given the status of another independent asset. Where a CGT event happens to a general insurance policy covering a CGT-exempt asset such as the insured's main domestic residence, any capital gain or loss arising from a claim is ignored for CGT purposes. However, where an asset that is subject to CGT, such as a rental property, is wholly or partially destroyed, receipt of insurance proceeds will have income tax and CGT consequences.

For businesses, the situation is different, as insurance premiums for most types of business insurances are generally income tax deductible. Insurance proceeds for the loss of trading stock or loss of profits as a result of fire or storm and tempest, for example, are assessable income. Where insurance proceeds are received following the partial or total loss or destruction of an asset, the compensation is treated as capital proceeds. If the asset was a pre-CGT asset, the claim proceeds would not be subject to CGT. However, if the asset was a post-CGT asset, a capital gain or loss might arise from the CGT event.

Other taxes

In New South Wales general insurance premiums can attract three cascading taxes: Emergency Services Levy (ESL), GST and stamp duty. Revenues collected through this levy are used to fund local and rural fire brigades. The levy is imposed on the insurance policy sum insured for property and on motor vehicles. Other states have abolished charging this levy on insurance policies and now impose the levy on property values or in the case of Western Australia, on the gross rental value and use of the property.

> ## At a glance
>
> - General insurance premiums are allowable deduction for businesses in Australia.
> - Premiums are generally deductible for a business when the policy proceeds are to replace revenue but not for capital purposes.
> - Payments received under a policy paying lump sums or making periodic payments are subject to tax.
> - General insurance premiums in Australia are subject to GST and the business is entitled to an input tax credit.
> - Insurance claim proceeds for loss of profits or loss of trading stock (both revenue generating items) are assessable items.
> - Insurance claim proceeds for property damage by fire, etc, is treated as capital proceeds and not assessable.
> - Stamp duty and an Emergency Services Levy (ESL) in some state applies.

10-150 Study questions

10.1   What is key-person insurance?

10.2   In what situations are premiums for key-person insurance not tax deductible?

10.3   Discuss the situations when the premiums for disability and trauma insurance are tax deductible.

10.4   Explain the circumstances in which the 10-year rule for an insurance policy will be restarted.

10.5   Discuss the tax effects of arranging life insurance under a superannuation plan.

10.6   Briefly outline the income tax treatment of general insurance claim proceeds.

10.7   Discuss the fringe benefits tax implications of the three life risk products.

10.8 Explain whether the insurance claim proceeds received for recently installed machinery represent assessable income for income tax purposes.

10.9 Explain the capital gains tax implications, if any, for insurance claim proceeds received with respect to the loss by fire of an office building that was bought some years ago and has increased in value substantially in recent years.

10-160 References and further reading

References

Releases

Australian Taxation Office, *Interpretative Decision* ID 2004/661

Australian Taxation Office, *Taxation Determination* TD 2000/31

Australian Taxation Office, *Taxation Determination* TD 94/40

Australian Taxation Office, *Taxation Determination* TD 95/41

Australian Taxation Office, *Taxation Determination* TD 95/42

Australian Taxation Office, *Taxation Determination* TD 97/14

Australian Taxation Office, *Taxation Ruling* IT 155

Australian Taxation Office, *Taxation Ruling* IT 2434

Australian Taxation Office, *Taxation Ruling* IT 2663

Australian Taxation Office, *Taxation Ruling* TR 95/5

Australian Taxation Office (ATO) (2012), *Deductibility under sub regulation 295-465.01(1) of the ITAR*. Available at *ato.gov.au*

Legislation

A New Tax System (Goods and Services Tax) Act 1999 (Cth)

Income Tax Assessment Act 1937 (Cth)

Income Tax Assessment Act 1997 (Cth)

Further reading

Articles and Books

CCH Australia Ltd (2016) *Australian Master Tax Guide*, 58th edn, CCH Australia Limited, Sydney.

Websites

Australian Taxation Office: *ato.gov.au*

Australian Treasury: *treasury.gov.au*

CHAPTER 11

PERSONAL RISK MANAGEMENT

RISK MANAGEMENT

11-000 Introduction

The risk management process as it applies to businesses was examined in Chapter 2. A similar process can be used for individuals and families, although it must be realised that individuals and families do not have the resources, sources of finance or access to risk management expertise that is available to organisations and small to medium sized enterprises (SMEs). Therefore, although loss retention and risk avoidance can still be used, insurance is a more likely risk management device than these risk management tools.

Essentially, the risk management process described in Chapter 2 remains the same for individuals and families:

1. Define objectives.

2. Identify and measure potential exposures.

3. Evaluate potential loss exposures.

4. Select the most appropriate risk management techniques.

5. Implement and monitor the personal risk management program.

The first four steps are discussed below in relation to personal, property and liability risks. The last step is discussed in relation to the entire risk management process. The discussion of property and liability risks is confined to domestic risks, which fall into the categories of house and contents and motor vehicle, the two principal forms of domestic property. Business risks are not covered in this chapter, as they are discussed in Chapters 12 and 13.

At a glance

- The business risk management process can also be used for personal risk management.

PERSONAL RISK MANAGEMENT

11-010 Introduction

The objective of personal risk management is to ensure that a catastrophic loss, such as premature death, will not jeopardise the financial plan or that the effect of such a loss will be minimised.

11-020 Define objectives

One of the major problems with most plans is that they do not have any direction or a statement about what the plan is trying to achieve. Therefore, for a plan to be effective, it must state the reasons for the risk assessment, what is going to be achieved and the time period in which this will occur. This gives the plan direction and purpose and something against which progress can be measured.

The overall financial plan objectives might be as follows:

To accumulate $2.5 million in assets, excluding the family home, within the next 15 years.

The financial plan will then detail the necessary steps to achieve these objectives, such as salary sacrificing 10 per cent of gross salary into superannuation, paying off the home mortgage in the next five years, etc. However, the world is full of risk and an unforeseen pure risk loss could jeopardise these plans, so this must be considered.

The risk management objective could be:

To put in place the necessary risk management processes over the next two months to ensure that the financial plan objectives will be achieved.

This statement of objectives is the starting point of the risk management process. Before an effective risk management strategy can be implemented, the next step is to establish the individual's or family's risk profile. In this context, risk profile means the degree of risk to which an individual or family is exposed. This exposure is demonstrated in the following illustrated example:

Illustrated example 11.1

Douglas and Shawna are a married couple living on the Sunshine Coast, both aged 35, with two children: Christopher, aged 12, and Kathleen, aged

9. Owns a bob cat and carries out sub-contracting work for builders and landscapers, earning $65,000 per annum after tax. Shawna is a full-time homemaker, but hopes to work part time in the future as a receptionist, where she anticipates she will earn about $10,000 per annum after tax. Both Douglas and Shawna are in good health, although there is a history of heart problems in Douglas's family, while Shawna's family has a history of diabetes.

Both children are healthy and have not had any serious medical problems.

They own a three-bedroom house worth $350,000, which has a $130,000 mortgage that costs $1,050 per month in repayments. They own two cars. Douglas's Toyota sedan, worth $8,000 was purchased with a personal loan that has repayments of $150 per month. Shawna's car is worth $3,000 and is fully owned. Their credit card debt is $1,200, which they are paying off at $100 per month, and their average living expenses are $1,200 per month. Household assets are worth $30,000 and they have a fixed term deposit worth $2,700 and a savings account with a balance of $1,200.

What is the couple's risk profile?

- They are still relatively young, but both have potential health issues.

- They have two young children, with one soon to start high school.

- They have very little surplus income (approximately $500 a month).

- They have liquid cash ($3,900), which gives them three weeks' consumption.

- They have moderate assets of $224,900, but most of this is tied up in their house and car, which are relatively illiquid assets.

It is apparent in the above example that Douglas and Shawna have a low risk-bearing capacity and are not able to afford the full range of insurances required to provide financial security. As they have only limited resources and three weeks' cash for consumption, to cope with any financial shocks, the use of excesses and longer waiting times will not be practicable. This couple does need budgeting advice and careful risk planning. Only when their risk capacity increases will they be able to start using higher excess and longer waiting periods on their insurances so as to obtain premium discounts.

11-030 Identify and assess potential loss exposures

Advisers are required by the suitability rule (referred to in RG 175.81 (Regulatory Guide RG 175 *Licensing: Financial Product Advisers*) and detailed in s 945A(1)(a) of the *Corporations Act 2001* (Cth)) to have a reasonable basis for the advice provided. Also known as the 'know your client rule', this reasonable basis is achieved by investigating the person's relevant personal circumstances (such as what regular income would be lost if they became disabled) and making reasonable inquiries into the person's ability to withstand this loss. Reasonable basis for inquiries is defined in RG 175.412, which reproduces the Revised Explanatory Memorandum to the Financial Services Reform Bill 2001, requires the providing entity:

> "... to ascertain the client's objectives, their financial situation and needs, investigate and consider the options available to the client, and base the advice on that consideration and investigation" (para 12.32).

The gathering of the information to allow an adviser to satisfy the suitability rule is made by using a confidential client questionnaire. By using this document, the adviser can gather the necessary information to investigate the client's financial and family circumstances, including financial needs, objectives, tolerance for risk (ie, financial ability to bear risk), retirement objectives, employment security, current insurances and superannuation, and the like. The fact-finding process sets out the client's financial situation so that the adviser is made aware of what the client owns and owes, what risks exist, their financial needs and the extent of their human capital.

The development of an individual's or family's risk profile begins with the identification of the types of risks that could jeopardise a financial plan. The types of losses that individuals and families face can result from personal income losses caused by human life contingencies, direct and indirect property losses and liability losses. Losses resulting from human life contingencies are discussed below, while property losses and liability losses are discussed separately in chapter 13.

Personal income losses

Personal income losses arise from a number of causes such as the premature death or long-term disablement of the breadwinner or primary carer of children, in which case alternative childcare arrangements need to be made and paid for. Losses can also be the result of high medical bills arising from an extended period of illness or from business risks. Each is examined in turn.

Premature death

The effect of premature death will depend on an individual's responsibilities for dependants, debts and business. The following situations are quite common.

- *Single person with no dependants.* There is generally very little need for cover at this stage, although an individual may be in business as a partner or sole trader. The types of allowances that should be made are final medical and burial expenses and any debt, although the financier may have required life insurance to cover the debt.

- *Single-parent families.* This category poses considerable problems because, although there is considerable need, the client may not have enough disposable income to support an insurance program. However, if the income-producer were to die prematurely, dependants would have to be provided for. Adequate provision for a reasonable standard of living and funding of education expenses would need to be made for children until they reach an age when they are self-supporting.

- *Two-income families.* This category accounts for the majority of families with dependants. In the early adult years, this group tends to have young children and accumulated debt, especially mortgage loans on first houses. If either or both breadwinners were to die prematurely, the family would suffer, as their disposable income would fall substantially, leading to a lower standard of living. Income is needed to provide financial support for the family so that future financial goals can be met. At least with two-income families there is still one income stream if one breadwinner dies, although the total income will be substantially reduced.

- *Families with additional dependants.* These dependants include aged parents and other relatives. They may not be readily identifiable, but may become financially dependent on the family in the future. This possibility needs to be factored into the calculation of the family's future financial needs.

Long-term illness or injury

Most people work for organisations that provide sick leave and workers compensation for work-related accidents. For most families these provisions and their own savings mean that short-term illness will not cause any significant deterioration in their standard of living. However, if a breadwinner is incapacitated for a long time, then the family's living standard can suffer, and the extent of any income shortfall needs to be quantified.

The situation is different for self-employed people, as they may not have sick leave or workers compensation and must always be able to self-fund any disablement. The business may be large enough to continue without the owner present, but additional expenses will generally be incurred because a replacement may have to be employed and funds found to finance this person.

Medical costs

The cost of medical care is a serious issue for families because health insurance costs are high and continually rising, making it unaffordable for some families. The alternative is to rely on the public health system. However, this system is overtaxed; there can be long waiting lists for treatment unless a condition is life threatening. The cost of health insurance should always be factored into a financial plan.

If an injury is work related or has resulted from a motor vehicle accident, then the medical costs arising from it are generally fully paid for by workers compensation insurance or by compulsory third party insurance. However, self-employed people may not have the benefit of workers compensation insurance and will have to fund their own health costs.

Business risks

Businesses have special risks that need to be identified and provided for.

- *Partnerships*. The expectation of most partners is that if one partner dies or becomes permanently incapacitated, then the other partner will purchase the incapacitated or deceased partner's share of the business. The death or permanent disablement of one partner results in the winding up of the business so the surviving partner has no claim on the deceased's share of the business. In most cases the surviving partner will not have the funds to do buy out the deceased or incapacitated partner and he/she may have to run the business with the deceased's spouse as a non-contributing partner. In other cases, the deceased's spouse may sell their share of the partnership to a third party, with whom the surviving partner may not want to be associated.

  However, term life insurance can be arranged to provide the surviving partner/s with sufficient funds to buy the incapacitated or deceased partner's share of the business so that these possible outcomes do not occur. The buy/sell agreement is an important document and needs to be arranged through a solicitor in order to provide certainty for the partners.

- *Buy/sell agreement*. A buy/sell agreement is a contract usually entered into between business partners , which commits the surviving partners to buy out the other partner's interest in the business should a specific event occur.

Specific events which may trigger a buy/sell agreement include death, divorce, long-term disability, retirement or bankruptcy.

The agreement is often linked to an insurance policy on each partner's life. The policy provides the surviving partners with the money to be able to buy out the deceased/disabled/departing partner's interest. Generally the agreement is structured in such a way that it does not matter what business structure has been used to own the business i.e. family trust, company, partnership.

The buy/sell agreement will take precedence over the will because the business will be transferred under the terms of the contract. The agreement must identify the owner of the interest being disposed of and the type of interest disposed of (shares, units, partnership). The agreement must also specify who is to acquire the interest (business partners, key personnel).

There are two types of buy/sell agreements:

1.   Cross-purchase agreement

This is an arrangement where the remaining owners are to be the purchasers. Upon the death or serious illness of the owner the other owner/s shall purchase the outstanding share. In a common scenario the executor of the estate will be required to sell the deceased's share and the co-owners will be required to purchase it.

2.   Corporate entity redemption agreement

Under this agreement the company will buy back the interest of the deceased/disabled owner. The owner, or the estate will receive cash from the company and the company will purchase and cancel the shares.

Funding the agreement

The buy/sell agreement is normally funded through an insurance policy. Depending on the parties and the circumstances, the policies can be held under any of the following arrangements:

- cross ownership, where the owners of the business hold policies on each other.

- principal ownership, where the owner holds the policy on himself/herself.

- discretionary trust, where the trustee holds the policies on behalf of all the owners.

- company ownership, where the business holds the policies on behalf of all the owners.

The buy/sell agreement will need to state either the value of the business or how the value is to be determined when the agreement is triggered. The agreement will state whether the value to be applied shall be: book value, the agreed value, the appraised value at the happening of the specific event, or capitalisation of earnings at the time of the specific event. Clients will need legal and tax advice on what is the most suitable agreement for them.

The tax deductibility of premiums and capital gains considerations are discussed in 10-070.

- *Key employees.* The loss of a key employee or key person (as defined in 10-060) can greatly disrupt the profitability of a company. Such an employee may be a highly skilled salesperson who services the company's key accounts, for example. In these cases, term life insurance can be arranged to provide sufficient funds to allow the business to continue operating by funding one or more of the following:

  » the loss of revenue the key person would have otherwise generated.

  » the additional costs associated with the recruitment and training of a replacement for the key person.

  » replacement of lost goodwill due to the key person's departure.

  » repayment of debts outstanding at the time of the key person's departure.

  Deductibility of premiums and capital gains tax considerations are discussed in 10-060.

- *Business loans.* In the case of many small businesses, a financier's willingness to continue business loans often depends on the skills and reputation of the business owner or other key person. Financiers are always more comfortable granting loans if they know the loan is covered by life insurance. The fact that life insurance is in place may result in a reduction or elimination of the 'risk margin' that is often added to the interest rate.

11-040 Evaluate the personal loss exposures

There are three key areas that must be considered when establishing the sum insured:

- a lump sum to meet 'final costs' associated with the income earner's premature death

- a provision to meet the ongoing needs of the dependants
- a provision to meet the needs of the dependants and the income earner in the event of his or her disablement.

Final costs

There are a number of expenses that generally arise and which must be provided for. These can include funeral costs, legal expenses, the costs of administering the estate, medical and associated care costs, and redemption of debt and adjustment expenses.

- *Funeral costs.* These can be quite high, so it is generally advisable to allow $10,000 to $15,000 to cover all associated costs. However, a funeral director can provide more accurate costs. Bear in mind that a family may have purchased a funeral plan and, if this is the case, many of these costs will be eliminated. Finally, as this provision relates to a future event, a reasonable allowance should be added to the estimated cost to allow for inflation.

- *Estate administration costs.* The amount allowed for will depend on the size and complexity of the estate, so professional advice may have to be sought in order to obtain an estimate. Legal fees, taxes and other costs will also have to be included. Taxes can be a significant factor, especially if the estate consists of property or a share portfolio and cash. In this instance, the person who inherited the property or share portfolio that is of equal value to the cash may receive an unfair distribution because the future value of the property and share portfolio may be substantially less than the value of the cash if these assets are sold and capital gains tax is deducted from the proceeds. If it is the intention of the beneficiaries to sell these assets, then the effect of capital gains tax should be included in the amount of the life sum insured.

- *Final medical and care costs.* These costs can be considerable, particularly as hospital and medical insurance do not always cover all costs. This could be the case if outside-of-hospital specialised nursing is required or if expensive, specialised tests not covered by health insurance are needed.

- *Debt elimination.* Debt is a significant element in most household budgets. The clearing of this debt may significantly reduce the amount of income required by the surviving spouse to maintain the family's standard of living. Debt might consist of home mortgage, credit card balances, the balance of hire purchase contracts and/or personal loans and charge accounts. Any anticipated future debt should also be allowed for.

- *Adjustment expenses.* These expenses refer to having sufficient funds available to ensure that there isn't any possible reduction in the family's standard of living that may result from a premature death. A lump sum calculated on six months' living expenses could greatly assist the family in adjusting to their new circumstances. For example, if the plan required that the wife of the deceased spouse was to return to work, then these funds would give her time to deal with her affairs without being forced to return to work prematurely.

Provision for dependants

Up to this point, data has been gathered and analysed and the client's exposures and needs identified. Once it has been determined that life insurance is required as part of a plan to provide for dependants, the next step is to determine how much life insurance is required. This process is important because buying too much life insurance is expensive and diverts funds away from other needed areas, like investments. On the other hand, buying too little life insurance could ultimately prove disastrous. To avoid these problems, a rigorous and accurate method is needed to calculate how much insurance is necessary. The approach used by financial planning industry is called the 'needs analysis' and this is described next.

Needs analysis

Needs analysis focuses on the actual income needs that the dependants will have if the income earner dies. A family's needs change over time, so an adviser will need to re-examine the plan periodically to check that the figures are still sufficient. This method involves three steps:

1. Calculate the total economic resources required by the dependants if the main income earner were to die.

2. Identify and quantify all financial resources available after death, including existing life insurances and superannuation death benefits.

3. Deduct available financial resources from the amount needed to arrive at the additional life insurance required.

Step 1: Assessment of family's total economic needs.

This step requires the preparation of a family budget of monthly expenditure required to live a comfortable life. This budget includes items such as expenses for clothing, education, housing, food, utilities, and dental and healthcare. Other items would be insurance costs, rates, recreation and travel. Children's needs change over time, consuming considerable financial resources in the early years but reducing substantially once they have grown up

This step also involves calculating the final expenses and the amount required to liquidate any existing debt and to look after any special needs. If there are elderly dependants, then an allowance may be necessary for the long-term care of disabled or chronically ill dependants. It may also be necessary to establish a special fund for financial emergencies or an education fund for the children's university education.

Step 2: Determine the availability of financial resources.

Once the dependants' financial needs have been estimated, it is then time to list all the available resources that can be applied to meet these needs. These could include money from savings, investments, proceeds from employer-sponsored group life insurance policies, and from superannuation funds. There may also be old whole-of-life policies available that have a term life rider attached to the policy. If the surviving spouse is able to work, their earnings will be an important resource for the family. It may also be possible to liquidate some assets such as jewellery, real estate or other investments in order to meet the financial needs. Once these resources have been identified, it should be possible to assign a reasonable estimate of their value.

Step 3: Calculation of additional life insurance requirements.

Finally, the total value of resources available is deducted from the total needed to satisfy the dependants' financial objectives. If the financial value of the resources is greater than the needs, then no further life insurance is needed. However, if the resources are less than the needs, then the difference represents the amount of life insurance needed.

Where there is more than one income earner, a separate calculation needs to be made for each person. The need for cover for each income earner should not be overlooked. The mathematical method used to calculate the amount of life insurance needed to finance future living is called the present value of an annuity.

Present value of an annuity calculation

This calculator is used to determine what a future income stream is worth in today's dollars. This is done by using the following formula:

$$PV = PMT \left(\frac{1 - (1 + i)^{-n}}{i} \right)$$

Where: PV = present value

PMT = periodic payment amount

n = number of compounding periods

i = interest (or, discount rate)

The PV of an annuity formula is used to calculate how much a stream of payments is worth *currently* where 'currently' does not necessarily mean right now but at some time prior to a specified future date.

In practice the PV calculation is used as a valuation mechanism. It evaluates a series of payments over a period of time and reduces or consolidates them into a single representative value at a certain date.

Note however that the PV of an annuity formula does not inherently take into account the effect of inflation. The value mechanism for the *current* value of a stream of *future* payments is the time value of money as represented by prevailing market interest rates, not the inflation rate.

The PV of the annuity equation above can be rearranged algebraically to solve for the payment amount (PMT) that will amortize (pay off) a loan or equate to a current sales price.

The formula above assumes an ordinary annuity, one in which the payments are made at the *end* of each compounding period. An annuity-due is one in which the payments are made at the *beginning* of the compounding period.

Distinction between an ordinary annuity and an annuity-due

Each payment of an ordinary annuity belongs to the payment period *preceding* its date, while the payment of an annuity-due refers to a payment period *following* its date.

The meaning of the above statement may not be immediately obvious until it is looked at it graphically.

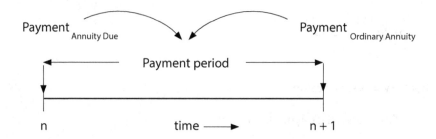

A more simplistic way of expressing the distinction is to say that payments made under an ordinary annuity occur at the end of the period while payments made under an annuity due occur at the beginning of the period.

A third possibility is to define an annuity due in terms of an ordinary annuity: *an annuity-due is an ordinary annuity that has its term beginning and ending **one period earlier** than an ordinary annuity.* This definition is useful because this is how an annuity due is computed, ie, in relation to an ordinary annuity (discussed below).

Most annuities are ordinary annuities. Instalment loans and coupon bearing bonds are examples of ordinary annuities. Rent payments, which are typically due on the day commencing with the rental period, are an example of an annuity-due.

Note that an ordinary annuity is sometimes referred to as an immediate annuity, which is unfortunate because it implies that the payments are made immediately (ie, at the beginning of the period, which would be the case with an annuity-due). However, ordinary annuity is the more widely used term.

Calculating the value of an annuity due

An annuity due is calculated in reference to an ordinary annuity. In other words, to calculate either the present value (PV) or future value (FV) of an annuity-due, the value of the comparable *ordinary* annuity is calculated and multiplied by a factor of *(1 + i)* as shown below.

$$\text{Annuity}_{Due} = \text{Annuity}_{Ordinary} \times (1 + i)$$

This makes sense because if the earlier definitions are considered, it can be seen that the difference between the ordinary annuity and the annuity due is one compounding period.

Note also that the above formula implies that *both* the PV and the FV of an annuity due will be greater than their comparable ordinary annuity values.

The following examples illustrate the mechanics of the ordinary annuity calculation and subsequent annuity due calculation.

Present value of an annuity

Using the present value of an annuity calculation formula above, the PV of an ordinary annuity of $50 per year over three years at 7% can be expressed as follows

$$PV_{ordinary} = PMT \left(\frac{1-(1+i)^{-n}}{i} \right) = 50.00 \left(\frac{1-(1+0.04)^{-3}}{0.07} \right) = 131.22$$

and the present value of an annuity due under the same terms is calculated as

$$PV_{due} = PMT_{ordinary} (1+i) = 131.22 (1.07) = 140.40$$

In this example, the PV of the annuity due is greater than the PV of the ordinary annuity by 9.18.

Putting it all together

The application of the needs approach is illustrated in the following example.

Illustrated example 11.2

The Morrison family has sought advice on the amount of life insurance cover needed to fully protect their family. John Morrison, aged 32, is an architect who has been in his own business for 12 months. His wife, Anna, aged 30, is a full-time homemaker. They have two children: Simon, aged four, and Kathy, aged two. John earned $100,000 in wages in his first year in business, with an after tax income of approximately $72,000.

The family's living expenses are $5,200 per month. Of this, $600 each parent is used for personal expenses and $2,500 is used for household expenses and a further $1,500 per month in mortgage repayments. The amount owing on credit cards is $6,000. John's car is leased through his business and Anna's car is owned outright.

The Morrisons' house is valued at $500,000 and has a mortgage of $250,000. They want their two children to attend a private school for their high school years and then university. They estimate that schooling will last from age 13 to 25 and cost, on average, $10,000 per year.

If Anna were to die prematurely, it is anticipated that John would need to spend $600 per month on assistance in raising the children. John's only personal insurance is a term life cover for $350,000, while Anna does not have any life insurance. The calculation for the sum insured would be:

Clean-up expenses

Funeral and other expenses	$15,000
Final medical expenses	$20,000
Mortgage repayment	$250,000
Credit cards	$6,000
Readjustment expenses	$25,000
Taxes	$5,000
Total	$321,000

Plus: dependants' support

Anna

Anna's life expectancy is approximately 83 years of age, so she will be a dependant for the longest time. Household expenses are $2,500 per month and Anna's personal expenses are included in her calculations. The mortgage repayments will cease, so expenses can be reduced by $1,500. The annual amount required is: ($2,500 + $600) × 12 = $37,200.

Anna is likely to live to age 83, so she will need to be provided for a total of 53 years. Therefore, using the present value of an annuity formula and a discount rate of four per cent, the amount required is $763,200.

Children

The children will need to be provided for until age 25, for which an amount of $600 per month has been allowed. Simon needs to be provided for 21 years and Kathy for 23 years. A separate calculation will need to be made for each child to age 25. Using the present value of an annuity formula and a discount rate of four per cent, the amount required per child is $207,979.

In addition, education expenses of $10,000 per annum per child from 13 to 25 have been allowed. The children's education requirements come to:

$10,000 × 24 = $558,000. The education funds will be required for 12 years and using a discount rate of four per cent, the amount required is $558,000.

Total insurance requirements

Anna	$763,200
Children's care	$207,979
Children's education	$195,209
Clean-up expenses	$321,000
Total sum insured	$1,487,388
Less: existing insurance	$350,000
Amount of insurance required	$1,137,388

Term life insurance cover of $1,137,388 needs to be arranged on the life of John. However, should John already have some life insurance, for example contained in his superannuation plan then this needs to be deducted.

Life insurance for a non-income earner

During this analysis, the value of the homemaker should not be overlooked, especially when there are young children. If the homemaker were to die or become totally disabled, then the family's financial situation could be severely compromised. It may be necessary for the surviving spouse to pay for childcare or for specialist nursing for the disabled spouse. These costs would also have to be considered and life insurance arranged to cover them.

In the previous example, if Anna were to die prematurely, then John's income would be sufficient to meet normal family needs. However, the children would need to be taken care of until age 13 and the amount allowed was $600 per month. This means that Simon would need care for nine years and Kathy for 11 years.

Childcare needs: Using the present value of an ordinary annuity a term life policy for an amount of $116,609 or more likely $120,000 (rounding) should be arranged on the life of Anna.

It is important to realise that life insurance needs do not stay the same forever, because the family situation changes over time. An adviser should conduct regular reviews, particularly when important life events take place, such as a promotion for the breadwinner, a new job, a new baby or an increase in debt.

Effect of inflation on the life insurance payout

The calculation of the death cover insurance requirements for the Morrisons (see illustrated example 11.2) has ignored the eroding effects of inflation. The proceeds from the insurance policies are calculated to meet future needs, but they may prove to be inadequate when ultimately received. For example, the Reserve Bank of Australia indicates that historically the inflation rate from 1951 to 2012 was 5.3 per cent. $100 worth of goods bought in 1997 would cost $131.53 at an inflation rate of 5.6 per cent in 2007.

Alternatively, $1,000,000 life insurance cover taken out in 1997 and paid out in 2007 would have a purchasing power of $684,742 at an inflation rate of 5.6 per cent. This is a significant reduction in purchasing power, particularly as this is not a particularly high inflation rate. So the question arises as to how to allow for the effects of inflation when it is not possible to predict what inflation will be over different periods.

The insurance proceeds will not all be needed at once, as only a small portion will be needed each year. Therefore, the balance can be invested and interest earned can be used to supplement the invested funds. The interest earned will help to offset inflation because, while inflation cannot be predicted, interest rates are historically higher than the inflation rate. The interest income will be subject to taxation, but future taxation rates cannot be predicted so it is not possible to allow for this charge. There are other variables to consider, eg, the dependent spouse may decide to work and so supplement the insurance proceeds.

Using interest to offset the effects of inflation is a reasonable approach given the unpredictable variables that may apply in the future. This approach ensures that the required amount will be available if and when it is needed.

Disablement

Death is not the only major peril that can destroy a family's financial plans. Another peril that can cause even greater disruption occurs when the main income earner becomes totally and permanently incapacitated (disabled). The insured may have substantial term life insurance to provide for any dependants on death, but this cover is useless unless the insured dies.

The term *disablement* in this context generally means that the insured is totally incapable of working in any occupation for which he or she is reasonably qualified by education, training and experience. In other words, the insured is unlikely to ever work again. This definition is more forgiving than the old definition which required a person to be 'totally incapable of *ever again* working in…'. The types of expenses that a permanently incapacitated person could expect to face are as follows:

- *Medical expenses*. Health insurance will cover many of these expenses, but some policies may not cover specialised nursing or specialised diagnostic tests.

- *Income for dependants*. Dependants still have to be provided for, so any lump sum payment from insurance will need to cater for this need. Included in this payment should be a lump sum to help family members readjust to their new circumstances.

- *Other costs*. These might include the purchase of a wheelchair, modifications to a car to allow the disabled person to drive, and modifications to the house (for example, the provision of ramps or lifts, widening of hallways, and enlargement of bathrooms and toilets to accommodate a wheelchair).

The types of covers that will provide for family protection in these circumstances are total and permanent disablement (TPD) insurance, which provides a lump sum as well as income protection that makes regular monthly payments for a designated period. These covers are discussed in detail in Chapter 13.

11-050 Select the most appropriate risk management technique

The risk management technique selected often depends on the risk control measures that are put in place. For example, certain control measures can be put in place to eliminate or reduce the likelihood of a risk. In regard to personal risks, these measures usually relate to lifestyle and can include keeping fit, maintaining an appropriate height/weight ratio, avoiding smoking or drinking too much and having regular medical checks.

Despite these control measures, losses will still occur, so provision needs to be made to finance these losses. The two methods discussed in Chapter 2 are as follows:

- *Retention*. Whether retention is active or passive, losses must be met out of an individual's own resources. Active retention is useful for small losses that a person can afford to finance. This is particularly the case with disability policies where a person may elect to exclude the first four weeks of a claim (known as the waiting period) for a substantial reduction in the premium. However, the selection of the waiting period is governed by the amount of available savings and sick leave provisions. Other areas where an individual may elect to retain the risk occurs where insurance cover is not available or the individual considers the risk of loss is remote.

Passive retention is most likely to occur if the individual thinks they are covered when in fact they are not. This might occur because the individual is unclear about definitions in a trauma policy or definitions of disablement in an income protection policy.

- *Transfer*. Transfer involves the passing of financial responsibility to another party and in this instance it will be by insurance, as discussed in Chapter 2 in the section on risk financing (see 2-040). In relation to personal risks, the types of policies that are available for use include life policies, disability policies, income protection policies and health policies. Life policies provide a lump sum in the event of death, TPD and specified traumas (critical illness). Income protection policies provide a monthly income for the period of the disablement or the term of the cover, whether temporary or permanent. These policies are discussed in Chapter 12.

When choosing the appropriate policies, an important part of the selection and costing process is considering the following factors:

- comparison of the features and costs of alternative policies
- selection of an insurance company
- choice of an adviser.

Because the selection of an insurance company and the choice of an adviser are part of buying insurance, these are discussed at 11-110 and 11-120 respectively.

Comparison of features and costs

It is important when comparing policies that the individual compares 'apples with apples'. Insurance policies are not all the same and it would be a mistake to think they are. For example, some mass-marketed life policies only cover death as a result of accident whereas term life policies cover death from all causes. The premiums for the former policies are quite low when compared to term life policies for the same sum insured, but care should be taken to read all the disclosures in the brochures, as accidental death policies may not suit an individual's financial plans. Definitions in trauma policies are often different, eg, whether the definition of a heart attack includes a heart attack while in a hospital. Most advisers have computer programs that compare the benefits offered by a large number of life companies and can rank policies according to an individual's specific requirements.

As indicated above, cost is not necessarily an indicator of a suitable policy. Costs will vary from company to company even for the same amount of coverage. Factors that will affect the premium include smoking, previous health history, high cholesterol or blood pressure, diabetes and other ailments. Companies may have differing views of these conditions and may apply premium loadings accordingly.

It can be misleading to consider only the current premium rates, as the accumulated rates should also be checked over, say, 10 years. It is also necessary to check that the projected rates are guaranteed and will not change in subsequent years. If a policy is going to be kept for a long period of time, then level premiums should be considered. With these premiums, the rates are higher than increasing term rates in the early years but lower than increasing term rates in later years. It may be the case that substantial premium savings can be achieved by opting for a level premium over the long term. These savings can be seen in the following example.

Illustrated example 11.3.

Case Study - Stepped and Level Premiums

Age: Male, 38 years old

Occupation: A class - professional and clerical

Salary: $80K - Monthly benefit $5,000, non-smoker.

Income Protection Premium comparison - annual (LCS)

The values below are examples only to demonstrate the difference between Stepped and Level premiums and may not be the same values applicable to you.

Age next birthday	Yearly Stepped Premium ($)	Yearly Level Premium ($)
39	1,193.07	1,805.55
40	1,256.86	1,805.55

45	1,754.50	1,805.55
50	2,647.70	1,805.55
55	4,204.42	1,805.55
60	5,461.28	1,805.55
65	5,346.44	1,805.55
27 year average	**3,477.57**	**1,805.55**
Total premiums to age 65	93,894.47	48,749.85
Inflation adjusted	2,164.51	1,262.34

Benefit details: Plus contract, $5,000 monthly benefit, inflation linked, agreed value, guaranteed renewal, benefit period to age 65, 1 month waiting period, no short waiting periods for accidents, no extra benefits option, indexed claim benefit, no aids exclusion. Premium excludes policy fee, premiums are not guaranteed and may be varied in the future.

Source: Rate detective

11-060 Implementation and review

By this stage, the plan's objectives have been established, the risks identified and control and financing measures developed to enable management of the identified risks.

The next step is to implement the plan. This involves the completion of the various proposal forms and other measures such as obtaining medical information or attending medical examinations. It is generally advisable to draw up an action list that details the actions that need to be taken, the person who is responsible for the completion of the tasks, and when they are to be achieved.

An adviser who wants to form long-term, ongoing relationships with clients will arrange for a regular review of the program, as the client's situation will change with significant life events such as promotion, pay increase, birth of a new child, or purchase of a new house. These events may alter the family's financial plans so that the risk component of the plan needs to be adjusted. A common premium instalment date on the insurance cover is an ideal time to undertake the review.

At a glance

- The risk management plan should contain both financial plan objectives and risk management objectives.

- Advisers must satisfy the suitability rule.

- Advisers must develop a client risk profile.

- Possible losses can be identified as personal income losses, direct and indirect property losses and liability losses.

- Losses are evaluated in terms of final costs, ongoing needs of dependants and the disablement of the main income earner.

- The amount of the required life insurance can be calculated by using either the human life value method or the needs analysis method.

- Clients can elect to either retain or transfer the identified perils through insurance.

- A periodic review of a plan needs to be undertaken so that it can be adjusted to take into account any changed or new needs.

PROPERTY AND LIABILITY RISK MANAGEMENT

11-070 Introduction

Protecting personal property is also an important part of the risk management process for families, individuals and businesses. Most individuals face two basic types of exposure: physical loss of property and loss through liability.

11-080 Exposure to property loss

The steps in the risk management process can be applied to property and liability risk assessment.

Identification of property risks

There are a range of perils that can cause loss or damage to personal property or motor vehicles and which result from legal liability:

- *Direct personal property losses.* Some of the perils that cause these losses are fire, storm or tempest, water damage, burglary, impact by a vehicle, earthquake, accidental damage, breakage of glass, fusion of an electric motor, and food spoilage.

- *Indirect property losses.* These perils are the result of damage to direct personal property. For example, a homeowner may be faced with the cost of alternative accommodation if their home is destroyed in a fire.

- *Liability losses.* These losses result from injury to third parties and damage to their property resulting from the negligence of the insured. Claims in this area are increasing.

Evaluation of property risks

In order for homeowners to be adequately insured, they need to calculate the maximum possible loss that could occur to their property and for which they could be legally liable. Losses may include:

- *Direct personal property losses.* It is relatively easy to determine the value of a house, whether the value is for replacement value or for indemnity value. The value that is being determined is for the house only and does not include the land, since the land will not suffer damage. However, it will be necessary to include an amount for the removal of debris in the event that the damaged structure needs to be demolished or fixtures dug up, and so on.

The valuation of home contents usually causes individuals a considerable amount of difficulty, as they generally own much more in contents than they imagine. Fortunately, insurance companies provide valuation checklists that list the more common items on a room-by-room basis, which greatly assists in the valuation process.

- *Indirect property losses*. These losses occur as a consequence of the main loss and can include the cost of alternative accommodation while the home is being repaired or rebuilt, or the cost of car hire following the theft of a car.

- *Liability losses*. Liability suits have the potential to cost individuals and households thousands, if not millions, of dollars in settlements, which could cause bankruptcy or ruin financial plans. Exposures can arise on the homeowner's property from such events as a visitor tripping over a garden hose left lying on the front lawn or being bitten by the family dog. Liability under tort can also arise away from the property, resulting from negligent acts that damage a third party's property or cause them injury.

People are more aware of their legal rights and are more inclined than in the past to pursue legal action against a negligent party. This attitude has been partly fuelled by the legal fraternity and by firms that provide representation on a 'no win no fee' basis. There has been a significant increase in the number of legal actions, which has resulted in a significant increase in liability premiums. However, recent tort reforms have reduced the number of court actions and led to a decline in liability insurance premiums to more realistic levels.

Control measures

Individuals are not powerless in protecting their property and can take positive steps to avoid or reduce the risk of a loss.

- *Personal property*. The possibility of loss and damage is always present, so it is important to minimise, through loss prevention and reduction, the chance of their occurring. The installation of security screens on external windows and deadlocks on external doors makes entry more difficult, thereby encouraging burglars to move on to a less secure property. Smoke detectors and burglar alarms (preferably back-to-base versions with 24-hour monitoring) ensure swift action, as local alarms are often ignored by neighbours. Items such as lawn mowers and small pleasure boats can be securely stored.

A further control method is to avoid the loss exposure. This is a sensible option when facing particular activities perceived as dangerous, or where the potential loss exposure cannot be transferred to another party. For example, an individual or family can avoid potential catastrophic loss to their property caused by flood by not purchasing a house in a flood-prone area. Because a property is flood prone, it may not be affordable to transfer the loss exposure, owing to the high cost of flood insurance.

- *Liability*. Most personal liability exposures can be covered by liability insurance that not only covers the losses resulting from legal settlements but also from the defence costs. Most household insurance building policies include liability protection for liability arising from events occurring on the insured's property. Household contents policies include personal legal liability protection for away-from-the-home events such as a carelessly driven golf ball causing injury to another player. Special care needs to be taken with liability cover relating to golf buggies, small pleasure craft, jet skis and other mechanical devices, as they may not be covered for damage or liability by some companies. Other activities that can result in legal liability exposures are as an executive member of an owner's corporation (strata scheme) or an office bearer in a body corporate. The cover provided by office bearers insurance is discussed in Chapter 13.

  It should be remembered that these policies only provide protection for non-business-related activities. These risks will need to be protected by particular liability policies designed for that situation, such as the activities of a plumber or accountant.

Financing measures

Financing of a loss is typically achieved through insurance. Some of the more common covers and pitfalls are as follows:

- *Personal property*. Retention of some of the amount can be undertaken by the use of a policy excess, but the premium discount is generally not enough to make this worthwhile. Remember: some policies, such as accidental damage policies, have compulsory excesses.

  There are generally two types of policy available for the insurance of personal property. Replacement value policies are referred to as 'new for old' policies, because in the event of a loss the damaged items are replaced with new items (although some exceptions apply for items such as clothing). Houses can also be insured on the same basis and, in the event of a loss, the damage will be repaired or the house rebuilt without any cost to the insured. Indemnity value policies pay only for the value of the property at the time of the loss, which would be its replacement value, less depreciation. These policies are discussed in greater depth in Chapter 13.

The calculation of the sum insured is critical if insurance is to provide the protection that it is designed for. With replacement value policies it is necessary to obtain a valuation for the rebuilding costs from a builder or professional valuer. With regard to contents, the valuation guide referred to above can be used, but items should be valued using their replacement cost, even though the items may have cost far less when purchased. This can be a time-consuming exercise but one well worth the effort, as most clients receive a shock when they realise what it would cost to replace their contents. Valuation guide can be found at most general insurance web sites.

When comparing insurance policies, it is dangerous to assume that they all provide the same coverage and differ only on price. Some of the cheaper policies may contain restrictive clauses, particularly the 'co-insurance or average' clause that was discussed in Chapter 7 (see 7-150). Insurance can be confusing for many people, so it may be a good idea to consult an insurance broker for advice.

Liability. The cost of most personal liability cover forms part of the overall householder policy premium, so no extra cost is involved. One exception to this is pleasure boats exceeding three metres in length, as they are not covered by a householders policy and have to be insured under a pleasure craft policy.

11-090 Motor vehicle risk management

For most people, their car is a significant investment and a valued possession. Unfortunately, cars have a major exposure to damage and theft. Also, their negligent operation leaves the owner open to the possibility of a significant loss through litigation from an injured party.

Identification and evaluation of motor vehicle risks

There are three types of motor vehicle risk: damage to the motor vehicle itself; theft; and loss or damage to third parties and their property, caused by the negligent operation of the motor vehicle.

- *Damage.* Motor vehicles run the risk of being damaged every time they are taken onto the road. This damage can range from minor panel damage to a total write-off following a major accident.

- *Theft.* Theft is an ever-present risk, as many cars are stolen from public car parks, home driveways, work parking spaces — in fact, from any place in which a motor vehicle is left unattended. Thousands of cars are stolen in Australia every day.

- *Legal liability*. The owner of a motor vehicle can be liable for the damage they cause, through the negligent use of their vehicle, to another's property such as a motor vehicle, fence, building or public utility. They can also be liable for any physical injury to third parties if they are proved to be negligent. All of this could cost the owner thousands, if not millions, of dollars.

Control and financing measures for motor vehicles

There are many ways an individual can prevent their car from being damaged or stolen. The following are some suggested strategies to control these risks:

- *Damage*. The following tactics reduce the chance of damage being caused to motor vehicles:

  » never speed

  » do not drive under the influence of alcohol

  » avoid aggressive driving

  » do not drive if fatigued

  » do not drive on bald tires

  » ensure your vehicle is mechanically sound

  » avoid driving if in poor health.

  » do not drive under the influence of drugs.

- *Theft*. The following ten control measures should aid in the prevention of motor vehicle theft:

  » fit an anti-theft device or alarm system to the car

  » never leave the car unlocked

  » do not leave the car keys in the ignition

  » always keep the windows wound up

  » have the windows tinted to stop potential thieves having a clear view of the car's interior

  » do not leave a spare key concealed on the car; instead, keep it on your person

  » etch the vehicle identification number on the glass and other major parts of the car as this makes the car more difficult to sell on the black market

> » always park in well-lit and heavily used areas where your car is visible to the public

> » purchase an anti-theft device (such as a steering wheel locking device that can easily be installed after parking) as an additional deterrent

> » do not leave personal items in the car such as mobile phones, laptop computers or handbags, especially if they are easily visible from the outside.

- *Financing.* There are three types of insurance relating to motor vehicles in Australia: compulsory third party; comprehensive; and third party property damage.

  > » Compulsory third party insurance is packaged with the yearly car registration renewal, which must be paid in order for cover to apply.

  > » Comprehensive motor vehicle insurance covers the insured vehicle for the cost of repairs if it is in an accident and it causes damage for which the owner is legally liable, such as damage to a third party's car or other property.

  > » Third party only cover provides protection for damage to a third party's car or property if the insured is liable for the damage. The cost for this insurance is considerably lower than for comprehensive insurance and is usually taken out for older, lower valued vehicles. The perils of fire and theft can usually be included for an extra charge up to a nominated figure such as $5,000.

At a glance

- Property losses can be classified as either direct, indirect or liability.

- Property losses are evaluated in terms of the economic losses they incur.

- The potential for losses can be controlled by loss prevention and reduction.

- Insurance is generally the main method used to transfer a loss.

- Motor vehicles have their own particular risk of loss, which must also be evaluated.

BUYING INSURANCE

11-100 Introduction

Once a decision has been made to transfer risk by purchasing insurance, decisions need to be made about which insurance company to select and whether to use the services of an insurance adviser, such as an insurance broker or agent.

11-110 Selection of the insurance company

Because of the strong regulatory environment in Australia and the history of life insurance company stability in Australia, the selection of a life company will most probably revolve around the choice of the adviser.

An individual can check the APRA website for information about the financial strength of a particular life or general insurance company, as shown by its individual solvency coverage (discussed in Chapters 8 and 9). Private rating agencies such as Standard & Poor's can also give an indication of the financial strength of an insurance company. The information provided includes an Insurer Financial Strength Rating, which is an indication of an insurer's claims-paying ability as well as an issuer credit rating report. This report gives an indication of a company's ability to meet its obligations to creditors and lenders. Table 11.1 shows the various ratings that are applied to insurance companies.

Table: 11.1: Standard & Poor's Credit Ratings

'AAA'	Extremely strong capacity to meet financial commitments. Highest Rating.
'AA'	Very strong capacity to meet financial commitments.
'A'	Strong capacity to meet financial commitments, but somewhat susceptible to adverse economic conditions and changes in circumstances.
'BBB'	Adequate capacity to meet financial commitments, but more subject to adverse economic conditions.
'BBB-'	Considered lowest investment grade by market participants.
'BB+'	Considered highest speculative grade by market participants.
'BB'	Less vulnerable in the near-term but faces major ongoing uncertainties to adverse business, financial and economic conditions.
'B'	More vulnerable to adverse business, financial and economic conditions but currently has the capacity to meet financial commitments.

'CCC'	Currently vulnerable and dependent on favourable business, financial and economic conditions to meet financial commitments.
'CC'	Currently highly vulnerable.
'C'	Currently highly vulnerable obligations and other defined circumstances.
'D'	Payment default on financial commitments.
Note: Ratings from 'AA' to 'CCC' may be modified by the addition of a plus (+) or minus (-) sign to show relative standing within the major rating categories.	

Source: Standard & Poor's Rating Services

Other factors to consider are the company's reputation; access to customer service personnel (particularly when it comes to making a claim); and the availability on the company website of information that will help an individual manage risk exposure.

11-120 Choice of adviser

Choice often boils down to trust and the adviser's perceived professionalism. A good adviser will have the skills to involve the family in the planning process and fully explain the planning steps in a client-friendly manner. Their report will be clear and concise and will provide a solution to the family's needs. The adviser's qualifications are important, as is their experience, but this does not mean that a relatively new entrant in the industry will not be competent. The advisor must be listed on ASIC's Financial Advisers Register and holding membership of professional associations is important because the adviser is required to comply with the professional body's standards of conduct and ethics. Examples of such associations are the Financial Planning Association (FPA), the Investment and Financial Services Association (IFSA) and, for insurance brokers, the National Insurance Brokers Association (NIBA).

Professional insurance advisers should have the following characteristics.

- They should be client-centred; ie, they should be interested in the client and how they can help the individual or family meet their financial goals, and be prepared to be part of the journey. This means that the relationship is likely to be for a long time, so the right choice is important.

- They should have a holistic view; ie, they should consider the client's entire financial position and the range of risks faced by their client.

- They should be prepared to work with their client over the long term. Product-based advisers are only interested in one-off sales and the commission that this returns, whereas a professional adviser will consider their client's financial situation and risk needs over the long-term and produce a plan that is optimal for their client.

- They should inform their clients at their first meeting about the services they provide and how they charge for their services. Generally, life insurance is arranged on a commission basis, but clients should be told this 'up front'.

- They must provide a Financial Services Guide (FSG) as required by the Corporations Act, which identifies who is responsible for the advice, what the remuneration is and how disputes are resolved.

- They must provide a Statement of Advice (SoA) that identifies the risks and provides a solution in a clear, concise and effective manner.

- They should provide advice on how their client can reduce risk and avoid losses.

- They should also be prepared to provide an ongoing review of the insurance program.

- They should put your interests before their own and only recommend policies or actions that benefit you.

11-130 Study questions

11.1 List and explain the different categories of family needs that life insurance can cover in the event of premature death. Separate the list into permanent and temporary needs.

11.2 Identify and briefly explain the five steps in the personal risk management process.

11.3 Briefly explain the needs analysis approach used in determining life insurance requirements.

11.4 Why is it important to establish a detailed record of home contents when seeking to arrive at a sum insured under a householders contents insurance.

11.5 Explain the difference between indemnity value and replacement value.

11.6 Explain the reasons why businesses purchase life insurance.

11.7 Identify the risks that can arise from the use of a motor vehicle.

11.8 Under what circumstances would a family retain a property exposure.

11.9   Why is it important for a family to review their life insurance program?

11.10 Explain some control measures that a family can take to protect their property against burglaries.

11-140 References and further reading

References

Releases

Australian Securities and Investments Commission Regulatory Guide 175, *'Licensing: financial product advisers — conduct and disclosure'*. Available at *asic. gov.au*

Further reading

Articles and Books

Dorfman, MS (2008), *Introduction to risk management and insurance*, 9th edn, Prentice Hall, Upper Saddle River, New Jersey, USA.

Rejda, GE (2007), *Principles of risk management and insurance,* 10th edn, Addison-Wesley, Boston, MA, USA.

Websites

Business Dictionary: http://www.businessdictionary.com/definition/due-diligence.html

Financial Advisers Register: http://asic.gov.au/for-finance-professionals/afs-licensees/financial-advisers-register/

Rate Detective: ratedetective.com.au/guides/stepped-vs-level-insurance-premiums.htm#.UXxh5aKBlF8

Reserve Bank of Australia (RBA): *rba.gov.au*

Standard & Poor's (S&P): *standardandpoors.com.au*

Chapter 12

LIFE INSURANCE PRODUCTS

TRADITIONAL LIFE POLICIES

12-000 Introduction

There are three types of policies that may be regarded as 'traditional': whole-of-life, endowment and annuities. They are considered traditional because they have been offered by life insurance companies for many generations and formed the foundation of insurance and savings for many Australians and New Zealanders. With the advent of managed funds, these policies have fallen out of favour.

12-010 Whole-of-life policies

Whole-of-life policies are bundled policies. That is, they have both a risk component and an investment component. Under a whole-of-life policy the policyholder pays a fixed regular premium for the duration of the policy and receives a specified sum of risk insurance. The amount paid out on termination may increase over time as bonuses accumulate on the policy.

Upon death, the beneficiary will receive at least the face amount of the whole-of- life insurance policy. Alternatively, the policyholder can choose to withdraw some or all of the cash value of the policy that is made up of dividends earnings, or even borrow against the cash value while keeping the policy active.

The policy's cash value increases over time and this allows the policy to have a cash surrender value. The surrender value is the value of the reserve fund minus the amount that is being paid for the life insurance death benefit (mortality charge), commissions, administrative expenses, fees and charges. This value arises because of the overpayment of insurance premiums in the early years, with the result that the policyholder builds cash equity in the policy.

When premiums are initially set, investment earnings are taken into account, but a conservative interest rate is used. Part of the premiums goes into a reserve fund, or accumulation fund that builds up over the years the policy is in effect. Periodically, a valuation of all policies held by the company is undertaken to determine the funds available to meet expected claims. Since a conservative approach was used when setting the premiums, this valuation generally produces a surplus, which is distributed back to the policyholders in the form of a reversionary bonus, which cannot be withdrawn by the life insurance company once it has been declared (ie, they are guaranteed). The declared bonuses accumulate and are paid along with the sum insured when the policy matures, generally at age 95 or 100 or a death claim arises.

In addition to the policy earning bonuses once a year, a policy may also earn a terminal bonus when it matures or when a death benefit is paid. A scale of terminal bonus rates is published in the policy, which varies according to the length of time the policy has been in force. For example, if the death benefit sum insured was $20,000, accumulated bonuses were $22,385, and the current terminal bonus scale was five per cent for a policy in force for three years, then the benefit paid would be: 105% × $22,385 = $23,504.

Terminal bonuses are not guaranteed and the insurer can vary the published scale at any time. Terminal bonus rates can even be reduced to zero.

Whole-of-life policies generally include a convertibility option that will allow the policyholder to convert the policy to an endowment policy by giving the insurance company five years' notice of the policyholder's intention to surrender the policy. The sum insured is adjusted to reflect the endowment sum insured (usually a lower amount) that the premium would have purchased at the time the policy was taken out.

Additionally, the policyholder can cease paying the premium (called 'paying up the policy') and the accumulated bonuses will continue to pay the life insurance component until they are exhausted (called the non-forfeiture option). The policyholder can also revive a lapsed policy (policy reinstatement) by paying outstanding premiums and interest.

There are also a number of optional benefits (called riders) that can be added to these traditional policies:

- *Total and permanent disablement*. This benefit is described in more detail at 12-100. In brief, this benefit provides a lump sum if the insured is classified as totally and permanently disabled.

- *Trauma cover*. While this cover is discussed in detail at 12-130, in brief, it provides for the payment of a nominated lump sum in the event that the insured is diagnosed with a specified life-threatening or major illness or disease.

- *Future insurability*. This option (also called guaranteed insurability) gives the insured the opportunity to purchase specified amounts of additional life cover, at standard rates, at future nominated dates without providing further evidence of health status. This option is of particular benefit to insureds who have developed a health condition that would preclude further cover being provided. It is possible that up to five opportunities will be provided to the insured up to the age of 45. The dates on which this option can be exercised are nominated in the policy, but in the event of certain nominated events, such as a house purchase or birth of a child, the date may be brought forward.

The premiums due do not increase with age but remain level for the duration of the policy. This means that the policyholder is overcharged in the early years for the insurance protection and undercharged in the later years when the insurance premiums are inadequate to pay for the death claims. A cash surrender value does not apply until two or three years after the inception of the policy. This means that if the policy is surrendered before that time, then the policyholder will not receive anything from the policy.

Whole-of-life policies are useful if a policyholder requires insurance for an entire lifetime and is able to budget for premiums over a relatively long period, thus eliminating the problems of unaffordability and uninsurability, particularly if the policyholder requires insurance after age 65. These policies were traditionally used to cover needs such as death duties in Australia and estate tax in New Zealand. Since the demise of these taxes, most people have few permanent insurance needs.

The major disadvantages of whole-of-life insurance are its lower yields (often only three per cent) compared with other investment vehicles and its cost. The premium is higher than a comparable term life cover because of the savings element. This expense is a major factor for policyholders when they need substantial life cover at a minimum cost. It is mainly these factors that have caused the virtual disappearance of this type of policy.

12-020 Endowment insurance

Endowment insurance is a combined death and savings policy where the policy owner nominates the sum insured and the policy term (eg, 20 years). It pays the sum insured plus bonuses at the end of the term or on death of the policyholder. The policy owner pays a level regular premium throughout the life of the policy. Each year, a share of the profits arising from the policy is distributed to the policy owner in the form of bonuses, which increase the potential benefits. Endowment insurance pays an effective investment rate of about 4.5 per cent and, apart from the savings element, the policy is the same as the whole-of-life policy in that it pays a surrender value, it allows the policy owner to convert to a paid-up policy, and it provides the same optional extras.

Endowment insurances were commonly sold in both ordinary and superannuation forms. With superannuation, the term of the policy was set to coincide with the planned retirement age of the policy owner, usually age 65. This is no longer a popular form of investment, and most life insurance companies no longer offer this policy for sale, although there are a significant number of policies in force.

12-030 Annuities

An annuity is a policy under which a person, called the annuitant, pays a single premium to a life insurance company which, in return, makes regular payments (usually monthly) to the annuitant for the rest of their life. An annuity may be paid to more than one person. This occurs, for example, when the annuity includes a reversionary beneficiary. A reversionary beneficiary is generally a spouse of the annuitant who receives a reduced payment, generally two-thirds of the full amount, on the death of the original annuitant.

A typical annuitant is a retired person who has received a large benefit from a superannuation plan and has purchased the annuity with the lump sum. The annuity will pay a regular income stream for the rest of the annuitant's life. This type of annuity is called a superannuation annuity because it was purchased with a superannuation benefit. All other annuities are called ordinary annuities.

An annuity includes a minimum payment period, such as five or ten years, which means that the insurer guarantees to make payments for that minimum period whether the annuitant lives or dies. However, the length of the guaranteed period will affect the minimum payment. Payments will continue beyond the guaranteed period for the annuitant's remaining lifetime.

During the minimum payment period, some insurers will allow the annuitant to commute the remaining payments into a lump sum payment. The payments beyond the end of the minimum payment period will still be made for the rest of the annuitant's lifetime.

Annuity investments

The life insurance company invests the lump sum in a variety of government bonds so that the income (interest payments and maturity payments) arising from the securities in each month match, as near as possible, the expected annuity payments for that month. Because the yields available on government bonds fluctuate, annuity prices are often quoted on a weekly basis. Therefore, if the government bond yields fall, the insurer must adjust its prices. Similarly, if government bond yields rise, then the insurer must adjust its prices or it will lose sales to its competitors.

The yield on government bonds is significantly lower than what can be obtained by investing in the share market. However, because of the volatility of share market returns, insurers avoid these investments because it would be too difficult to predict future returns and hence annuity prices. As a result of annuity returns being lower than those which annuitants can obtain from other market-linked investments, such as allocated pensions, the market for annuities has declined.

Types of annuities

There are basically three types of annuities: *immediate* (or ordinary annuity), *deferred* and *term certain*. Under an immediate annuity, payments to the annuitant commence within one year of the initial single premium being paid. Under a deferred annuity, payments to the annuitant may not commence until some future specified date, such as when the annuitant reaches 65 years.

Term-certain annuities make payments for a fixed period of time even if the annuitant dies. These annuities generally allow for a residual capital value (RCV) on maturity. This means that if an annuitant purchased a 10-year annuity with a 50 per cent RCV, then the annuitant would receive regular payments for 10 years and 50 per cent of the initial payment would be returned at the end of 10 years. The size of the RCV, which is generally negotiable, will affect the regular payments. Thus the regular payments for an annuity with a 100 per cent RCV will be lower than for an annuity with a 50 per cent or zero RCV.

At a glance

- A whole-of-life policy combines a death benefit with a modest savings element.
- Whole-of-life policies are not meant to mature, so a policy terminating at the age of 95 or 100 is set.
- Bonuses are added to the policy each year and, once set, cannot be withdrawn by the life insurance company.
- The death benefit and a proportion of the bonuses on death is paid.
- The policies can be surrendered, paid up and revived if the policy owner chooses.
- Endowment insurance is a combined death and savings policy.
- Endowment policy owners nominate the term of the policy.
- Annuities are another type of policy offered by life insurance companies.
- Annuities are classified as immediate, deferred or term certain.

TERM LIFE INSURANCE

12-040 Introduction

Term life insurance has become an important component of many financial plans, as it guarantees the future financial wellbeing of an insured's family. Since it is a relatively low-cost product in comparison to whole-of-life and endowment policies, insureds are able to cover themselves for large amounts and may still have money available for other investments. This section examines term life basics, premium options, policy features, rider benefits, how TPD fits into superannuation and common policy exclusions.

12-050 Basics

Term life insurance is generally known as 'annual renewable term insurance' and is often described by the abbreviations ART or YRT (yearly renewable term). The policy owner purchases a set amount of cover for a specified period of time with a guarantee of renewal. Upon the death of the insured, the insurer will pay the chosen sum insured and the policy ceases. It is considered pure insurance because it does not provide a cash value on surrender. This is because the policy does not participate in any of the profits made from investing the premiums. Hence, it is called a non-participating policy. The policy owner pays premiums each year throughout the life of the policy, and these generally increase with age, although level premiums are available.

The policy is renewed by the insurer sending the policy owner a written invitation to renew the policy for another year. This invitation is sent just before the policy anniversary, and the process occurs each year until:

- the death benefit is paid following the death of the life insured
- the policy owner elects not to pay the premium, so the policy *lapses*; or
- the insured reaches the 'expiry age', in which case the policy ceases without the benefit being paid.

Expiry ages are generally in the range of 70 to 90 years, although some companies offer expiry ages between 95 and 100 years.

Premiums can be paid monthly through a bank deduction authority or annually, so the policy owner can discontinue a monthly premium policy simply by cancelling the deduction authority. Unlike a whole-of-life or endowment policy, term life does not have any surrender value. The most common form of YRT is a stepped premium guaranteed renewable policy.

12-060 Premiums

Policy owners have an option of choosing either stepped or level premiums.

Stepped premiums

Stepped premiums are those that are set according to the insured's age at the beginning of the year, so that each year the premiums generally rise in accordance with the increasing death risk that results as the insured gets older. However, for ages 20 to 30 mortality rates are fairly equal, and for males the premiums may even decline. Premiums are adjusted on the policy anniversary, so that for a monthly policy the policy owner will pay 12 level premiums before any increase or decrease can occur.

The problem with stepped premiums is that the premiums increase each year, so if the insurance is required for a long time, eventually they become quite expensive. By the time the insured reaches age 60, the premiums are virtually unaffordable. This is a significant problem where term life insurance is required for partnership or key-man insurance.

On the other hand, most people find that their need for death cover ceases before they reach the age of 60. It is unlikely their children will still be dependent on them, and any mortgages the insured holds are often paid off. They may have accumulated enough savings and investments for retirement and for taking care of a dependent spouse or partner in the event of the insured's death. If there are insufficient funds, the surviving spouse or partner may be able to qualify for the age pension and other social security benefits.

Death cover is generally required between the ages of 20 and 40 when there are dependent young children and home mortgages to be repaid. Yearly renewable term insurance offers low-cost cover for these ages.

Level premiums

Although not offered by all insurers, level premiums are calculated by averaging the premium over the lifetime of the policy. Therefore, in the early years, the premiums will be higher than comparable stepped premiums for the same age of the client, but will be less in later years. The amount paid in excess of the death risk amount in the early years is invested, with the earnings used to supplement the amount paid in later years, so the insurer receives the full risk premium.

Level premiums offer a solution to the increasing nature of stepped premiums. Level premiums would be chosen only if the insurance were needed for an extended period, because if a level premium is cancelled in the first five or six years, the policy owner will have paid an excessive price for the insurance.

Table 12.1 shows a comparison of stepped and level premiums for a professional 27-year-old male non-smoker with a sum insured of $300,000.

Table 12.1: Comparison of stepped and level premiums.

Age next birthday	Premium cost (stepped)	Premium cost (level)
27	$298.08	$322.08
28	$297.63	$324.63
29	$297.26	$326.26
30	$299.97	$329.97
31	$302.76	$332.76
32	$302.63	$335.63
Cumulative to age 50	$10,517.96	$8,616.93

Source: Based on information from OneCare Product Illustration, ING Life Limited, *ing.com.au*

Note: OneCare is a life policy that provides a range of insurance covers issued by ING Life Limited. This table is not an endorsement of ING Life Limited products, nor encouragement to favour any one particular payment type. The premiums quoted are correct as at 8 January 2008.

The difference between stepped and level premiums can be appreciated from table 12.1. Note that premiums are actually lower for younger ages. It must be appreciated that over the long term the accumulated level premiums are generally less than accumulated stepped premiums. Also, the table illustrates that a level premium should not be selected if the policy is intended for only a short period.

Stepped verses level premiums

Any insurance advice should address the question of stepped verses level premium. In the Commonwealth Financial Services Limited v Couper discussed in section 5-050 the SoA prepared by Mr Couper recommended stepped cover without highlighting how the premiums rise over time and only made a comparison of the first year's premiums. This comparison showed that the stepped premiums were considerably cheaper than the level premiums, but a comparison over the life of the policy may have shown that the accumulated level premiums were less than the accumulated stepped premiums. The Court emphasized that it is misleading to do a stepped/level premium comparison by only looking at the first year's premium.

The premium and policy comparison software used by financial advisers allows policy benefits of different competing policies to be compared and a comparison to be made of the premiums over time. A graph is available which shows the breakeven point where the level premiums and stepped premiums intersect as well as accumulated premiums for the selected period, which should be at least to age 65 years.

12-070 Guaranteed renewal

Term insurance policies are guaranteed renewable. This means that:

- the policy owner is not under any obligation to renew the policy

- the policy is underwritten only once and, if the insurer accepts the insured at standard premium rates, it must continue to offer renewal of the policy at the then standard rate for as long as the policy owner elects to pay, subject to the maximum expiry age

- the premium rates are not guaranteed. The insurer is able to alter the premium rates for all policy owners if there is an increase in mortality rates. The increase will apply on the next policy anniversary, but it cannot be applied to a particular policy or a small subset of all policies. This allows insurers to adjust premium rates if there is an unexpected increase in mortality rates. Mortality rates could be affected, eg, by epidemics that continue for a long time.

It is a matter of history that in the 1980s life insurers were concerned about how HIV may affect the mortality rates of males aged between 20 and 40. Most of the deaths from HIV at this time were occurring among male homosexuals between these ages. If mortality rates did, in fact, increase as a result of HIV, then life insurers would have been able to adjust the premium rates for all males between the ages of 20 and 40. The insurers would not have been able to re-underwrite existing policies, but they would have the option of asking questions about an applicant's sexual preferences for new policies. In fact questions regarding homosexual activities were introduced into proposal forms.

12-080 Cancellable versions

Some insurance companies offer a renewable version of the yearly renewable term insurance. Under the cancellable version, the insurer has the right to re-underwrite the policy on each policy anniversary date and to decline to renew the policy if it sees fit. This type of policy is generally offered to those who do not qualify for the renewable term policy because of some health problem. However, if the insured's condition should deteriorate during the policy year, then the insurer will almost certainly discontinue the policy at the next renewal date.

12-090 Policy options

Over the years a number of options have been developed to make YRT policies more attractive. The following features are found in most policies.

Indexed sum insured

The indexed sum insured option allows the policy owner to have the insured sum automatically increased each year without any evidence of their state of health. Generally, if the indexed increase is declined three years in a row, then the automatic index benefit ceases. This benefit can be reinstated, but it will be subject to a medical check.

Future insurability

This option is described in 12-010 and can be included in an YRT policy. The main value of this option is that no medical check is required, so if an insured develops a condition that would preclude the issue of death cover, this policy option will allow the insured to obtain further cover subject to the maximum and minimum amounts specified and the frequency with which these increases can be made.

Multiple lives

Life insurers generally allow more than one life to be covered under the one policy. The insured lives have their own sum insured and if an insured dies, the insurer pays that person's death benefit and the policy continues as either a single life policy or a duel policy. The effect from the customer's point of view is that it is almost identical to purchasing individual YRT policies. The benefit of this is that the insurer makes some administrative savings when it insures multiple lives and these savings can be passed on to the insureds in marginally lower premiums than would have resulted from multiple policies. In addition, only one policy fee is charged. This means that for a family policy, there is a saving in multiple policy and administration fees.

Convertibility

This option allows the policy owner to change the policy to any other type of policy offered by the insurer, provided the sum insured remains the same. A medical examination is not required and the option can be exercised at any time to age 65. This feature may be of benefit if the health of the insured person deteriorates to such an extent that it is no longer possible to obtain further life insurance or it could only be obtained with a large premium loading or policy exclusion. This feature also allows a policy owner to change cover to better suit their changed needs. For example, the initial cover may have been for stepped premiums, but level premiums may be required at a later date so that the premiums do not become prohibitive.

12-100 Rider benefits

In life insurance, a rider benefit changes or amends the original policy. Such benefits include the following.

Accidental death benefits

This rider provides an additional sum insured (often double the sum originally insured) that is payable if the death of the insured is as a result of accident. The term *accident* is defined in the policy, but generally the accident must be caused directly and independently of any other cause by accidental means. For example, if the insured fell from a roof and was killed, the accidental benefit would apply and an amount would be paid in addition to the death cover, because the direct cause of death was an accidental bodily injury. However, if the insured had a heart attack and then fell from the roof and was killed by the fall, the rider would not be paid, because a heart attack was the direct cause of the accident. In addition, death must occur within 90 days of the accident and cover may cease upon attaining some specified age such as 60, 65 or 70 years.

The additional premium for an accidental death rider can be very low because the chance of death occurring through accidental means is relatively rare. While this rider is offered to most policies offering a death benefit, the cover does not satisfy a primary need for death cover from all causes and could be considered a marketing gimmick.

Terminal illness benefits

This rider pays a benefit if the insured suffers a terminal illness and is unlikely to live beyond six or, for some companies, 12 months from the date of diagnosis. This rider is generally available as a standard feature on ordinary YRT insurance and superannuation term life policies. The terminal illness benefit involves the payment of part of the YRT death benefit, whereas the TPD rider involves the total payout of the whole death benefit if both benefits were for the same amount. When a terminal illness benefit is paid the remaining life insurance reduces by the amount paid under the terminal illness benefit.

The purpose of this rider is to allow the insured early access to part of the death benefit in order to put their affairs in place and have the funds to carry out any final arrangements. Although the cover is termed a rider, most YRT policies include this in the policy as a standard benefit without any cost to the policy owner.

Many insureds hold their term life insurance in their superannuation plans. Under the provisions of the *Superannuation Industry (Supervision) Act 1993* (Cth) (SIS Act) trustees are not permitted to release funds until a condition of release is achieved such as retirement or death. However, should an insured member suffer a terminal illness special rules apply to the release of the funds from their plan. A terminal medical condition exists if:

- two registered medical practitioners have certified jointly or separately that the member suffers from an illness, or has incurred an injury, that is likely to result in the member's death within 12 months of the date of certification

- at least one of the registered medical practitioners is a specialist practicing in an area related to the illness or injury, and

- the certification period has not ended for each of the certificates.

How payments are taxed

A payment is made as a superannuation lump sum payment. These payments are non-assessable non-exempt income (ie, tax-free) regardless of the member's age and the underlying tax components, if the member has the required medical certification stating that a terminal medical condition existed either:

- at the time of the payment, or

- within 90 days of receiving the payment.

Many insureds are members of multiple superannuation funds. A terminally ill member may consolidate their funds into one fund when cleaning up their affairs before declaring terminal illness. Terminal benefits can only be paid out of a superannuation fund as a lump sum or a pension – they cannot be rolled over into another superannuation fund. Concessional tax treatment does not apply to a terminal medical condition income stream; any taxable component is taxed at marginal rates, but a 15% tax offset applies. However, the tax offset only applies between preservation age and age 60 or if the disability super benefit definition has been met. A terminal medical condition income stream can only be commenced from the client's existing fund.

Dread disease insurance

This rider is also called trauma insurance or crisis insurance (discussed in detail at 12-130) and can be added to a death benefit policy other than superannuation policies. The dread disease rider is generally expressed as an early payment of a percentage of the death benefit. Once a claim is made, the benefit ceases. The operation of this rider is shown in the following illustrated example.

Illustrated example 12.1

Stefanie holds a term life cover with a sum insured of $300,000. A dread disease rider will pay 20 per cent of the death benefit if she contracts one of the listed conditions. Stefanie contracted an eligible condition and received a payment of $60,000 ($300,000 × 0.20). She was paid this benefit immediately and the rider benefit ceased. Her term life policy continued, but the sum insured was reduced to $240,000 ($300,000 − $60,000) with subsequent premiums reduced to reflect the reduction in the sum insured.

Total and permanent disablement insurance

By paying an additional premium, this rider can be added to a policy containing death benefits. It causes the death benefit to be paid upon either the death or the total and permanent disablement (TPD) of the life insured. The TPD rider does not provide extra cover, so once the TPD benefit is paid, the policy ceases if the amount paid is equal to the death benefit, or the remaining amount of cover is reduced by the amount of benefit paid.

The definition of TPD contained in the policy is critical, but TPD definitions generally include the following requirements:

- the insured must have been unable to work for at least six months

- the insured must be so severely injured that it is unlikely he/she will ever be able to work again in any occupation for which they are reasonably qualified by education, training or experience.

The insured will automatically be classed as totally and permanently disabled if they lose two limbs, two eyes or one limb and one eye.

Since the definition of TPD is based on the insured's inability to work, this benefit usually ceases at age 65. This means that if the insured reaches the age of 65 and has not made a TPD claim, the TPD cover ceases along with the TPD premium but the underlying cover, to which the TPD rider was added, continues.

Several companies also offer TPD cover for home duties. The 'home duties' occupation is part of the 'any' occupation definition and is applicable to persons who are disabled when occupied at home. A careful examination of the definition used in a particular policy is important, as different companies have variations to the definition that may be restrictive for a particular insured. For example, some definitions require that the insured is unable to work in any 'gainful occupation' (paid work), while others require the inability to carry out 'any work', which can include unpaid charity work.

Some definitions are flexible, so that in the event of a claim, the insured will be allowed to perform a small amount of work and earn a percentage of their pre-disability income without it affecting their claim. This is because returning to some form of work usually aids in a person's rehabilitation and longevity.

The 'homemaker' definition of TPD is adjusted slightly due to the unique tasks carried out by the homemaker and the fact that they do not generate any income. Any claim is generally assessed against their ability to:

- perform normal domestic tasks — some companies require that the level of disability results in the insured being housebound

- engage in any occupation for which they are reasonably qualified by education, training or experience.

If the homemaker were to recommence paid work, they would be covered by the 'any' occupation definition, generally without the need for medical underwriting.

The broadest definition is one that covers the life insured for their 'own occupation'. This cover is generally restricted to professional white-collar occupations. It stipulates that the life insured must be unable to work in their occupation for at least six consecutive months and is so incapacitated that, in the opinion of the insurer's professional adviser, the insured is unlikely to be able to resume their own occupation or profession ever again. Therefore, if a surgeon lost the use of his/her hand used for operating, the surgeon would qualify under this definition, even though he/she could hold down another occupation. However, the definition would need to be checked to ensure that the insurer does not assess the claim against surgeon's ability to be a general practitioner. The cost of this definition is generally higher than the 'any' occupation definition.

Some life companies extend TPD coverage by including a number of additional benefits, such as loss of limbs or sight, significant cognitive impairment, and long-term care.

Loss of limbs or sight

This benefit provides cover if the life insured suffers the loss of any of the following:

- two limbs
- two hands
- two feet
- two eyes
- one limb and one eye
- the use of one hand and one foot
- the use of one hand and the sight of one eye
- the use of one foot and the sight of one eye.

The main problem with this definition is that some life companies define the term *loss of use* as meaning 'loss by severance' rather than the preferred 'loss of use of'. Such a distinction could have a significant bearing on a claim in which the insured has retained the limb but cannot use it.

Because this tier overlaps with the 'unable to work' tier, the cost is generally minimal, but it will be of particular benefit for those insureds who are not in full-time employment.

Significant and permanent cognitive impairment

If the insured suffers significant and permanent cognitive impairment, there is a deterioration or loss of intellectual capacity that requires continuous care and supervision. This mainly refers to dementia-type illnesses and can be the result of Alzheimer's disease or stroke.

This benefit is important because companies generally cease the 'unable to work' tier at age 65 but will allow the TPD tiers to continue up to age 99.

Dementia-type claims are related to age, so maintaining the cover past age 65 may be important to some insureds.

Long-term care

This benefit relates to the insured's inability to perform at least two (or, with some companies, three) of the five activities of daily living: washing, dressing, feeding, toileting and moving about independently. Generally, when companies assess this type of claim they determine whether the insured can perform these activities with the aid of specialist equipment. If they can, they will *not* be considered as unable to perform that activity.

Some companies may offer only one or two of these tiers, such as 'unable to work' and 'loss of limbs', or they may offer all four tiers under their definition. From the point of view of pricing, the majority of the TPD premiums are based on the 'unable to work' tier and vary according to whether the policy owner selects the 'any occupation' or 'own occupation definition'.

Some companies offer a 'non-occupational' TPD rider by removing the 'unable to work' tier and leaving the remaining three tiers. This is the cheapest form of TPD cover. It is important to be aware that having this choice of cover places considerable responsibility on the adviser to recommend the appropriate cover for their client.

12-110 Policy exclusions

There are very few exclusions in a YRT policy, and exclusions vary between insurers. The following are some of the more common exclusions:

- *Suicide.* No cover is provided if the insured commits suicide within the first 13 months of the commencement date of the policy. In addition, no cover is provided in relation to the terminal illness benefit where the terminal illness is a result of an intentionally self-inflected injury or disease.

- *Other exclusions.* Not all insurers apply these exclusions, but they can include the following:

    » *war:* this term excludes not only death resulting from war and warlike activities, but can also exclude death resulting from civil commotions and other similar events

    » *pre-existing conditions:* this exclusion prevents the payment of the sum insured if the cause of death resulted from a known pre-existing condition that was not disclosed to the insurer before entering into the contract.

12-120 Life insurance held in superannuation

Many people hold their death and TPD insurance as part of their work superannuation fund, retail superannuation fund, or in their own self-managed superannuation fund. For self-employed persons this allows these persons to claim a tax deduction for the premium, but this can have an opposing disadvantage of reducing the funds available for investment. Despite the tax advantages of holding death and TPD insurance within a super fund, the potential effects of how provisions contained within the *Income Tax Assessment Act 1997* (Cth) (ITAA97) can affect a future payout must be understood.

Taxation of insurance benefits

Death benefits

This section introduces the special rules that apply when calculating the tax components of a lump-sum superannuation death benefit when the benefit is paid from a superannuation fund. Any benefits paid from a superannuation fund, whether as a lump sum or income stream payment, will consist of two components:

- a tax-free component, and
- a taxable component.

The taxable component may be split into two elements – the taxed element and the untaxed element (only lump-sum benefits are considered in this discussion). The tax treatment of a lump-sum superannuation death benefit will depend on whether the recipient is a dependant for tax purposes or a non-dependant.

A dependant for the purpose of receiving tax concessions on benefits received from a superannuation fund includes:

- any spouse or former spouse of the member
- any child, aged less than 18 years, of the member, and
- any person who is financially dependent on the member or who has an interdependency relationship with the member, just prior to the member's death.

Upon death of a superannuation fund member, the member's benefits (made up of the member's account balance and any life insurance proceeds) will be paid to the beneficiaries or the member's personal legal representative. Where the proceeds of a lump-sum superannuation death benefit are to be paid to a dependant for tax purposes, all the proceeds (regardless of the amount) will be tax free.

If the proceeds of a lump-sum superannuation death benefit are to be paid to a non-dependant, the tax-free component will be tax free. The taxable component will be subject to tax at up to either 16.5 per cent or 31.5 per cent (including the Medicare levy) depending on whether the taxable component is a taxed element or an untaxed element. However, where life insurance policy proceeds are included as part of a lump-sum superannuation death benefit, special rules may apply to calculate the taxable component.

Complying superannuation funds are allowed a tax deduction under s 295-465 of the ITAA97 in relation to premiums paid for providing death benefits, disability superannuation benefits and certain temporary incapacity benefits. Section 295-470 of the ITAA97 also allows a tax deduction for a complying superannuation fund in respect of the future service element of a superannuation death benefit, disability superannuation benefit and certain temporary incapacity benefits.

If the trustee of the superannuation fund paying the lump-sum superannuation death benefit has never claimed, or never intends to claim, a tax deduction (under s 295-465 of the ITAA97 in respect of premiums paid for providing superannuation death benefits, or under s 295-470 of the ITAA97 in respect of the future service element of a superannuation death benefit), then the whole of the taxable component will be a taxed element. However, if a tax deduction was claimed or is to be claimed, under either s 295-465 or s 295-470, then the taxable component will be made up of a combination of taxed and untaxed elements.

The taxable component has two elements – taxed and untaxed elements. Where the trustee claimed or intends to claim a tax deduction, the taxable component will be calculated as follows.

Step 1 – Determine the tax-free component

This amount can be obtained from the superannuation fund and consists of items such as non-concessional superannuation contributions.

Step 2 – Calculate the taxable component – taxed element

Step 2 is made up of two steps:

Firstly, work out the amount under the following formula, which is found in s 307-290(3) of the ITAA97:

Amount of superannuation lump sum X $\dfrac{\text{service days}}{\text{service days} + \text{days to retirement}}$

where:

Service days = the number of days in the service period for the lump sum

Days to retirement = the number of days from the day on which the deceased died to the deceased's last retirement day.

Secondly, from the result arrived at by the formula, deduct the tax-free component.

Step 3 - Calculate the taxable component – untaxed element

The untaxed element of the taxable component will equal the total lump-sum superannuation death benefit, less the amounts of the tax-free component determined in step one and the taxable component – taxed element calculated in step two.

Unless the individual has reached a particular age, or completed a period of service the last retirement day is taken to be 65 years. How this works is shown in illustrated example 12.2.

Illustrated example 12.2

Mark (date of birth 1 February 1966) started work with XYZ Pty Ltd on 2 January 1995. He has a superannuation fund with an account balance of $100,000, which is made up of the following components:

Tax-free component $20,000

Taxable component $80,000

Total $100,000

In addition to his retirement benefits, Mark also has $400,000 of life insurance through his superannuation fund. Unfortunately on 25 October 2010, while still an employee of XYZ Pty Ltd, Mark is involved in a motor vehicle accident on his way home from work and dies. At the date of his death Mark's lump-sum superannuation death benefit is $500,000, which includes $400,000 from the life insurance policy. Mark does not have any tax dependents and has left his estate to his married brother (a non-tax dependent).

Since the trustee of Mark's superannuation fund has been claiming a tax deduction in relation to the life insurance premiums, the formula in s 307-290 of the ITAA97 must be applied to determine the extent to which the taxable component of the lump-sum superannuation death benefit consists of taxed and untaxed elements.

Step 1 - Determine the tax-free component

Mark's tax-free component is $20,000.

Step 2 - Calculate the taxable component – taxed element

Firstly, calculate the amount under the following formula:

Amount of superannuation lump sum X $\dfrac{\text{service days}}{\text{service days} + \text{days to retirement}}$

$= \$500,000 \times \dfrac{5,775}{13,180}$

$= \$219,082$

Note: The days used can be found in table 12.2 – see step 3.

As no alternative last retirement day has been nominated or Mark under the terms of his employment or an award, then his last retirement day is taken to be when he turns 65.

Secondly, from the result arrived at by the formula, deduct the tax-free component from step one:

$= \$219,082 - 20\ 000$

$= \$199,082$

Therefore the taxable component – taxed element is $199,082.

Step 3 - Calculate the taxable component – untaxed element

The untaxed element of the taxable component will equal the total lump-sum superannuation death benefit, less the amounts of the tax-free component determined in step one and the taxable component – taxed element calculated in step two and shown in table 12.2.

Table 12.2 : Basis of calculating the taxed and untaxed elements of a super payment

Item	Explanation	Days/Amount
Amount of superannuation lump sum		$500,000
Service days	Number of days in the service period for the lump sum (2/1/1995 to 24/10/2010)	5,775 days
Days to retirement	Number of days from the day on which the deceased died to the deceased's last retirement day (25/10/2010 to 1/2/2031)	7,405 days

= $500,000 – 20 000 – 199 082

= $280,918

The taxable component – untaxed element is $280,918.

Mark's lump-sum superannuation death benefit is made up of the following components:

Tax-free component $20,000

Taxable component – taxed element $199,082

Taxable component – untaxed element $280,918

Total $500,000

Therefore, the maximum tax payable on the lump sum death benefit would be **$123,737.70**

($199,082 x 17.0% + $280 918 x 32.0%)

However, if the proceeds of Mark's lump-sum superannuation death benefit, including any taxable component – untaxed element, are paid to a tax dependant they will not be subject to tax.

The introduction of the transfer balance cap (TBC) from 1 July 2017 has important implications for holding insurance inside superannuation. Following the death of a client proceeds from life insurance cover held inside superannuation form part of the deceased's superannuation account. This superannuation death benefit must be cashed as a lump sum, one or more retirement phase income streams (only if it is paid to the deceased's spouse, minor child, a child who is severely disabled, adult child under 25 and financial dependent, or interdependent relation) or a combination of both.

The TBC restricts the amount of superannuation, including insurance proceeds, that can be received as a death benefit income stream to $1.6 million and any excess must be cashed out of the superannuation system. This restriction now questions whether large life insurance policies should continue to be held inside superannuation, as the payment of a death benefit income stream will effectively 'use up' the beneficiary's TBC, leaving little or no cap available for the beneficiary's retirement. However, compared to investing insurance proceeds outside of superannuation, the difference in taxation mean that death benefit income streams may provide a better outcome.

TBC is a lifetime cap so the commencement of a death benefit income stream will use up some or all of the beneficiary's TBC, reducing the amount available at retirement to commence further retirement phase income streams. In addition, if the death benefit income stream equalled or exceeded the TBC, the beneficiary will not be able to increase their unused TBC by future indexation.

Total and permanent disablement benefits

TPD can be included in a policy written under superannuation, because its objective is to provide benefits to the member. For a member of a superannuation fund to receive the proceeds of a TPD insurance policy, the first step is satisfying the insurer's definition of TPD. If the member cannot satisfy this first definition, the insurer will not accept the member's claim and will not pay the sum insured to the trustee of the superannuation fund.

Essentially, there are two main types of TPD definitions:

- *own occupation*, which covers the insured if they are incapacitated to the extent that they are unable to work again in their own occupation. This definition is not available to all job categories, and

- *any occupation*, which covers the insured if they are incapacitated to the extent that they will never return to work in any occupation for which they are suited by education, training or experience.

Purely from the perspective of choosing a definition under which the member is more likely to be able to submit a successful TPD claim, an 'own occupation' definition is preferred. However, in order for the member to access the proceeds of a TPD insurance policy that has been paid by the insurer to the trustee of a superannuation fund, the member will have to satisfy an 'any occupation' definition of TPD.

A potential problem could occur under the SIS Act where an 'own occupation' definition has been selected and a benefit is paid to the trustee of the superannuation fund. The funds might be inaccessible because if the trustees assess that the member can engage in other gainful employment for which the member is reasonably qualified by education training and experience, then the trustee cannot release the policy proceeds. The policy proceeds will be trapped in superannuation until the member does satisfy the SIS Act TPD definition or satisfies another condition of release such as having reached preservation age and retired.

New legislation effective from 1 July 2014 prevents individuals from holding own occupation TPD insurance in their super fund. Although the legislation allows current own occupation policies to continue to be help in super any payment will be trapped in the super fund as the trustees will not be able to release the funds to the member.

Permanent incapacity – satisfying a condition of release

The trustee of a superannuation fund is able to release benefits paid from a TPD claim under the conditions of release rules contained in the SIS Act. Under reg 6.01(2) of the *Superannuation Industry (Supervision) Regulations 1994* (SIS Regulations), 'permanent incapacity', in relation to a member, means

> "ill health' (whether physical or mental), where the trustee is reasonably satisfied that the member is unlikely, because of ill health, to engage in gainful employment for which the member is reasonably qualified by education, training or experience."

If a member satisfies this definition, they meet a condition of release and the trustee can pay the balance of the member's account (both account balance and TPD insurance proceeds) to the member, regardless of their age. This definition of permanent incapacity applies from 1 July 2007 and has changed slightly from the previous definition. There is no longer a requirement that the member must have ceased a gainful employment arrangement to satisfy the definition of permanent incapacity.

The implication of this change is that it is now possible for a person who has never worked, such as a non-working spouse, to take out TPD insurance through a superannuation fund and be able to meet the permanent incapacity definition in reg 6.01(2) of the SIS Regulations.

This incapacity definition within superannuation has caused real problems to claimants on a number of occasions. In the case *Manglicmot v Commonwealth Bank Officers Superannuation Corporation Pty Ltd* [2011] NSWCA 204 the Judge stated that the permanent incapacity clause requires unfitness to work, without distinction between full time and part time work provided the member is reasonable capable of performing the work by reason of the member's education training or experience. The judge went on to say that a person who is capable of undertaking regular part-time work is not totally and permanent disabled provided the work is not casual. Finally, the judge ruled that the plaintiff had to show that he is not capable of doing any part-time work.

In the case *Hannover Life Re of Australasia v Dargan* [2013] NSWCA 57, the judge ruled on the issue of retraining and further education. His honour ruled that a short training course or retaining may qualify the plaintiff to find work within the plaintiff's education, training or experience. Furthermore, the injured person must satisfy the insurer that they are permanently disabled at the date of the disablement. If this cannot be done then the insured's claim is likely to fail (*Chapman v United Super Pty Ltd* [2013] NSWSC 592).

The potential problems that can arise with an 'own occupation' TPD definition is demonstrated in illustrated example 12.3.

Illustrated example 12.3

A superannuation fund trustee takes out a TPD insurance policy with an 'own occupation' definition of TPD for a member, David, who is 50 years old and works as a surgeon. In this scenario, the 'own occupation' clause contained in the insurance policy states that a benefit will be payable by the insurer should the insured be unable to perform the duties of their regular occupation at the time of the disability. Therefore, if David hurt his hand to the extent that he may not be able to perform surgery in the future, under this definition the insurer would be able to pay a benefit to the trustee of the superannuation fund.

However, as David has previously worked as a lecturer at a medical college, and the injury does not prevent him from being employed in the future as a lecturer, the trustee may not be able to pay a benefit to him as the permanent incapacity condition of release, or any other condition of release, has not been met.

Disability superannuation benefits – concessional tax treatment

Assuming that the member satisfies the insurance policy definition of TPD and the permanent incapacity definition under the SIS legislation, the trustee will be able to pay the member's retirement benefits and insurance proceeds to the member. This payment will be taxed as a lump-sum superannuation benefit. A lump-sum superannuation benefit may be made up of two components:

- tax-free component, and

- taxable component.

Table 12.3 outlines how the components of a lump-sum superannuation benefit, paid from a taxed superannuation fund, will be taxed in the 2019/20 tax year.

Table 12.3: Components of a lump-sum superannuation benefit

Age at date of payment	Tax-free component	Taxable component – Taxed element[1]	
Under preservation age	Tax free[2]	Total amount	22.0%
Preservation age to age 59	Tax free[2]	First $210,000 Balance	0% 17.0%
60 and over	Tax free[2]	Tax free[2]	

1. Rates shown include Medicare levy, where relevant. Tax rates shown are maximum rates. Where a person would be subject to a lower marginal rate of tax than the maximum specified, the lower rate applies.

2. Non-assessable non-exempt income.

Illustrated example 12.4

Tony is 56 years old and is retired. He receives his first lump sum super payment of $350,000 on 25 July 2018. His fund tells him this amount consists of $100,000 tax-free component and $250,000 taxable component. All the taxable component was taxed in the fund.

Tony includes the $250,000 taxable component as income on his 2018–19 tax return. This results in him paying the following effective rates of tax:

Effective tax rates paid by Tony

Type of super	Effective tax rate (including Medicare levy)
Tax-free component: $100,000	No tax
Taxable component – taxed element (up to the low rate cap): $205,000	0%
Taxable component – taxed element (over the low rate cap): $45,000	17%

Source: ATO (2019

If a member can satisfy a third definition, the definition of a disability superannuation benefit in s 995-1(1) of the ITAA97, the benefit paid by the superannuation fund may include an increased tax-free component. Section 995-1(1) defines a disability superannuation benefit to mean a superannuation benefit if:

"(a) the benefit is paid to an individual because he or she suffers from ill-health (whether physical or mental); and

(b) two legally qualified medical practitioners have certified that, because of the ill-health, it is unlikely that the individual can ever be gainfully employed in a capacity for which he or she is reasonably qualified because of education, experience or training."

The increased tax-free component is calculated as follows:

Amount of benefit x $$\frac{\text{days to retirement}}{\text{service days} + \text{days to retirement}}$$

where:

Days to retirement = the number of days from the day on which the person stopped being capable of being gainfully employed to his or her last retirement day. Unless otherwise stated the last date of retirement is age 65.

Service days = the number of days in the service period for the lump sum.

The increased tax-free component associated with a disability superannuation benefit will only be created if there is a payment of a superannuation lump sum to the member or a rollover of benefits by the member to another superannuation fund. The increased tax-free component is not available when the benefit is paid as a pension.

Where TPD insurance is owned outside of superannuation and the policy is taken out for personal protection reasons:

- the proceeds will not be subject to income tax, and

- the proceeds will not be subject to CGT where they are paid to either the life insured or a defined relative of the life insured.

The tax effects of a TPD payment from a complying superannuation fund are explained in illustrated example 12.4.

Illustrated example 12.5

Bob (date of birth 24 July 1968) works as a forklift driver for Safety Pty Ltd. He started working for Safety Pty Ltd on 15 March 1998. He has a superannuation fund with an account balance of $125,000, which is made up of the following components:

Tax-free component	$35,000
Taxable component	$90,000
Total	$125,000

In addition to his retirement benefits, Bob also has $400,000 of life and TPD insurance through his superannuation fund. As a result of a workplace accident on 24 October 2010, Bob loses the use of both of his legs. The accident will require him to be wheelchair-bound for the rest of his life and he will be unable to work as a forklift driver/storeman, which are the only types of jobs that Bob is reasonably qualified for by reason of his education, training or experience. The insurer agrees that he satisfies the TPD definition in its insurance policy and it pays the proceeds to the trustee.

This being the case, the trustee can pay the proceeds of Bob's account (both account balance and TPD insurance proceeds) to him as he satisfies a condition of release. At this stage, his lump-sum superannuation benefit is made up of the following components:

Tax-free component	$35,000
Taxable component	$490,000
Total	$525,000

Bob will receive the tax-free component tax free, but will have to pay 22.0 per cent tax on the taxable component, as he is under his preservation age (Bob's preservation age is 60 – see table 12.4, below). The amount of tax payable on the taxable component reduces his net benefit by $107,800 ($490,000 x 22.0 per cent). However, Bob is able to produce evidence from two medical practitioners stating that his disability is likely to result in him being unable to ever be gainfully employed in a capacity for which he is reasonably qualified for because of education, training or experience.

As the definition of disability superannuation benefit in s 995-1(1) of the ITAA97 is satisfied, Bob's superannuation benefit will include an additional amount

of tax-free component, which is calculated as follows:

Amount of benefit X   days to retirement

service days + days to retirement

= $525,000 X 8,309

12,916

= $337,738

The basis for calculating Bob's benefit is shown in table 12.4.

Table 12.4: Basis for calculating the additional tax-free amount of a disability payment from a super fund

Item	Explanation	Days/Amount
Amount of benefit		$525,000
Days to retirement	Number of days from the day on which the person stopped being capable of being gainfully employed to his or her last retirement day (25/10/2010 to 24/7/2033)	8,309 days
Service days	Number of days in the service period for the lump sum (15/3/1998 to 24/10/2010)	4,607 days

As no alternative last retirement day has been nominated for Bob under the terms of his employment or an award, his last retirement day is taken to be when he turns 65. Therefore, after taking into account his increased tax-free component, Bob's disability superannuation benefit is made up of the following components:

Tax-free component $372,738

Taxable component   <u>$152,262</u>

Total $525,000

Bob will receive the tax-free component tax free, but will have to pay 22.0 per cent tax on the taxable component, as he is under his preservation age. The amount of tax payable on the taxable component now reduces his net benefit by only $33,497.64 ($152,262 x 22.0 per cent). Therefore, the increased tax-free component associated with a disability superannuation benefit will save Bob $74,302.36 in tax.

An interesting observation about the formula used to calculate the increased tax-free component of a disability superannuation benefit is that the further the client is from their last retirement day, when they are forced to terminate their employment as a result of disability, the higher their increased tax-free component will be.

Preservation age

Generally, members must reach preservation age before they can access their super. A member's preservation age is dependent on his/her date of birth and will vary between 55 and age 60. Table 12.5 contains this information

Table 12.5: Preservation age

Date of birth	Preservation age
Before 1 July 1960	55
1 July 1960 - 30 June 1961	56
1 July 1961 - 30 June 1962	57
1 July 1962 - 30 June 1963	58
1 July 1963 - 30 June 1964	59
From 1 July 1964	60

Source: Australian Taxation Office

At a glance

- YRT provides death benefit only, with no savings element.

- These policies are guaranteed renewable, with premiums that can be stepped or level.

- The policy has optional features, such as indexed sum insured, future insurability, the provision for multiple lives and convertibility.

- There are some rider benefits that can be attached, such as accidental death benefits, terminal illness, dread disease insurance and TPD.

- TPD can be based on 'any occupation' or 'own occupation' definitions.

- The cover offered by the TPD rider can be extended to include loss of limbs or sight, significant cognitive impairment and long-term care benefits.

- YRT contains some exclusions, such as suicide and war.

- Death and TPD insurance can be included but any payment by the trustee of the fund can be subject to taxation.

TRAUMA INSURANCE

12-130 Introduction

The purpose of trauma insurance is to provide a lump sum on the diagnosis of any of the listed traumas. This is a kind of 'living insurance' that provides protection against events that result in a financial loss or otherwise. The benefits from these policies can be used to assist in a number of costs that can be incurred following a trauma event, such as:

*   out of pocket medical expenses

*   repayment or extinguishment of debt

*   ongoing nursing care

*   rehabilitation expenses, such as the cost of speech therapy

*   readjustment expenses, such as home modifications to accommodate a wheelchair

*   pre- and post-retirement goals.

12-140 Conditions covered

Trauma insurance is an extremely flexible product that can be offered in two forms: basic cover and an extended list of major and ancillary trauma conditions. Trauma insurance in either form can be included with life cover and TPD benefits or purchased as a stand-alone policy.

Basic cover

Basic cover includes the conditions that account for the majority of claims: cardiovascular conditions, cancers and strokes. Cardiovascular conditions include heart attack, coronary artery bypass surgery and heart surgery (including aorta and heart valve replacement). Partial benefit payments can also be made for coronary artery angioplasty and other less invasive coronary procedures. Many life companies define the conditions differently, and care needs to be taken to ensure that the correct policy is selected for clients.

Some companies also include paraplegia, quadriplegia and occupationally acquired HIV. The tendency is for the traumas listed under basic cover to increase.

Broader cover

In addition to the major trauma conditions, some insurers include a further 35 or more relatively rare or extremely rare conditions that can affect individuals. These conditions include:

- those caused by injury, eg, blindness, severe burns, major head trauma, paralysis, coma, medically and occupationally acquired HIV and serious accidental injury

- acute conditions such as bacterial meningitis, those requiring intensive care, encephalitis, and out of hospital cardiac arrest

- slowly debilitating conditions, which may result in events such as deafness, dementia or the need for major organ transplant, eg, motor neurone disease, multiple sclerosis, Parkinson's disease, kidney failure, liver failure, lung failure and muscular dystrophy

- other conditions such as cardiomyopathy, peripheral neuropathy and primary pulmonary hypertension.

The list of trauma conditions is becoming more extensive, but the majority of claims are covered by basic cover. However, these policies can be difficult to understand, as they define the traumas using medical definitions that do not have a great deal of meaning to the average insured. Also, as occurs for the basic cover, many insurers use differing definitions, so care needs to be taken when recommending a particular policy.

Some conditions are triggered only after a qualifying period, eg, cancer (malignant tumours), coronary artery surgery, heart attack, hemiplegia and stroke. These will not be covered if they occur within 90 days of the inception of the policy. This waiting period is intended to exclude any pre-existing traumas; that is, those that were present when the policy was taken out but were not apparent at the time.

Severity conditions

Over the years, insurance companies have tended to increase the number of traumas covered by their policies and to loosen the policy wordings without increasing their premiums. This has resulted in many products that are underpriced and instances where claims have exceeded expectations. In an effort to remain competitive, some companies have introduced severity criteria (or claim limitations) to their existing event wordings. These severity criteria can allow companies to maintain existing premiums and in some cases to actually reduce their premiums.

In addition to the policy's medical definition of a condition, the severity conditions mean that a claim can only be admitted when it satisfies the additional requirements. There are three approaches that are taken when assessing the degree of severity:

- at least 25 per cent impairment of 'whole person function' must be permanent

- there must be permanent inability to perform at least two of the 'activities of daily living' *or* cognitive impairment that requires continual supervision to protect the insured. The activities of daily living are bathing, dressing, toileting, mobility and feeding

- the insured must be permanently unable to perform more than 50 per cent of their usual activities, pursuits and processes of everyday life.

The operation of the severity conditions is shown in the following illustrated example.

Illustrated example 12.6

Benjamin has taken out a trauma policy with XYZ Insurance Company. He has elected to include the company's Premium Saver Option, which gives him a premium discount. As a result of selecting this option, Benjamin must satisfy the following conditions before he can claim on the policy.

1. He must survive the condition for at least 46 days after first being diagnosed with the condition.

2. He must not be able to undertake any active employment as a result of the condition for at least 46 days after diagnosis of the condition.

3. He must not engage in any occupation, whether or not for reward, during the 46 days and must be under regular treatment from, and following the advice of, a registered medical practitioner.

If Benjamin were to contract an insured condition and die before the 46 days elapsed, any payment in relation to the insured condition would not be paid by the company.

Exclusions and limitations

Trauma policies exclude suicide within 13 months of the commencement of the policy, intentional self-injury or intentional infection, and trauma from war or civil commotion. The maximum amount of cover provided by insurers appears to be limited to $1 million.

12-150 Combined policies

Trauma cover can be attached to life cover as an optional rider in the same way as TPD insurance, with the trauma rider having the same sum insured as the death cover. Trauma riders are an acceleration of the death cover, so any level of trauma benefit paid is deducted from the death cover. The trauma rider can be added in three ways:

1. *As a linked policy.* Under this type of policy, death, TPD and trauma are covered in the one sum insured. If a claim is made under the policy (for example, under the trauma rider) all cover is suspended for up to three years. However, a buy-back option is available, which allows the cover to be reinstated straight away.

2. *As a combined policy.* Under this type of policy, death, TPD and trauma are included in the same policy and a claim on one event does not affect the cover under the others, except where the first claim is for death.

3. *As a hybrid policy.* This type of policy combines some life cover with trauma rider benefits as bundled benefits. Under this policy the trauma benefits are stand-alone, and a claim on the trauma rider will not affect the death benefit cover.

At a glance

- Trauma insurance provides cover for a defined list of medical conditions.
- The policy benefit is paid on the diagnosis of a defined event.
- The trauma rider is an accelerated benefit, so its payment extinguishes the policy unless a buy-back option has been purchased.
- Trauma cover can be added to a death policy in the same way as TPD, or it can be issued as a stand-alone policy.

INCOME PROTECTION INSURANCE

12-160 Introduction

The success of personal financial plans depends on the continuation of the breadwinner's income. Therefore, any cessation of regular income can totally unravel a carefully implemented plan. The aim of income protection insurance is to replace lost earnings of the life insured and so minimise the financial impact of long-term sickness or accident.

12-170 Policyowner

Under the provisions of the *Insurance Contracts Act 1984* (Cth), a policyowner does not need an insurable interest in the life of the insured in respect to life insurance. Therefore, anyone is able to effect an income protection policy on the life of another, such as a business taking out a policy on the life of a key employee. However, a problem can arise if a wife, for example, effected a policy on the life of her husband and they subsequently parted. If the estranged wife refused to assign the policy to the husband and kept the policy in force, then the wife would receive any claim payments and the husband would not. (This example ignores any possible settlement arrangements.) Because of such potential problems, insurers generally insist that the life insured be that of the policy owner.

12-180 Benefits

An income protection policy provides cover for up to 75 per cent, or in some policies 85 per cent of the insured's pre-disability earnings (PDEs) and fringe benefits, if applicable. For higher earnings, such as $240,000, the insurable income reduces to 50 per cent. These lower percentages are applied as an incentive for individuals to return to work and not simply rely on the income benefit.

For employees, insurable income will generally be their base salary or salary package, which can include fringe benefits. The value of a fringe benefit can be determined by calculating the taxable income needed to provide that benefit.

Insurable income for self-employed individuals is taken to be the gross income earned from the business less the business expenses incurred in generating that income. In all cases, investment income (or passive income) is not taken into account, as this will continue regardless of incapacity.

Different policies may define PDEs differently. Some policies define PDEs as the 12 consecutive months immediately prior to the disability, while others may define PDEs as the highest 12 consecutive months in the five years prior to the disability. This may result in a higher insurable amount than the prior definition. These different definitions can cause problems when an additional income protection policy is taken out and the existing policy cannot be replaced because the insured has developed a condition that could result in a premium loading or a policy exclusion. There are two possible ways to arrive at the maximum total disability benefit:

- add the benefit amounts of the two policies together and compare the total to 75 per cent of PDEs

- assume the second policy is to top up the benefit of the first policy to 75 per cent of PDEs.

However, as income protection contracts generally do not specify how the maximum total disability benefit is calculated, an adviser would be prudent to obtain written agreement from the insurer as to what approach should be taken. This agreement should be obtained at the time of writing the policy.

Offsets

The policy document lists a number of payments that, if received by the insured, will be offset against or reduces the benefit amount. The wording in the policy could appear as:

> Benefits can be reduced by the receipt of other payments such as workers compensation or similar legislative benefits, or from other sources such as disability, group, sickness or accident insurance cover.

However, the particular wording that appears in a particular policy should be read carefully, as offset wording may vary between companies. The better income protection policies do not contain offset clauses.

It is also possible that insurers will apply these other payments differently. Some insurers will offset the full amount of the 'other payment' while other insurers will offset only if 'other payments exceed 10 per cent of pre-disability earnings'.

12-190 Benefit period

The benefit period is the length of time that the insurer will pay the claim. Historically, there are two types of benefit periods:

- *Coterminous benefit.* Under this benefit the payment period for disabilities caused by accident is the same as that for sickness. For example, the payment period extends to age 65 for both accident and illness.

- *Non-coterminous benefit.* Under this benefit the payment period for a disability arising from accident is generally longer than the payment period for sickness. For example, an accident payment period extends to age 65 but a sickness payment period is for only five years.

Generally, non-coterminous payment periods are not encouraged because of the possible confusion that could arise in the minds of some insured persons, as they may think that it is a coterminous benefit and take legal action against the insurance company and adviser when a claim ceases at the expiry of the shorter payment period.

A number of other payment benefit periods are generally available, such as two years, five years, to age 55, to age 60, and lifetime. With a lifetime payment period, the benefit (subject to some conditions) will be paid until the insured dies. The longer the payment period, the higher the premium.

Income protection policies usually contain a return to work clause, which allows the insured to reactivate the claim if they return to work and the condition recurs — as long as it is from the same cause and within a specified time, such as six or 12 months. In this clause, the policy waiting period is waived because the second claim is deemed to be a continuation of the first claim. In this instance, the two claim periods are added together when determining the benefit period.

The termination date of the policies offered may also be defined differently by different insurers. Some insurers terminate their policies on the exact date of the life insured, while others terminate on the policy anniversary before or even after the pre-set age of the insured. This difference can have a significant impact on an insured person's long-term claim. For example, if a policy starts on 1 January 2001, with an insured date of birth of 31 December 1951, and the policy expires on the insured's 65th birthday, then the policy expiry date will be 31 December 2016. In contrast, if the policy expires on the policy anniversary prior to the insured's 65th birthday, then the expiry date will be 1 January 2016. The difference will be 12 months of benefit payments.

12-200 Waiting period

The waiting period (or qualifying period) refers to the period of time when no cover is provided under the policy. It refers to:

- the period of time for which the insured must be 'disabled' to qualify for a benefit payment
- the period of time in which the insured bears the risk of a disablement occurring and not receiving a benefit payment.

Disablement refers to both total and partial disablement. The specific requirements and conditions vary between different company contracts and occupation categories. Waiting periods can range from 14 days to 720 days, as follows:

- 14 days or two weeks
- 30 days or four weeks
- 60 days or two months
- 90 days or three months
- 180 days or six months
- 360 days or one year
- 720 days or two years.

Some companies offer a lifetime benefit where the benefits, subject to some restrictions, are paid until the insured dies. The longer the waiting period, the cheaper the premium.

Choice of waiting period

The choice of the waiting period will generally depend on:

- the availability of other resources that can be used to provide for the insured while disabled
- the existence of accumulated sick leave, salary continuation through superannuation, and workers compensation
- affordability — the shorter the waiting period, the more expensive the premium. Many applicants may be forced to choose a longer waiting period because of price considerations.

Under taxation rules that applied until March 2007, salary continuation through superannuation was only allowed to have a two-year benefit payment period. Since an additional income protection policy would also have a two-year waiting period, a claim on the new policy would commence after the two-year benefit ceased under the salary continuation policy. However, Taxation Determination

TD 2007/3, released in March 2007, declared that a tax deduction will be allowed for premiums paid where income payments are made to members for temporary disablement lasting more than two years. Following this ruling, superannuation product providers now offer income protection benefits to age 65 in superannuation funds.

While this tax determination increases the options available under superannuation, it does raise an important issue that must be considered before including a salary continuance policy in a superannuation plan. A key issue to consider is when a temporary disability claim becomes a permanent disablement. Under *Taxation Determination* TD 2007/3, the ATO uses the term *temporary disability*, so trustees may not be willing to incur the additional cost of regularly establishing whether or not the member still meets the temporary incapacity definition. Additionally, benefits tax may be payable on any lump sum payments from superannuation following a commutation of benefits arising from permanent incapacity for persons under 60 years of age.

The waiting period commences when the insured first consults a doctor or when the insured stops work, provided they consult a doctor within a specified number of days after ceasing work. Policies generally allow the insured to return to work for a period ranging from five to 10 days during the waiting period, with the days actually worked being added to the waiting period. For example, if an insured had a 30-day waiting period and returned to work for two days and stopped work again, the two days would be added to the end of the 30-day waiting period. Therefore, the insured would be away from work for 30 days over a 32-day period. Benefit payments would commence at the end of the 32-day period.

12-210 Guaranteed renewal

Income protection policies are guaranteed renewable until a stated age. The premium rate will change only if the entire underwriting class is increased. In comparison, under a non-cancellable policy, both the renewal and premiums are guaranteed. The insured can discontinue the policy by not paying the premium by the expiry date or requesting cancellation.

12-220 Agreed value policies

An agreed value policy will pay the amount insured even though the insured suffers a decline in earnings after the policy is taken out. For example, a person might earn $150,000 and insure 75 per cent of this under an income protection policy with a monthly benefit of $9,350. If an insured suffers a serious illness and claims on their policy and, when proof of income is provided, it is found that the insured's income has declined to $95,000, the insurance company will still pay $9,350 per month, even though the claimant would only be entitled to insure for $5,937 if they were to take out the same policy at this time.

12-230 Indemnity policies

Under indemnity value policies, the monthly benefit indicated in the policy is not guaranteed, because if the insured suffers a reduction in income between the inception of the policy and a claim, there will be a comparable reduction in the disability benefit that is paid. In the example of the person who had an initial income of $150,000, which dropped to $95,000, under an indemnity policy the insured would be paid only $5,937 per month and not $9,350 (see ¶13-220).

Indemnity value policies are generally useful for employees whose incomes are relatively stable and not likely to decline.

12-240 Total disablement

What constitutes total disablement is defined in the various life insurance policies, and claimants must satisfy the relevant definition described in the policy if their claim is to be successful. The definition of total disablement (often referred to as total disability) contains three criteria, and a claimant must satisfy all of the three criteria in order to be deemed totally disabled. The insured must be:

- under the care (or in some cases 'advice') of a medical practitioner
- not working
- unable to perform some aspect of their occupation.

A common definition of total disablement for a white collar worker or professional is that

> 'you are totally disabled if, solely because of sickness or injury, you:
>
> » are not capable of doing one of the important duties of your regular occupation or are not capable of doing the important duties of your regular occupation
>
> » are not working in any gainful occupation, and
>
> » are following the advice of a doctor (who is not a relative or partner).'

For those in a manual occupation, a common definition is that *'you are totally disabled if, due to injury or sickness:*

» during the first two years, you cannot do at least one of the income-producing duties of your occupation; and

» after the first two years, because of the same injury or sickness, you are unable to perform any occupation for which you are reasonably qualified by education, training or experience; and

» *you are not working and are under medical care.'*

The terms *advice* and *care* often cause difficulty. *Advice* can be taken to mean that the insured is following the attending doctor's instructions, which may not actually require regular visits to the surgery. In contrast, *care* can be taken to mean that the insured must be attending the doctor's surgery on a regular basis, generally weekly. Therefore, if the doctor tells the insured to go home and rest for one month before reassessment, then it could be considered that the insured was not under the doctor's care. An adviser would need to clarify the meaning of these words in writing with the insurer.

12-250 Partial disablement

After a sickness or injury, recovery is sometimes gradual and the insured can often return to work in a reduced capacity. In this event, most policies will pay a reduced monthly benefit if:

• the insured returns to work in any occupation for more than 10 hours per week (hours-based definition)

• the insured's income is reduced below pre-disability income (often specified to be at least a 20 per cent reduction) (income-based definition), and

• the insured is under unable to perform their normal tasks at work (duties-based definition).

Hours-based definition

Policies containing this definition will allow a client to return to work for up to 10 hours per week and still receive a full total disability benefit. Hours-based definition works best for self-employed individuals who may have 'lumpy' (inconsistent) earnings, where income may be received for a job that was performed prior to the disability.

Income-based definition

Under this definition, regardless of how many hours the client works or how many duties they can perform, as long as they are still suffering an injury or illness and there has been a reduction in their income, then they are entitled to a benefit.

Duties-based definition

Once the criteria are met, the partial disability payment is based upon an income-based formula:

Benefit payable =

$$\frac{\text{Pre-disability monthly income} - \text{Earnings while disabled}}{\text{Pre-disability monthly income}} \times \text{Monthly benefit}$$

The calculation of a partial income protection claim using this formula is shown in the following illustrated example.

Illustrated example 12.7

Michael is a self-employed computer technician. He was involved in a motorbike accident and broke both his legs. He was not able to work for 12 weeks but was then able to return to work on a reduced basis. His pre-disability income was $16,000 per month, but this dropped to $1,000 per month following the accident. His income protection policy had an income benefit of $12,000 per month. He will be able to claim:

$$\text{Benefit} = \frac{\$16,000 - \$1,000}{\$16,000} \times \$12,000$$

$$= \$11,250 \text{ per month}$$

The duties-based definition is the industry standard and works best for salaried employees.

23-260 Additional benefits

Insurance companies generally offer several different types of income protection policy, ranging from a basic cover to extensive cover, each including different levels of additional and optional benefits. The following additional benefits are an indication of what can be automatically included in these policies.

Accommodation benefit

This benefit reimburses the accommodation expenses of an immediate family member (such as a spouse) who accompanies the insured if:

- the insured is confined to bed, and

- the insured becomes totally disabled more than 100 kilometers from home or the insured has to travel more than 100 kilometers to seek independent medical advice.

This benefit usually pays to a maximum amount, such as $200 per day for up to a maximum amount of time (say, 30 days) in any 12-month period.

Bed confinement benefit

If the insured receives care from a registered nurse for more than 72 hours during the waiting period, then the policy generally pays 1/30th of the monthly benefit amount for each day of confinement. There are two conditions for this benefit to apply:

- It must be medically necessary for the insured to remain in or near a bed for a substantial part of the day.

- If the insured is at home, they must be under the continuous care of a registered nurse.

The bed confinement benefit generally ceases at the end of the waiting period or when an amount equal to three times the monthly benefit amount has been paid — whichever is earlier.

Crisis benefit

If the insured suffers one of the crisis events listed in the policy, such as heart disorder, nervous system disorder, body organ disorder or blood disorder, the policy will pay the monthly benefit amount in advance for a minimum payment period, provided the waiting period is 90 days or less. (*Note:* Some policies pay an extra amount, such as one-third above the insured monthly benefit.) Table 12.6 gives an example of the minimum payment periods for a crisis benefit payment.

Table 12.6: Minimum payment period for a crisis benefit

Waiting period	Crisis benefit
30 days or less	6 months
60 days	4 months
90 days	3 months
Over 90 days	Nil

This benefit normally does not apply until after a three-month waiting period has expired. However, the waiting period generally does not apply to events such as stroke, heart attack, coronary artery surgery, repair or replacement of aorta, and repair or replacement of valves.

Death benefit

This benefit applies if the insured dies while in receipt of a monthly benefit. The death benefit is usually made by continuing to pay the monthly benefit to the insured's estate for a further period after death. Although this period can vary between policies, it is generally paid for a period of three months.

Elective or cosmetic surgery benefit

This benefit is paid if the incapacity results in total disablement following elective or cosmetic surgery where the policy has been in force for more than six months. Some companies also include, as part of this benefit, total disablement resulting from organ donation.

Expense reimbursement benefit

Up to six months benefit will be paid for money spent on rehabilitation, and engaging or attempting to engage in gainful occupation as part of rehabilitation. Examples of these expenses could include wheelchairs, artificial limbs, travel and education expenses, and structural changes to a home.

Family support benefit

This benefit generally pays the benefit for a certain period (such as six months) if the total disablement monthly benefit has been paid for at least six months. This benefit applies if the insured needs someone to look after them at home and they are looked after by an immediate family member who gives up full-time paid employment to look after the insured.

Indexation benefit

This benefit ensures that the monthly benefit is not eroded by inflation, so the monthly benefit is increased each year generally by the Consumer Price Index (CPI) or three per cent, whichever is greater. The insured does not have to accept this increase but, if they do accept, the premium is increased accordingly.

There are instances when the policyholder should consider not accepting this increase. For example, when a policy was written, the monthly benefit was set at 75 per cent of salary and when a claim occurs the claim benefit will be set at the same percentage. If indexation increases the monthly benefit above the insured's salary, then the insured will be paying for higher benefits than they will be paid for. In this instance, the insured should reduce the monthly benefit to 75 per cent of salary and have the premium concomitantly reduced.

This benefit does not apply when a claim is being paid, as the amount paid will be based on the sum insured applying at the time of the claim. For example, if the policy commenced several years ago with a sum insured of $40,000, but this has increased to $48,000 with CPI increases, the claim will be paid on the $48,000 sum insured for the entire length of the claim (assuming that this does not exceed 75 per cent of pre-disability salary for an indemnity policy). If this claim were to be paid for a number of years (say, 30), then inflation would severely erode the purchasing power of the payment. In order to overcome this problem, the insured would need to include the optional 'increasing claims benefit' described below.

Rehabilitation benefit

An extra 50 per cent of the monthly benefit for up to 12 months is generally paid if the insured participates in an approved rehabilitation program while totally disabled.

Overseas assist benefit

If the insured becomes totally disabled while out of Australia for a defined period of time (eg, more than a month) following an incident that results in a continuous disability, this benefit will reimburse the monthly benefit up to a number of times (eg, three times) for the cost of an economy airfare back to Australia by the most direct route, less reimbursements from elsewhere (such as travel insurance). The operation of this benefit is shown in the following illustrated example.

> ### Illustrated example 12.8
>
> Bronwyn was holidaying in Austria, where she broke both her legs in a skiing accident. She holds an income protection insurance policy in Australia that contains an overseas assist benefit, which will pay a maximum of three times the monthly benefit. Therefore, if her monthly benefit was $3,360, the policy would pay a maximum of $10,080. However, if the most direct economy airfare back to Australia, including connecting flights, and less a reimbursement by another policy, was $5,000, the policy would pay only $5,000.

Scheduled injury benefit

This benefit will pay the monthly benefit amount if the insured suffers a listed injury for the indicated period, even if the insured is still working. For example, the insurer could pay for paralysis for as long as 60 months. If the insured is still disabled at the end of the specified payment period, the monthly benefit amount continues under the total disability benefit.

Transportation benefit

If the insured is disabled and requires emergency transportation (other than by ambulance) within Australia, this benefit will reimburse the transportation costs, generally up to three times the monthly benefit amount once in any 12-month period. The amount paid under this benefit depends on the particular company, as some companies will only pay an amount of $200 towards these expenses.

Unemployment benefit

The name of this benefit suggests that the insured will be paid a benefit if they are unemployed, but this is not the case. Under this benefit, the policy premiums are waived for a maximum period of up to six months if the insured is unemployed. It is a condition that the insured is registered with a recognised government or non-government employment agency.

Waiver of premium benefit

Under this benefit the premiums are waived while the insured is being paid a disability benefit. The premiums recommence when the insured is no longer disabled or at the end of the payment period for the crisis benefit or scheduled injury benefit.

12-270 Optional benefits

These benefits allow individuals to extend the cover provided by the standard income protection policy by paying an additional premium.

Increasing claim benefit

This option increases the monthly benefit amount every year in line with the CPI while the insured is on claim. The increase is usually capped at a certain percentage such as seven per cent.

Superannuation benefits

This option allows cover to be increased above 75 per cent of earnings, with the extra cover being used to reimburse the claimant for contributions made to a superannuation fund while disabled. This option is generally restricted to 10 per cent of earnings.

Severe disability benefits

This option allows cover to be increased above 75 per cent of earnings, with the additional cover being based on a more severe definition of disability, such as the permanent inability to perform at least two of the five activities of daily living.

Guaranteed future insurability

The insured may develop a condition or enter a situation that makes them less insurable in the future. This option allows the insured to take out additional cover at standard rates. The trigger for future increases could be marriage, the birth of a child or a specified anniversary of the income protection policy (eg, the third anniversary).

Readers should be aware that available income protection policies may contain different benefits to those listed above. Therefore, Product Disclosure Statements need to be examined carefully so as the product recommended fully meets the client's needs.

12-280 Group Income protection policies

Group income protection insurance (more commonly called salary continuance insurance) is a regular monthly benefit paid to an employee who is unable to work in the event of an accident or illness. Group income protection insurance provides employers a device to pay their employees a monthly income during the disablement period.

The income – related benefits are paid if an injured member is:

- Unable to work through injury or sickness (definitions vary by company)
- Totally disabled, or
- Partially disabled (generally after 14 consecutive days of total disablement)
- Is still injured or sick after the waiting period
- Under medical care (some policies state under medical advice)

Payments from group salary continuance policies are paid to the employer who is the owner of the policy and not directly to the insured person. In effect, employers are insuring their payroll.

Although policies can differ between companies, a person can become a *person insured* if they satisfy the eligibility criteria for cover and the person is either a full-time employee or a contractor. Generally, a contractor must have worked an average of 15 hours or more per week over a period of three consecutive months up to the date they became totally disabled, partially disabled or suffered a listed specific sickness or specific injury. In most cases the person insured must be aged 15 year or more and be less than age 65 on the first day they became eligible for cover. Also, they must be an Australian resident.

 The maximum sum insured is limited to 75% of pre-disability incomes and in some cases up to $480,000 per annum, or $30,000 per month. An option is generally available to purchase an additional 10 per cent to cover superannuation contributions.

The product has a number of payment periods with a maximum expiry age of 65 years. For limited term schemes payment period range from 2 to 5 years which can include rehabilitation in the event of an injury or illness. Qualify (waiting) periods range from 30 days up to two years. Longer the waiting periods attract lower premiums.

Cover can be granted in one of three ways: under automatic acceptance terms, through transfer terms, or by individual underwriting.

Automatic acceptance terms (AAT)

Under AAT conditions, certain criteria must be met. Although the following may vary among underwriters, there must be:

- clearly defined eligibility for the plans, or for each category of membership
- clearly defined and fixed benefit formulae for determining the level of benefit amounts
- at least 10 people with insurance
- membership restrictions of employees
- only one insurer of the benefits defined under the plan
- no more than 10 per cent of members resident overseas
- at least 75 per cent participation of eligible members at the inception of the policy and at least 75 per cent of those eligible to join in the future must do so within three months of becoming eligible
- the member was at work on the day cover commences

Transfer terms

In most cases all of the following conditions must apply:

- the previous policy was a group salary continuance policy
- the previous policy provides insurance for similar events
- there were at least 10 people with insurance for similar insured events under each category of persons insured
- the member provides all requested information about the previous insurance within 90 days of the policy commencement date
- the member was at work on the day immediately preceding

Individual underwriting

Individual underwriting is undertaken for members who do not meet the AALs or apply for monthly benefits above the maximum generally allowed. The individual underwriting process is similar to that discussed in section 8-080.

Optional benefits

Optional benefits are generally available and can include: cover to age 70 years, a claim payment escalation benefit ranging between 5 and 7.5 per cent, an option to continue the salary continuance plan under a personal protection plan should the member leave their current employer, a nursing care benefit which will pay 1/30th of the monthly benefit up to $500 per day for a maximum of 90 days, a family carer benefit subject to limits and a trauma benefit.

Gaps in group salary continuance cover

Many people have basic income protection cover under a group scheme that provides benefits for up to two years. In order to provide the client with more extensive cover, financial planners routinely recommend that a retail income protection policy with a two-year waiting period and a longer benefit period.

While this structure would appear to cover any gaps in the current income protection insurance arrangement, problems can be encounted if the client returns to work after the initial claim and the injury/illness is exacerbated. The waiting period for the retail policy may recommence, depending on the level of work undertaken.

Most retail policies have a maximum number of days that an insured person can return to work during the waiting period without restarting it. For example, some policies allow an insured to return to work for five days during a waiting period of 30 days and up to 10 days during a waiting period of more than 30 days. If they return to work at full capacity for longer than this, the waiting period will recommence.

Financial planners need to consider whether adding a group policy could result in a gap in cover and whether an alternative solution should be considered. The following illustrated example highlights this potential gap in cover.

Illustrated example 12.9

Douglas has a group income protection policy with a waiting period of 30 days and a benefit period of two years. In addition, he has a retail income protection policy with a waiting period of two years and a benefit period to age 65.

Douglas is disabled for one year owing to an illness and receives income protection payments under the group policy. Douglas returns to work for one month, but his condition relapses to a point where he must temporarily cease working once again.

Under Douglas's group policy he can claim for a further year. However, as Douglas has worked more than 10 days during the waiting period for the retail policy, the waiting period will restart. Therefore, this will push out the date when the first monthly benefit can be received from the retail policy (in this case, three years and one month after the initial claim) and a gap is created.

Alternatively, Douglas could have replaced his group income protection policy with a retail policy that has a waiting period of 30 days and a benefit period to age 65. When he relapses, the waiting period is waived (due to the recurring disability benefit). Therefore, Douglas can immediately go back on claim.

Note: Care needs to be taken when replacing this group policy to ensure that the three-year non-disclosure period discussed in section 4-200 has not been refreshed.

12-290 Income protection policies held in superannuation

Where income protection benefits are held in a superannuation fund, different rules apply to the calculation and payment of benefits. There are some circumstances where part of the income protection insurance proceeds may be retained within the super fund as it does not meet a condition of release. In this situation, part of the income protection proceeds is transferred to the client's superannuation balance.

The SIS Regulations, Schedule 1, lists the various conditions of release from superannuation. An income-based policy held within a superannuation fund meets the condition of release under item 9, *Temporary incapacity*. These rules state that the payments must be a non-commutable income stream cashed from the super fund for:

a. the purpose of continuing (in whole or part) the gain or reward which the member was receiving before the temporary incapacity, and

b. a period not exceeding the period of incapacity from employment of the kind engaged in immediately before the temporary incapacity.

So what does all this mean? The income protection (temporary incapacity) benefits paid from superannuation are based on an income-based definition. Therefore, the member is not entitled to earn more money than they were prior to disability (rule (a) above).

In those cases where a client has the ability to carry out limited tasks per week after injury, but hold a policy under their superannuation fund, they would not be able to utilise the hours-based definition, where a member is permitted to work up to 10 hours per week with no reduction in their income protection benefits. This means the member receives less income from the policy held within super, than held individually outside super. Table 12.7 illustrates this difference.

Table 12.7: Benefits held within super vs. individually outside of super

Details	Policy held outside super	Policy held within super
Hours worked in a typical working week prior to injury	37.5 hours	37.5 hours
Annual salary	$50,000	$50,000
Monthly salary	$4,167	$4,167
Value of annual insurance	$37,500	$37,500
Hours worked in a typical week after injury	10	10
Monthly salary after injury	$1,111	$1,042
Monthly full disability benefit from the policy	$3,125	$3,125
Total monthly earning post injury	**$4,236**	**$4,167** (limited to pre disability earnings)

Table 12.7 highlights the difference of $69 per month in earnings for the two scenarios. The excess amount for a client who holds their policy within their super fund would need to be retained within the super fund.

To be eligible to claim income protection benefits through a super fund, the insurer's definition of a claimable event must be met. After that, the income protection benefit will be paid to the super fund. Then, the trustee of the superannuation must be satisfied that the insured meets the definition of temporary incapacity, before releasing the benefit.

When the temporary incapacity condition of release is met, the income protection benefit gets paid from the fund to replace in part or in full what salary the insured received before becoming incapacitated. In some cases, the trustee of the superannuation may find that the insured has not met the condition of release and thus restricts the money released.

Other disadvantages include:

- The policy terms and conditions are generally weaker. Group income protection policies usually require the insured to use all their sick and holiday leave before the waiting period will start

- Group policies are generally not renewable, meaning the fund or insurer can down grade the policy terms and conditions at any time.

- Salary continuance in super might be limited to a maximum 2-year benefit period.

- Policies do not include 'extra benefits' usually built-into self-owned retail income protection policies.

- No tax advantage as premiums are paid from your fund and any tax deductions will be provided to your fund

- Less money goes toward retirement savings because income protection premiums are paid out of the superannuation balance

- Claiming can be more complicated and time-consuming.as both the policy definition as per the PDS and the SIS condition of release must be met

Temporary incapacity v permanent incapacity

Temporary incapacity is defined in regulation 6.01(2) of the Superannuation Industry (Supervision) Regulations (SISR) to mean: "Temporary incapacity, in relation to a member who has ceased to be gainfully employed (including a member who has ceased temporarily to receive any gain or reward under a continuing arrangement for the member to be gainfully employed), means ill-health (whether physical or mental) that caused the member to cease to be gainfully employed but does not constitute permanent incapacity."

We now contrast this definition with that of permanent incapacity as we will examine a number of interesting points that arise from the comparison.

Firstly, we note the definition of *temporary incapacity* is ceasing gainful employment due to illness that falls short of permanent incapacity. Secondly, there is no express criteria such as medical certification being required. Thirdly, the ATO has confirmed its view in Taxation Ruling 2012/6 at paragraphs 149, and 162 to 167 as:

"149. A disability superannuation benefit is defined in subsection 995-1(1) of the *Income Tax Assessment Act 1997* (ITAA) to mean a superannuation benefit where:

a. the benefit is paid to a person because he or she suffers from ill-health (whether physical or mental); and

b. two legally qualified medical practitioners have certified that, because of the ill-health, it is unlikely that the person can ever be gainfully employed in a capacity for which he or she is reasonably qualified because of education, experience or training.

The *permanent incapacity* of a member is listed in item 103 of Schedule 1 to the SISR as one of the conditions of release under which a superannuation fund can provide a benefit to a member and is the relevant condition of release that would have to be satisfied, in conjunction with the requisite two medical certificates, in order for a superannuation fund to provide a 'disability superannuation benefit'.

Sub-regulation 6.01(2) of the SISR defines permanent incapacity in relation to a member as: ill-health (whether physical or mental), where the trustee is reasonably satisfied that the member is unlikely, because of the ill-health, to engage in gainful employment for which the member is reasonably qualified by education, training or experience.

The degree of ill-health that the trustee of a fund must be reasonably satisfied exists in order that a member meets the definition of permanent incapacity under sub-regulation 6.01(2) of the SISR is for all practical purposes is identical to that which two medical practitioners must certify for the payment of a disability superannuation benefit.

While the trust deed may not require certification by two medical practitioners for the purpose of satisfying the permanent incapacity condition of release, it would be expected that the trustee would rely on the advice of at least two medical practitioners in order to be reasonably satisfied that this condition of release has been met. For the purpose of obtaining a deduction within subsection 295-465(1), this would equate to the certification required for a 'disability superannuation benefit'."

Sickness benefits

In the event that the member receives sick leave benefits from his/her employer, a similar situation arises. Many insurance companies do not offset sickness benefits on their income protection policies. When the policy is held outside a client's super, the client benefits from receiving both the regular sick leave income from their employer plus the normal monthly income protection benefits.

Table 12.8 illustrates compares the sick leave benefits paid to a client within and outside of super.

Table 12.8 Sick leave payments outside super vs. inside of super

Details	Policy held outside of super	Policy held within super
Hours worked in a typical working week prior to injury	37.5 hours	37.5 hours
Annual salary	$50,000	$50,000
Monthly salary	$4,167	$4,167
Value of annual insurance	$37,500	$37,500
After injury sick leave paid monthly by employer	$4,167	$1,042
Monthly full disability benefit from the policy	$3,125	$3,125
Total monthly earning post injury	**$7,282**	**$4,167** (limited to pre disability earnings)

Table 12.8 illustrates a difference in monthly earning capacity of $3,125 per month. The excess amount for the client who holds their policy within their super fund would be retained within the super fund and added to the member's super balance. This situation would be relatively rare as the client will only be paid this 'boosted' benefit until their sick leave benefits are exhausted. In most cases there is a 30-day or 60-day waiting period on the policy, so the sick leave payments will most likely be exhausted prior to the first payment from the income protection policy. However, this discussion demonstrates the care that needs to be exercised when recommending that income protection policies be held within super, as the entire benefit may not always meet a condition of release.

12-300 Business expenses protection

Business expenses protection (sometimes called business overheads protection and not to be confused with general insurance's loss of profits cover) is a variation of the income protection policy and is specifically designed for small business. This cover allows small business owners to keep their businesses afloat if they are disabled through accident or illness and absent from their businesses.

Business protection insurance allows the small business owner to insure a proportion of their gross income that normally meets the business's standing charges. These are the expenses that must be met even though the business is not operating.

Income protection insurance can provide a benefit until the insured turns 65 years. However, business expenses protection has a benefit period of only 12 or 24 months. The following example illustrates how business protection operates.

Illustrated example 12.10

Melissa is an insurance broker who generates a gross income of $10,000 per month. Her monthly operating expenses are as follows:

Monthly Expenses	Cost
Office lease	$3,000
Computer lease	$800
Accounting and insurances	$1,800
Account executive's salary	$4,000
Business expense total	**$9,600**

If Melissa insures her gross income, she will receive $7,500 per month from her income protection policy if she is totally disabled. However, she still needs to find $9,600 per month to keep her business going, which she can claim through her business expenses protection. By insuring her business expenses, Melissa ensures that her business will not collapse while she is absent.

There are a number of allowable business expenses listed in the policy, and these generally include the following:

- **Premises**
    - » rent or interest/fees on a loan to finance premises
    - » insurance premiums (fire, etc)
    - » property rates and taxes
    - » security costs

» repairs and maintenance

- **Services**
    - » telephone
    - » gas
    - » electricity
    - » water
    - » mobile phone
    - » cleaning and laundry

- **Equipment**
    - » lease or financing costs (excluding payments attributable to the initial cost)
    - » car lease
    - » registration and insurance of vehicles and equipment
    - » repairs and maintenance of equipment

- **Salaries and related costs**
    - » salaries of employees
    - » payroll tax
    - » compulsory superannuation for employees

- **Other**
    - » regular advertising costs
    - » accounting and auditing fees
    - » bank fees/charges and account transaction taxes
    - » interest/fees on loans to finance the business
    - » professional association fees and subscriptions
    - » business insurance (liability, etc)
    - » postage

It is important to note that the amount paid is not the benefit stated in the policy, as this represents the maximum amount payable. The amount paid is the total amount of expenses that accrue in that month. Unlike income protection policies, the benefits are only paid while the insured is unable to work; ie, there is no partial benefit available.

12-310 Study questions

12.1 Discuss the key differences between a traditional whole-of-life policy and a term policy.

12.2 Discuss the bonus structure of traditional life policies.

12.3 Describe the options that are available on a term life policy.

12.4 Why do life insurance premiums start to become significantly higher from about the age of 65?

12.5 When is the use of term insurance appropriate?

12.6 What is TPD insurance? Describe its features.

12.7 Bob Brown purchases a *renewable, convertible, non-participating* term insurance policy. Explain the precise meaning of the italicised words.

12.8 Explain the main differences between TPD and income protection insurance.

12.9 Name two advantages and two disadvantages of holding TPD cover in superannuation.

12.10 Explain a significant tax disadvantage of including TPD cover in a superannuation plan.

12.11 What is trauma insurance and what is it designed to cover?

12.12 Under disability income insurance policies there are two definitions that some insured persons can select. Explain the difference between the two definitions of disability, the classes of occupation that would qualify for each definition, and which definition is more advantageous to the client.

12.13 What is the rationale for having a waiting period in an income protection policy? In general, what is the effect of having different combinations of waiting and benefit periods on the premium payable?

12.14 A client is very concerned that the monthly benefit payable under his income protection policy will be eroded by inflation in the event of a claim. Discuss how this concern can be provided for under such a policy.

12.15 What is the relevance of family health history, personal health history, occupation and leisure pursuits to the underwriter when assessing an application for life insurance?

12-320 References

Websites

ING Life Limited, OneCare Product Illustration. Available at ing.com.au

Releases

Australian Taxation Office (ATO) 2019, Key superannuation rates and thresholds. Available at *ato.gov.au*

Australian Taxation Office (ATO) 2007, Taxation Determination TD 2007/3

Legislation

Income Tax Assessment Act 1997 (Cth)

Insurance Contracts Act 1984 (Cth)

Superannuation Industry (Supervision) Act 1993 (Cth)

Superannuation Industry (Supervision) Regulations (SISR) 1994 (Cth)

Superannuation Legislation Amendment (Further MySuper & Transparency Measures) Bill 2012 (Cth)

CHAPTER 13

GENERAL INSURANCE PRODUCTS

13-000 INTRODUCTION

The following section examines the common general insurance products available to householders and small business

DOMESTIC INSURANCE POLICIES

13-010 Introduction

General insurance principally covers assets associated with real property, motor vehicles and various liabilities. General insurance can be divided into five areas:

- domestic

- motor vehicle

- liability

- strata title

- commercial.

Commercial insurance (including marine cargo and hull insurance) is a highly technical area and represents a field of study in its own right. In this chapter, only the fundamentals of commercial insurance available to small business owners will be discussed, enabling clients to be referred to an insurance broker if assistance is required in these areas. Other commercial policies, such as industrial special risks, marine insurance, farm insurance and crop insurance, will not be discussed.

Certain insurance contracts are prescribed contracts under Pt V of the *Insurance Contracts Act 1984* (Cth) (IC Act). The Act and accompanying Insurance Contracts Regulations 1985 (IC Regulations) prescribe minimum cover that must be provided to insureds who have not been given a notice advising a variation to standard cover. Generally, giving the insured a copy of the policy document with the terms clearly set out in plain English is sufficient to provide notice. However, if this is not done, and an insurer wishes to rely on the terms of its standard contract, it must prove that the insured knew or should have known the extent of cover provided by the insurer.

The prescribed contracts which provide standard cover under the IC Regulations are:

- motor vehicles (reg 5)

- home buildings (reg 9)

- home contents (reg 13)
- sickness and accident (reg 17)
- consumer credit (reg 21).
- travel insurance (reg 25)
- Limits on minimum amounts (reg 29)
- Flood insurance (reg 29A)

13-020 Domestic insurance

When reference is made to domestic insurance it generally refers to houses and their contents and motor vehicles, as these are the most common and most valuable property assets owned by individuals. The protection of these assets is an important consideration when considering a family's risk management plan.

Householders policies combine several types of cover into one policy, which allows an individual to insure his or her house, its contents, specified valuable property, public liability, specified personal property and unspecified personal property without having to take out individual policies. Because these individual policies are packaged into one policy, there are premium savings for the insured.

Householders policies are now required to include a summary of the various insured events covered by the policy (discussed further in the Key Facts Sheet section below), a summary of the additional features, and a list of the optional covers available through payment of an extra premium. This is generally followed by an explanation of the terms used in the policy (eg, flood), followed by a discussion of the insured's responsibilities, including their duty of disclosure.

Insurance can be taken out to insure property for either its:

- indemnity value
- replacement value (Capped (fixed) sum insured), or
- Full replacement

Indemnity value: provides cover for the depreciated value of assets. These policies cover assets for damage caused by a list of defined perils, some of which are limited to defined amounts and subject to a list of exclusions. Replacement value policies (or, Capped (fixed) sum insured) replace most assets for their replacement cost (ie, new for old) up to the sum insured following damage caused by accidental means. Replacement cost means there is no deduction for depreciation in determining the amount paid for a loss. For example, assume that the roof of a house if five years old and has a useful life of 20 years. The roof is damaged by a storm and the cost of replacement if $10,000. Under an indemnity policy the insured would receive only $7,500 ($10,000 - $2,500). Under replacement conditions, the insured would receive the full $10,000 (less any applicable policy excess). Because the insured receives the value of a brand new roof instead of one that is five years old, the principle of indemnity is technically violated.

Replacement value policies: will repair a damaged building or a totally rebuild destroyed dwelling to the same size, with similar materials at the same site or on a different site, but only to the cost of rebuilding the destroyed home. If the insured elects to be paid out in cash, the policy generally reverts to an indemnity policy with a reduced payout. If the insured elects to rebuild on another site, he/she still retains owner ship of the land as the value of the land is not included in the sum insured.

Under these policies, the responsibility for calculating the sum replacement value (or capped amount) is the responsibility of the insured. Many insurance companies provide online calculators to allow insureds to estimate the replacement value. Values can be also obtained from a builder, architect, quantity surveyor or valuer. When making these calculations, insureds must add an inflationary component to the sum insured and review the value each year. Remember, the replacement value is established by the insurer at the time of the loss so inflationary increases in costs may mean the dwelling is underinsured.

Full replacement value policies: cover accidental loss or damage to the dwelling and rebuild it to the standard it was prior to an insured event.. These policies will cover the full replacement or repair to the insured dwelling to the same floor area, irrespective of the cost to repair or replace. These policies reduce the risk of underinsurance and generally also include features, such as swimming pools, fences, sheds and paving. However, these features may vary between different company's offerings, but only a few companies offer this product.

Contents such as furniture can also be insured for their replacement but not items like clothing. Again, there are some exclusions such as damage caused by vermin, and some limits placed on certain occurrences such as deterioration of frozen food and loss of credit cards.

13-030 Prescribed contracts and flood coverage

Section 37B of the IC Act prescribes a new definition of flood that must be included in an expanded list of prescribed contracts. Regulation 29C of the

IC Regulations prescribes the following contracts that must have compulsory flood cover included in the policy terms:

- home building insurance
- home contents insurance
- combined home and contents insurance
- residential strata title insurance
- small business insurance that cover loss or damage of the equipment, stock, inventory or premises.

A small business is defined as having turnover in the last financial year less than $1 million and the total hours worked each week by the employees is no more than 190 hours, or if it has five or less employees (reg 29B).

Regulation 29D of the IC Regulations defines flood as the covering of normally dry land by water that has escaped or been released from the normal confines of any lake, river, creek, another natural water course (whether or not any are altered or modified), a reservoir, canal or dam.

Insurers are still able to continue using standard limitations such as exclusions for: flood cover in the first 72 hours of a policy or request for cover; high risk property such as pontoons; buildings which breach building laws and regulations; and flooding that is the result of deliberate damage to a dam. Insurers are also able to allow insureds to 'opt-out' of flood cover if they so desire. Many insureds will generally 'opt-out' because their property is in a flood prone area and the cost of flood insurance is considered unaffordable. In contrast, some insurers offer their policies on a 'no opt-out' basis, which gives insureds no option than to pay the extra for flood cover other than moving to another insurer who does offer the 'opt-out' option.

Insurers must clearly inform insureds of whether an insurance policy that is a 'prescribed contract' contains flood cover under s 37C of the IC Act. However, insurers do not have to re-supply insureds with flood cover information upon renewal, extension or reinstatement of a prescribed contract. Where a prescribed contract is varied, the duty will only operate in relation to variations that impact upon an insured's flood cover.

Key fact sheets

The key fact sheet (KFS) is a one-page document for prescribed contracts to provide consumers with easy access to key information in relation to home building and home contents insurance policies. The KFS will reduce consumer confusion regarding what is and is not included in insurance contracts and provide consumers with a mechanism to easily compare key aspects of insurance contracts.

The KFS contains an outline of the difference between:

- sum-insured policies
- sum-insured policies plus margin, and
- total replacement policies.

The outline will be accompanied by a clear statement specifying which of these categories of cover is held by the insured. It also details what is covered in the policy, including a list of natural disaster events, and what is not covered in the policy. Also included in the 'what is covered' section, is a list of the amounts of any standard sub-limits or excesses. In addition, a warning in the KFS refers consumers to the product disclosure statement (PDS) for the product where there is an option for one or more sub-limits or excesses to apply to the policy and a statement outlines the cooling off period that applies to the policy.

The KFS's standard set of warnings state that the KFS is merely an outline of the policy and not a comprehensive disclosure document, and consumers are advised to consider their own particular financial needs and risks when deciding whether to take out the policy (general consumer warning). There is also a warning that underinsurance may cause financial hardship which may in turn have negative health implications for consumers (health warning) and a brief explanation of the *'Wayne Tank* principle' stating that where there are two or more concurrent causes of damage and one cause is excluded from the policy then any claim in respect of that damage may be excluded.

Buildings

The building that is insured as the insured's home is generally defined as a residential structure and its domestic fixtures and domestic structural improvements. Depending on the insurance company's policy, other items such as garages and other domestic buildings, pergolas, insulation for roofs or walls, in- ground swimming pools, spas, saunas and jetties, fixed light fittings, wall and floor coverings, paved paths and service connections are included in the home definition. Therefore, adequate allowance must be made in the sum insured for these additional items.

The definition of the term *'building'* contains several exclusions or part exclusions. These exclusions may mean that coverage will not be provided for the construction of a new home or for temporary homes and structures, caravans, motor vehicles, trailers, mobile homes, tents, rail carriages, trams, aircraft or water craft. Part exclusions often relate to the use of the premises for business purposes unless the company agrees to the business activity, such as where part of the home is used for a home office or where a tradesperson parks their vehicle at the insured address.

An examination of many householders insurance policies reveals two important points. First, exclusions are not always called exclusions. They may appear as 'we do not cover' or 'not insured at your home' or following the word 'except'. Second, they may appear anywhere in the policy, not just under the heading 'Exclusions'.

Contents

Depending on the particular policy, contents may mean an insured's unfixed household goods, valuables and personal effects, including an extensive list of items such as: carpets (fixed and unfixed); internal blinds and curtains; furniture and furnishings; electrical appliances; wheelchairs and medical equipment; household tools and gardening equipment, including ride-on mowers; golf buggies; portable and above-ground swimming pools and spas in a temporary site, and their accessories; and canoes, sailboards and boats no more than three metres in length.

Provision is also made for fixtures and fittings in a unit. For insurance purposes, this cover includes fixtures and fittings that are not legally part of the unit building. These include light fittings, wall paint, wallpaper, wall coverings, floor coverings (such as floating floors and linoleum), and a heater or air conditioning unit that the insured owns.

A list of exclusions is generally contained in the policy, and these deny cover for such items as motor vehicles and their accessories or spare parts; items permanently connected or plumbed to the electricity or gas supply; pets, domestic animals and livestock; shrubs, hedges, lawns, trees and plants other than pot plants; and caravans and trailers. Some of these excluded items, such as plumbed-in dishwashers, will be covered under the building section of the policy.

Generally, certain items are covered only up to set limits, such as:

* home office equipment — up to $10,000 in total

- tools of trade — up to $1,000 in total
- refrigerated or frozen food — up to $500 in total
- uncut and unset gems, gold or silver nuggets and ingots (not jewellery) — up to $500 in total
- cash, smartcards, phone cards and documents able to be cashed — up to $300 in total.

These items and limits vary between policies, and care needs to be exercised when recommending these policies to ensure that the cover meets the client's requirements.

There are generally other contents items that are covered for a specified amount but which can be insured for more by listing each for its replacement value on the certificate of insurance. This cover can include items such as the following (the indicated values are examples only):

- jewellery and watches — up to $1,000 for each item or set, but not more than a total of $4,000
- CDs, DVDs, audio and video tapes, records, computer discs, computer software, game cartridges and consoles — up to $5,000 in total
- hand-woven carpets or rugs —up to $2,000 for each carpet or rug
- silver and gold items, either plated or solid — up to $2,000 each item or set
- paintings, pictures, works of art, sculptures and art objects — up to $10,000 for each item or set but not more than a total of $50,000 in total
- stamps and coin collections — up to $2,000 in total
- collections and memorabilia — up to $2,000 in total

Policies covering contents normally have a rider that covers unspecified and some specified personal property if it leaves the home and travels anywhere within Australia and New Zealand, and anywhere else in the world for up to 30 days. Policies will usually offer a choice of a specified per-item sum insured and an aggregate cover for personal effects lost or damaged by accidental means. For example, the following item may insured as a specified item: one Sony Digital 8 Handycam, insured for $2,000. For example, an aggregate sum insured (ie, total cumulative loss) for non-specified items would appear as follows: general effects are covered for $500 per item to a maximum aggregate loss of $3,000.

Unspecified personal property normally includes:

- jewellery, spectacles and watches
- sporting equipment
- photographic and video equipment
- portable sound equipment
- binoculars
- clothing and luggage.

Unspecified personal property normally does not include:

- road, water or air craft
- business assets
- cash, stamps or negotiable securities
- contact lenses
- bicycles
- portable computers
- mobile phones
- camping equipment.

Perils covered

The common perils covered include:

- fire, lightning (including power surge caused by lightning) and explosion
- bursting, leaking, discharging or overflowing of liquids
- damage by animals
- earthquake and tsunami
- flood
- impact
- malicious damage
- riot and civil commotion
- storm and rainwater run-off
- theft, burglary and house-breaking

- fusion of electric motors
- accidental breakage of glass and ceramic fittings.

Most of these perils are listed along with some explanation of what they involve, as well as specific exclusions.

Fire-related perils

Fire does not include scorching, heat, smoke, ash or soot damage when the home or contents have not caught fire (ie, where there is only smouldering), or where there has been no flame, or from heating or cooking food. However, if a fire does break out (ie, there is a flame) and spreads from the heating or cooking appliance, damaged items will be covered. Marks and burns caused by cigarettes and cigars, and damage by power surges are not covered, unless the power surge results in fire damage.

Stormwater and flood-related perils

Storm and rainwater run-off is covered but not if rain, hail or wind entered the home because of a building, design or structural defect, unless the policy modifies this exclusion. Flood coverage normally contains a number of exclusions such as loss or damage caused by:

- landslide, subsidence, erosion or any earth movement
- hydrostatic pressure
- flood for a period of five days from the date cover was initially provided
- loss or damage to retaining walls, paths, driveways or landscaping.

Some companies also include an exclusion relating to damage to in-ground swimming pools. However, conditions and exclusions can vary widely among policies and care needs to be exercised when choosing an appropriate cover.

Unless the insurance commences directly after another insurance policy covering the same property expired, without a break in cover, home and contents policies generally don't provide cover for a period of 48 hours from the time of the commencement of the insurance for physical loss, destruction or damage caused by:

- bushfire or grassfire, or
- a named cyclone.

Water-related perils

Other water-related perils covered by domestic insurance are those caused by bursting, leaking or overflowing of water or liquids from a variety of containers such as pipes and taps; roof gutters and rainwater downpipes; tanks, swimming pools and spas; waterbeds; dishwashers and washing machines; baths, sinks, toilets and basins; drainage and sewerage systems; and water collection trays in freezers, refrigerators and air conditioners. However, such damage is not covered if the insured knew about the leak and did not fix it before the loss or damage occurred, or if the leak originated from shower floors or bases or shower cubicle walls. The exploratory costs incurred in searching and locating a leaking pipe that is causing damage *is* included in the cover.

Burglary (theft)-related perils

Policies cover loss or damage caused by theft but not if:

- the theft is perpetrated by someone who lives in the home or enters the home with the owner's consent

- the loss or damage occurs without forced entry when a tenant or boarder occupies the home or part of the home

- the theft is the result of loss from a common area such as a garage or a community clothesline of residential flats, units, townhouses or villas.

Therefore, if an insured made a claim for the theft of a bicycle from a common parking area, the claim would not be paid. However, if the bicycle was stolen from an enclosed garage of a townhouse and the garage was reserved for the insured's own use only, or if the bicycle was damaged during the process, it would be covered.

Insurance policies generally contain specific conditions relating to security devices. An insurer may refuse to pay for loss or damage caused by burglary or housebreaking if:

- additional security devices (eg, window locks and detection systems) as specifically required by the insurer are not installed within a reasonable time following the insurer's request

- any security device installed or declared to be installed is not maintained in an efficient working order and is in operation whenever the risk address is left unattended by the insured or any other person.

Animal-related perils

Damage caused by animals requires comment. This cover generally does not indemnify the insured for damage caused by animals or birds belonging to or in the control of anyone living at the home. This would include damage caused by animals or birds pecking, biting, clawing, ripping curtains or chewing the home or contents. However, damage caused by an animal accidentally trapped inside the home that does not belong to the insured or anyone living at the home is normally covered.

Additional benefits

In addition to the basic cover, a number of additional benefits are often provided by insurers. These normally include:

- removal of debris and extra building costs, usually up to a percentage of the sum insured
- cost of temporary accommodation, although the amount tends to be limited to a percentage of the sum insured
- replacement of locks when keys are stolen, usually to a dollar limit
- contents in the open air at the insured address
- spoilage of food, up to a dollar limit
- uninsured visitors' contents, up to a dollar limit
- loss of rent if the insured is the owner of the building
- cover for contents temporarily removed from damaged premises
- legal liability arising out of the occupation or ownership of the premises.

Specific exclusions

Several exclusions and limitations in the cover have been commented on above, but policies generally include a list of specific exclusions. Such exclusions can include:

- situations where the residence has been left unoccupied for more than 60 consecutive days
- damage to walls, gates and fences caused by abnormal weather conditions
- damage to electrical equipment caused by electric current
- damage arising from the application of heat

- accidental damage to television screens, radio sets and clocks
- glass in picture frames, hand held mirrors and the like
- scratching, dinting or chipping
- intentional loss or damage
- lawful seizure, confiscation or nationalisation of property
- war
- radioactivity
- tidal waves or high water
- wear and tear, rust
- mildew, mould and algae
- loss of electronic data
- damage by vermin, insects or wildlife
- damage by tree roots.

The former Insurance Ombudsman Service (now the Financial Ombudsman Service) criticised the way policy exclusions were noted in insurance policies, because they were generally not noted in one place and appeared in different parts of the policy (such as in the definition section or in the limitations to cover section) (Hardman, 2007). Therefore, advisers need to be particularly careful when interpreting policy exclusions.

Legal liability

Insurance against legal liability is normally included in householders policies up to a maximum payable (usually A$10 million), where a home is insured and/or where contents are insured. Where a home is insured, the legal liability cover provides compensation for death and/or bodily injury to other people or loss or damage to their property arising out of the ownership of the home and at the insured address. For example, liability could arise when a visitor or trespasser trips over a hose or other obstruction negligently left on the front lawn, causing them to suffer an injury.

On the other hand, when contents are insured, the legal liability cover provides compensation for a negligent incident causing death or bodily harm to other people, and/or loss or damage to their property, if it happens away from the insured address but within Australia or New Zealand. For example, the insured could be held legally liable for an injury caused by a ball striking an innocent third party while the insured and friends were playing cricket in a public park.

Cover is generally not provided for:

- members of the insured's family who do not normally reside with the insured (ie, they would need to have their own legal liability policy)
- any person who normally resides with the insured, such as family, for injury or damage to their property. (These family members cannot sue the policyowner, the insured's employees or those connected with a business.)

The policy usually defines the 'address' of the property as the land on which the building is located, including the yards and garden areas used for private and domestic purposes. Sometimes, the policy defines the address as an area not comprising more than two hectares of land. This definition could be particularly important where the insured lives on a hobby farm and runs horses or cattle. In this instance, the insured may not be indemnified for injuries or damage to a third party or their property caused by a horse or cow breaking through the boundary fence.

As an adviser, it is necessary to examine any policy carefully and either arrange for the client to put in place appropriate insurance, such as a stand-alone public liability policy, or to advise the client to consult an insurance broker.

Liability insurance is important cover because of the duties of a property owner to a wide class of persons who may enter the property. These can include tenants, tenants' family members or associates, visitors and even trespassers. Therefore, risk management is an important consideration for property owners.

If a person is injured and brings a claim in negligence against a property owner, three key elements need to be present in order to establish liability:

1. There was a property defect.
2. The owner had notice of the defect.
3. There was an unreasonable response to addressing the defect following the notice of the defect.

The leading case in this area is that of *Jones v Bartlett* [2000] HCA 56; 75 ALJR 1, in which the High Court set some boundaries to actions brought in negligence:

- The landlord is only required to take reasonable steps to remedy defects in the premises.

- There is no such thing as absolute safety. All residential premises contain hazards to their occupants and to visitors, but the fact that a house could be made safer does not mean it is dangerous or defective.

- The landlord is largely only required to identify defects that a reasonably prudent person would be capable of identifying (ie, patent defects).

In all cases, a property owner would be wise to keep their property well maintained and free of any obstructions that may cause injury. In any event, advisers should always refer clients to a legal adviser in relation to legal issues and should never attempt to give legal advice.

Specific policy conditions

Although these conditions may vary from company to company, insurers often require their insureds to advise them immediately if during the period of insurance the insured:

- commences to use any part of the home for business, trade or professional purposes

- removes any security devices that were specifically required by the insurer, or

- alterations, additions, demolition, repairs or decorations to the buildings are carried out costing more than $50,000.

Upon receiving this information an insurer may alter the terms and conditions of the policy, charge an additional premium or decide not to offer to renew the policy.

13-040 Strata title insurance

Definition of strata title

Strata title is a form of ownership devised for multi-level apartment blocks and horizontal subdivisions with shared areas. The 'strata' part of the term refers to apartments being on different levels, or 'strata'.

Policy benefits

Policies generally provide accidental damage and new for old cover for buildings, common contents and common property caused by land slide or subsidence but only if it occurs as a result of and within 72 hours after one of the following events:

- storm, rainwater or wind
- flood
- earthquake
- explosion
- liquid that escapes from a fixed pipe or something attached to a pipe, fixed gutter, fixed tank or drain.

This cover also applies to gates, fences and retaining walls that are attached to, and are part of, the structure of the buildings.

Cover is available for buildings, common contents and common property, liability up to $20 million, fidelity guarantee, office bearers' liability, personal accident, and workers' compensation in New South Wales, Western Australia, Tasmania and the Northern Territory.

Policies also generally include cover for additional costs required to comply with government or local authority bylaws provided the sum insured has not been exhausted. Cover for burning out of electric motors no bigger than 40 kilowatts (5hp) is included provided they are less than 10 years old.

Additional benefits

Policies generally pay for the reasonable costs of replacing trees, scrubs if damaged by a vehicle, stolen, burnt or maliciously damaged. Usually a limit applies such as $5,000 per policy period.

Exclusions

Some common exclusions include loss or damage caused by:

- erosion
- rust, corrosion, gradual deterioration, depreciation, wear or tear
- defect in an item, faulty workmanship, structural defects or faulty design.

Terrorism insurance

Some companies offer insurance against acts of terrorism. A typical policy wording states that cover for damage caused by a terrorist act is covered where the sum insured as for the buildings, common contents and common property is $50 million or less.

Terrorism is defined as any act which may, or may not, involve the use of, or threat of, force or violence where the purpose of the act is to further a political, religious or ideological aim or to intimidate or influence a government (whether lawfully constituted or not) or any section of the public.

Policy excesses

Policies may or may not have excesses on claims but typically a $250 excess will apply to earthquake claims.

13-050 Motor vehicle insurance

Domestic motor vehicle insurance is normally provided in four forms:

- compulsory third party
- comprehensive motor vehicle
- third party property damage
- fire, theft and third party.

Of these four insurances, only the last three forms are examined, as compulsory third party insurance (CTP) is mandated by law and must be effected at the time of motor vehicle registration. Thus, a vehicle cannot be registered and legally used on public roads unless it is covered by CTP insurance. CTP insurance indemnifies drivers against actions brought over personal injury suffered by third parties as a direct result of a motor vehicle accident.

Extent of cover

Comprehensive motor vehicle insurance

Comprehensive motor vehicle (CMV) insurance covers a vehicle for accidental loss or damage anywhere in Australia, which includes loss caused by collision, theft, storm, hail, malicious damage, flood and similar perils. In addition, it covers third party damage and liability. Some types of vehicles that can be covered by CMV insurance are cars, four-wheel drives, utilities, vans with up to two tons carrying capacity, trailers and caravans.

The sums insured are either market value or a specific agreed value (or, nominated value). Agreed value is a fixed value agreed between you and your insurer and is the maximum amount that the insurance company will pay for the vehicle in the event of a claim, so it is important that the agreed value accurately reflects the value of the vehicle. This cover is usually restricted to vehicles under a certain model age, such as two years. On the other hand, market value is calculated by insurers at the time of the loss and represents what the car would be sold for on the open market at any point in time and may include reference to industry publications, such as Glasses' Guide, to compare a motor vehicle of similar age and condition as the insured vehicle.

The policy can cover the vehicle for private, business or goods carrying or trade use. Private use can be defined as not being used in connection with earning income but includes driving to and from work and occasional use in connection with work, such as doing the daily banking. However, this may not be the case with all companies, so the wording should be carefully checked.

Third party property damage

Third party property damage (TPD) insurance covers amounts for which the insured is legally liable to pay another person to compensate for loss or damage to their property caused by the use of the motor vehicle. Cover is generally limited to $20 million and it includes legal and other costs approved by the insurance company.

Fire, theft and third party property damage

Fire, theft and third party property damage (FT&TP) insurance covers an insured vehicle for accidental damage caused by fire or theft, generally up to an amount stated in the policy, such as $5,000. Third party property damage is generally covered up to a maximum of $20 million.

Additional features

The following additional features generally apply only to CMV cover, not to TPD and FT&TP.

- *New vehicle after total loss.* Some policies will replace an insured vehicle with a new one of the same make, model and series if the vehicle is a total loss (ie, a write-off) owing to an insured event that occurred within the first two years of the vehicle being registered. This cover generally includes all on-road costs, and the insurance policy may continue to its expiry date.

- *Hire car after theft.* Some policies cover the hire of a car for up to 13 days if the insured vehicle is stolen. The cover ceases if the vehicle is returned undamaged or when the vehicle is repaired and returned to the insured or the claim is settled. The insured is responsible for all running costs.

- *Emergency repairs, travel and accommodation.* Some policies will pay up to a stated figure, such as $300, if an insured vehicle needs emergency repairs in order to get to a destination. Some will also pay up to a stated amount, such as $500, for emergency travel and overnight accommodation if the event was more than 100 kilometres from home and the vehicle is unroadworthy or unsafe to drive.

- *Medical expenses*. A policy may cover the reasonable costs of hospital, medical, dental, pharmaceutical or ambulance expenses if the insured is injured as a result of the event, provided the costs are not covered under another policy or scheme. The costs are generally restricted to a specified amount, such as $500.

- *Driver fatality*. Some policies will pay a stated amount, such as $5,000, to the estate of the insured if death results from injuries caused by an event while driving the vehicle and if death occurs within 12 months of the event.

- *Locks and keys*. This cover pays the difference between the cost of replacing keys and/or recoding a vehicle's locks and the policy excess. The amount payable is generally restricted to an amount such as $300.

- *Damage by uninsured drivers*. Provided the car is insured for comprehensive cover, the policy will pay loss or damage to the insured vehicle if the other vehicle is being driven by an uninsured driver.

- *Towing and storage costs*. This feature covers the reasonable costs of towing the insured vehicle to the nearest repairer and storage costs.

- *Two-wheel trailer cover*. A two-wheel trailer is generally covered for comprehensive cover while attached to the insured vehicle, but is subject to a stated amount (eg, $500).

- *Third party property damage for caravans and trailers*. This cover will pay for loss or damage to a third party's property caused by the caravan or trailer while it is being towed or by property falling from the caravan or trailer while being towed.

- *Substitute vehicle*. This cover provides third party damage for a vehicle that does not belong to the insured if the insured vehicle cannot be driven. This cover generally only lasts for a limited period, such as 13 days.

- *Contents cover for caravans*. This feature provides cover for up to a stated amount for loss or damage to contents in the insured caravan (or annex or garden shed) caused by theft, wind, flood, storm or accidental damage. The amount payable is generally restricted to a maximum amount such as $500.

- *Glass cover* (windscreen or window glass). This cover is included in most policies, but generally for only two or three replacements with the policy excess not applying and no loss of no claim bonus. The policy excess will apply to further replacements. For some policies, this cover is an optional extra.

Exclusions

There are a number of exclusions that apply to all types of car insurance and voids cover. For example, cover does not apply if:

- the vehicle is loaded beyond specifications

- the driver is under the influence of alcohol or drugs

- the driver refuses to take a legal test for alcohol or drugs

- the vehicle is being driven by an unlicensed driver

- the driver is not licensed or not correctly licensed, or is not complying with conditions of their license

- there is damage to tyres caused by braking, punctures, cuts or bursting

- the vehicle was damaged, unsafe or unroadworthy at the time of the event

- the caravan or trailer was being used for business or carrying goods for trade purposes.

These are some of the more common exclusions. Some policies also exclude cover to vehicles if they are parked on the street overnight.

Premiums

Premiums for motor vehicle insurance are based on the make of the vehicle, its age, whether the car is used for private or business purposes, the age of the driver and the location of the vehicle. Location is important because premium rates are higher for cars permanently located in a metropolitan area than for cars permanently located in a country area. This is due to the higher risk of theft in a city and of accidents caused by the increased traffic.

Vehicle makes and models are grouped according to their potential expense of repair after accidents. Generally, the common Australian family car models attract lower premiums, as they are less expensive to repair than other less popular models. Additionally, drivers are rated according to their accident history, which determines whether a driver is classified as a preferred or substandard risk. The longer the accident-free period, the lower the premium rating. A rating 1 driver, for example, normally receives a no-claim bonus of up to 60 per cent. Premiums are higher for drivers under the age of 21 years or 25 years, owing to the higher probability of their having an accident. Policies held by these drivers generally have a higher policy excess than those held by drivers aged over 25 years. Indeed, some companies will not insure drivers below the age of 21 years — particularly if they have high-powered vehicles.

The gender of the driver is taken into account because claims experience shows that men drive more aggressively than women, are prone to more accidents and the prices they are charged for insurance reflect this. Overall, women pay 12 per cent less than males with similar age and driving history.

How can premiums be reduced? Insurance companies generally provide a lot of options to reduce the cost of premiums. Actions an insured is able to consider to keep costs down. These include:

- Parking vehicles safely. Vehicles that are securely parked either off street or in a lock-up garage can reduce the cost of theft, vandalism, flood or storm damage claims.

- Maintaining a good driving record. A good driving record reduces the risk to the risk of damage and claim. Many insurers offer sizeable discounts for drivers with good driving records.

- Safety and security devices. Cars fitted with safety and security devices like alarms or immobilisers to reduce the risk of theft and damage, or have them installed.

- Driving less often. Some insurers offer lower premiums for drivers who don't drive much or only drive short distances.

- Limiting the number of nominated drivers. Some of the nominated drivers may have a poor claim and traffic infringement history. Lastly, under 25 year old drivers should not be included as nominated drivers.

- Choosing a higher excess. Higher excesses can be a good option if the insured is confident that their probability of having an accident is low. The higher the excess, the lower the premium.

- Choosing to insure for market value instead of agreed value. For newer vehicles this isn't usually an issue, but as the value of a vehicle depreciates quickly, the insured value may be overpriced and may result in the market value being paid in the event of a total loss.

- Bundling car insurance with other types of insurance. Bundling car insurance with home a contents or travel insurance may result in a premium discount.

- Multiple policies. Having multiple policies with an insurance company may quality the insured of a loyalty premium discount.

Extras

As with most types of insurance product, insurers will offer a range of extras to the basic policy however, these extras will attract an additional cost. These extras include:

- no claim bonus protection
- rental car hire following an accident (sometimes this extra is an automatic inclusion in some policies, as mentioned above)
- windscreen and glass damage protection cover
- cover for theft of work tools or stock
- road side assistance

13-060 Pleasure craft/boat insurance

The cover provided by pleasure craft insurance is somewhat similar to a comprehensive motor vehicle policy, as insurers generally cover the boat for all accidental loss, damage and legal liability in relation to the operation of the boat.

The insured boat generally includes:

- hull(s)
- motor(s)
- masts, spars, rigging and sails
- trailer (but only if specifically noted as covered on the schedule)
- equipment and accessories
- boat tender
- personal effects (but only when on the insured boat or the boat tender).

Policies generally cover accessories and equipment, emergency expenses, loss prevention and recovery costs, medical expenses, towing costs, and rescue expenses up to a specified limit, and provide an amount of cover for the death of the authorised operator/driver. Additionally, boat trailers can be insured under these policies.

Optional covers may include cover while racing yachts and sailing craft, subject to restrictions on distance from the Australian mainland and on race distance; and water skiers' liability cover. Water skiers' liability insurance covers the operator of the boat or on board observer if a water skier towed by the boat accidentally dies or suffers bodily injury or death or injury is caused to a third party or damage caused by a water skier who is being towed by the boat. This extension also includes aquaplaning activities, provided that commercially manufactured items are used. Therefore, the use of car tyres and the like are not covered under this extension.

Exclusions

Pleasure craft insurance policies contain a number of exclusions in addition to any restrictions noted in the policy definitions. Some of the more common exclusions are:

- operating the boat while under the influence of alcohol or drugs
- using the boat while in an unsafe, unseaworthy or unroadworthy condition
- operating the boat by an unlicensed person
- using the boat while unregistered when legally required to be registered
- using the boat in ways other than for private use
- fitting the boat with a motor that has a horsepower rating greater than that recommended by the hull manufacturers
- overloading the boat
- carrying passengers for payment or reward
- operating outside the policy navigation limits
- loss or damage to sails from wind or water.

13-070 Personal sickness and accident insurance

These policies compensate the insured for loss of income resulting from injury or accident. Examples of events that are covered by these policies include:

- accidental death
- accidental permanent disabling injury
- temporary total or temporary partial disablement as a result of accident or sickness.

This cover is quite restrictive, in that:

- the benefit insured is limited to the average weekly income
- the renewal of the policy is not guaranteed

- the period of indemnity is generally only 52 or 104 weeks
- an excess of seven to 13 days applies to all claims
- claim payments are reduced if compensation is received from other sources
- the policy contains a list of defined events and the amount of cover provided for that event. For example, death is generally covered for 100 per cent of the sum insured, permanent loss of hearing in one ear is covered for 25 per cent, and permanent loss of one joint in any finger is covered for 7.5 per cent.

Additional benefits

Some sickness and accident policies include the following additional benefits:

- *Exposure.* Compensation will be payable if, as a result of exposure, the insured suffers a defined event.
- *Disappearance.* The death benefit is generally payable if the insured is travelling in a conveyance that disappears, sinks or is wrecked and the body of the insured has not been recovered in one year.
- *Hijack.* Compensation is payable in the event of injury or sickness suffered as a result of unlawful seizure of a conveyance.
- *Rehabilitation.* This benefit provides payments to an approved rehabilitation centre if the insured suffers total disablement for a period in excess of 26 weeks as a result of injury by accident.
- *Indexation of compensation.* This benefit indexes the weekly benefit by movements in the consumer price index up to a maximum, such as two per cent, after three months of benefit payment.
- *Funeral expenses.* The reasonable cost of funeral or cremation expenses, including the cost of returning the remains to their normal place of residence, is covered by this benefit. It is generally subject to a specified limit such as $5,000.

Some companies offer an optional renewable benefit that guarantees to renew the policy for a maximum of two years, and a business expenses cover. A further option allows voluntary workers to be insured while they are engaging in voluntary work.

Exclusions

There are a certain number of exclusions that apply to personal sickness and accident insurance, including:

- AIDS and HIV
- flying or other aerial activity unless as a fare-paying passenger on an airline with scheduled flights
- certain diseases
- existing medical conditions
- injury caused by alcohol or drugs
- mental conditions
- certain occupations and sporting injuries
- pregnancy
- suicide or any attempt at suicide and intentional self-injury.

Policy conditions

Personal sickness and accident insurance policies are subject to a number of conditions such as the following:

- There must be immediate notification of any change in the insured's usual occupation.
- There must be immediate advice of the existence of any other accident, disability or sickness insurance held with another insurer.
- If the insured becomes affected by any disease, physical defect, infirmity, sickness or injury, then the insurance company must be immediately advised.
- The insured must consent to a medical examination if they are making a claim.
- The insured must follow the medical treatment prescribed by a legally qualified medical practitioner.

13-080 Travel insurance

Travel insurance provides protection for people travelling domestically or overseas for a host of benefits. Examples of the benefits include:

- cancellation fees and lost deposits

- overseas emergency medical assistance
- additional expenses
- accidental death
- loss of travel documents, credit cards and travellers cheques
- loss of luggage and personal effects
- alternative travel expenses
- personal liability
- medical expenses and cancellation costs related to pregnancy (conditions apply).

Exclusions

Travel insurance has a number of exclusions in relation to medical expenses, cancellation costs and additional expenses. The travel cover does not apply, for example, if the insured:

- has been given a terminal prognosis for any condition with a life expectancy of under 24 months
- requires home oxygen therapy or will require oxygen for the journey
- has chronic renal failure treated by haemodialysis or peritoneal dialysis
- has been diagnosed with congestive heart failure
- has full-blown AIDS
- is on a waiting list for an organ transplant
- has any specified pre-existing medical conditions such as cancer.

13-090 Consumer credit insurance

Consumer credit insurance (CCI) covers the insured if something affects their capacity to meet the payments of their personal loan mortgage. CCI is usually offered when a person takes out a loan, and the premium is included in the amount of the loan. There are three types of risk that can be covered:

- death
- sickness or accident (disability)
- involuntary unemployment.

Some companies offer CCI to protect credit cards, motor vehicle finance, business or commercial loans, and personal loans and mortgages. For business or commercial loans, CCI provides cover in the event that a guarantor of the loan dies. The premiums for CCI are generally financed into the loan for up to five or seven years, while some companies will allow the premiums to be paid monthly via direct debit.

Death insurance benefit

In the event of death, the insurer will generally pay an amount sufficient to pay out the loan at the date of death plus a maximum of two months arrears, or the amount financed in the application/certificate of insurance, or a stated sum insured (such as $100,000).

The operation of the death benefit in CCI is shown in the following illustrated example.

Illustrated example 13.1

Mario chose to purchase death cover under CCI when he arranged his $35,000 loan in February 2007. On 16 April, Mario suffered a fatal heart attack. At the time of Mario's death, the amount outstanding on his loan was $32,000 and there were no arrears. As the amount outstanding on Mario's loan was less than the amount financed in the application and less than $100,000, the insurance company paid a benefit of $32,000.

Disablement benefit

This benefit generally pays $1/30^{th}$ of the monthly benefit (excluding the first 13 days), provided the insured is engaged in permanent and gainful employment at the date the disablement commenced. This cover generally has a maximum benefit payable, such as $75,000.

The operation of the disablement benefit is shown in the following illustrated example.

Illustrated example 13.2

Bevan is a full-time accountant. He has a regular monthly loan repayment of $600. He suffered an accident and couldn't work from 15 February 2007 to 30 April 2007 inclusive. He has a medical certificate from his doctor for this period. His CCI will make the repayments on his home loan during this period, less the first 13 days, when no benefit is payable. The total period of the claim equals 60 (74 − 13) days. The amount payable under the policy would be 60/30 × $600, which equals $1,200.

Involuntary unemployment

This benefit can generally only be taken in combination with disability cover, and will pay 1/30th of the monthly benefit for each day of involuntary unemployment for up to six months. There is usually a maximum benefit payable for each claim, such as $3,000, and a maximum benefit payable for multiple claims, such as $6,000. After an involuntary benefit claim, there is generally a waiting period of six months before a new involuntary benefit claim is paid.

Involuntary unemployment has the potential of causing home loan borrowers considerable financial pain. The following illustrated example shows how Debbie received a payment under this benefit.

Illustrated example 13.3

Debbie was made redundant on 22 June 2007 and was involuntarily unemployed until 22 October 2007 inclusive — that is, for a total of 122 days. She has a regular monthly loan of $400. The number of days that Debbie is able to claim is 108 (122 − 13). The total benefit payable is 108/30 × $400, which equals $1,440.

Eligibility

Applicants must be in generally good health, ie, not suffering any serious health problems, and must be over 18 and less than 60 years of age at the cover commencement date. Applicants must be employed on a permanent full-time basis or working on a permanent part-time basis for at least 20 hours per week.

Also, applicants must never have had a life, accident or sickness insurance policy declined, cancelled or offered on special terms.

Exclusions

There are various consumer credit insurance exclusions. The cover does not apply, for example, if the insured:

- commits suicide within 13 months of the cover commencement date
- is involved in war or warlike activities
- dies while flying or engaging in aerial activities other than as a passenger in an aircraft
- is involved in terrorist activities
- dies or suffers disablement as a result of a known pre-existing condition.

The first 13 days of a claim period are also excluded.

At a glance

- Householders policies allow insured persons to insure multiple risks in one policy.
- Assets can be insured for either their indemnity value or replacement value.
- Exclusions can appear in a variety of forms throughout the policy.
- Motor vehicles can be insured under comprehensive, third party property damage or fire, theft and third party property damage policies.
- Premiums and acceptability of risks are influenced by a number of factors.
- Pleasure craft policies mainly cover the hull, its contents and legal liability.
- Personal accident and sickness policies are designed to cover short-term disabilities.
- Travel policies allow insured persons to insure their baggage, legal liability and other risks while travelling.
- Consumer credit insurance protects insured persons if they are unable to meet debt repayments resulting from death, disablement or involuntary unemployment.

LIABILITY INSURANCE

13-100 The law

Liability exposure can arise out of statute or common law. Statute law refers to the body of written law created by legislature, whereas common law is based on custom and court decisions. Liability can fall within both criminal law and civil law. Criminal law is concerned with acts that are a wrong against society (crimes), such as burglary and murder. In contrast, civil law deals with acts that are not a wrong against society, but which cause injury or loss to an individual or organisation, such as carelessly running a car into the side of a building. A civil wrong may also be a crime; eg, murder attacks both society and individuals. Civil law has two branches, known as the law of contracts and the law of torts. Civil liability may arise from either contracts or torts.

Contractual liability arises in many settings. For example, a rental agreement for the hire of machinery may stipulate that the machinery will be returned to the owner in good condition — ordinary wear and tear excepted. If the machinery is stolen or damaged, then the hirer is liable for the loss. Contractual liability is beyond the scope of this text and is not examined further.

A *tort* is a civil wrong other than a breach of contract. It generally involves infringing the rights of another, and the law redresses this injury by an award of damages. That is, all civil wrongs with the exception of a breach of contract are torts. Torts may be intentional; ie, they are committed for the purpose of injuring another person or damaging their property. Examples of intentional torts include libel, slander, assault and battery. Torts may also be unintentional. These are the most frequent source of liability and involve negligence.

A person may be liable for damages if they commit some act that results in bodily injury to another party or damage to their property as a result of their negligence. It may arise from the act of doing something or failing to do something that should be done. In other words, the person has failed to act reasonably towards another. The existence of negligence is usually determined by proving the existence of three elements:

- there was a duty to act, or not to act, in some way — known as the duty of care

- there was a breach of that duty of care

- the breach caused damage or injury to the person who was owed that duty.

For example, when a person drives a motor vehicle, that person has a duty to obey the traffic rules and to drive with reasonable care, given the state of the roads. If a person drives too fast on a wet road, they have breached the duty to drive safely. If, as a result of driving too fast, the car skids off the road and damages property, all elements of negligence exist, and the driver will be legally liable for all damages.

Liability for damages can arise from:

- conscious acts

- unconscious or unthinking acts

- dishonest or fraudulent acts

- self-interested, biased acts

- errors.

From a business perspective, liability can arise from many areas, examples of which are listed below.

- Employment of labour in relation to:
  - » employers' liability
  - » directors' and officers' (D&O) liability, arising from errors, misleading statements, conduct, omission, neglect or breach of duty in an individual's capacity as a director or officer in the management of a company (including an incorporated club).

- Sale of goods and services in the form of:
  - » product liability (or manufacturers' liability) arising from a breach of a duty of care owed to consumers for the quality and the safety of a product
  - » electronic commerce arising from the use of electronic networks, including electronic data interchange (EDI) and the internet
  - » professional indemnity arising from people in business providing advice and acting on behalf of others (eg, financial advisers, insurance brokers, doctors and lawyers)
  - » directors' and officers' liability.

- Site operations:
  - » public liability arising from personal injury or damage to property caused to third parties by the actions and operations of the insured.

The liabilities arising from the situations mentioned above can be covered under various insurance policies. However, underwriters exclude cover for conscious, dishonest and fraudulent acts so that wrongdoers may not profit or be protected by their insurance policies. Many of the above liabilities are beyond the scope of this text, but interested readers can obtain more information about these liabilities by referring to the Australian Business Law text noted in the recommended reading section at the end of this chapter. The types of liability insurance that are examined here are:

- public liability
- products liability
- professional liability.

Insurance policies contain a large number of definitions that reduce the likelihood of disputes by making clear the intention and meaning of policy terms. This is preferable to having the courts interpret the meaning of the terms after the loss has occurred.

Historically, public liability policies had to be endorsed to specifically remove limitations in order to include the cover required. Modern 'broadform' policies overcome this limitation by providing cover for any liability that is not specifically excluded. In addition, public liability and products liability are generally combined into the one policy because most legal jurisdictions now recognise that all clients have a products exposure, even if that exposure relates only to serving food and drink in an office.

13-110 Public and product liability

These two sections of a public and products liability policy are taken out by a business owner and provide indemnity cover for material, physical or financial loss directly attributed to negligent acts that occur during the period of insurance.

In respect of personal injury or damage to property, public liability policies cover the insured's liability to pay:

- compensation for damages
- all costs that are awarded against the insured.

These policies are 'occurrence based' policies, as they allow claims to be admitted after the policy has expired, provided that the event happened 'during the period of insurance.' The occurrence causing the liability must happen in connection with the insured's business and within the territorial limits imposed by the policy. The sum insured is referred to as the limit of liability and represents the maximum amount that the insurance company will pay, including costs of defence, for any one claim (or series of claims from the one incident). The limit of liability applies to each separate event that falls within the terms of the policy during the period of insurance and not to the aggregate of all claims.

Defence of claims

The insurer will pay all legal costs, expenses and awards of interest associated with defending any claim or legal action against the insured for personal injury or property damage, provided the insured obtains the permission of the insurance company to incur these expenses. These costs generally include the reasonable cost of providing first aid to others at the time of personal injury to others.

Words with special meanings

Most people think that all insurance policies are the same, but this is not the case — especially with liability policies. Therefore, the wording contained in each policy needs to be carefully analysed.

It is critical that the insured is described correctly in the policy, as only those named will be covered. The definition of the insured (which can be either an individual, proprietary limited company or organisation, such as 'The Bindy Creek Yacht Club Inc') should include:

- the named organisation and all subsidiary companies, existing or subsequently constituted, provided that they are incorporated within Australia or its territories

- every director, executive officer, employee, partner or shareholder, partner, joint venturer, co-venturer joint lessee, voluntary worker or work experience student

- any principal arising out of the performance of work on their behalf

- every office bearer or member of social and sporting clubs, canteen and welfare organisations or childcare groups, first aid, fire and ambulance services, fund raising and charity committees

- any director or senior executive who has organised private work to be undertaken by employees for the director or senior executive.

The definition of the products should include any goods, products and property (after they have ceased to be in the insured's possession or under the insured's control), which are deemed to have been manufactured, grown, extracted, assembled, erected, installed, repaired, serviced, treated, sold, supplied or distributed by the insured.

Personal injury includes more than just bodily injury, death and illness. It can also include disability, shock, fright, mental anguish or mental injury, effects of false arrest, wrongful detention, false imprisonment, malicious prosecution, effects of wrongful entry or eviction, libel or slander, breach of confidentiality, defamation, invasion of privacy and assault and battery.

Property damage not only includes damage, loss or destruction of tangible property, but also loss of use of tangible property that has not been physically damaged. An example of this might be the prevention of access to property as a result of an occurrence negligently caused by the insured.

The definition of territorial limits is important, as cover is generally restricted to 'anywhere in the world' excluding the USA and Canada, other than for business visits by executives and sales representatives. These restrictions could cause difficulties for manufacturers whose products are exported, unknown to them, by resellers to these countries. However, some companies will extend the policy to include these countries.

Exclusions

Some of the more important liability insurance exclusions are listed below:

- *Professional indemnity*. Most policies exclude this risk because liabilities of professionals are a specialist area and can be covered under a separate professional indemnity policy. A liability policy should be endorsed to include advice given during the normal course of selling a product.

- *Property in custody or control*. Most policies exclude any liability for damage to third party property in the insured's physical or legal control. However, the exclusion may provide some limited cover to leased premises; vehicles in the insured's car park; employees' or visitors' clothing and personal effects; and property temporarily in the insured's physical and legal control, such as premises and property temporarily occupied for work.

- *Pollution liability*. All policies exclude pollution damage from a number of listed causes such as discharge, dispersal, release, seepage and so on, but policies may allow cover for the escape of pollutants from a sudden and accidental cause.

- *Asbestos liability*. This risk has caused substantial liability to companies in Australia and the USA, with the effect that most insurers now exclude this exposure.

- *Product recall*. Product recall, and the cost of removing or recalling defective products, is excluded by most insurers.

- *Product defect*. If the insured's products are defective and this defect causes property damage, this is excluded from liability policies.

- *Employment liability*. There is a common law duty of care to maintain a safe workplace. This duty is owed by an organisation and its employees to other employers and contractors and their employees who may be engaged on the premises to do work. Most policies exclude liability for personal injury imposed by any workers' compensation law, industrial award or contract of employment or workplace agreement. However, cover is available, except for direct employees, for incidents that would be covered under workers' compensation. Cover can also be obtained for subcontractors under a cross-liability clause, which treats each party as a separate insured, thereby allowing cover.

Additional cover

Some insurers include additional benefits such as:

- expenses incurred in providing first aid and medical treatment to third parties

- expenses for temporary repair, shoring up or preservation of property that has been damaged

- interest accruing after a judgement has been made against the insured until payment is made by the insurer.

13-120 Professional liability

Professional people in the business of giving advice in their specialist areas — eg, doctors, financial advisers, solicitors, barristers, company directors, insurance brokers, architects and stockbrokers — take out professional indemnity insurance to cover their legal liability if they are negligent or breach their duty of care. In many instances this insurance is compulsory under legislation. Indeed, holders of an Australian Financial Services License (AFSL) who provide services to retail clients are obliged to maintain compensation arrangements under s 912B of the *Financial Services Reform Act 2001* (Cth) (FSR Act).

Liabilities can also arise from such things as design work, providing advice or technical information or management of a project on behalf of other joint venturers. An increasing number of claims have been made under the former *Trade Practices Act 1974* (Cth) (now *Competition and Consumer Act 2010* (Cth)), claiming misleading conduct or advice rather than negligence. In most cases, this additional cover can be included in a professional indemnity policy.

Basis of cover

Professional indemnity insurance indemnifies the insured for amounts up to the policy limit if they are found legally liable as a result of actual or alleged acts, errors or omissions incurred by them in the conduct of their business or profession.

Costs and expenses incurred to investigate, defend or settle any claim are also included. In some policies these are in addition to the sum insured.

Wording difficulties

Claims-made policies

These policies will respond only to claims made against the insured during the policy period, irrespective of when the act of negligence was actually committed. This means that once a professional indemnity policy expires, then no claims can be made on the policy unless the claim was made on the insurer during the currency of the policy.

Retroactive cover

This covers the activities of the insured (eg, a financial planner) undertaken before the current insurance policy was taken out. Retroactive cover is often provided in conjunction with claims-made cover. It insures against claims arising out of incidents that occurred before the commencement of the current claims-made policy, but which are notified during the term of the current claims-made policy. Without retroactive cover, these claims would be declined.

Some companies will provide this cover only if the exposure (financial planning activities) was previously insured. It should be noted that retroactive cover generally excludes any circumstances (ie, possible claims) known prior to the inception of the policy, as these should have been reported to the previous insurer. The operation of retroactive cover is shown in the following illustrated example.

Illustrated example 13.4

Peter Smith and Associates are two partners in a financial planning practice located in a suburb of a large town. They have held professional indemnity insurance since they commenced business in 1995 and have just renewed their policy for the 2008–09 year. During the 2007–08 year, the partners were contacted by an upset client who felt that the advice they had provided about a certain property trust was inappropriate and had caused him financial loss. The partners met with their client and, after what appeared to be a very satisfactory resolution to the meeting, the client appeared to be satisfied and left the office. The partners thought no more about the incident and got on with their business.

Not long after the renewal of their professional indemnity insurance, the partners received a letter from their client's solicitor holding them liable for their client's financial loss plus damages. This letter referred to the meeting between the partners and their client. The partners reported the claim to their professional indemnity insurers and were horrified when they were advised that their claim had been rejected. Although the partners' professional indemnity policy included unlimited retroactive cover, it did not cover instances that occurred and were reported to the partners in the previous policy period.

The partners should have reported the incident to their previous professional insurer as soon as possible after their meeting with their client as there was a possibility that a claim could have been made against them. Had they done so, the claim would have been covered by their previous professional indemnity policy.

Some companies offer continuous cover extension or it may be included in the policy. This provides cover for any claim that should or could have been notified under a previous policy period, as long as the same company provided the professional indemnity insurance on a continuous basis since the date when the notification should have been made.

Civil liability

Traditionally, professional indemnity policies covered only negligent acts. Policies that provide coverage on a civil liability basis will indemnify the insured for any act or omission, whether it is negligent or not.

Proposal forms

A new proposal form must be completed each year for every risk, even if the insured is renewing with the same insurer. The full description of the business is important, as the policy may not respond if it is incorrect. All professional activities must be listed, including the income earned from these activities.

The insured must be carefully described to include all parties to be covered by the policy, including employees such as insurance broker account executives, who could be named as defendants in a claim. Vicarious liability can also arise out of work completed by consultants, subcontractors, agents and previous corporate entities, and through mergers, acquisitions, affiliations and joint ventures.

Exclusions

The more usual professional liability exclusions include the following:

- *Known claims and known circumstances*. These refer to circumstances known to the insured before the policy was entered into, such as those described in illustrated example 13.4.

- *Loss of documents and computer records*. This refers to misplaced or incorrectly destroyed information. The policy can generally be extended to include coverage for this event.

- *Dishonest, fraudulent, criminal or malicious acts or omissions of the insured or of any person employed at the time by the insured*. Generally the policy can be extended to cover this event.

- *Trade practices and related legislation*. Policies can be extended to cover claims brought for reason other than for negligence under trades practices legislation and state fair trading legislation.

- *Contractual liabilities*. Most policies exclude cover for liabilities assumed under contracts, except to the extent that the organisation would have been liable if the contract had not been in force.

- *Excesses*. The excess in many policies is defined as 'costs inclusive'. This means that the insured has to pay the excess in respect to costs before a defence can begin. However, some insurers provide coverage on a 'costs exclusive' basis.

- *Jurisdiction.* Some policies exclude any action brought against the insured in any country outside the territory in which the policy was issued. However, some insurers can provide cover on a worldwide basis, including or excluding USA and Canada.

At a glance

- Liability can arise from both intentional and unintentional acts.
- Public liability policies cover legal liability for both personal injury and damage to third party property caused by negligent acts.
- Professional liability policies cover negligent advice given by professionals.

SMALL BUSINESS POLICIES

13-130 Introduction

Insurance for small to medium-sized enterprises (SMEs) is generally only available via a bundled business insurance policy. These policies are custom contracts offered to SMEs by brokers and insurers that bundles together specific covers from a variety of policies into a single contract for the client, which creates economies of scale for the insurance companies in relation to administration, policy issue, claims and so on. The benefits to the individual are the cost savings through lower premiums (in comparison to those for multiple individual policies) and the convenience of having only one document

Much of the insurance cover described in this section is specialised and financial and other advisers would need to have a licence or be an authorised representative of an insurance broker to give advice. It would be advisable to refer an individual to a general insurance professional such as an insurance broker listed on the website of the National Insurance Brokers Association (NIBA).

Small business insurance policies generally offer cover under multiple sections of the policy, each of which must be specifically taken up with a separate sum insured. Some of these sections include:

- fire and other defined events
- business interruption
- theft
- money
- general property
- glass
- public and products liability
- personal accident and sickness
- employee dishonesty
- machinery breakdown
- computer/electronic equipment
- transit.

Insurance policies for large commercial risks tend to be insured under an industrial special risks policy, which are usually arranged by insurance brokers. These policies are often restricted to property with an asset value exceeding $5 million.

13-140 Fire and defined events

Fire and defined events insurance covers the insured's business premises at the situation indicated in the proposal form, eg.

> 32 Rudd Street,
>
> Small Town, Qld 4560

Cover can be arranged on either a replacement value or indemnity basis. The perils covered include:

- fire
- lightning
- explosion
- earthquake
- storm, tempest, cyclone, tornado, wind and water
- flood
- leakage of water and liquid
- riots, civil commotion or labour disturbance
- accidental damage
- vehicle, aircraft or animal impact.

Property covered includes:

- buildings, though definitions vary between insurers
- contents, including plant and machinery and other contents not specifically excluded.

Exclusions

There are many exclusions and restrictions on cover provided in the various sections of small business insurance policies, and these need to be examined carefully. However, some of the more prominent exclusions are:

- construction, erection, alteration or addition to property

- premises being empty during demolition
- jewellery, furs, bullion, precious metals or precious stones
- curios and works of art
- motor vehicles, trailers, caravans or motorcycles registered or licensed to travel on a public road
- flood (generally included in most domestic policies)
- Terrorism.

Underinsurance

Business insurance policies also contain a co-insurance clause (fully explained in Chapter 8), which is generally based on 80 per cent of:

a). where the Basis of Settlement is Reinstatement or Replacement, the reinstatement or replacement cost of the Property Insured;

b). where the Basis of Settlement is Indemnity, the value of the Property Insured, taking into account wear, tear and depreciation; on the day of commencement of the Period of Insurance.

Underinsurance will not apply if the amount of the Damage is less than 5% of the Sum Insured.

Every Situation insured is separately subject to this clause.

However, an insurer may not rely on an average provision included in a contract of general insurance unless, before the contract was entered into, the insurer clearly informed the insured in writing of the nature and effect of the provision including whether the provision is based on indemnity or on replacement value of the property that is the subject-matter of the contract.

13-150 Business interruption

Business interruption insurance indemnifies an insured for loss of gross profit after the insured property is damaged or lost following a catastrophic event and is generally only payable if the loss is triggered by a loss claimable under the fire and perils section of the policy or other stated section. It operates to cover business cash flow and in the process also protects the owner's income stream and their investment in the business.

The cover pays for ongoing costs that continue regardless of whether the business is closed or substantially affected; e.g. rent, fixed electricity, gas and water charges. It also covers additional costs incurred to minimise the effects of the closure or downturn, plus net profit and/or loss

Protecting business priorities. Emerging risks can range from increased frequency and severity of existing risks, such as climate change impacts on storms, water levels, bushfire risk; to new risks that develop through advances to technology and social or political changes, including terrorism, regulatory changes, pollution and other environmental impacts or food supply.

But the risks faced by a business will vary based on the company, it's critical operations, the risk management options available and a business owner's risk appetite.

In terms of purchasing business interruption cover, the business owner has three concurrently operating areas of interest:

*   paying ongoing business expenses to ensure the business is not wound up, and to protect the capital already invested into that venture

*   meeting personal guarantees given in connection with the business, and

*   maintaining personal income

The indemnity period. The indemnity period is the amount of time during which a business owner can claim the benefits of their business interruption insurance policy.

The indemnity period is selected by the insured depending on their needs, but can range from three months to 24 months or more. The indemnity period generally operates from the date of property damage caused by an insured event. Although some wordings extend the start date to the date when the financial results are first impacted.

Cover does not automatically cease when the building, or other damaged property, has been repaired or replaced. It will continue, subject to the indemnity period selected, until the results of the business are no longer adversely affected.

The period required will depend on the circumstances of each business but because maintenance of income is a primary consideration to owners and employees, the period selected should not be so short as to create a risk of business failure through shortage of cash-flow in the final stages of the recovery process. It is also wise to also consider any lease requirements if the business operator is a tenant, in terms of liability for rent and other outgoings.

Underinsurance

Co-insurance applies if the sum insured for gross profit at the commencement of the period of insurance is less than the sum insured by applying the rate of gross profit to 80 per cent of the annual turnover. The co-insurance calculation is arrived at by applying the Rate of Gross Profit, Revenue or Rentals (as applicable); these factors first being appropriately adjusted as provided for in the "Trend of Business" or "Other circumstances" clauses in the policy.

Policy extensions

Extensions to the cover can be obtained to cover loss of gross profit resulting from:

- damage to adjoining properties, which restricts access to the insured's premises
- damage to the property of a supplier or customer
- damage to a public utility
- the maintenance of employee wages
- closure by government authorities.

The insurer may also pay, up to certain limits, the costs involved in:

- avoidance of reduction in turnover
- temporary business premises
- loss of accounts receivable value due to records being destroyed.

The policy exclusions are the same as for the fire policy.

13-160 Burglary

Burglary insurance generally offers burglary/theft cover following forcible and violent entry to a securely locked building, or any attempt at theft, or theft by someone feloniously concealed in the building. It also covers theft following assault or armed hold-up. Generally, the sum insured is reduced when a claim is paid and not reinstated after loss payments during the period of insurance, but is fully reinstated at the commencement of the next period of insurance.

13-170 Money

Money insurance covers the loss of cash or negotiable instruments in a number of situations, such as when money is on the premises during business hours; when money in a building is held in a securely locked safe outside business hours; when money is in transit to and from the bank; and when money is contained in a night safe or automatic teller machine.

The exclusions include losses:

- that are the result of clerical error
- of money from unattended motor vehicles
- not discovered within seven working days of the occurrence
- caused by fraudulent embezzlement by the insured, its directors, partners or employees
- of money carried by professional carriers
- of money from a strongroom opened by a key left on the premises or by a combination code, details of which have been left on the premises
- caused by dishonest manipulation of any database of computer system
- of money outside the territorial limits.

13-180 General property

General property insurance generally offers cover for property, such as notebook computers, mobile phones, surveying equipment and the like, which is listed in the certificate of insurance for accidental loss or damage. These items can be covered for their replacement or their indemnity values.

This insurance also offers a restricted cover where the listed property is covered only for loss or damage resulting from a collision, overturning of a conveying vehicle, and flood.

There is generally an extensive list of exclusions that could affect the success of a claim.

13-190 Glass

Glass insurance generally covers all glass, both external and internal for its replacement value, against accidental breakage at the situation (address) noted in the proposal. Breakage is defined as a fracture extending through the entire thickness of the glass.

External glass is defined as fixed glass, perspex or plastic material used in external windows, doors, skylights and showcases at the premises. Glass includes external and internal glass for which the insured is legally liable, which means that a tenant is able to insure glass belonging to a landlord when required by the tenancy agreement to do so.

Additional benefits

Additional benefits under glass insurance include damage to window frames, tiled shop fronts, stock in trade, cost of temporary shuttering and security, signwriting, ornamentation, reflective material and alarm tapes. Generally these benefits require a separate sum insured or are limited to a maximum amount, such as $5,000, for any one event.

13-200 Employee dishonesty

Employee dishonesty insurance covers losses from within the insured's business. The usual perils include embezzlement and misappropriation of property or money by employees. Insurers attempt to limit their liability by listing a number of provisions in the cover. For example:

- the loss must be discovered not later than 12 months after the expiry of the period of insurance or termination of employment of the employee

- the sum insured for any one employee is reduced by the total of any claims payable in respect to that employee (this can be covered by paying an extra premium)

- the loss must be reported to the police for a claim to be triggered.

There are a number of specific conditions and exclusions applying to this insurance that need to be carefully considered.

13-210 Machinery breakdown

Machinery breakdown insurance covers either specified machinery, as shown in the policy schedule, or machinery that has blanket coverage against breakdown. A property insured against machinery breakdown would be covered against breakdown of electrical, electronic and mechanical machinery, including their interconnecting cabling and piping and/or boilers and pressure vessels.

Basis of settlement

The insurer will choose to either repair or replace the broken down equipment. Some policies cover electronic equipment, such as electronic scales and cash registers, for its indemnity value only.

Additional benefits

Additional benefits may include:

- hire of temporary machinery and expediting costs

- the reasonable cost of replacing insulating oil and refrigeration gas or liquid

- the automatic cover of additional machinery acquired during the period of insurance, usually subject to conditions.

Optional benefits

Optional benefits can be included by the payment of an extra premium, covering deterioration of stock, limited to a specific sum insured, including seasonal increases.

Machinery breakdown insurance includes a number of exclusions such as wear and tear; losses covered by fire; replacement of belts, ropes, moulds, dies; and the costs associated with submersible pumps.

13-220 Computer/electronic equipment

This section covers accidental loss or damage to the property insured. The policy will repair or replace the property with new or equivalent makes and models if it is uneconomical to repair the equipment and it is less than six years old. Otherwise the replacement property will be depreciated by 10 per cent per annum for each year in excess of six years up to a maximum depreciation of 70 per cent.

Additional benefits

Additional benefits include:

- removal of debris

- temporary removal — damage to the property while it is temporarily removed from the premises

- additional computer/electronic equipment — automatically covered up to a maximum percentage of the sum insured, such as 25 per cent.

Optional benefits

Optional benefits include:

- restoration of data — covered to the sum specified by the insured
- increased cost of working — covering the cost actually incurred by the insured, which is above the normal expenses that would have been incurred.

There are a number of exclusions applicable to this section and conditions such as adequate maintenance of the equipment and co-insurance.

13-230 Transit

Transit insurance provides cover for items such as whitegoods and freight being transported from one place to another. Generally, the cover provided will be either 'all-risks' or damage caused by 'fire, flood, collision and overturning and theft' with the 'all risks cover' being the most expensive. Cover is generally extended to include damage arising during the loading and unloading of goods and the removal of debris following a loss.

If a business carries high-value goods such as cigarettes, machinery or the like, it is best to obtain cover from a specialist insurer under a declaration policy.

Exclusions

There are a large number of exclusions in transit cover, including:

- damage caused by insufficient or unsuitable packing or preparation of the property insured
- damage or expenses caused by inherent vice or the nature of the property insured
- loss or damage caused by the unseaworthiness of the vessel or craft, or unfitness of any other conveyance, container or lift van
- loss through capture, seizure, arrest, restraint or detainment (piracy excepted)
- the conveyance being driven by any person whose facilities are impaired by any drug or intoxicating liquid
- hazardous goods.

The notable exclusion is that of hazardous goods, which excludes cover if hazardous goods such as hairspray, paint and inflammable liquids are carried as part of the load. Some companies will include hazardous goods as an extension to the policy for an extra premium, but subject to restrictions.

13-240 Terrorism insurance coverage

The terrorist attack on the World Trade Center in New York on 11 September 2001 caused a major upheaval in the insurance industry that affected most insurers. Because the potential scale of terrorist attacks could not be accurately assessed, reinsurers globally sought to exclude terrorism coverage from their property and business interruption policies. As a result, some countries, including Australia, established 'pools' where funds could be collected to help cover the costs stemming from a future terror attack.

The scheme covers insurance for loss of or damage to commercial property that is owned by the insured, insurance for business interruption arising from loss of or damage to or inability to use eligible property, and insurance for liability of the insured arising from ownership or occupation of eligible property. Private residential property is not included in the scheme. Risk cover is for any declared terrorist incident, except events involving damage from nuclear causes.

The Federal Government established the Australian Reinsurance Pool Corporation (ARPC) which is a statutory corporation established under the Terrorism Insurance Act 2003 (Cth) (TI Act) to offer reinsurance for terrorism risk in Australia. Under the TI Act the Commonwealth provides a guarantee of $10 billion to back ARPC's liabilities.

During 2017-18, ARPC had funds available for claims of $13.4 billion. This capacity was provided through a combination of ARPC net assets, $3.065 billion of retrocession reinsurance purchased from 68 global reinsurers and the $10 billion Commonwealth guarantee. This resulted in cover being provided to 235 insurer customers, totalling approximately $3.7 trillion sum insured.

The terrorism reinsurance scheme is an excess of loss scheme with reinsurance premiums are set at 12 per cent, 4 per cent and 2 per cent of underlying premiums for property and business interruption insurance for CBD, urban and other properties, respectively. ARPC can only charge premiums on those sections of an insurance policy that are eligible.

A claim on the scheme may be made for eligible terrorism losses arising from any declared terrorist incident covered by an eligible insurance contract where the insurer has a reinsurance agreement with the ARPC. The scheme will not be triggered unless the Minister who has administrative responsibility for the Act declares that a terrorist incident has occurred for the purpose of the Act.

There has been one declared terrorist incident in the history of the scheme – the siege incident at the Lindt Café, Martin Place, Sydney in December 2014. The ARPC's claims system recorded 92 claims totalling $2.3 million of insured claims from 20 insurers as a result of the Lindt Café siege. Treasury understands the insured losses were for minor property damage and business interruption. As such, there has been no call on the Commonwealth guarantee in the history of the scheme.

The scheme was established as an interim measure and is only intended to operate while terrorism cover is unavailable commercially on reasonable terms. The TI Act requires that the scheme is reviewed every three years and last reviewed in 2018 when it was recommended that the arrangement continue for another three years, subject to review as stipulated in the TI Act.

At a glance

- Small business insurance is offered under bundled business insurance policies.
- Packaged policies offer economies, convenience and one review date.
- The various covers are contained in individual sections that have their own terms, conditions and exclusions.
- Business policies tend to offer wider cover than was available under traditional stand-alone policies.
- Business policies allow business owners to more easily manage risk through insurance.

GENERAL INSURANCE CODE OF PRACTICE

13-250 History of the Code

The first General Insurance Code was developed by the Insurance Council of Australia in 1994 in anticipation of the legislative changes to the *Insurance Act 1973* (Cth), which required all authorised general insurers to adopt an approved code of practice. The objective was to raise the service standards offered by the general insurance industry. It was intended that over the years the Code would develop and be modified as the insurance environment changed. The Code was reviewed independently in 1998, and most of the recommendations of the review were adopted in the new Code, which was approved by ASIC on 28 July 2000.

Since then the regulatory environment has changed with the introduction of the FSR Act. Additionally, consumers now expect more and better service from their insurers. As a result, a new voluntary Code of Practice was developed by the industry, which became fully operational on 18 July 2006. The objectives of this Code were to set minimum service and training standards to complement the new regulatory system that now governs Australia's financial services sector. This Code is a world first in the insurance industry, as it addresses the needs of both individual consumers and business customers. The Code is reviewed every three years with the last review being conducted in February 2014, with a new Code: General Insurance Code of Practice 2014 applying from 1 July 2014. This Code replaces all previous Codes.

In addition to service standards, the Code sets out timeframes for insurers to respond to claims, complaints and requests for information from customers. The Code covers many aspects of a customer's relationship with their insurer, from buying insurance to making a claim, to providing options to those experiencing financial hardship, to the process for those who wish to make a complaint.

The Code covers all general insurance products except reinsurance, workers' compensation, marine insurance, medical indemnity insurance, compulsory third party insurance (even if driver protection cover is linked to it), and life and health insurance products issued by life insurers or registered health insurers.

A dispute can be lodged by an individual, partnership, trustee, club or association. If the entity lodging a dispute (the applicant) carries on a business, the business must be a small business, which is defined by the Australian Financial Complaints Authority (AFCA) as an organisation of less than 100 employees.

As an external complaints authority AFCA is able to resolve a wide range of disputes that small business have with their financial services providers. Time limits within which complaints must be provided and monetary compensation limits apply. Table 13.1 provides details of monetary limits applying in respect to claims involving Life Insurance Policy or a General Insurance Policy. Information regarding compensation limits applying to other financial complaints, such as claims arising from a credit facility can be found on the AFCA web site.

Table 13.1: AFCA compensation limits

Row	Type of claim	Compensation amount limit per claim	Monetary restriction on AFCA's jurisdiction
1.	**Income Stream Insurance** Claim on a Life Insurance Policy or a General Insurance Policy dealing with income stream risk or about such a contract. If the claim is in excess of this monthly limit, the monthly limit will apply unless: • the total amount payable under the policy can be calculated with certainty by reference to the expiry date of the policy and/or age of the insured: and • that total amount is less than the amount specified in row 4. If this is the case, then the limit will be the amount in row 4.	$13,400 per month	Amount claimed by Complainant must not exceed $1 million
2.	**General Insurance Broking** Claim against a General Insurance Broker except where the claim solely concerns its conduct in relation to a Life Insurance Policy (in which case row 1 to 4 applies, as the case may be)	$250,000	The amount claimed by Complainant must not exceed $1 million
3.	**Uninsured Motor Vehicle** Claim under another person's Motor Vehicle Insurance Policy for property damage to an Uninsured Motor Vehicle caused by a driver of the insured motor vehicle	$15,000	Amount claimed by Complainant must not exceed $1 million

4.	**All other claims (excluding Superannuation Complaints)** In all other circumstances by a Complainant (whether or not a Small Business or Primary Producer)	$500,000	Amount claimed by Complainant must not exceed $1 million
5.	**Claim for indirect financial loss**	$5,000	Not applicable
6.	**Claim for non-financial loss**	$5,000	Not applicable

Source: AFCA 2014

In relation to superannuation products, AFCA is able to resolve a number of disputes subject to section 1055 of the Corporations Act 2001. Additionally, there is no monetary limit on the remedies .

13-245 Cyber insurance

Technology, social media and transactions over the Internet play key roles in how most organizations conduct business and reach out to prospective customers today. Those vehicles also serve as gateways to cyberattacks. Cyber-attacks are becoming more common and likely to cause severe losses to small and large business. In addition, businesses have a responsibility to protect sensitive customer and employee information. A cyber-attack can result in severe financial loss and damage to a firm's reputation. Therefore, small business proprietors have a need to include cyber protection insurance in their risk management plan.

What is cyber insurance?

Cyber insurance is an insurance product used to protect businesses and individual users from Internet-based risks, and more generally from risks relating to information technology infrastructure and activities. Risks of this nature are typically excluded from traditional commercial general liability policies or at least are not specifically defined in traditional insurance products. As well as directly improving security, cyber-insurance is enormously beneficial in the event of a large-scale security breach. Insurance provides a smooth funding mechanism for recovery from major losses, helping businesses to return to normal and reducing the need for government assistance.

What it covers

Cyber insurance typically covers expenses related to first parties as well as claims by third parties. There are many cyber insurance policies available in the insurance market and coverage can vary between these policies so a prospective customer needs to be sure that the policy will cover their needs. The following is a general overview of the types of coverages that are available:

First Party Coverages

Cyber liability policies typically include various property and crime coverages. These policies also cover certain costs, such as notification expenses and are often subject to a deductible. Cyber liability policies can provide cover for:

- **Loss or Damage to Electronic Data** - Many policies cover losses caused by damage, theft, disruption or corruption of a firm's electronic data. These policies also cover damage or theft of data stored on a computer system that belongs to someone else. For a loss to be covered, it must result from a covered peril such as a hacker attack, a virus, or a denial of service attack. The policy generally covers the costs to restore or recover lost data. It may also cover the cost of outside experts or consultants hired to preserve or reconstruct data.

- **Loss of Income or Extra Expenses** - Many policies cover income lost and extra expenses incurred to avoid or minimize a shutdown of a business after the computer system fails due a covered peril. The perils covered may be the same as those covered under Damage to Electronic Data. The loss of income and extra expense coverages afforded under a cyber liability policy differ from those provided under a commercial property policy. Cyber policies cover income losses and extra expenses that result from an interruption of a computer system by a covered peril. In contrast, property policies cover income losses and extra expenses that result from an interruption in business operations caused by physical damage to covered property, which does not include electronic data.

- **Cyber Extortion Losse**s - Cyber extortion coverage applies when a hacker or a cyber thief breaks into a computer system and threatens to commit a nefarious act. For instance, a hacker may threaten to damage data, introduce a virus, or shut down a computer system unless they are paid a sum of money. The perpetrator may also subject the computer system to a denial of service attack or threaten to release confidential data unless they are paid the sum demanded. Extortion coverage typically applies to expenses incurred (with the insurer's consent) to respond to an extortion demand, as well as the money paid to the extortionist.

- **Notification Costs** - Policies may cover the cost of notifying parties affected by the data breach by government statutes or regulations. They may also include the cost of hiring a solicitor to assess the firm's obligations under applicable laws and regulations. Some policies cover the cost of providing credit monitoring services for those affected by the breach. Some also cover the cost of setting up and operating a call center.

- **Damage to Your Reputation** - A data breach can severely damage a firm's reputation. Thus, some policies cover the costs incurred for marketing and public relations to protect a company's reputation following a data breach. This coverage may be referred to as Crisis Management.

Third-Party Liability Coverages

Most cyber policies include more than one type of liability coverage. These coverages apply to damages or settlements that result from covered claims. They also cover the cost of defending against such claims. Note that defense costs may reduce the limit of insurance. Virtually all cyber liability policies are claims-made (i.e., claims made and notified during the policy period – see section 13-120). Some third-party coverages may be subject to retention. Third party liability coverages can include:

- **Network Security Liability** - Network security liability insurance covers legal action against a company due to a data breach or to the inability of others to access data on a computer system. Coverage may apply if the data breach or inability to access the system is due to a denial of service attack, a virus, malware or unauthorized access and use of the system by a hacker or rogue employee. Policies may cover legal action alleging that the company failed to adequately protect data belonging to customers, clients, employees or other parties.

- **Network Privacy Liability** - Network privacy liability insurance covers legal action based on allegations that the company failed to properly protect sensitive data stored on the computer system. The data may belong to customers, clients and other parties. Some policies cover liability arising from the release of private data belonging to the company's employees.

- **Electronic Media Liability** - Electronic media liability insurance covers legal action for acts like libel, slander, defamation, copyright infringement, invasion of privacy or domain name infringement. Generally, these acts are covered only if they result from publication of electronic data on the Internet.

- **Errors and Omissions Liability** - Some cyber liability policies include coverage for errors or omissions that arise out of professional services the insured provides. For example, a policy purchased by a software developer covers claims arising out of coding mistakes and other errors or omissions that arise out of the company's software services. Likewise, a policy purchased by an architect covers claims alleging design flaws, faulty drawings, and other errors.

Other Coverages

Other coverages that may be available under a cyber liability policy include various crime coverages such as computer fraud, funds transfer fraud, and cyber terrorism (acts of violence committed for political purposes). Some insurers have developed cyber liability policies tailored to specific industries. For example, one policy may be designed for businesses in the healthcare industry while another policy is intended for financial institutions.

Common exclusions

- Patent, software and copyright infringement: Patents, software, and copyright are covered by intellectual property insurance policy, and not by a cyber policy.

- Wars and invasions

- Failure in security measures: When an organization claims on the cyber risk insurance policy, it will be handed a number of questions regarding the steps taken to safeguard the data. If the Insurer finds that the firm has failed to implement all the security measures, the claim will be denied

- Bodily injury and damage: Some policies may cover the emotional distress and anguish caused by such events

- Loss of electronic device: When an employee loses a company-issued portable electronic device, the coverage for this item is excluded from the insurance

- Vicarious liability: When an organization passes the data to a third-party vendor, and the breach occurs at the vendor's system, the claim may be denied

- Government Entity or Public Authority: Any recommendations or orders from government authority or public authority are generally excluded

- Specific Network Interruption Condition: If data is lost due to any technical or network interruptions, it may be excluded

Illustrated example 13.5 shows the operation of a cyber insurance policy following the actions of a rogue employee.

Illustrated example 13.5

Yourwardrobe, an online shopping website had been in online business since past 5 years. It had a good amount of traffic on its website daily. Revenue figures showed year-on-year growth for this online firm.

However, an inside rogue employee got access to personal information of thousands of customers including their address and credit card details. Yourwardrobe had obtained a cyber risk insurance policy which protected it against:

• The costs of notifying the thousands of customers whose data had been stolen.

• The costs of credit monitoring for the affected customers. This ensured that they suffered minimal losses after the information theft.

• The costs of representing and defending the online business against the legal action that was brought against them.

Due to the security breach of the website, the sales of this online shopping website slumped in the coming months. The online business claimed for the loss due to reduced sales. However, the claim was denied by the insurer, stating that loss of future revenue is not covered in cyber risk insurance policy.

In addition, illustrated example 13.6 highlights the importance of keeping security systems updated .

Illustrated example 13.6

A car-component manufacturing company had obtained a Cyber risk insurance policy to safeguard itself against cyber-crimes and malware. Since the business was mostly into manufacturing segment, management paid less importance to software updates. Because of which the system had become outdated.

One day, an employee of this manufacturing company clicked on a malicious link in an email. A malware was downloaded onto the company server, encrypting all information. The company telephoned its insurance provider for assistance. When the IT forensic investigators came to assess the problem, they found that the system was poorly maintained with no malware protection. This resulted in the claim being denied by the insurance company.

13-260 The Code

The General Insurance Code of Practice (the Code) comprises 15 parts. The first part, the introduction, sets out the objectives of the Code which are "We have entered into this voluntary Code with the Insurance Council of Australia (ICA). This Code commits us to uphold minimum standards when providing services covered by this Code". The remaining sections explain the standards that apply to those sections, but this text will address the following sections:

- buying insurance
- making a claim
- responding to catastrophes and disasters
- providing information to customers
- handling complaints
- monitoring and enforcing the Code.

Buying insurance

This section applies to Retail Insurance only. It promises that the sales process and the services provided will be conducted in an efficient, honest, fair and transparent manner.

The Code promises that all communications by the company and its authorised representatives will be in plain language and promises to only use, ask for and rely on information and documents relevant to their decision in assessing an application for insurance. If the policy is subsequently cancelled, a refund will be sent within 15 business days.

The Code also promises that if errors are detected or if the company is advised of errors or mistakes in the application then they will be immediately corrected and not relied on in assessing the application.

Making a claim

This part of the Code applies to Retail Insurance only. Claims handling will be conducted in an honest, fair, transparent and timely manner and only relevant information will be asked for and relied on when assessing the claim. If mistakes or errors are identified by the company you claimant, then will be immediately corrected.

Sections 7.7 applies to financial hardship experienced by clients.

- The company will fast-track the assessment and decision process and in some cases make an advance payment to alleviate hardship within five days of the claimant demonstrating financial hardship.

Repair workmanship and materials

The company will accept responsibility for the quality of workmanship and materials if they have authorised the repairer.

Financial hardship

Section 8.1 states that should an individual Insured or third party beneficiary owe the company money under an insurance policy that has been issued, or if the company is seeking recovery for damage or loss caused by the insured to another insured or third party beneficiary covered under an insurance policy and the insured is experiencing financial hardship then the insured can apply for assistance. This section makes it clear that the financial hardship provisions do not apply to the payment of insurance premiums.

Responding to catastrophes and disasters

Section 9 of the Code requires companies to promise to respond in a fast, professional and practical manner. This section also stipulates that the claimant can request a review of the claim within 12 months of the catastrophe or disaster.

Handling complaints

Section 6 of the Code details how companies must handle disputes and mistakes in a transparent and efficient manner and in a specified time and have internal and external dispute resolution facilities.

With regard to internal dispute resolution, insurers are required to respond to complaints within 15 business days of a complaint but this can be extended by agreement to a reasonable time frame if further investigation is required. If agreement cannot be reached, the complaint will be treated as a dispute and the complaint can be reviewed by another employee.

The company must respond to the dispute within 15 business days, provided all the necessary information has been received, and keep the claimant informed about the progress of the dispute within the 15 business day timeframe. If the complaint is not resolved to the claimant's satisfaction within 45 days after receiving the complaint, the claimant can refer their complaint to AFCA.

The determinations made by AFCA are binding on the insurance company, but not on the claimant, who is free to pursue their own legal action.

Monitoring and enforcing the Code

Section 13 of the Code stipulates that the Code will be monitored by he Code Governance Committee (CGS). The companies pledge to have appropriate systems and processes in place to enable the CGC to monitor compliance with this Code; to prepare an annual return to the CGC on their compliance with the Code and have a governance process in place to report on our compliance with this Code to their Board of Directors or executive management.

If a company identifies a significant breach of the Code by their employees or authorised representatives they will report the breach to CGC within 10 business days.

Should the company fail to correct a Code breach then CGC is empowered to impose sanctions on the company.

Objectives of the Code

The objectives are listed in section 2.1 of the Code and commits participating companies to:

- promote better and more informed relations between insurers and customers
- improve consumer confidence
- provide better mechanisms for better complaints resolution and disputes
- provide higher standards of customer service.

Adoption of the Code

All members of the insurance industry are encouraged to adopt the Code, although its adoption is not compulsory. However, members of the Insurance Council of Australia, which represent 90 per cent of the general insurance market, are required to adopt the Code.

The Code is intended to be a 'living Code', which is reviewed every three years through consultation with AFCA, CGC, the Insurance Council of Australia, insurers, consumers and business representatives. Any subsequent amendments to the Code will be subject to the approval of ASIC.

13-270   Study questions

13.1   List three events that are not covered under most general householders insurance policies.

13.2   Briefly describe the cover provided by the three principal motor vehicle insurance policies.

13.3   List the types of insurance that are described as 'prescribed contracts'.

13.4   A financial adviser gave advice on a general insurance product to manage risk, which was later found to be incorrect. Explain the options open to an insured to seek redress.

13.5   A patient suffers extensive and continuous pain from the negligent action of his/her doctor. Assuming that the doctor has public liability insurance, discuss whether this insurance will give protection him from any action taken by the patient.

13.6   At any one time, a business may be holding substantial inventories of raw materials and finished products. Explain whether the business will be sufficiently covered under a standard commercial fire policy.

13.7   An insured is away on a holiday when a wild storm hits his/her suburb. The television antenna is blown down and wrecked when it lands on the side fence. Hail comes at such an angle that it breaks all the windows on one side of the house, causing rainwater to enter and damage the carpet and walls. Before the insured arrives home to survey the damage, a thief enters through one of the broken windows and steals the DVD recorder and television and some expensive jewellery. Discuss which of the above items will be covered by the householders insurance policy.

13.8 An insured owns an old car that is not maintained very well. On a rainy night the insured skids on the wet road and write the car off when it hits a lamp post. The insurance company declines the claim because it became apparent that all four tyres were bald and the car registration had expired. Discuss whether the insurance company's decision to reject the claim was justified.

13.9 Warren is an insurance agent who has taken out a professional indemnity policy to cover his activities as an insurance adviser — ie, selling and advising on insurance products. While reviewing the insurance for one of his business clients, he recommends that his client insure some machinery for $10,000, which the client does. This machinery is destroyed by fire and the insurance company pays the sum insured of $10,000, but the client finds that the machine will actually cost $20,000 to replace. Discuss the insurance agent's potential legal liability and whether he is covered by his professional indemnity policy.

13.10 Explain the importance of correctly describing the names of those to be insured in a general insurance policy and involving them in the completion of the proposal form.

13-280 References and further reading

References

Articles and Books

Hardman, P 2007, 'Personal lines insurance: the looming challenges', *Australian and New Zealand Institute of Insurance and finance journal,* vol 30, no 3, June/July 2007, pp 24–25.

Releases

Insurance Council of Australia, General Insurance Code of Practice, Available at *codeofpractice.com.au*

Insurance Ombudsman Service 2007, *IOS terms of reference*, 1 June, IOS, p. 2. Available at *insuranceombudsman.com.au*

Reports

Accident Compensation Corporation (ACC) 2006, *ACC injury statistics 2006*, 1st edn. Available at *acc.goz.nz*

Accident Compensation Corporation Annual Report 2012. Available at *acc.co.nz*

Australian Competition and Consumer Commission, *General Insurance Enquiries and Complaints Scheme (GIECS)*. Available at *accc.gov.au*

Legislation

Insurance Contracts Act 1984

Insurance Contracts Regulations 1985

Terrorism Insurance Act 2003

Further reading

Books

Berwick, G 2007, *The executive's guide to insurance and risk management,* 2nd edn, Fast Books, Sydney.

Latimer, P 2013, *Australian business law,* 32nd edn, CCH Australia, Sydney.

Websites

Financial Ombudsman Service (FOS): *fos.org.au*

National Insurance Brokers Association, niba.com.au.

CHAPTER 14

MANDATED AND HEALTH INSURANCE

14-000 Introduction

This chapter discusses the major mandated insurance programs available in Australia. The programs discussed include social security, compulsory third party insurance, workers compensation and Medicare. Private health insurance and government initiatives to encourage greater participation are also examined.

SOCIAL SECURITY

14-010 Introduction

Social security benefits can play an important part in private risk management. They are designed to provide a 'safety net' by helping people become self-sufficient and support those in need. Many people who are unemployed or unemployable, or are retired with limited assets, rely on government assistance. This section outlines the basic benefits available in Australia and includes a brief discussion of benefits available for the unemployed and for people who are ill, injured or disabled. Information about other benefits and allowances can be obtained from the websites listed at the end of this chapter. Information was current as at 1 July 2019.

14-020 Australian social security

Social security in Australia is provided by Centrelink, which is an Australian government statutory agency responsible to the Minister of Human Services. Centrelink was established to provide Australian government service arrangements under the *Commonwealth Services Delivery Agency Act 1997* (Cth) (the CSDA Act). The CSDA Act was amended by the *Human Services Legislation Amendment Act 2005* (Cth), which commenced on 1 October 2005. Centrelink is now virtually the sole provider of social security programs. Table 14.1 provides a list of the main social security benefits available and gives a brief description of the purpose of each benefit.

Table 14.1: Centrelink benefits

Benefit type	Purpose of benefit/beneficiary
For people who are retired:	
Age pension	Provides a minimum level of income to elderly people who have reached pension age and are retired
Pension bonus scheme	Provides a tax-free lump sum as an incentive to the elderly to defer claiming the age pension and stay in the workforce if registered for the scheme before 1 July 2014. Participants may be eligible for the Commonwealth Seniors Health Benefit Card. The scheme is closed to new entrants
Widow allowance	Paid to a woman born before 1 July 1955 who is not a member of a couple, and who is widowed, divorced or separated since turning age 40 and meet resident and work test rules
For people who are ill, injured or disabled:	
Disability support pension	Provides a minimum level of support to a person who is over 16 years old and under pension age who cannot work because of a physical, intellectual or psychiatric impairment
Sickness allowance	Provides assistance to a person aged 21 and over but under age pension age who is temporarily unable to work or study because of sickness, injury or disability
Mobility allowance	Paid to a person aged 16 or over who have a disability that prevents him/her from using public transport without substantial assistance
Bereavement allowance	Paid to a recently widowed person for up to 14 weeks from the date of death of their partner. The payment is subject to income and asset tests

Benefit type	Purpose of benefit/beneficiary
For people raising children:	
Family tax benefit Part A	Paid to parents and guardians, including foster parents and grandparents, with dependent children who are either 0-15 or 16-19 and meet the study requirements, to help with the cost of raising children
Family tax benefit Part B	Paid to a single-income family or sole parent to help support a child under 13 (or up to 18 if he/she is a full-time student) who does not receive youth allowance
Child-care subsidy	Provides financial assistance for child-care fees for a child 13 or younger, or 14 to 18 with a disability attending an approved child care service and not attending secondary school. All families may claim the minimum benefit. Residency rules do apply
Parenting payment	Paid to a parent, grandparent or foster carer who is single and has a qualifying child under age 8 or, who is partnered with a qualifying child under age 6
For people who are unemployed:	
Newstart allowance	Paid to an unemployed individual aged 22 or over who is available for work, actively looking for work
Youth allowance	Paid to an individual aged 16 up to 25 who is studying or undertaking a full-time Australian apprenticeship or is looking for work full time or undertaking any other approved activity.

Benefit type	Purpose of benefit/beneficiary
People caring for others:	
Carer payment	Paid to a person who provides constant care for one or more people; for a person who has defined care needs and who needs care for an extended period. The person being cared for must receive social security income support or meet the special care receiver income and assets limits
Carer allowance	Paid to a person who provides daily care for either an adult aged 16 years and over or a child under 16 years who is frail, chronically ill or disabled and being nursed at home or in hospital
Double orphan pension	Paid to a person who has the care and control of a child under age 16 or a full-time student aged 16 to 19 who does not receive a youth allowance; where the child's parents or adoptive parents have both died; or one parent is dead and the other is serving a long-term prison sentence or is on remand for an offence punishable by long-term imprisonment, or lives in a psychiatric institution or nursing home on a long-term basis, or their whereabouts is unknown

Benefit type	Purpose of benefit/beneficiary
For students:	
Youth allowance	Paid to a full-time students age 16 and older who is studying in an approved course at an approved institution, or a full-time Australian apprentice. Also available to 16-year-olds who have left school and are living independently
Austudy	Paid to a student aged 25 years or over who is studying in an approved full-time course or undertaking a full-time Australian apprenticeship
Pensioner education supplement	Paid to a full time student who is studying full time and is receiving an income support payment because he/she is disabled, a sole parent or carer
Abstudy	Paid to Aboriginal and Torres Straight Islanders who are at least 14 years of age at 1 January of the year of study and are studying an approved course at an approved education institution. Also applies to apprenticeships, traineeships or trainee apprenticeships
Assistance for isolated children (AIC) scheme	Paid to the families of full-time primary and secondary students under age 19 who are isolated from an appropriate state school; where the student boards away from home or lives at home and is enrolled at an approved distance education institution

Source: Department of Human Services (2019)

The Australian government pays a range of welfare benefits to people, as shown in table 14.1. This section, however, discusses only the benefits provided to those who are ill, injured or disabled. Full details of the other benefits and eligibility can be found on the Centrelink's website.

Disability support pension

The disability support pension (DSP) provides a level of income for people who have an illness, injury or disability and who:

- are aged 16 or over and under age pension age, and are unable to work or undertake vocational training for work of at least 15 hours per week within two years
- are permanently blind, or

- participate in the Supported Wage System.

The maximum rate of disability support pension for people under age 21 with no children, under age 21 with children, and over 21, are shown in table 14.2.

Table 14.2: Maximum rate of disability support pension, as at 20 March 2019

Status	Pension rate per fortnight*
Single, under 18, at home	$379.00
Single, under 18, independent	$585.00
Single, 18–20 years, at home	$429.60
Single, 18–20 years, independent	$585.00
Member of a couple, 18–20 years	$585.00
Over 21, or under 21 with children	
Single	$926.20
Couple	$698.10 (each person)
Couple separated by ill health	$926.20 (each person)

Note (1): Payment rates for those under 21 without children are updated 1 January each year.

Note (2): Payment rates for those 21 years of age and over or under 21 years of age with children.

* Payments are taxable and subject to income and assets tests.

* Pharmaceutical allowance may also apply.

Source: Department of Human Services (2019b)

These payments are subject to the income test and assets test, but the DSP is not taxable where the person is under the age pension age. Also, the person must have lived in Australia as an Australian resident for a total of 10 years, or the disability must have occurred while the person was an Australian resident. In addition, the following benefits may be available:

- a one-off employment entry payment; education entry payment
- pensioner education supplement (including a fares allowance)
- an advance payment of disability support; pharmaceutical allowance
- rent assistance

- remote area allowance
- telephone allowance
- utilities allowance
- pensioner concession card where a number of different benefits apply
- school kids bonus.

Sickness allowance

The sickness allowance provides assistance for people who are currently employed but are temporarily unable to work owing to a medical condition, but have work to return to. The commencement date of payment is affected by the payment of sick leave, annual leave and other leave payments made by an employer. Self-employed people may receive a sickness allowance if they intend to resume their employment when they are fit to do so. The benefit may also be available to full-time students.

Payment is made for the period of incapacity shown on each medical certificate up to a maximum of 13 weeks per certificate. The payment is subject to income and assets tests, and the payments are taxable. The payment rates are shown in table 14.3.

Table 14.3: Sickness allowance payment rates, as at 20 March 2019

Status	Allowance rate per fortnight
Single, aged 22 years or older but under age pension age, with no children	$555.70
Single, aged 22 years or older but under age pension age, with dependent children	$601.10
Single, aged 60 years or older but under age pension age, after 9 continuous months of payment	$601.10
Partnered	$501.70 (each person)

* Pharmaceutical allowance may also be paid.

Note: Payment rates are updated 20 March and 20 September each year

Source: Department of Human Services (2019c)

Additional benefits that may be payable include:

- pharmaceutical allowance

- rent assistance
- remote area allowance
- telephone allowance
- health care card.

Mobility allowance

A mobility allowance may be payable to a person who is aged 16 or older, who has a disability that prevents them from using public transport without substantial assistance, and who is undertaking paid or voluntary work or vocational training for a minimum of 32 hours every four weeks.

Since 1 July 2006, two rates of mobility allowance apply — the standard rate of $97.90 per fortnight and a higher rate of $136.90 per fortnight. A lump sum equal to 26 weeks' allowance may be paid once a year. The higher rate is payable if the person is receiving the disability support pension, Newstart allowance or youth allowance as a job seeker, is working 15 hours per week or is looking for work with an employment services provider (Human Services 2019d).

Payments are not subject to income or assets tests and are not taxable.

Bereavement payment and allowance

This benefit pays a lump sum or short term payment when your partner, child or the person you were caring for has died. Centrelink has two methods of compensating partners or families following a person's death. The first option is a lump-sum payment called a bereavement payment. To be eligible, the person who dies must have been one of the following:

- a pensioner
- a person being cared for by someone receiving a carer payment
- a long-term allowance recipient (more than 12 months)
- a child of a family who receives or qualifies for a family tax benefit.

For a bereaved partner, the lump-sum payment is made up of seven payments (14 weeks) of the amount paid to the couple if the deceased partner had not died minus the single rate paid to the remaining partner. When a single pensioner dies, the estate receives one extra payment of their pension or allowance.

The second option is the payment of a bereavement allowance for up to 14 weeks from the date of death of the partner, which can be extended if the widow is pregnant. This allowance is payable to people not eligible for widow B pension, parenting payment, service pension or the war widows' pension. The maximum rate of bereavement allowance is $843.60 per fortnight, which excludes a pension supplement of $68.50 single and $51.60 each for a couple. Rent assistance may also be payable. The bereavement allowance is taxable and subject to income and assets tests (Department of Human Services 2019e).

To qualify for the bereavement allowance, the widow or widower must have been living with the partner immediately before the partner's death and not be re-partnered, and must not have any children.

14-030 Waiting periods

A range of different waiting periods apply to income support payments benefits. These waiting periods include:

- ordinary waiting period
- liquid assets waiting period
- income maintenance period
- seasonal workers preclusion period
- newly arrived residents.

If more than one waiting period applies, the benefit is not payable until all the waiting periods have ended. Most waiting periods are served concurrently, with the exception of the liquid assets waiting period, which is served before the ordinary waiting period. Therefore, a person may have a 13-week liquid assets waiting period but will have to wait 14 weeks, as they will have to serve the additional ordinary waiting period of one week after serving the 13 week period.

Ordinary waiting period

The Newstart and sickness allowance have an ordinary waiting period of one week. However, the waiting period can be waived if the person is returning to the benefit within 13 weeks of having received it previously or is in severe financial hardship.

Liquid assets waiting period

A person applying for Newstart, Austudy, youth or sickness allowance may have a liquid assets waiting period applied if they have liquid assets above a specified amount. Liquid assets include cash, term deposits, bank accounts and other investments that can easily be converted into cash.

The liquid assets waiting period is between 1 and 13 weeks. It applies if the applicant has funds equal to or more than:

- $5,500 for a single person with no dependents

- $11,000 if the person has a partner or single with dependents

Liquid assets are any funds readily available to the applicant or the applicant's partner. This includes money your employer owes the applicant. The Department of Human Services determines the liquid assets waiting period based on the applicant's personal situation and the amount of funds the applicant has. A sample of the waiting periods applying to different levels of liquid assets is shown in table 14.4.

Table 14.4: Liquid assets waiting periods

Waiting period (weeks)	Partner or single – with dependants and liquid assets of	single with no dependants with liquid assets of
Nil	$0 - $10,999	$0 - $5,499
1	$11,000 - $11,999	$5,500 - $5,999
2	$12,000 - $12,999	$6,000 - $6,499
9	$19,000 - $19,999	$9,500 - $9,999
13	$23,000 or more	$11,500 or more

Source: Department of Human Services (2019e)

The liquid assets waiting period may be waived if the applicant is experiencing severe financial hardship because of unavoidable or reasonable expenses. The may also be exempt if:

- The applicant or his/her partner have been subject to a liquid assets waiting period that started within the last 12 months

- transfer from one payment to another within a 14 day period

- have self-served this waiting period before claiming

- qualified for Newstart Allowance after getting another payment

- are in a rehabilitation program with a Disability Management Service Provider

- are doing a Stream C activity with your employment services provider

- are doing an activity equivalent to a rehabilitation program or Stream C as part of the Community Development Program

Income maintenance period

An income maintenance period is applied when a person applies for a social security payment and has received a payment on the cessation of work. These entitlements are treated as income from the date of payment and include:

- unused annual leave

- unused long service leave

- unused sick leave

- redundancy payments.

They exclude:

- eligible termination payments

- tax-free amounts on bona fide redundancy payments.

An income maintenance period may apply if the applicant is claiming or getting any of these payments:

- Newstart Allowance

- Partner Allowance

- Parenting Payment

- Sickness Allowance

- Youth Allowance

- Widow Allowance

- Farm Household Allowance.

It may also apply to:

- Austudy

- Disability Support Pension, except if you're permanently blind.

For example, a 10-week redundancy payment would result in a 10-week income maintenance period from the date the applicant or his/her partner received the redundancy payment. How the Income Maintenance Period (IMP)works is shown in the following illustrated example.

Illustrated example 14.1

Michael has been made redundant from a company and on the day of leaving he receives a redundancy payment consisting of:

- 5 weeks annual leave

- 10.5 weeks long service leave

- $25,500 gratuity payment (also known as a 'golden handshake'), and

- 4 weeks payment in lieu of notice.

Michael's IMP will be calculated as follows:

- 5 weeks annual leave = 5 weeks IMP

- 10.5 weeks long service leave = 10.5 weeks IMP

- $25,500/$1,000 (Michael's gross weekly income) = 25.5 weeks rounded down to 25 weeks IMP, and

- 4 weeks payment in lieu of notice = 4 weeks IMP.

The total IMP period will be 44.5 weeks. Michael's total redundancy payment will be apportioned as ordinary income over this 44.5 week period and assessed under the applicable income

Seasonal workers preclusion period

If an individual or their partner has finished doing seasonal, contract or casual work in the six months before a claim is made, the person may need to wait for a period of time before payment is received.

Newly arrived resident's waiting period

As from 1 July 2019 waiting period of four years applies to newly arrived residents.

At a glance

- Centrelink is the provider of social security in Australia.

- Centrelink provides are a wide range of pensions, allowances and benefits.

- Receipt of payments is affected by waiting periods such as the ordinary waiting period, compensation payments, liquid assets and the receipt of unused leave entitlements.

COMPULSORY THIRD PARTY INSURANCE

14-040 Introduction

Compulsory third party (CTP) insurance is an involved area of insurance, with different legislation applying in different states and territories. Therefore, only a general overview is presented here.

14-050 The scheme

The emergence of CTP insurance in Australia relates directly to the growth of motor vehicles as a preferred mode of transport. At first CTP insurance was optional, which meant that many vehicle owners did not have this insurance, so crash victims missed out on compensation because the person at fault was uninsured and could not afford to pay. Consequently, the state governments passed laws to make CTP insurance compulsory. South Australia first legislated in the 1930s.

Early CTP was based on common law, which meant an injured person had to show that the driver was at fault and negligent. This system created a problem for an injured person where no other party was at fault; hence, the fault-based system has been subject to much debate.

Since 1974 some states have departed from the fault-based system and developed a no-fault system in which the amount of compensation is limited, precluding the large awards for damages that were being made under the fault-based system. Limiting the amount of compensation has meant that in most cases injured parties are forced to revert to common law.

No-fault CTP insurance schemes usually have two components:

- Injured parties are given access to medical and rehabilitation assistance regardless of fault.
- The option of seeking damages under common law against a negligent third party is still available to seriously injured people.

CTP insurance indemnifies vehicle owners and drivers who are legally liable for personal injury to any other road user in the event of a motor vehicle accident. This insurance covers personal injury claims made against vehicle owners and drivers by other road users such as third party drivers, passengers, pedestrians, cyclists, motorcyclists and pillion passengers anywhere in Australia.

CTP insurance premiums are included with the registration of a motor vehicle, so a motor vehicle cannot be registered without the owner arranging CTP coverage. In those states that allow a choice of insurers, the registered owner is not obliged to stay with the same insurer and may change the insurer when the registration falls due, usually by completing a 'Compulsory Third Party Nomination' section on the back of the registration renewal form.

Actions brought against vehicle owners and negligent drivers are conducted under the jurisdiction of the legal system where the accident occurred and are subject to the CTP insurance legislation applying in the state. However, where, for example, an interstate driver of a vehicle registered in Queensland injures a person in another state, the driver's Queensland CTP insurance will respond to any action brought against them.

CTP insurance schemes generally include a clause for a Nominal Defendant, which is a statutory office that enables persons injured by vehicles without CTP insurance or by unidentified vehicles, eg, hit-and-run accidents, to be compensated. The Nominal Defendant is generally funded by levies on the CTP insurer. In some cases, the costs of claims brought against the at-fault driver of an unregistered vehicle are also covered.

In those states where the CTP insurance market has been deregulated (eg, Queensland), insurers compete for business on the basis of price and policy coverage. For example, in Queensland at-fault driver protection is available that guarantees benefits of up to $1 million for drivers aged 25 or older who drive specified classes of vehicles.

In 2016 the Queensland government introduced a version of the National Injury Insurance Scheme (NIIS). Under the NIIS, Queensland drivers who suffer a serious personal injury (such as severe burns or spinal cord injuries) in a car accident may be eligible to receive necessary and reasonable lifetime treatment, care and support, regardless of whether or not they were at fault. Drivers in Queensland have paid an NIIS levy on top of their vehicle registration costs since the scheme's introduction. Typically, this levy forms part of each driver's CTP premiums.

Exclusions

Common exclusions that apply to CTP insurance include the following:

- the insured fails to lodge a claim within a specified time
- the motorist is injured in an organised motor race

- injuries occur in the course of employment, because the claim would be made under workers compensation
- injuries occur after the vehicle registration has expired, or after any relevant days of grace in those states where this may apply
- the driver for personal injury if they are the at-fault driver (unless the driver has at-fault driver protection)
- damage to property and other vehicles.

Wording difficulties

The common assumption is that CTP insurance will cover all motor vehicle-related accidents; however, this may not be the case with all schemes. Some states and territories leave vehicle owners open to potential exposures owing to restrictions in the definition of the 'use' of a vehicle. In some jurisdictions, CTP applies only when the injury is caused as a result of driving the vehicle or running it out of control. As a consequence, liabilities caused by a stationary vehicle may not be covered. Injuries involving stationary vehicles include those suffered when opening a car door of a parked vehicle, when an unattended vehicle rolls away, when filling a petrol tank, during loading or unloading of a vehicle, or when a detached trailer rolls away.

Summary of CTP schemes

Table 14.5 provides a summary of the various CTP insurance schemes available across Australian states.

Table 14.5 Summary of the main features of Australian CTP insurance schemes

	Administration / Underwriter	Type of scheme	Coverage	Legislation
ACT	Department of Treasury / choice of four insurers	Common law	Use of a vehicle	*Road Transport (General) Act 1999* (ACT)
NSW	Motor Accidents Authority /choice of five insurers	From 1 December 2017 a no fault scheme	Use/ operation of a vehicle	*Motor Accidents Compensation Act 1999* (NSW)
NT	Motor Accident Compensation Authority / Territory Insurance Office	No fault for residents and non-residents	Use of a vehicle	*Motor Accidents (Compensation) Act 1979* (NT)

QLD	Motor Accident Insurance Commission (MAIC) / choice of four insurers	Common law	Driving a vehicle, collisions, vehicle out of control	*Motor Accident Insurance Act 1994* (QLD)
SA	Motor Accident Commission (MAC) / choice of four insurers	Common law with statutory limits	Driving a vehicle, vehicle out of control	*Motor Vehicles Act 1959* (SA)
TAS	Motor Accidents Insurance Board (MAIB) / MAIB	No fault with limited common law rights	Use of a vehicle	*Motor Accidents (Liabilities and Compensation) Act 1973* (TAS)
VIC	Transport Accident Commission (TAC) / TAC	Common law with statutory limits	Motor vehicles, trams and trains	*Transport Accident Act 1986* (VIC)
WA	Insurance Commission of Western Australia (ICWA / ICWA	Common law with statutory limits, emergency treatment on a no-fault basis	Driving a vehicle, vehicle out of control	*Motor Vehicle (Third Party Insurance) Act 1943* (WA)

14-055 National Injury Insurance Scheme

As shown in table 14.5 several Australian states and territories operate a common law fault-based CTP system. Under these systems no cover is available for those considered to be "at fault" or in a situation where there is no negligent party involved. This means that a large number of people catastrophically injured in a road traffic crash are not eligible to claim against CTP insurance. These injured people rely on their own assets, taxpayer funded health care and support services, family members and friends for their care and support.

In order to rectify this situation, in 2011 the Productivity Commission recommended the establishment of a state and territory funded National Injury Insurance Scheme (NIIS) as part of a National Disability Insurance Scheme (NDIS) enacted by the *National Disability Insurance Scheme Act 2013* (Cth). The NIIS is designed to provide nationally consistent no-fault life time care for catastrophic injuries caused by four types of accidents: motor vehicle accidents, workplace accidents, medical accidents and general accidents (occurring in the home or community). A catastrophic injury is defined as a life-changing injury that leaves a person with permanent disability requiring assistance in everyday life.

Catastrophic injuries include: spinal cord injuries; traumatic brain injury; severe burns; permanent blindness and multiple amputations (eligibility rules apply). The scheme is a no-fault scheme and will be extended to include injury arising from medical accidents, criminal injury and injury occurring at home or in the community.

The NIIS builds on existing State and Territory accident compensation schemes (for example, for motor vehicle and workplace accidents) to complement the National Disability Insurance Scheme (NDIS).

To implement the NIIS for motor vehicle accidents, minimum benchmarks (or national standards) have been developed for State and Territory motor vehicle accident compensation schemes.

Support will be provided on a no-fault basis, significantly reducing legal disputes so that catastrophically injured people will benefit from early access to medical and disability care. Support may include medical treatment and rehabilitation, support for personal care needs, home and vehicle modifications, aids and appliances, educational support, vocational and social rehabilitation and domestic assistance.

The minimum benchmarks for motor vehicle accidents have been agreed by the seven jurisdictions that have committed to the rollout of the NDIS: New South Wales, Victoria, South Australia, Tasmania, the Australian Capital Territory, the Northern Territory and Queensland. The commencement dates for a NIIS for motor vehicle accidents aligns with the commencement of the National Disability Insurance Scheme in that jurisdiction.

The agreed minimum benchmarks for motor vehicle accidents include people who suffer the following catastrophic traumatic injuries in motor vehicle accidents:

1. Spinal cord injury — based on evidence of a permanent neurological deficit (principally paraplegia and quadriplegia).

2. Traumatic brain injury — based on evidence of a significant brain injury which results in permanent impairments of cognitive, physical and/or psychosocial functions. A defined period of post traumatic amnesia plus a Functional Independence Measure (FIM) at five or less, or two points less than the age appropriate norm (or equivalent where other assessment tools are used), would be required.

3. Multiple amputations of the upper and/or lower extremities or single amputations involving forequarter amputation or shoulder disarticulation, hindquarter amputation, hip disarticulation or "short" transfemoral amputation involving the loss of 65 per centor more of the length of the femur.

4. Burns — full thickness burns greater than 40 per cent of the total body surface area (or greater than 30 per cent in children under 16 years) or full thickness burns to the hands face or genital area, or inhalation burns causing long term respiratory impairment, plus a FIM score at five or less, or two points less than the age norm (or equivalent where other assessment tools are used).

5. Permanent traumatic blindness, based on the legal definition of blindness.

As the NIIS is a federated model, States and Territories have some flexibility in how they implement a NIIS, including providing higher standards of service or eligibility than set by the minimum benchmarks. However, if a jurisdiction does not fully meet the minimum benchmarks, individuals who are catastrophically injured in a motor vehicle accident and not covered by the relevant State or Territory accident compensation scheme will receive lifetime care and support through the NDIS. States and Territories will be responsible for 100 per cent of the cost of people who enter the NDIS because their motor vehicle accident compensation scheme does not meet the minimum benchmarks.

The NIIS will cover injuries that arise from accidents which:

• involve at least one registrable vehicle

• occur on a public road or other locations where registrable vehicles are commonly driven including driveways, car parks and adjacent areas, such as nature strips, footpaths and other related areas

• are the result of driving the vehicle, the vehicle running out of control, action taken to avoid a collision with the vehicle, or collision with the vehicle while it is stationary and includes injuries to pedestrians and cyclists injured as a result of such accidents

Individual jurisdictions may extend the coverage to include:

• unregistered vehicles on private property such as farm vehicles

• unregistrable vehicles such as motor cross bikes, quad bikes, trikes, offroad or racing vehicles

• bicycles

- other modes of transport (trains, trams, waterborne craft)
- injuries arising from organised motor sports
- injuries arising from acts of terrorism involving the use of a motor vehicle

Cover provided by the NIIS

- at a minimum each jurisdiction's NIIS will cover people who are catastrophically injured in motor vehicle accidents which occur in that jurisdiction. Jurisdictions may, if they wish, provide broader coverage extending beyond their jurisdiction
- state and Territory NIIS schemes will establish arrangements to purchase care and support services from each other when a scheme participant resides in a different jurisdiction to that which assumes funding responsibility
- a review will be undertaken every five years to assess the extent to which State and Territory NIIS schemes face differential (net) financial burdens in relation to liability for services provided to a nonresident
- in all cases the jurisdiction assuming financial responsibility should retain the right to seek recovery from the CTP insurer of an interstate registered vehicle
- there are a number of exclusions which are limited to persons who: have received a common law compensation payment in respect of their care and support needs resulting from the motor vehicle accident, have an existing catastrophic injury; or are already a participant of the National Disability Insurance Scheme in respect of the costs of care and support already being provided by the NDIS

Entitlements

A minimum level of entitlement in each jurisdiction's NIIS will include reasonable and necessary needs for eligible persons for the following services to the extent that they arise from the motor vehicle accident:

- medical treatment (including pharmaceutical)
- dental treatment
- rehabilitation
- ambulance transportation
- respite care
- attendant care services

- domestic assistance
- aids and appliances
- artificial members, eyes and teeth
- education and vocational training
- home and transportation modification

The NIIS is being rolled out in Australian states and territories on a progressive basis with Queensland commencing to provide these services from 1 July 2016. The funding of the NIIS in Queensland will be by a loading on car registration premiums. Readers should follow developments as the NIIS is rolled out in their states and territories.

At a glance

- CTP insurance indemnifies injured third parties for personal injuries caused by negligent drivers.
- Each Australian state and territory has its own CTP insurance scheme.
- These schemes are either at-fault or no-fault based.
- A Nominal Defendant clause applies to all schemes.
- At-fault cover is available in some states.
- Different definitions of 'use' of a vehicle may cause difficulties.
- All schemes have a range of exclusions.
- The new NIIS will provide life time no-fault care for persons who experience catastrophic injuries in motor vehicle related accidents.

WORKERS COMPENSATION INSURANCE

14-060 Introduction

Workers compensation has become an important component of workers' financial protection in Australia. In the 2017-2018 year, 536,600 Australians experienced a work-related injury with an economic cost of $61.8 billion (ABS 2018). This section traces the history and purpose, entitlements and premium structures of workers compensation in Australia.

14-070 History and purpose

Little is known about how workers fared in Australia before the introduction of workers compensation, but it is known that extensive accident compensation arrangements existed independently of the courts. Prior to the introduction of workers compensation, injured workers in Australia were largely reliant on the charity of employers and others; the benefits of mutual societies such as friendly societies, trade unions and health societies; employer-sponsored sickness and accident schemes; government-provided medical hospital care, free dispensaries and other institutions; and sometimes the common law.

To a large extent, workers compensation replaced these former, largely private arrangements. For example, union membership often included disability benefits. At the turn of the century, about one-third of the Australian population was covered by friendly societies in some way. Coverage was concentrated in manual trades with high accident rates in sectors such as mining.

At the beginning of the twentieth century, state governments introduced social welfare benefits indirectly. Hospitals were heavily subsidised; fees accounted for only about 10 to 15 per cent of total hospital revenues, with half of the remainder coming from government grants and the balance from private charity and fund raising. Additionally, aged and invalid pensions were introduced into Victoria in 1901. New South Wales introduced an aged pension in 1901 and disability pensions in 1907; the Commonwealth did the same in 1908 and 1910 respectively. The schemes were non-contributory with flat-rate, means-tested benefits. Disability pensions covered permanent incapacity, irrespective of the source of that incapacity.

The British *Workermen's Compensation Act 1897* served as the model for the introduction of similar legislation in Australia. Workers compensation laws were introduced by South Australia in 1900, Western Australia in 1902, Queensland in 1905, New South Wales and Tasmania in 1910, and Victoria in 1914. This legislation effectively replaced employer–employee bargaining and imposed conditions on the employment contract with respect to safety and accident compensation. However, the early workers compensation schemes were restrictive, eg, employers were exempted from liability for injuries that did not disable the worker for a minimum period. Additionally, not all workers were covered initially as coverage was restricted to manual labour employed in high-risk industries such as the railways, mines and quarries.

The evolution of the current compulsory system has been characterised by increasing government involvement over the terms and conditions under which insurance is supplied. Indeed, workers compensation legislation makes employers liable for government-prescribed disability benefits if employees are injured or killed at work, or on their way to or from work.

All political jurisdictions in Australia, including the federal government have legislated for employers to provide a no-fault employee injury benefit scheme commonly known as workers compensation. This means there are 12.8 million workers in Australia covered by 11 major workers compensation schemes (safe work Australia 2019). This has caused difficulties for a growing number of Australian corporations that operate across state borders. Hence some large Australian companies, such as Optus, Linfox, the Toll group and the National Australia Bank, have exited state and territory workers compensation systems to join the federal Comcare scheme as national self-insurers – that is, employers who are entitled to administer the Comcare legislation for their own workers.

The schemes are run by a statutory authority as a central fund or managed fund with the premium rates set by the various authorities and operated by either the statutory authority or approved private insurers. For example, Victoria's workers compensation scheme is characterised by public underwriting (risk bearing), but with private marketing, premium collection and claims administration. All jurisdictions allow self-insurance, which is subject to prudential requirements.

Broadly speaking, workers compensation cover has two components:

- a no-fault benefit that provides compensation for loss of earnings, medical expenses and rehabilitation
- a common law right to allow workers who have been seriously injured through employer negligence to bring action.

The common law right to sue for negligence has been abolished in most jurisdictions in Australia but has been retained in South Australia, the Northern Territory and the federal government's Comcare and Seacare schemes.

14-080 Entitlements

The employee is usually covered for personal injury arising out of or in the course of employment, including death and occupational diseases. Some schemes include travel to and from work. However, the benefit payable is subject to certain maximum levels, which results in a deficiency with respect to normal earnings in some cases.

Weekly benefits

Injured workers are paid a weekly benefit according to the number of weeks the employee is injured. For example, Comcare will pay normal weekly earnings if the injury lasts 45 weeks or less, while South Australia will pay the worker's average weekly earnings up to a maximum of twice the state average weekly earnings for claims for 52 weeks or less. Weekly benefits decrease as the length of the claim increases. For example, in Victoria the weekly benefit reduces to 80 per cent of the worker's pre-injury average weekly earnings after 130 weeks if they have no current work capacity. In all cases, weekly benefits cease when the injured worker reaches age 65, when they will qualify for the age pension.

Lump sums

Impairment/non-economic loss

The schemes pay varying amounts for impairment/non-economic loss caused by physical injuries, psychiatric injuries, hearing loss, loss of limbs, and so on. The amount paid is often based on the percentage of permanent impairment; for example, the New South Wales scheme pays a maximum of $598,560 (indexed each year) for permanent injuries incurred on or after 5 August 2015 plus an additional five per cent for permanent impairment for the back. In addition, the worker can receive a maximum of $50,000 for pain and suffering (WorkCover NSW 2019).

Death benefits

Death benefits are paid by all schemes, with an additional amount paid where there is a partner and dependent children. For example, as at 1 July 2015 Comcare pays a lump sum of $562,978.81 for death plus $154.82 per week for each dependent child (Comcare 2019). Funeral benefits are also paid by all schemes up to differing amounts.

Medical and hospital

All schemes pay medical and hospital benefits, but subject to different limits. For example, there are no limits to the benefits for Queensland, South Australia, Tasmania, the Northern Territory, the Australian Capital Territory, and the federal government (but entitlements cease after nine years).

Journey claims

Journey claims refer to the extent to which employees are covered while travelling to and from work or during their lunch hours, and vary considerably between schemes. New South Wales, Queensland, the Northern Territory, the Australian Capital Territory ACT and the federal government provide this cover while Victoria, Western Australia, South Australia and Tasmania do not.

Extra-territorial employees

Many organisations have employees, such as transport drivers, salespersons and engineers, who travel interstate. While many workers compensation schemes provide a level of cover for employees while working in other places, the level of cover may not be adequate. In addition, employees may have the option of claiming under the jurisdiction in which they were injured, particularly if the benefits offered are higher. Therefore, the organisation may be exposed if the injured employee exercises this option and the employer does not pay a premium to this jurisdiction.

The Australian Capital Territory, New South Wales, Queensland, Victoria, Western Australia and Tasmania have addressed this issue by establishing a series of cross-border cooperative workers compensation arrangements. However, employers need to establish their 'state of connection' by using one of three tests:

- Test A relies on where the worker 'usually works'
- Test B relies on where the worker is 'usually based'
- Test C relies on where the employer's principal base of business is located.

Exclusions — stress claims

All jurisdictions contain a number of exclusions relating to stress that centre on claims arising from the worker being dismissed, disciplined, redeployed, demoted, reclassified, retrenched, transferred, granted leave of absence or not being promoted, or from performance appraisal.

14-090 Premiums

Premiums are set following an actuarial analysis of claims and wages data so as to cover the estimated total costs for all claims to be incurred in the next financial year. Common elements to all schemes influence premium calculations and the final cost to the particular business. These include:

- wages paid per annum, which generally includes superannuation contributions and the monetary value of other earnings such as fringe benefits – there are variations between schemes as to the inclusion of such things as meal, car and clothing allowances as assessable wages

- the industry and the degree of hazard presented to workers – some schemes allow separation of workers and/or sites into numerous classifications

- the organisation's unique claims history

- work safety and rehabilitation practices undertaken by the insured.

Others schemes, such as Queensland's WorkCover, use an experience-based rating system that takes into account the employer's individual wage and claims history and the wage and claims experience of the employer's industry to determine how much premium the employer will pay.

Australia's standardised average premium rate is currently 1.61 per cent of payroll. Comcare has the lowest Australian standardised average premium rate for 2018/19 of 1.06 per cent of payroll (Finity 2018). The different premium rates charged across the jurisdictions can be explained by the differences in the entitlements that workers receive for work-related injuries or work-related disease.

A unique feature of Australian workers compensation schemes is the concept of employers' excess. This means the employer is directly responsible for a short initial income maintenance period as well as a maximum level of initial medical expenses. The objective is to provide an incentive for employers to prevent losses, raise the likelihood of prompt payment of income maintenance benefits and reduce system administration costs.

At a glance

- Workers compensation provides benefits to workers injured at work.

- The cover includes a no-fault benefit and a common law right if the injury is serious.

- The common law right to sue has been abolished in most jurisdictions.

- A range of weekly, lump-sum and death benefits, and hospital and medical expense coverage, is available.

- Extra benefits can apply to extra-territorial employees and to and from work cover.

- Claims due to stress have a range of exclusions in all jurisdictions.

- Premiums are based on annual wages, industry classifications, claims history, and safety and rehabilitation practices employed.

- Some jurisdictions calculate premiums on experience-based rating.

- Premiums differ between jurisdictions, as do the benefits.

PUBLIC HEALTH INSURANCE

14-100 Background

The idea of health insurance was initially proposed in England by Hugh the Elder Chamberlen in 1694. By the late nineteenth century health insurance was generally available in some countries, although this was in fact disability insurance in the sense that it covered the cost of emergency care for injuries that could result in disabilities. In Australia, public health was initiated in 1788 in south-east Sydney with the opening of convict hospitals. These convict hospitals passed into civilian control in 1841 when transportation of convicts to New South Wales ceased. The government provided some financial assistance but exercised little control over their operations.

Today, the Commonwealth Government and state governments jointly fund public hospitals and community care for aged and disabled persons. The states and territories are primarily responsible for the delivery and management of public health services and for maintaining direct relationships with most health-care providers, including the regulation of health professionals.

Immediate attention is given to those who are ill or require emergency treatment, but if patients do not qualify they are subject to an assessment process to determine their need for elective services. If patients do not qualify for publicly funded surgery, they will have to pay for surgery in a private hospital. The alternative to self-funding of surgery is to purchase private health insurance.

14-110 Medicare

Public health insurance is provided by Medicare Australia, which is a statutory agency under the *Public Service Act 1999* (Cth). On 1 October 2005 the *Human Services Legislation Amendment Act 2005* (Cth) was passed, which placed Medicare under the authority of the Department of Human Services (DHS). Medicare Australia administers a range of health and payment programs, such as for the Department of Veterans' Affairs, and manages claims processing for the payment of benefits for Medicare.

Medicare, the Commonwealth-funded health insurance scheme, provides free or subsidised health-care services to the Australian population. Medicare:

- provides free hospital services for public patients in public hospitals
- subsidises private patients for hospital services (75 per cent of the medical benefits schedule fee)

- provides benefits for out-of-hospital medical services such as consultations with GPs or specialists (85 per cent of the schedule fee).

These benefits are available to:

- Australian citizens who reside in Australia
- New Zealand citizens or holder of permanent visas
- people visiting Australia and temporary residents from countries with which Australia has reciprocal health-care arrangements, such as the United Kingdom and Italy.

Medicare levy

When Medicare began in 1984 the Medicare levy was introduced as a supplement to other taxation revenue to enable the Commonwealth Government to meet the additional costs of providing the same level of care for the whole population. This levy provides only about 27 per cent of Commonwealth funding for Medicare, with the balance coming from a range of taxes such as income tax, GST and consolidated revenue.

The Medicare levy is paid by individuals resident in Australia at a basic rate of 2.0 per cent of taxable income above certain income thresholds, with no limit on the quantum of the levy payable. For 2018/19 low-income single taxpayers do not pay the levy until their income reaches $22,398. A reduced levy is paid for taxable income between $22,398 and $27,997. For individuals who qualify for the senior and pensioners' Australians tax offset, the lower threshold amount is $35,418 and upper threshold is $44,272. Incomes between lower and upper limits pay a levy of 10% of the excess (ATO 2019a).

Medicare levy is not payable if an individual's income is equal to or less than $22,398 ($44,272 for seniors and pensioners). A part pension is payable if the individual's income is between $22,398 and $27,997 ($35,418and $44,272 for seniors and pensioners) (ATO 2019a).

Section 251U of the *Income Tax Assessment Act 1936* (Cth) provides relief to the following 'prescribed persons':

- someone who is entitled to full medical treatment as a member of the Defence Forces or as a relative of, or a person otherwise associated with, a member of the Forces
- a person entitled under veterans' entitlement legislation to full free medical treatment

- someone who is not an Australian resident for tax purposes
- a resident of Norfolk Island
- persons not entitled to Medicare benefits
- a blind pensioner or sickness beneficiary.

Medicare levy surcharge

Individual taxpayers on higher incomes who do not have adequate private patient hospital health insurance for themselves and their dependants may be liable for an additional amount up to 1.5 per cent Medicare levy (MCL) surcharge. The rates of the MCL surcharge (MLS) applicable to various income bands is shown in table 14.6.

Table 14.6 Medicare levy surcharge for 2018/19

Income	Surcharge
Singles	
$90,000 or less	0%
$90,001 - $105,000	1%
$105,001 - $140,000	1.25%
$140,001 and over	1.50%
Families	
$180,000 or less	0%
$180,001 - $210,000	1%
$210,001 - $280,000	1.25%
$220,001 and over	1.50%

For families, the income thresholds increase by $1,500 for each MLS dependent child after the first.

Source: Australian Taxation Office (2019b)

The operation of the MLS is shown in the following illustrated example.

Illustrated example 14.2

Example: Medicare levy surcharge for a single adult

Josh is 35 years old, single, and doesn't have the appropriate level of private patient hospital cover. In 2018–19, Josh's taxable income is $90,000.

When Josh completes his tax return, he also completes the income test section of the tax return and declares:

- reportable fringe benefits of $20,000

- net investment losses of $7,000.

Josh's total income for Medicare levy surcharge purposes is $117,000 ($90,000 + $20,000 + $7,000.

The amount of Medicare levy surcharge is only calculated against his taxable income and reportable fringe benefits. In 2018–19, Josh's Medicare levy surcharge liability is:

- ($90,000 taxable income + $20,000 reportable fringe benefits) × 1.25% = $1,375.

If the combined income of a couple exceeds the family surcharge threshold, but the taxable income and reportable fringe benefits of one member of the couple does not exceed the MCL low income threshold of $22,398 then that member is not liable for the surcharge.

Medicare benefits

A listing of the Medicare services subsidised by the federal government is contained in the Medicare Benefits Schedule (MBS). Most medical practitioners charge more than the Schedule fee with the patient paying the difference. Medicare provides benefits for:

- consultation fees for doctors, including specialists
- tests and examinations by practitioners needed to treat illnesses, including x-rays and pathology tests
- most surgical and other therapeutic procedures performed by doctors
- some surgical procedures performed by approved dentists

- specified items under the Cleft Lip and Palate Scheme.

Public patients at public hospitals receive free in-hospital treatment from professionals nominated by the hospital. For private patients at private and public hospitals, the choice of practitioner remains with the patient, with Medicare paying 75 per cent of the schedule fee. Some or all of the outstanding balance (including accommodation, theatre fees and medicines) can be covered by private health insurance.

Items not covered by Medicare

Medicare does not cover such health services as:

- private patient costs (eg, theatre fees and accommodation)
- dental examinations and treatment
- ambulance services
- home nursing
- physiotherapy, occupational therapy, speech therapy, eye therapy, chiropractic services, podiatry or psychology
- acupuncture (unless as part of a doctor's consultation)
- glasses and contact lenses
- hearing aids and other appliances
- the cost of prostheses
- medicines not subsidised under the Pharmaceutical Benefits Scheme
- medical and hospital costs incurred overseas
- medical costs for which someone else is responsible (eg, a compensation insurer, an employer, a government or government authority)
- medical services that are not clinically necessary
- cosmetic surgery
- examinations for life insurance, superannuation or membership of a friendly society, and
- eye therapy. (Medicare Australia 2007a)

However, these products and services can generally be covered by private health insurance.

How Medicare works

The payment of health services can be made by direct billing by the medical service provider or by the patient paying the account to the practitioner and then claiming a refund direct from Medicare. With direct billing (bulk billing) the practitioner bills Medicare directly and accepts the benefit as full payment for the service. Most practitioners bulk bill particularly for pensioners and health-care cardholders mainly because of federal government incentives. Otherwise, patients can pay the account and then claim the benefit from Medicare or claim on Medicare for the unpaid account and receive a cheque made payable to the practitioner, which is then forwarded to the provider together with any difference owing.

Medicare pays 85 per cent of the schedule fee other than for general practitioners' services. The patient pays the difference between the schedule fee and the rebate (known as the gap), plus the difference between the schedule fee and the practitioner's charge (if the practitioner decides to charge above the schedule fee).

Pharmaceutical Benefits Scheme

The Pharmaceutical Benefits Scheme (PBS) provides access to necessary and life-giving medicines at an affordable price. Access is restricted to Australian residents and visitors from those countries with which Australia has a reciprocal health care agreement. These include the United Kingdom, Ireland, New Zealand, Malta, Italy, Sweden, the Netherlands and Finland.

The maximum contribution for a pharmaceutical benefit item on the PBS is currently $40.30 (2019) for general patients and $6.50 for concessional patients (health-care cardholders and pensioners). Individuals and families are protected from large overall expenditures for PBS-listed medicines by 'safety nets' whereby expenditure is subsidised or free once a certain threshold is exceeded. The general patient safety net threshold for 2019 is $1,550.70 and $390.00 for concessional cardholders and pensioners (Department of Health and Ageing 2019).

All pensioners receive a pharmaceutical allowance of $6.20 fortnightly for a single person and $3.10 per fortnight each for a couple to help defray their out-of-pocket pharmaceutical expenses. These payments are made by Centrelink as part of the pension payment (Department of Health and Ageing 2019).

At a glance

- Public health insurance in Australia is provided by Medicare Australia.
- Medicare health insurance provides free hospital, subsidised private patient hospital care and out-of-hospital medical services.
- Medicare is funded by a levy imposed on most wage earners and from a range of taxes.
- A Medicare levy surcharge is imposed on some income earners.
- Medicare provides a range of benefits, although not all hospital-related services are covered
- A pharmaceutical benefits scheme is in place to keep important medicines affordable.
- This system provides in-hospital care for emergency treatment, but not elective treatment.
- A wide range of conditions are classified as elective.
- A range of extra services are either fully or partly funded.

PRIVATE HEALTH INSURANCE

14-120 Introduction

Private health insurance entitles those insured to obtain refunds for specific health services. It also helps the insured avoid long waiting times for elective surgery by having the surgery performed in a private hospital and consulting a doctor of their choice.

14-130 Australian private health

There are two types of private health insurance available:

- hospital cover
- ancillary cover.

Hospital cover

Hospital cover helps pay for the cost of treatment and accommodation in a private hospital or as a private patient in a public hospital. It generally covers in-hospital treatments where Medicare pays a benefit. Excesses or co-payments can apply although with some policies the excess does not apply to dependent children.

Ancillary cover

Ancillary or 'extra' cover helps with day-to-day extras such as dental, optical and physiotherapy, and a wide range of extras not covered by Medicare. Some funds also cover alternative therapies and wellness programs. Many of these ancillary covers are subject to a waiting period. For example, 'major dental' work, which includes the provision of crowns, bridges and the like, may have a waiting period of 12 months and be subject to a maximum dollar amount of coverage per person.

Ancillary cover may be offered as a stand-alone policy or as part of a package with hospital cover. Each scheme pays a different benefit for a different service with a different range of exclusions, caps and waiting periods applying before an individual can make a claim. Most of the larger health funds have special deals with 'approved providers'. Members get a higher benefit if they use these providers.

As from April 2007, insurers have been allowed to offer some ancillary services within their hospital cover. Cover can be provided for private hospital outpatient services; out-of-hospital visits to dentists, psychologists and podiatrists; fitness and smoking cessation programs; and treatment for chronic conditions such as asthma and diabetes.

Types of fund membership and tables

A general classification of types of fund membership and tables can be organised along the following lines:

- *Front-end deductible.* This is payable when a claim is made for a hospital stay. This type of cover is favoured by those who have joined a health fund to avoid the one per cent Medicare levy surcharge and to secure a place in the Lifetime Health Cover system. These policies generally have a maximum deductible, such as $500 single / $1,000 family, built in and without the no-gap benefits.

- *Exclusions.* Certain types of treatment, such as maternity, cataract and eye lens procedures and hip replacement, are generally excluded. All rating tables are required to provide cover for psychiatric, rehabilitation and palliative care.

- *Single membership.* Provides cover for the member named on the application form.

- *Family membership.* This covers the contributor, one other adult and one or more dependent children.

- *Single-parent family membership.* This covers the contributor and one or more dependent children.

- *Couple membership.* This covers the contributor and one other person who is not a dependent child of the contributor.

- *Ancillary membership.* This cover is available with hospital cover from health insurance providers or as a stand-alone product, and includes a range of benefits as described above.

Community rating

Community rating refers to the system of determining premiums based on the average cost of insuring a broad age group, and forms the basis of the current private health insurance system. With community rating, insurers must accept all applicants, and when setting their premiums and benefits they cannot discriminate on the basis of health status, age, race, sex, use of hospital or medical services, or general claiming history.

The principle of community rating is supported by a reinsurance system administered by the Private Health Insurance Administration Council (PHIAC). Reinsurance in the health insurance context involves sharing between health insurers the hospital and medical costs of high-risk members admitted to hospital. Insurers with a greater proportion of low-risk members (the young) pay contributions into the reinsurance pool, while those with a greater proportion of high-risk members (the aged and chronically ill) receive transfers from the pool.

Lifetime health cover

Lifetime health cover is a government initiative introduced on 1 July 2000 to encourage people to take out hospital insurance earlier in life and to maintain that cover. Under Lifetime health cover, funds can charge different premiums based on the age of each particular member when they first take out hospital cover with a registered health fund.

Lifetime health cover recognises the length of time a person has had private health insurance and rewards loyalty by offering lower premiums. People who take out hospital cover early in life will be charged lower premiums throughout their life, relative to people who take out cover later.

People who delay taking out hospital cover will pay a two per cent loading on top of their premium for every year they are aged over 30 when they first take out hospital cover. For example, a person who delays joining until the age of 40 will pay 20 per cent more than someone who joined at age 30. The maximum loading a person can be required to pay is 70 per cent, payable by people who first take out hospital cover at age 65 or older.

Lifetime health cover encourages more people to take out private health insurance at a younger age and to maintain their membership. This improves the overall health profile of health insurance members, which contributes to making premiums more affordable for all members. It should be noted that there are no age penalties for ancillary cover.

Gap insurance

The 'gap' represents the difference between the MBS fee for a medical service and what the health practitioner charges for this service.

Medicare does not always provide a full rebate for the fee. The Medicare rebate applicable to services is shown in table 14.7.

Table 14.7 Medicare rebate

Service	Medicare rebate (percentage of scheduled fee)
GP consultations	100%
All other services provided by a community medical practitioner	85%
All services provided by a medical practitioner during hospital treatment when the patient is admitted as a private patient	75%

Source: Department of Human Services (2019f)

Previously health funds were prevented by law from covering the gap; it all had to be paid by the patient. The passing of the *Health Legislation Amendment (Gap Cover Schemes) Act 2000* (Cth) means health funds are now obliged to offer 'gap insurance'. If they do not, the fund will not be able to offer the federal government's 30 per cent rebate on health insurance premiums. Gap insurance covers all or most of the gap between the Schedule fee and what the doctor actually charges.

Gap cover is available only if the doctor has agreed to participate in this arrangement with the fund. To be included in a gap scheme, doctors must agree to cap their fees, so many specialist doctors don't participate. It is important to appreciate that gap cover applies only to medical procedures performed by specialists in hospital or day hospital facilities.

Under this 'no-gap' arrangement, the medical practitioner who provided the in-hospital service can decide to accept the health insurer's payment as full settlement of the account. For example, some doctors may use the gap scheme for pensioners but not for other patients. In effect, agreement needs to be reached between the patient and the doctor for the doctor to adhere to the no-gap agreement.

If the doctor does not agree to the capped fee, the health fund will pay the difference between the MBS fee and the capped fee and the patient will pay the balance. For example, suppose the fee charged by the doctor was $3,000. If the MBS fee was $1,000, Medicare would pay $750 and the health fund would pay $250. If the capped fee was $2,000, the heath fund would pay $1,000 under the gap insurance and the patient would have to pay the $1,000 balance.

Gap cover schemes for each registered health insurer are approved by the Minister for Health and Ageing. These agreements offer cover under Medical Purchaser — Provider Agreements (MPPA), Hospital Purchaser — Provider

Agreements (HPPA) and Practitioner Agreements (PA). The benefits paid to participating doctors are determined by reference to the relevant insurer's private schedule of benefits. These benefits are usually set at a fixed amount or percentage above the MBS.

The law requires that a patient be provided with informed financial consent. This means that the doctor who will provide treatment under a fund's gap scheme must provide written information about fees and likely out-of-pocket costs. The patient will be asked to sign an acknowledgement that they have received this information.

Federal government rebate

In 1998 the proportion of Australians covered by health insurance fell to an all-time low of 38 per cent (ABS 1999). Over the years the federal government, concerned about the growing costs of health, has introduced a series of measures designed to attract people back into the health system. As part of these initiatives, all Australians who are eligible for Medicare and who are members of a registered health fund may be eligible for up to a 40 per cent rebate on annual private health fund premiums, with the rebate based on a combination of age and income.

From 1 July 2012, the private health insurance rebate and the Medicare levy surcharge are income tested against three new income thresholds. The amount of private health insurance rebate an insured is entitled to receive is calculated by the Australian Taxation Office when the insured lodges their tax return. These income thresholds for 2020-21 are shown in table 14.10.

Table 14.10: Income thresholds 2014-15 to 2020-21

	Base tier	Tier 1	Tier 2	Tier 3
Singles	$90,000 or less	$90,001 – $105,000	$105,001 – $140,000	$140,001 or more
Families*	$180,000 or less	$180,001 – $210,000	$210,001 – $280,000	$280,001 or more
Private health insurance rebate				
Less than 60 years old	27.820%	18.547%	9.273%	0%
69 – 69 years old	32.487%	23.184%	13.910%	0%

70 years old or over	37.094%	27.820%	18.547%	0%

*The family income threshold is increased by $1,500 for each dependent child after the first.

Source: Australian Taxation Office (2019c)

Table 14.10 shows that a single person earning in excess of $300,000 will not receive a rebate on his/her private health insurance premiums. Similarly, a family with a combined income in excess of $280,000 will not receive a rebate.

A person can choose to receive the rebate as a tax credit or have their premiums reduced instead of claiming the tax offset and rebate adjusted when their annual income tax return is lodged.

At a glance

- There are two types of private health cover in Australia: hospital cover and ancillary cover.
- A variety of deductibles are available.
- Premiums are calculated using community rating.
- Lifetime health cover helps to reduce premiums.
- Gap insurance provides cover for the difference between the MBS fee and the health practitioner charge.
- The federal government rebate is means tested.
- Community rating is used plus people are grouped into 5 year age bands.

14.140 Study questions

14.1   Discuss how public health insurance is funded in Australia.

41.2   Describe the hospital coverage provided by public health insurance in Australia.

41.3   Discuss the present and future benefits to insureds to be gained from the following initiatives:

   a.   Lifetime health cover

   b.   gap cover

    c.   the income tested rebate on private health insurance.

14.4   What is the difference for gap cover purposes between the Medical Benefits Schedule (MBS) and a private schedule of benefits?

14.5   A friend drives off the road in the middle of the night and is seriously injured and unable to work for several months. No-one else is involved in the accident. Will your friend receive any benefits from compulsory third party insurance? If so, discuss the benefits available.

14.6   Explain the two ways that Medicare can pay for a medical service provided by a medical practitioner when the practitioner does not bulk bill.

14.7   What are the implications for workers compensation payments with respect to the social security system in Australia?

14.8   Give a brief explanation of how a person's income and assets can affect the level of payments they can receive from a range of social security benefits in Australia.

14.9   Explain how the premiums for health insurance are calculated.

14-150 References and further reading

References

Articles and Books

Finity 2018, d'finitive: Workers compensation, October. Available at *finity.com.au*

Releases

Australian Bureau of Statistics (ABS) 2018, 'Work-related injuries', *6324.0 Work Related Injuries in Australia*. Available at *abs.gov.au*

Australian Taxation Office (ATO) 2019a, 'Medicare levy income thresholds' Available at *ato.gov.au*

Australian Taxation Office (ATO) 2019b, 'Medicare levy surcharge income thresholds' Available at *ato.gov.au*

Comcare 2019, 'Statutory rates'. Available at *comcare.gov.au*

Department of Health and Ageing 2019b, 'Pharmaceutical allowance'. Available at *health.gov.au*

Department of Human Services (2019a), 'Australian government payments'. Available at *health.gov.au*

Department of Human Services (2019b), 'Payment rates for disability support pension'. Available at *humanservices.gov.au*

Department of Human Services (2019b), 'Payment rates for sickness allowance'. Available at *humanservices.gov.au*

Department of Human Services (2019c), Payment rates for mobility allowance'. Available at *humanservices.gov.au*

Department of Human Services (2019e), 'Liquid assets waiting periods' Available at *humanservices.gov.au*

Department of Human Services (2019f), 'Medicare rebate'. Available at *human services.gov.au*

Department of Social Services (2019), 'Social Security Guide'. Available at *dss. gov.au*

Icare (2015), 'Permanent impairment claims'. Available at *icare.nsw.gov.au*

Medicare Australia 2019b. Available at *medicareaustralia.gov.au*

Legislation

Income Tax Assessment Act 1936 (Cth)

Medicare Levy Act 1986 (Cth)

National Disability Insurance Scheme Act 2013 (Cth)

Social Security Act 1991 (Cth)

Further reading

Articles

Pharmaceutical Benefits Pricing Authority (PBPA) 2004, , 'PBS pricing'. Available at *health.gov.au*

CHAPTER 15

THE CONCEPT OF ETHICS

Why ethics is important in financial advising

15-000 Recent history and origins of ethics

Ethics is a subject that has become to the forefront of financial planners' minds in recent years. The Federal Government had been concerned with the number of scandals involving the financial advice industry for several years, which culminated in the scandal involving Storm Financial, a Townsville based financial planning group. The main issue that ASIC had with this group was the giving of inappropriate advice to vulnerable investors and Storm's business model. In short, the directors failed in their duty as directors to their clients. The upshot of this and other managed investment schemes (MIS) in timber, fruit and other projects where investors were recruited by a number of financial advisers, the federal Government took steps to enact legislation to increase the education standards of financial planners and implement and industry wide code of ethics.

Financial planning is an important sector of the financial space with research by Roy Morgan showing that as at May 2018 nearly 1.96 million Australians use a financial planner or adviser to purchase managed funds or superannuation. This group of almost two million Australian accounts valued at approximately $703 billion in total wealth management products (of over 27% of the wealth management market) with an average value of $360,000. These figures highlight how important this industry is to the financial welfare of Australians and as such its practitioners must adhere to the highest standards of ethics in their business.

15-010 Business ethics

Business ethics is a social science whose origins date back some 4,000 years to the time of Mesopotamia with the Code of Hammurabi, which was a legal code dealing with criminal and civil matters to give order to society. The main aim of business ethics is to define and examine the responsibilities of businesses and their agents as a part of the general moral environment of a given society. A set of rules and codes of conduct has developed, which serve as a means of protection from the possible infringements of moral codes as a result of the general activities and responsibilities of a firm to its stakeholders (e.g. generating profits for shareholders and taxes for government). (See Section 15-100 and Table 15.2 for further discussion).

Two terms; *ethics* and *morals* have been introduced. The meaning of these terms and how they interact needs to be examined.

The concept of ethics

15-020 Ethics vs morals

Both ethics and morals relate to 'right' and 'wrong' conduct. While they are often used interchangeably, they are different: **Ethics** is a branch of philosophy that deals with morality. It refers to the rules provided by an external source, e.g. professional codes of conduct and focuses on weighing the pros and cons of competing values and interest, which help the individual or group to decide what is good or bad. In other words, ethics is a process which requires the decision maker to consider facts in light of important values and morals, in the context of explicit forms of codified behavior. Ethical principles can be seen as a map of how one makes choices. It is like the 10 commandments of the holy Bible, which tells a person how to behave with another person. For example, is it ethical to state the truth in a particular situation?

Each person has his/her own set of ethical values, but there can be 'grey areas' in interplay between these ethical values that guide a person's moral obligations. A person may be strictly following Ethical Principles, but not have any morals. Likewise, one could violate Ethical Principles within a given system of rules in order to maintain moral integrity. Illustrated example 15.1 highlights an unethical action.

Illustrated example 15.1

A very close friend or relative of an interviewer comes for a job interview and without asking a single question, the interviewer selects him. This act is unethical because the selection process must be transparent.

On the other hand, **morals** refer to an individual's own or group principles (or values) regarding right and wrong, which are usually based on religious tenets generally expressed in the form of general rules and statements, which inform ethical decisions. Morality is something one feels intuitively and its principles can be used to judge behavior. For example, we should speak the truth. As morals are framed and designed by the group, there is no option to think and choose; the individual can either accept or reject. To refer to a person as 'ethical', we would be saying that the person is honest and follows good moral standards.

However, the 'grey areas' mentioned above can also arise in relationship to morals.

A moral person although bound by a higher covenant, may choose to follow a code of ethics as it would apply to a system. That is, "make it fit". Illustrated example 15.2 highlights and immoral action.

Illustrated example 15.2

If the son of a prominent politician has committed a crime and the politician uses his powers to free his son from the legal consequence. Then this act is immoral because the politician is improperly trying to save a culprit from justice.

Table 15.1 provides a useful comparison chart of ethics vs Morals.

Table 15.1: Morals vs ethics comparison chart

Basis for comparison	Morals	Ethics
Meaning	Morals are the beliefs of an individual or group as to what is right or wrong.	Are the guiding principles that help an individual or group to decide what is good or bad.
What is it?	General principles set by group.	Response to a specific situation.
Root word	Mos means custom.	Ethikos which means character.
Governed by	Social and cultural norms.	Individual or Legal and Professional norms.
Deals with	Principles of right and wrong.	Right and wrong conduct.
Applicability to business	No	Yes
Consistency	Morals may differ from society to society and culture to culture.	Ethics are generally uniform.
Expression	Morals are expressed in the form of general rules and statements.	Ethics are abstract.

Source: Difference between morals & ethics, Surbhi, S. (2018a)

15-030 Defining ethics

Ethical derives from the Greek *ethos, ethikos*, meaning 'character' which referred to the authority of custom and tradition. The term 'moral' is roughly its Latin equivalent *(mores, moralis), meaning 'custom'.* To say that a person or behavior has 'moral character' describes a person or behavior as right in the moral sense – truthful, fair and honest. Examples of societal ethical behavior can include such things as: respect for another's property, putting another's interest before your own, refraining from violence against another, treating others with civility, telling the truth, adhering to the principle of confidentiality. All these decisions impact on moral decision making.

The Macquarie Concise Dictionary (1988) defines the term 'ethics' as a system of moral principles, by which human actions and proposals are judged good or bad or right or wrong. This dictionary also describes 'ethics' as the rules of conduct recognized in respect of a particular class of human actions for example, medical ethics and the moral principles of an individual.

If ethics were only a matter of rules, customs and contracts then questions of right or wrong would be easy to answer. But ethical issues are often grey; people can differ on ethics as they do not on other rules, such as the laws of physics or the rules of calculus. This does not mean that ethics is soft or trivial. Ethics is not poor reasoning or vague custom, but one of the most important sources of motivation and guidance of human conduct. In order to help clarify these dilemmas, Guy (1990, pp.14-17) and Smith (2002, pp.1-4) identified 10 core ethical principles to guide decision making. These are listed and explained in table 15.2.

Table 15.2: Ten core principles to guide decision making

No.	Principle	Definition
1	Justice	What is right, fair or just in any social arrangement.
2	Honesty	To be truthful and not deceive or distort.
3	Accountability/ Personal responsibility	To accept the consequences of one's actions and accept responsibility for one's decisions. This includes setting an example for others and avoiding the appearance of impropriety.
4	Keeping promises	To keep one's commitments. Promises and agreements to stakeholders create expectations and obligations that must be met.
5	Pursuit of excellence	Being diligent, industrious and well prepared (commonly called exercising 'due care and skill').

6	Loyalty	Being faithful and loyal to those with whom the person has dealings.
7	Fairness/ Justice	This requires impartiality and being loyal to those with whom the person has dealings.
8	Integrity	Judgement should be exercised with the objective of improving a situation. If the harm outweighs the good, then prudence dictates a return to the status quo. This is often referred to as the principle of 'do no harm'.
9	Responsible citizenship	A person's actions should accord to societal values and he/she should apply appropriate standards when exercising discretionary judgement.
10	Respect for others	There is an obligation to act with dignity, respect and courtesy in dealing with all stakeholders. A person should also be prompt and decent whilst recognizing each person's rights.

It should be recognized that different cultures have different ethical standards. For example, some cultures allow female circumcision, torture, religious intolerance and racial discrimination. No doubt that you would find these practices ethically impermissible.

Now that we have identified what ethics is, we need to define what ethics is not.

15-040 What ethics is not

When thinking about what ethics is not, it is useful to consider the following quotation. "Ethics is not for wimps. It is not easy being a good person. That's why it is such a lofty goal and an admirable achievement." (Josephson, M., n.d.). In defining what something is not can provide valuable insight to the term itself and can help us in clarifying our own definitions and questions about what ethics is. Ethics is not:

Feelings. Feelings can often diverge from what is ethical. However, feelings can often provide us with insight and information to what is ethical; what we should or should not do. For example, we generally feel a sense of wellbeing when we do something good, even when it is difficult. In contrast, most people feel bad when they do something wrong. However, there are those people who feel good despite doing something wrong. This dichotomy illustrates that feelings do not always coincide with what is ethical.

Religion. If we were to hold the view that ethics was limited to one's personal religious beliefs, then it could be concluded that ethics could only apply to the religious, or to those who hold religious beliefs. This is not true. Ethics applies to everyone irrespective of their religious beliefs. Religions can set high ethical standards and provide personal motivation for certain behaviors and choices, so religions can set a solid foundation to practicing good ethics. However, ethics is not confined to religion. A person can be moral and ethical and not be religious.

Legality. Law is a system of rules and guidelines, which are enforced through social institutions to govern behavior. However, ethics and law are not the same thing. It is true that laws often incorporate ethical standards as they set the minimum standards of behaviors however, ethics can vary from person to person because different people have different opinions on certain issues, but laws are defined and precise. Nobody will be punished when they violate ethics, but they will be punished if they violate the law. Besides, an action can be illegal, but morally right. For example, consider the actions of Robin Hood, who robbed from the rich and gave to the poor. This action is considered morally correct although it was illegal. Similarly, an action that is legal can be morally wrong. For instance, some people spend thousands of dollars on their pets while some poor people do not have enough food or shelter. Finally, ethics is grounded in positive aspects of human behavior, while laws are concerned with negative actions. Because of these differences, it is not appropriate to rely on laws to govern ethical behavior.

Culturally accepted norms. Most societies have standards of social behavior that can be viewed as ethical. Of course, there are cultural and individual differences. In some cultures people may think it is wrong to place your elbows on the dinner table, while in others it is totally acceptable. While we should be tolerant and respectful of cultural differences, should we also accept that all cultural practices are morally right?

When considering this question we need to clarify that *normative ethics* deals with how we should behave and live our lives, particularly when our actions affect others. However, we do not always, as individuals or societies, do what we should. Looking at specific times and places we understand why people behave the way they do. This, however, does not mean that they should have behaved in this way.

Take slavery for example. It was legal in the UK until 1833 and in the US until 1855. In Australia, the indentured labour of Indigenous people and South Sea islanders in the 19th and 20th centuries was akin to slavery. Yet many Europeans at the time saw nothing wrong with the practice.

Even when we agree that certain behaviours are wrong, they may still be widespread. For instance, bribery is considered wrong and is illegal in every nation, but in some countries it is very common and an essential part of doing business in that country. If we were to agree that moral values differ from culture to culture or from society to society, or from one person to another, then it means that any individual ought to behave in the manner seen to be moral within the environment in which they are operating (when in Rome, then…. when doing business Beijing, then….). We cannot adopt that standard when making decisions, or even justifying a decision that we have made. Just because everyone is doing it does not make it right.

Science. Science provides a lot of information about how to make better choices, but science cannot tell us what we should do ethically. In essence, science does provide us with explanations for what humans are like; but when we look at ethics, we find that ethics provides reasons or explanations for how we should act as humans. It is important; again, to know that just because something is scientifically possible, does not make it ethical. For example, consider the ethical anguish nuclear physicists experienced when developing the atom bomb.

15-050 Understanding ethics

The question arises, why is it important to have a complete understanding of the term ethics and what it means to us? There is a large grey area when it comes to ethics. In order to act ethically, we need to understand what guides our decision-making, what affects our decisions and what is the basis for the decisions that we make? Are there rules we need to follow, such as professional rules of conduct? How do we approach ethics? How do we evaluate and work through professional situations? How do we solve ethical dilemmas in our own lives?

As mentioned above, although ethics is not specifically legality, it is important to understand both the moral and legal implications of any decision we make or action we take.

- Legal and Moral: A decision can be legal and moral. This decision would have both no legal implications and it would be ethically sound. For example, the *Ant-Discrimination Act* 1977 (NSW), which is a legal document relating to discrimination in employment, the public education system, delivery of goods and services, and other services such as, banking, health care, property and night clubs. This Act is intended to reflect and enforce the moral and ethical standards of a civilized society.

- Legal and Immoral: A decision can be legal and it can also be immoral. A decision such as this would have no legal implications, but it would definitely have a questionable ethical basis. For example, not to long ago it was the law in the United States that black people had to sit at the back of the bus. Legal but not ethical.

- Illegal and Immoral: A decision could also be illegal and immoral. This type of a decision would have both legal implications and poor ethical standards attached to the choice. For example, the possession of pornography.

- Illegal and moral: A decision could be illegal and moral. While the decision may have legal implications and against the law there could be grounds to argue that it is ethically sound and be the right thing to do. For example, it is illegal to run a traffic light or speed, but might be ethical and legal to do so if the act was necessary to rush a critically ill person to hospital.

The process of ethical decision making

15-060 Ethical decision making

In the preceding sections we have looked carefully at what ethics is and what ethics is not. But how do we apply this information to the inevitable difficult decisions that we confront in our professional life where we need to make tough ethical decisions? Since making the right choice is not always clear cut we need to form a solid foundation of how we decide and why we decide. Questions arise such as, where do our ethical principles come from? What do they mean? Some will say that they are social inventions, while others will say that they are universal truths and yet others will say that they are the 'will of god'. It is clear that making the right choice is not always obvious or clear cut. Therefore, we need a solid grounding on how we decide and why we decide. There are several theories of ethics that we can use to guide our decision-making: meta-ethics, applied ethics and normative ethics.

Meta-ethics. Meta-ethics is a branch that examines the role of reason by examining a broad range of questions and puzzles such as, is morality more a matter of taste than truth? Are morals standards culturally relative? These questions lead to puzzles about the meaning of moral claims as well as about moral truth and the justification of our moral commitments. It also examines the connections between values, reasons for action and human motivation, asking how it is that moral standards might provide us with reasons to do or refrain from doing as it demands. It also addresses many of the issues commonly bound up with the nature of freedom and its significance (or not) for moral responsibility (Stanford Encyclopedia of Philosophy 2012).

Applied ethics. Applied ethics looks at how we can achieve moral outcomes in respect to real world actions and their moral considerations in certain situations such as, private and public life, the professions, health, technology, law and leadership. It also examines controversial issues such as: war, capital punishment, environmental issues and animal rights.

Normative ethics. Normative theory is the study of ethical action. It is the attempt to provide a general theory that tells us how we ought to live. For any act there are three things that might be thought to be morally interesting: first, there is the agent, the person performing the act; second, there is the act itself; third, there are the consequences of the act. Normative ethics looks at certain duties that we should follow, and the consequences – both direct and indirect - of our behaviors and decisions on others. Within normative ethics, the goal is to arrive at moral standards that regulate right and wrong conduct. The goal is to determine what will lead us to the right decision, and what will lead us to the wrong decision, and the process by which to choose a course of action.

Unlike metaethics, normative ethics does not attempt to tell us what moral properties are; and unlike applied ethics, it does not attempt to tell us what specific things have these properties. Normative ethics simply seeks to tell us how we can find out what things have what moral properties, to provide a framework for ethics.

The golden rule that is thought of by many people is: "Do unto others as you would have them do unto you". However, some people use a different rule: "Do unto others as they would have done unto them". It's not about what we think is right and good; it's about what is going to be the best for the person at the end of the ethical decision.

Normative ethics assumes that we can establish a single principle, and that principle is one by which we can judge and guide each ethical choice of action. We can look at a set of traits or principles that should be the foundation for our ethical decisions. Additionally, there is one key assumption that an ultimate criterion of moral conduct exists, although there is not 100% agreement on what this criterion is. The key is to identify the single principle, the single standard or criterion. How do we find that principle? We know that we might agree 'in principle,' but we don't all have the same principle in mind. As an individual we need to determine the basis on which we ground our standards. Then, we can figure out how to apply the standards to our ethical decisions.

We know that we need this single principle; we know we need a criterion by which to judge our actions. We know we have to pinpoint something on which to base the standard; but how do we figure out what our standards are and how we are going to apply them? The solution is to refer back to the list of things that ethics is not. It is not our feelings, or religion; it's not law, it's not social norms or science …so what is it? What is ethics? This is where it truly can become very complicated. However, the following five approaches will help us answer this question.

15-070 Five approaches to judging ethical decisions

In addition to the ethical theories discussed above, we will discuss five approaches to help determine and settle upon the ultimate criterion by which we judge our actions. The five approaches are:

1. Utilitarian
2. Rights

3. Fairness/Justice

4. Common good

5. Virtue

Utilitarian. This approach is also known as consequentialism. Figure 15.1 shows a popular cartoon used to illustrate the Utilitarian approach, known as the Trolley Problem. The trolley tracks split and branch off into two separate directions. To the right, one person is tied to the tracks. To the left, five people are tied to the tracks. The operator is unable to stop the runaway trolley and he must choose on which track the trolley will travel. How does the operator choose? Pull the lever and drive the trolley onto the right track will kill one person, but diverting the trolley onto the left track will kill five people. In essence, the operator will choose the lesser of two evils.

Figure: 15.1: The trolley problem

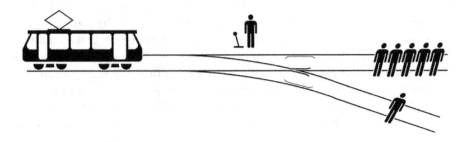

Source: Trolley problem (2018)

The basis of the utilitarian approach is the idea that we will choose to do either the most good or the least harm. Then we have to look at the consequences of trying to increase the good done, while simultaneously reducing the harm by that exact same decision. A tally of the good against the bad can be kept. In doing this, the assumption is that if there is 'more good' than it is ethical. If there is 'more bad' then it is unethical. It seems like a simple clear cut decision, but not everyone is going to agree on what is good and what is bad and so we end up in a grey area.

Rights. With the Rights Approach, the best decision is one that protects and respects the moral rights of those affected. This quote by the philosopher Immanuel Kant embodies what the rights approach is about. "Always recognize that rational human individuals should be treated as an end in themselves, and do not use them as means to your ends" (Wikipedia n.d.). With the rights approach we do have to recognize that others are an end and not simply a means to our end.

It's a duty-based approach. We have a duty to respect and protect the rights of others. We have a duty to respect others in not only in what we choose, but also in the consequences of the choices that we make. At the heart of this approach are the rights that we have a duty to protect. These rights are varied and debated, but most include several key rights, such as the rights to make your own choice regarding what type of life you want to lead. As an example, you may choose to be a vegetarian. You have that right and people have a duty to respect that right. You are not hurting anybody by choosing that lifestyle. Other rights include the right to be told the truth, the right not to be hurt or not to be injured and the right to a certain degree of privacy.

Fairness/justice. The fairness/justice approach embodies the idea that we should treat everybody equally and if not, we must be able to defend 'why'. When using this approach, we want to ask ourselves three different questions in the decision-making process:

- What is the fair thing to do?
- What has been done in the past?
- Are my decisions consistent both with what has been done in the past and with what my choice have been?

As an example, let's say you have two employees who have the same job, but one is paid a higher wage than the other. On the surface, this seems like it is unfair. However, there could be a difference in education, there could be a difference in experience, and there could be a difference in years of service with the company. These differences may allow you to justify and defend why there is an inequality in wages and so the inequality can be considered as ethical. If you treat people unequally without any defense, the justice approach holds that it is an unethical decision.

Common good. The common good approach can be useful when the issue involves, or should involve, the overall picture or environment. The common good approach regards all individuals as a part of a larger environment and that we should do whatever is necessary to contribute most to the common good. An example of this approach is Robin Hood, as mentioned above. His actions were not always legal (stealing from the rich to give to the poor), but in the grand scheme of things, they were ethical. He was doing what was in the best interests of the people in the community. It is the common good and our intentions with those around us that are the basis of our ethical decisions.

We not only look at the common good of society as a whole, but also how the decisions that we make affect our interactions with neighbors, coworkers, clients or whoever it may be. We must have respect and compassion for others and the conditions that might affect their welfare. We need to take into consideration the consequences of any decision that we make and the effect it will have, both short-term and long-term, in essence life in a community is good and our actions should contribute to that life.

Virtue. The virtue approach is the belief that our actions should be consistent with certain values or virtues that we hold in high regard. The virtue approach is in contrast to the approach that emphasizes duties or rules or that emphasizes the consequences of actions. It is these value or virtues that provide for our full development. When we consider any action that we are about to take we ask ourselves a series of questions:

- What kind of person will I be if I do this?
- If I make this choice, how does that define me?
- Is this action consistent with me acting at my best?

We also have to ask ourselves, 'by what criteria are we judging our actions? What are the virtues that we should be holding in high regard?' A number of these virtues have been identified that are critical in helping to guide our decision-making to keep us at our best selves and to stay true to ourselves through any type of decision making process.

Virtues that help that help us become our best possible self include:

- Fidelity. The duty to keep promises to those with whom we interact.
- Reparation. The duty to compensate others when we do harm. (for example, saying "I'm sorry")
- Gratitude. The duty to thank those who help us.
- Justice. The duty to recognize merit.
- Beneficence. The duty to improve the conditions of others; always striving to do better, to be better.
- Self-improvement. The duty to improve ourselves and further our knowledge, never to become complacent, always work to know more, to be more.
- Non-maleficence. The duty not to injure others.

15-080 Applying these approaches

We have addressed the topic of ethics and ethical decision-making. We have introduced multiple ethical theories and a number of different approaches. A list of virtues that we should follow when facing ethical decisions has just been provided. Making ethical choices is not always easy or clear cut as there are many grey areas. In order to make ethical decision making easier, we will now examine six key underlying values that lie at the heart of nearly every ethical choice that we may have to make.

Regardless of the theory or the ethical approach that we use, or the virtues that we hold and find very important, the following six key underlying values will help guide decision making:

1. *Trustworthiness.* A person who is trustworthy is reliable; they have consistent positive behavior and keep their promises. In essence, they do what they say they will do. A trustworthy person is honest; they are not deceptive as they say what they mean and mean what they say. They act with integrity by standing up for what is right and are loyal to others even when no one is watching. Trustworthy people are viewed as credible as they are honest and reliable, and have a strong character by maintaining good reputation, which is good for business. If your clients trust you, if your coworkers trust you, if your community trusts you, you in turn will have a very good reputation as a professional.

2. *Respect.* People are not things and have the right to be treated with dignity. While there is no ethical rule to hold everyone in high esteem we should treat everyone with respect regardless of what they have done. We have a responsibility to be the best we can be even when dealing with unpleasant people.

   The Golden Rule – do unto others as you would have them do unto you – nicely illustrates the pillar of respect. Respect prohibits violence, humiliation, manipulation and exploitation. It reflects notions such as civility, courtesy, decency, dignity, tolerance and acceptance.

3. *Responsibility.* Life is full of choices. Being responsible means being in charge of our choices and by extension, our lives. It means recognizing that our actions matter and that we are morally responsible for the consequences. The consequences may not be immediate, but actions will always create consequences. Our capacity to reason and our freedom to choose make us morally autonomous and, therefore, answerable for whether we honour or degrade the ethical principles that give life meaning and purpose.

Ethical people show responsibility by being accountable, pursuing excellence and exercising self-restraint. They exhibit the ability to respond to expectations.

4. **Fairness.** Fairness involves issues of equality, impartiality, proportionality, openness and due process. Fairness also requires playing by the rules, to take turns, to share, not to pass blame onto others and to accept the consequences of your words and your actions. Fairness also involves consistency, so it would be unfair to handle similar matters inconsistently. It would also be unfair to impose punishment that is not commensurate with the offence. The basic concept seems simple, even intuitive, yet applying it in daily life can be surprisingly difficult. Disagreeing parties tend to maintain that there is only one fair position (their own, naturally). But essentially fairness implies adherence to a balanced standard of justice without relevance to one's own feelings or inclinations.

   Process is crucial in settling disputes, both to reach the fairest result and to minimize complaints. A fair person scrupulously employs open and impartial processes for gathering and evaluating information necessary to make decisions. Fair people do not wait for the truth to come to them; they seek out relevant information and conflicting perspectives before making important judgements.

   Impartiality. Decisions should be made without favoritism or prejudice.

   Equity. An individual, company or society should correct mistakes, promptly and voluntarily. It is improper to take advantage of the weakness or ignorance of others.

5. **Caring.** Caring is the heart of ethics and ethical decision-making. It is scarcely possible to be truly ethical and yet unconcerned with the welfare of others. That is because ethics is ultimately about good relations with other people.

   People who consider themselves ethical and yet lack a caring attitude toward individuals tend to treat others as instruments of their will. They rarely feel an obligation to be honest, loyal, fair or respectful except insofar as it is prudent for them to do so, a disposition which itself hints at duplicity and lack of integrity. A person who really cares feels an emotional response to both the pain and pleasure of others.

   Of course, sometimes we must hurt those we truly care for and some decisions, while quite ethical, do cause pain. But one should consciously cause no more harm than is reasonably necessary to perform one's duties.

544

The highest form of caring is the honest expression of benevolence, or altruism. This is not to be confused with strategic charity. Gifts to charities to advance personal interests are a fraud. That is, they aren't gifts at all. They're investments or tax write-offs.

6. **Citizenship.** Citizenship includes virtues and duties that prescribe how we ought to behave as part of a community. The good citizen knows the laws and obeys them. A good citizen volunteers and stays informed on the issues of the day, the better to execute his/her duties and privileges as a member of a self-governing democratic society. A good citizen is a good neighbor; they protect the environment by conserving resources, recycling, using public transportation and cleaning up litter. At the end of the day the good citizen seeks the common good.

15-090 The path for ethical decisions

Incorporating these different components into your decision-making can be difficult. Choosing the correct component can be difficult when there are so many different factors to consider, so the question is how do we choose? However, the choices are not always clear. The following step-by-step method will help guide and direct your ethical decisions.

Steps on the path of ethical decisions are:

- Stop and think
- Clarify goals
- Get the facts
- Evaluate alternatives
- Consider the consequences
- Decide and test

Stop and think

When faced with ethical dilemmas, we need to take a moment to pause and think carefully about the issue. This gives us time to recognize and assess the situation. It also prevents us from making a rash decision that we might later regret. It is often recommended to walk away from the situation and reflect on the situation. This gives you time to think about the decision you are faced with and it gives you the chance to move forward.

Clarify the goals

Goal clarification is an important step as short-term and long-term goals must be identified. Once identified, the question is "will achieving a short-term goal prevent me from achieving my ultimate goal?" Identifying our goals is an important step in determining the end result that we want to achieve.

Get the facts

So far we have taken the time to stop and think, and to clarify our end goal; now we have to get the facts. This is not always as easy as it seems. Some facts are relatively easy to obtain, but these will not be the only information required to make a sound decision. Other facts need to be discovered that are missing; in other words, what do we not know? This can be hard because we don't know what we don't know. We have to be prepared to accept information that isn't readily available. Once information is received, it must be assessed. Consider the source: who is giving us that information? How reliable are they? What are their motives? Why are they giving us this information? Do they have an ulterior motive, or are they genuinely providing information to allow an ethical choice to be made?

Obtaining and analyzing information can be difficult; we have to use our best judgement. While you must be open to information, you must be smart. Don't be complacent and just look at the surface. You must dig deep especially when making touch, ethical decisions. Even though we might not have ulterior motives, those giving you information might have ulterior motives.

Evaluate alternatives

It is now time to evaluate alternative options and/or actions. Once we have identified our end goals and evaluated all the facts, we need to make a list of choices to help us reach our goal. Sometimes this step can be difficult so help may be required such as talking to a trusted coworker, which may allow you to see things from a different perspective.

Consider consequences

Once we have made our list of potential actions, we must consider the consequences of each and every option or action that we are considering. If any of these options go against our ethical standards then they are rejected and we find another option. We need to consider everyone and everything that our decision is going to affect and how it is going to affect them. Again, we need to look at both the short-term but also the long-term result of our action or decision. While we are free to choose, we are not free from the consequences of our choice. There can be a lot of ethical dilemmas in our decision. In order to avoid these dilemmas, any decision must be made with a full understanding of their overreaching impact, not only to ourselves and our business, but also to those who are inadvertently or directly affected by it.

Decide and test

The option has been selected so now it is time to move forward with it. If at this point we are still unsure, we may consider seeking assistance from someone who has high moral standards we trust by asking them what they would do in this situation. We also need to consider that when our decision become known by others, will be we proud of our decision? The test really is whether you are willing to put your name to the decision.

Reflect on the outcome

Once the decision has been tested, it is then helpful to reflect on the outcome of the choice. When making decisions it is always important to monitor the outcome of decisions. Monitoring allows us to change or alter our decision if the outcome doesn't turn out the way we wanted it. If the decision cannot be changed, evaluating our choices helps us to make better decisions in the future.

Illustrated example 15.3 is a real-life success story about a person who made an ethical decision that resulted in a positive outcome.

Illustrated example 15.3

In 2009, Captain Chesley Sullenberger was piloting an airliner with 155 passengers and crew. Immediately after takeoff the plane struck a flock of Canadian geese, which disabled the aircraft. Captain Sullenberger had about 30 seconds to make a decision about how to avoid a disaster. In that 30 seconds he had to think, he had to clarify his goal and he had to get information about how to achieve that goal. Then he had to decide and he had to test.

Captain Sullenberger's goal was not to save the aeroplane; his goal was to save the passengers and to not injure those who were on the ground. There were two airports nearby, but he was unsure whether he could clear the buildings, or even if he would be able to reach either of these airports. Also, if he chose to attempt to reach a nearby airport he would be risking injury or death to many people on the ground. His choice? To land the airliner on the Hudson river.

As with any choice there will always be "what ifs". There will always be questions that emerge after the fact; but we can only do the best with the information that we have at the time. If we use the *path of ethical decisions* framework, if careful thought is given to the available options, and we adhere to our values we will almost always make the right choice. As for Captain Sullenberger, he achieved his goal. There was not one fatality as the passengers and crew all survived and there weren't any injuries to people on the ground.

So far we have examined ethics and morals in respect to individuals. How are these principles and actions applied in a professional setting?

Ethics in the professions

15-100 Professional ethics

When discussing professional ethics it is necessary to understand how the ethical environment in which professions operate differs from that of business. Many people in business certainly act professionally – they are upright, act with integrity, display competence and have gained the trust of their customers. The main objective of a business is to earn a profit. However, while a professional will aim to make a profit from his/her activities they must adhere to and abide by the professional body's code of conduct while conducting their business activities. The key differences between a business and a profession are shown in table 15.2.

Table 15.2 Business vs profession

Basis of Comparison	Business	Profession
Meaning	Business is an economic activity concerned with the production or purchase and sale of merchandise and rendering of services with the purpose of earning a profit.	Profession is a form of economic activity, wherein special skills, knowledge and expertise is required to be applied by the person, in his/her occupation.
Basic objective	Earning a profit	Rendering a service
Establishment	On the decision of the entrepreneur and fulfilment of legal formalities.	Membership of the respective professional body and certificate of practice.
Qualification	No minimum qualification	Specialized knowledge through formal study is required.
Reward	Profit	Professional fees
Code of conduct	No prescribed code of conduct.	Code of conduct prescribed by the professional body's needs to be followed.
Advertisement	Product and services are advertised to increase sales.	Promoting services by telemarketing, mail outs prohibited.

Source: Surbhi, S. 2017b

Therefore, business refers to the regular occupation of a person in which they engage in an occupation to earn profit and acquire wealth. There isn't any requirement to belong to an industry body nor are business people required to follow a code of conduct. In contrast, the profession is defined as a paid occupation in which a person is formally qualified follows a code of conduct and has undergone prolonged training to render services to the general public. Some examples include: doctors, accountants, lawyers and financial advising.

When giving advice the professional must survey the entire landscape, having the client's interest as the focus. In contrast, the business person, say a Holden dealer has a duty to survey the Holden landscape, that is, the Holden range of vehicles. The difference is that the Holden dealer is restricted in his/her offering, which may not fully satisfy the client's requirements. The client may later see a vehicle of a different make which may have suited his needs better. While the Holden dealer may have acted ethically he/she is not independent, which for some professions is an ethical requirement. The professional, but not the business person – also has a duty to have regard for the broader public interest. It is virtually universal that the code of ethics for every professional body includes the following three focuses:

- The client's interest

- The public interest

- The profession's interest: the professional's duty not to engage in conduct that could bring the profession into disrepute.

Professional ethics is not a special type of ethics, but the application of professional judgement in a professional practice. This application can sometimes be forgotten in business settings as organizational culture can impact on how people behave. For example, management emphasizing commission (or, fee) income above acting in their clients' best interests (See 5-050). This example (Commonwealth Financial Planning v Couper) illustrates a violation of trust and emphasizes that practitioners are not exempt from common morality. The requirements of professions add to, rather than replace, ordinary ethical obligations.

One mark of a profession is a commitment to values expressed in codes of conduct and related documents. Professional practice requires that practitioners:

- Adhere to the rules of their profession formally set down by their professional body, and comply with the directions of the regulatory bodies

- Exercise professional skills and expertise on behalf of clients for their benefit

- Adhere to the principles of ethical conduct that govern professional practice, that is, to the minimal principles of professional practice

These requirements dovetail into the three focuses listed above (client's interest, public interest and professional's interest). The following table 15.3 lists the professional values that are built on the three requirements of a professional practice.

Table 15.3 The minimum principles of professional practice

Beneficence	Doing good
Non-maleficence	Not doing harm
Confidentiality	Respecting the privacy of clients
Avoiding conflicts of interest	Keeping private interests separate from those of clients
Respectability	Behaving in ways that do not bring the profession into public disrepute
Competence	Keeping up with the latest developments in the profession, and carrying out work at an appropriately high level

Source: Grace, D. & Cohen, S., (2013)

Care

Professional codes prescribe principles and standards of conduct. A caring person cares *for* someone or *about* something. A caring person becomes involved with the concerns of people when they care for them. Therefore, a caring professional is likely to be more understanding of, and attentive to, clients' interests and be a better practitioner.

Confidentiality

Confidentiality is one of the most important values for professionals and the most important in professional ethics. In the course of providing professional advice, the client discloses personal information. Clients are willing to disclose this information because of confidentiality. The practitioner is promising the client that he/she will keep the client's affairs private. Confidentiality is a contractual term upon which information is given and the terms on which it can be given to others.

The handling of personal information is also governed by Australian Law. The *Privacy Act 1988* (Privacy Act) regulates the handling of personal information about individuals. The Privacy Act defines personal information as information or an opinion about an identified individual, or an individual who is reasonably identifiable. The Privacy Act includes thirteen Australian Privacy Principles (APPs). The APPs set out standards, rights and obligations for handling, holding, use, accessing and correction of personal information (including sensitive information).

Confidentiality is not an absolute principle as it is elastic enough to allow, for example, consultation with colleagues about the best way to construct a client's investment portfolio or to meet legal requirements or if written authority has been given by the client. The most serious breach of confidentiality is when private information is used for personal gain.

All personal information gained during disclosure either gained directly or inadvertently in the course of offering personal services is subject to confidentiality. A relationship with clients is based on trust and a foundation of this trust is that personal information will be stored securely and safe from cyber-attacks. Professionals, including financial advisers are natural targets for hackers because they manage large amounts of money. Therefore, clients trust that professional and financial advisers will be diligent in checking the security of all their third-party vendors.

Responsibility and accountability

Professionals and financial advisers must be accountable for the advice they give. The Business Dictionary defines Accountability as: "The obligation of an individual or organization to account for its activities, accept responsibility for them, and to disclose the results in a transparent manner. It includes the responsibility for money or other entrusted property" (Business Dictionary (N.D.)). For example, financial advisers are required by section 946C of the Corporations Act (2001) (CA) to deliver Statements of Advice (SOA) to their clients within five days after providing the advice or sooner if practicable. Should they fail to deliver the SOA within the prescribed period they will be held accountable and be subject to penalties as prescribed by the CA.

Responsibility should not be confused with accountability. Responsibility is defined as: "A duty or obligation to satisfactorily perform or complete a task (assigned by someone, or created by one's own promise or circumstances) that one must fulfil and which has a consequent penalty for failure" (Business Dictionary (N.D.)). Therefore, failing in one's requirement to act responsibly would lead to the individual being called to account and to answer for one's conduct. That is, the individual is able to choose for oneself between right and wrong. Being responsible invokes the notion of being trustworthy. It is about responsibility when things go wrong "Yes, I did it" and about taking responsibility (ownership) for its rectification - "I am going to do something do about this and its mine". A professional or financial adviser is accountable for providing competent advice and be responsible for the outcome of that advice. In other words they are responsible for their professional judgement.

Professional judgement

Professional judgement is defined as: "The discretion of an individual with the educational, work-related or other experience to make a decision"

(Financial Dictionary (N.D.)). Professional principles and standards enable good judgement. A person should be able to give an account of such judgement, so the question 'Could I justify my decision to my peers?' should be uppermost in one's thinking. If you cannot account for your actions, then those actions are likely to be unjustified. Professional judgement needs to be responsible, not only in making justified decisions, but also to be willing to engage with an issue by being proactive in dealing with it.

Professional moral obligations can be thought about through the notion of a person's role. A person's role in financial advising is to take responsibility for their decisions. However, conflict can arise when a person has several roles and they conflict. What should the person do, for example, if professional services are required at a time when their child is performing in a school choir? Our values will ultimately guide our decision.

Professional ethics are guided by the norms, regulations and law that relates to that profession and act as constraints upon that which a professional may do for a client. Among these constraints are the profession's professional Codes of Ethics.

15-110 Professional codes of ethics

Professional codes of ethics are a guide outlining the principles designed to help professionals conduct business honestly and with personal integrity that the profession expects of the professional. A code of ethics document outlines: the mission and values of the business or organization, how professionals are supposed to approach problems, the ethical principles based on the profession's core values and the standards to which the professional is held. Breaking the code of ethics can result in termination or dismissal from the organization.

There are both federal guidelines and professional codes that financial advisers must follow. The federal guidelines are contained in the *Financial Planners and Advisers Code of Ethics* (2019) (the Code). Section 921E of the *Corporations Act* (2001) (CA) states that financial advisers must comply with the Code and section 922HD requires that from 1 January 2020 financial advisers must advise ASIC of any failures to comply.

The Code imposes ethical duties on financial advisers that go beyond the requirements of law. The Code is designed to encourage higher standards of behavior and professionalism in the financial services profession. The Code states that a financial adviser must always act in a way that demonstrates, realizes and promotes the following five values:

(a) trustworthiness
(b) competence
(c) honesty
(d) fairness, and
(e) diligence

Trustworthiness. This value requires financial advisers to act in good faith in their relationships with other people. Good conduct inspires trust, which can be easily broken by unethical conduct. A trusting relationship is built and maintained with dealings that exhibit integrity and honesty in all dealings.

Competence. This value requires financial advisers to acquire and maintain the knowledge, skills and experience to professionally advise clients. In order to demonstrate competence, financial advisers will need to demonstrate that they have assessed the professional services that the client requires and to assess individual needs, priorities, circumstances and preferences, expressed or identified. This value stresses that the duty of competence is personal and cannot be outsourced to others when third party assistance is used.

Honesty. The value of honesty requires that financial advisers conduct themselves with complete integrity in all professional dealings. It requires transparency, frankness and fairness to each client, even where this may cause personal detriment.

Fairness. The value of fairness requires that financial advisers bring professional objectivity when advising clients and when recommending financial products and professional services. It requires a thorough investigation, evaluation and diagnosis of a client's needs for professional services. It also requires financial advisers to ensure that they have the necessary skills and knowledge to provide the required service.

Diligence. This value requires that financial advisers exercise due care and skill in all professional engagements. It also requires time and resources to deliver professional services in a timely, efficient and cost effective way.

This standard says that "all advisers must act at all times, in all cases in a manner that is demonstrably consistent with the 12 standards, which will be monitored by ASIC's monitoring schemes".

The 12 standards are split into four main categories:

- ethical behavior
- client care

- quality process, and

- professional commitment

The following list details extracts from the 12 standards. Full details of the Explanatory Statement accompanying the *Financial Planners and Advisers Code of Ethics* (2019) can be accessed by following the link at the end of the chapter.

Ethical Behaviour

Standard 1

This standard requires, as an ethical duty, that you comply with your legal obligations and not seek to avoid or circumvent them. This is a minimum ethical obligation.

Standard 2

This standard requires, as an ethical duty, that you act with integrity and in the best interests of your clients.

Standard 3

The primary ethical duty in this standard is that, if you have a conflict of interest or duty, you must disclose this conflict to the client and you must not act. If the client wishes you may refer the client to another relevant provider if neither you nor your principal will receive any benefits from the referral.

Client care

Standard 4

This standard requires that you only act for a client with the client's free, prior and informed consent.

This means that before you start to act, you must have explained to your client, clearly and simply:

- what services will be provided; and

- the terms on which they will be provided; and

- the records that will be made of the services, and the privacy and confidential arrangements applicable to them.

Standard 5

This standard elaborates on the "best interest of the client" in standard 2 and also requires that you satisfy yourself that the client understands your advice and the products and services you recommend. This requires detailed engagement with and assistance with the client.

This standard emphasizes the need for the advice and recommendations to be appropriate to the client's individual circumstances (which will require you to take into account the client's broader long term interests and the client's likely future circumstances).

Standard 6

This standard expressly requires you to take into account the broad effects of the client acting on your advice. These effects are not limited to effects on the client. For example, your advice may have implications, not just for the client personally, but also for other family members of the client.

Quality process

Standard 7

This standard requires the client's free, prior informed consent to all relevant remuneration agreements for you and your principal. To meet this standard, the client must be given a clear and simple explanation of the fees and charges, and the benefits you and your principal will receive, that are attributable to you or your principal acting for the client.

Standard 8

This standard requires that a relevant provider keep complete and relevant records of advice and services provided.

Standard 9

This standard requires that all financial product advice, and all financial products, offered to a client be offered in good faith. This means that you must act honestly, and in the best interest of the client, in giving the advice and making the recommendations. You will not be acting in good faith if there is something you are aware of that would lead to the conclusion that your advice is not in the client's best interests, taking into account the broad effects from the client acting on your advice and the broader, long-term interests and likely circumstances of the client.

Professional commitment

Standard 10

This standard imposes, as an ethical duty, a requirement to develop and maintain a high level of relevant knowledge and skills. For example, if you specialize in a particular area, you should not provide advice outside that area unless you have the necessary skills and competencies to do so in a professional way.

Standard 11

This standard is a positive duty to cooperate with any investigation in a breach or a possible breach of the Code by a monitoring body or ASIC. This duty applies in addition to the offences in sections 921M and 921P of the Corporations Act (2001).

Standard 12

This standard deals with relevant provider's professional relationships with each other, emphasizing the need to be supportive and aligned to the profession as a whole – being and being seen to be, a profession that acts ethically and professionally.

One element of this duty affects relevant providers who are acting as supervisors for provisional relevant providers undertaking the professional year (see the *Corporations (Provisional Relevant Providers Professional Year Standard)* Determination 2018). This Standard requires that you must provide supervision that is in the best interest of the provisional relevant provider, that is, supervision that actively assists them is getting the full benefit of the professional year.

15-120 Enforcement of the code of ethics

Section 921M of the CA states that a relevant provider must comply with the Code. Although, a failure to comply with the Code is not a criminal offence and does not attract civil penalties, sanctions may be applied by an authorized monitoring body, or ASIC.

Enforcement of the Code is made by monitoring bodies appointed by ASIC. Monitoring bodies have the power to investigate breaches and potential breaches of the Code and impose sanctions if they determine a breach has occurred. Potential sanctions that may be applied are:

- a warning or reprimand; and

- requiring the relevant planner to undertake additional training or counselling; and

- requiring additional supervision on a relevant provider; and

- requiring specified corrective action; and

- requiring an independent compliance audit of the relevant provider (if it is a licensee); and

- requiring the relevant provider to provide the services to the retail client again at no cost, or to reduce or waive fees.

ASIC's Role in Contraventions

ASIC may suspend or terminate the financial services license of a relevant provider that is a licensee for a breach of the Code (sec 921E – comply with the Code), paragraph 912A(1)(a) of the CA, but its powers to ban a provider who is not a licensee is limited to actions contained in section 920A(1)(e) of the CA.

ASIC retains the power to investigate contraventions of the Act including a failure of a relevant provider to comply with the Code (sec 921E)(CA). ASIC is able to make a banning order in the following circumstances:

- ASIC suspends or cancels an Australian Financial Services License (AFSL) held by the person; or

- The person has not complied with their obligations under the code (sec 921A); or

- ASIC believes that the person is likely to contravene their obligations under section 912A; or

- the person becomes insolvent under administration; or

- The person is convicted of fraud; or

- ASIC has reason to believe that the person is not of good fame or character; or

- ASIC has reason to believe that the person is not adequately trained, or is not competent, to provide financial services; or

- The person has not complied with his or her supervisory obligations of provisional relevant providers; or

- The person has not complied with financial services law; or

- ASIC believes the person is likely to contravene financial services law

If ASIC believes that a person is not of good fame or character, the following circumstances will be taken into account:

- Any conviction of the person, within 10 years before that time, for an offence that involves dishonesty and is punishment by imprisonment for at least three months; and

- Whether a person has held an AFSL that was suspended or cancelled; and

- Whether a disqualification or banning order has been made against the person

However, the person concerned has the right to:

- appear or be represented at a private hearing, or

- to make submissions to ASIC on the matter

Financial advisers must also abide and comply with the codes of conduct prescribed by their professional bodies.

15-130 Professional bodies

Section s.912A(1)(g) and 912A(2) of the *Corporations Act 2001* (CA) requires all Australian Financial Services organizations that give financial advice must have a dispute resolution system available to retail clients and belong to an External Dispute Resolution Service, which is the management group licensed by the regulator, ASIC (for a description of retail clients see section 4-130).

There are three financial professional financial adviser bodies registered with the Tax Practitioners Board (TPB). These are:

- The Financial Planning Association of Australia Ltd. (FPA)

- Association of Financial Advisers Ltd. (AFA)

- SMSF Association

The Financial Planning Association of Australia Ltd (FPA).

Being a member of the FPA requires its members to follow and adhere to three sets of standards: Code of Ethics; Professional Standards and the Rules of Professional Conduct. The code of ethics contains eight principles that apply when providing financial advice:

- Principle 1: Client first

- Principle 2: Integrity

- Principle 3: Objectivity
- Principle 4: Fairness
- Principle 5: Professionalism
- Principle 6: Competence
- Principle 7: Confidentiality
- Principle 8: Diligence

FPA's Conduct Review Commission

The Conduct Review Commission (CRC) is an independent disciplinary body put into place to ensure members are held accountable to the FPA Code of Professional Practice and Code of Ethics. The CRC plays a vital role in regulating the conduct of FPA members and upholding the highest ethical standards within the financial profession.

Key functions of the CRC:

- Determining whether disciplinary proceedings should be commenced against members;
- Hearing and determining complaints against members in respect to breaches; and
- Hearing and determining appeals.

The Association of Financial Advisers Ltd.

The AFA is guided by six principles of professionalism:

- Principle 1: Integrity and Professional Conduct
- Principle 2: Best Interests
- Principle 3: Conflict of Interest
- Principle 4: Informed Client Consent
- Principle 5: Service Standards
- Principle 6: Rules of Professional Conduct

Self-Managed Superannuation Fund Association

Members of this association must adhere to and follow the following major principles:

- Principle 1: Safeguard the Public Interest

- Principle 2: Integrity

- Principle 3: Objectivity and Independence

- Principle 4: Confidentiality

- Principle 5: Competence

- Principle 6: Knowledge

- Principle 7: Ethical Behaviour

15-140 Do codes work?

Until the passing of the *Financial Planners and Advisers Code of Ethics* 2019, financial advisers were not required to act ethically unless it was a condition of belonging to a professional body. This industry code of ethics permeates every aspect of how an adviser thinks and behaves – or at least should have. There are examples of companies with substantial code of ethics statements that have been found to be acting contrary to their code. For example Enron was the company that espoused wonderful core values and made compelling statements in its 64-page code of ethics booklet. However, it was found to have acted anything but ethically by falsifying its financial accounts over a number of years. There are many institutions with codes of ethics statements who were involved in the financial skullduggery that lead to the 2008 financial crisis.

In order for codes to be a success, codes must be integrated into the organizational culture and work. This integration of an ethical culture is created and fostered by senior management, who manifest their commitment to ethical practice through their attitudes and behavior. According to Webley and Werner (2008) and numerous other authors, having a code of ethics without creating an ethical culture and a comprehensive ethics program is like having a Ferrari without wheels—i.e., it looks good, but you're not going anywhere. You can't create an ethical culture if employees and other stakeholders perceive the company to be dishonest or unfair in its business dealings, or if they believe the company does not value its employees or clients. Therefore the first step in positively influencing employee behavior must come from top management.

The fact that the Code is a legislated requirement monitored by ASIC appointed monitoring bodies makes it more likely that its requirements will be observed and practiced.

15-150 Study questions

15.1 It is claimed that a salaried professional has conflicting obligations; the obligations to one's employer can conflict with one's professional obligations.

    (a)   Is it clear why this claim has been made?

    (b)   Do you think this is correct?

15.2 A variety of different responses could be appropriate to the identification of a conflict of interest, given the different contexts in which a conflict of interest might be identified. How might you decide what the appropriate response would be in any particular occurrence of a conflict of interest?

15.3 You are faced with a situation where you are uncertain whether the action will involve a conflict of interest. What steps could you take to avoid committing a breach of you professional duties?

15.4 Explain the seven virtues that can help us to develop our best selves.

15-160 Discussion questions

1. What is ethics?

2. If "business is business", what is business ethics?

3. Define ethics.

4. Discuss, how would you propose to live an "ethical life"?

5. Why do professionals have a code of ethics?

6. If a person or business is interested in operating ethically, it seems that beliefs must be examined.

    Questions to discuss:
    What does a person who is greedy and determined to crush or cheat others, believe?
    What does a person who gets pleasure from dominating others believe?
    What does the person who only ever conforms and complies, believe?
    What does a conceited or self-important person, believe?

7. What is the need for professional ethics?

8. What is the purpose of strong ethical beliefs in the workplace?

9. What is the purpose of professional codes of ethics?

10. If the essence of ethics is concern for the wellbeing of others, what values would you expect to see in a person (or business) that was behaving ethically?

11. Why do people behave unethically?

15-170 References and further readings

References

Articles and Books

Ayer, A. J., 1946. "A Critique of Ethics," in *Language, Truth and Logic*, London: Gollanz, pp. 102–114.

Grace, D. & Cohen, S., (2013), *Business ethics*, 5th edn, Oxford University Press, Sydney, p. 152.

Guy, M.E. (1990), *Ethical decision making in everyday work situations*, Quorum Books, New York.

Josephson, M. (N.D.), It's not easy. Available at http://whatwillmatter. com/2017/01/ethics-not-easy/

Roy Morgan (2018), Nearly two million Australians use a financial planner of adviser – worth $703b, July 16. Finding No. 7655. www.roymorgan.com/findings

Simon Webley & Andrea Werner (2008), *Corporate codes of ethics: necessary but not sufficient*, Business Ethics: A European Review. Volume 17, Number 4.

Surbhi, S. (2018a), Difference between morals and hazards. Available at https://keydifferences.com/difference-between-morals-and-ethics.html

Surbhi, S. (2017b), Difference between business and Profession. Available at: https://keydifferences.com/bifference-between-business-and-profession.html

The Macquarie Concise Dictionary (1998), 2nd edn, The Macquarie Library, Macquarie University, NSW.

Smith, B.D. (2002), 'An Ethics Primer', CPCV *e journal*, editorial, May, vol. 55, issue 3, pp. 1-5.

Wikipedia Contributions (2019), Trolley problem, *Wikipedia, the free encyclopedia*. Available at https://en.wikipedia.org/w/index.php?title=Trolley_problem&oldid=911324470

Wikipedia (n.d.), Immanuel Kant, *Wikipedia, the free encyclopedia*. Available at https://en.wikipedia.org/wiki/Immanuel_Kant

Releases

Australian Securities and Investments Commission (ASIC) Regulatory Guide 165: Licensing: Internal and external dispute resolution. Available at https://download.asic.gov.au/media/4772056/rg165-published-18-june-2018.pdf

Legislation

Corporations (Provisional Relevant Providers Professional Year Standard) Determination 2018 (Cth)

Corporations Act 2001

Financial Planners and Advisers Code of Ethics 2018 (Cth)

Privacy Act 1988 (Cth)

Websites

Business Dictionary**.** https://www.businessdictionary.com/definition/accountability.html

Business Dictionary**.** https://www.businessdictionary.com/definition/responsibility.html

Financial Dictionary. https://www.financial-dictionary.thefreedictionary.com/Professional+Judgement

Financial Planning Association of Australia Ltd: Conduct Review Commission: https://fpa.com.au/professionalism/conduct-review-commission/

Financial Planning Association of Australia Ltd: Code of Ethics; Professional Standards and the Rules of Professional Conduct: https://fpa.com.au

Self-Managed Superannuation Fund Association: https://www.smsfassociation.com/

Stanford Encyclopedia of Philosophy (2012): https://plato.stanford.edu/entries/metaethics/

The Association of Financial Advisers Ltd: https://www.afa.asn.au/

Index

CPSIA information can be obtained
at www.ICGtesting.com
Printed in the USA
LVHW081303080223
738983LV00004B/48

9 780646 812816